Major Themes in Modern European History: An Invitation to Inquiry and Reflection

Volume I

THE INSTITUTION OF THE STATE

By

Harold T. Parker

and

Marvin L. Brown, Jr.

Moore Publishing Company

Durham, North Carolina

CONTENTS

VOLUME I   THE INSTITUTION OF THE STATE

MAPS

PREFACE

This textbook on modern European history should commend itself to college teachers and beginning students for several reasons.

It is selective, concentrating on four themes: the rise of national states and the conflict between authority and liberty within them; the problems of peace and war among these states; the economic and technological changes which have taken place under the aegis of capitalism and alternatives to it; and the ideas and faiths by which men live and die.

It has a simple principle of organization. As it describes the development and expansion of Europe, it brings in other areas as Europe affects them or they affect Europe. By the twentieth century the entire world, so to speak, is in the book.

The book adheres to a simple theory of presentation: that it is presenting data for discussion, reflection, and further inquiry rather than for mere memorization. The concentration on a few themes enables the authors to offer data and to explain what happened in greater depth. They have the time to tell the story of what occurred in terms of individuals and their motives and actions, which give momentum to history; of identifiable social groups; of institutions which individuals and groups build, sometimes unconsciously; and of processes of continuity and change in which individuals and groups are involved. Indeed, in several chapters the presentation moves at three levels of understanding. Chapters 3 and 11, for example, tell how the activities of the central governments in France, England, and Prussia contributed to bring their respective peoples together to form a nation. At one level the story is told as a sequential narrative of unique events. At the same time the story is recounted in such a way as to offer data for comparison and for the formulating of generalizations about how nation-states emerged in the early centuries of Western culture. This is a second level of understanding. Then the story is narrated in such detail that the student has data to devise his own theories about the deeper processes of historical continuity and change. The phenomena of overseas settlements, of liberal revolutions, and of social and technological invention, to mention only a few items, are presented in equal depth. At the end of each chapter questions lead the student into these profounder reflections. Selective bibliographies for general and specialized reading indicate routes for further inquiry.

The division of the book into three paperback volumes and also into nine paperback booklets promotes flexibility of use. Each of the nine parts is available as a booklet. In addition, the first three parts form the first paperback volume, entitled *The Institution of the State*. The word "institution" is here used both actively (individuals by their day-to-day actions gradually instituted the state) and passively (the state became an intricate, complex institution). Parts four, five, and six constitute the second volume, *The Institution of Liberty*. Again, there are subtle dialectics within the title: within the word "institution," between its active and passive meanings; between "institution" and "liberty" — how can liberty endure if it is not institutionalized? how can it remain free if it is?; and between the institution of liberty and the institution of the state. Such considerations form part, but only a part, of the interplay of thought within these volumes. Parts, seven, eight, and nine deal with the multi-rich, multifarious *Twentieth Century*. The instructor may choose to use all three volumes, or any two, or one. Similarly, he may select among the narrative booklets, picking those that fit his course.

The basic draft of chapters 1-24, 26, 35, 38 and 41 was written by Harold T. Parker. Marvin L. Brown, Jr., who gave his collaboration after most of the nineteenth-century chapters were in first draft, wrote chapters 25, 27-34, 36, 37, 39, 40, and 43. Chapter 42 is the result of drafts of both authors. As in any prolonged collaboration, there was an exchange and interpenetration of views throughout the text.

The authors wish gratefully to acknowledge the professional copyediting of the first draft of the entire manuscript by Mrs. Barbara Reitt. They also wish to thank Mrs. Marvin L. Brown, Jr. for her imaginative copyediting of most of the manuscript and for her practical suggestions. They express their gratitude to Dr. Parker's students in the introductory courses at Duke University for their emendations of the text in its final draft. Special credit is owed to Mr. J. M. Martin for his assistance in the final rewriting of chapters 1-24. For chapters 18-21 and 23-24, he prepared a detailed line-by-line commentary on the text, leading to an imaginative redoing of the entire presentation. His aid throughout the first two volumes was indispensable and deeply appreciated. To Richard L. Watson, executor of the estate of William B. Hamilton, the authors owe permission to reprint material written by Dr. Parker for a synopsis entitled *Historical Background of the World Today*, a permission that was graciously accorded and gratefully received. Despite the aid the authors acknowledge, they are themselves fully responsible for any errors and lapses that remain.

Harold T. Parker
Marvin L. Brown, Jr.

PART I

BACKGROUND: ASPECTS OF THE EMERGENCE OF MODERN EUROPE – THE RISE OF TOWNSMEN, THE RISE OF MONARCHS, AND THE EXPANSION OF KNOWLEDGE

Introduction to Part I

Ostensibly this book begins in 1492, with the expansion of Europe overseas to the Americas. Conceivably we could open with a static cross-sectional description of aspects of European civilization in 1492: the vigorous commerce and its capitalistic organization and technological base; the monarchical states, and the associated national consciousness; the expanding knowledge of the natural world and of history. Such information is indeed indispensable for understanding modern Europe on the eve of overseas expansion. However, if we give this information in a series of flashbacks and show *how* commerce, capitalism, and technology came into being, *how* the nation-state emerged, and *how* knowledge increased, we gain a plus value: we come to understand some of the processes by which change has occurred in Western culture and new institutions and ideas have come into existence. For this reason Part I is so organized by flashbacks that it offers the student the opportunity to get in mind (1) the emergence of a new European culture from the decay and wreck of the western half of the Roman Empire, (2) the basic elements of European society as it existed in the latter part of the tenth century, (3) how and by what processes, commerce, capitalism, technological advance, the nation-state, and new knowledge emerged from tenth-century society, and (4) aspects of European civilization in 1492 on the eve of expansion. Our stance is in 1492 and we are looking back, bringing certain elements of an emerging culture toward us.

CHAPTER I

THE EUROPEAN WILDERNESS

What American is not familiar with at least one picture of Christopher Columbus striding ashore at Watlings Island on October 12, 1492? The details of the scene vary with the imagination of the artist, but the elements are always the same: the courageous explorer, the royal standard, a cross, and in the middle distance the three ships. Those who know the story endow the scene with dramatic impact — the Europeans have discovered a New World — and also with dramatic irony — Columbus who has sailed west to reach Asia believes that he has reached it and is unaware of what he has actually achieved. This event is a supreme example of the familiar historical phenomenon, of men doing other than what they intend.

However, to note the scene's dramatic impact and irony is not to exhaust its historical significance. If we look again at such a painting, we shall perceive that each element in it represents a characteristic aspect of the European civilization from which Columbus came. The royal standard, with F on one side for Ferdinand and Y on the other for Ysobel, bespeaks the emerging nation-state, which was to be the characteristic political structure of European culture. The cross reminds us that the civilization was Christian. The woven cloth of the royal standard, of the uniforms of Columbus and his followers, and of the sails of the three ships as well as the construction of the three ships themselves tell us of an advanced and perhaps advancing technology. From the three ships, built in all probability for trade, we may infer an active commerce. Columbus and his followers came from an expanding European civilization that had been developing for a thousand years, from the decay and wreck of the western half of the Roman Empire.

That empire, centered on the Mediterranean Sea, had been formally structured by the first Roman emperor, Caesar Augustus (27 B.C.-14 A.D.), and by his immediate successors. Within the empire a vigorous commerce binding together Greek and Roman civilizations had sustained a sophisticated urban life. A common government had insured domestic peace and order. A universal Christian Church, by the fourth century after Christ, had attained predominance and given to all its members a treasured unity of belief. Then, in the fifth and sixth centuries, under the triple burden of internal decay, top-heavy government, and barbarian invasions, the western, Latin-speaking part of the Roman Empire broke up into warring units. What else happened in western Europe from the fifth to tenth centuries, and especially why, is still a subject of historical inquiry and dispute. It is evident, however, that in certain categories of social existence, disintegration and retrogression took place. Population declined; commerce decayed; towns shriveled or vanished; vast cultivated areas returned to forest; the arts and learning in the classical tradition were barbarized and neglected. Though shadows and memories of a universal state and a universal law remained to shape men's thoughts and actions in the west and the church survived and grew, the reality of a universal political organization was gone.

Amid this disintegration, on the other hand, while classical learning was fading to a stale echo of the past, fresh new ideas, new attitudes toward life, new values, and new productive forces were coming into play. The fourth and fifth centuries were one of the great ages in the formation of Christian theology. Christian leaders, notably St. Augustine, bishop of Hippo in North Africa, were constructing from theology, philosophy, and history a vital, original interpretation of man's destiny that supported Christians in their concern for salvation and expressed fundamental assumptions which were to form the bases of Western thought for the next fifteen hundred years. Soon, the two chief ecclesiastical institutions of the era, the papacy and monasticism, were spreading the gospel to the pagan rural areas of Spain and France and to the heathen peoples of England, Germany, and the Scandinavian countries. In 529, St. Benedict (480-543), abbot of the monastery of Monte Cassino, formulated his Rule, which became the basic guide of Western monasticism. It exacted a threefold vow of poverty, chastity, and obedience, and prescribed a daily life of prayer and work. In 597 Pope Gregory the Great dispatched a mission of Benedictine monks to Anglo-Saxon England. Later from Christian England other Benedictine missionaries, led by St. Boniface (675-755), undertook the conversion of Germany. Wherever the Benedictine monks went, they were more than preachers of the new religion, they were teachers, builders, physicians, metalworkers, and above all farmers among farming people, demonstrating a superior quality of life and civilization. In many ways, both obvious and subtle, it was important that social disintegration and reconstruction during these centuries was proceeding in the atmosphere of the Christian religion.

At the same time gains were made in technology. As might be expected, most of the new devices were answers to problems of an agrarian society. Roman agriculture, though painstaking and deft, had been held back by certain limitations of equipment and practice. Roman farmers had used a scratch-plow, which did not cut very deeply and required cross-plowing; they had used ox teams, which moved very slowly; they had employed a two-field system that each year left one half of the land fallow. During the seventh, eighth, and ninth centuries (it would be scholarly imprudence to be more

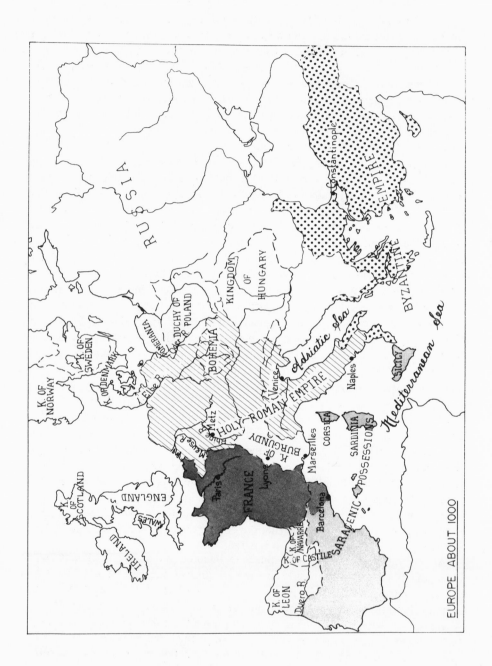

EUROPE ABOUT 1000

precise) farmers in northern Europe began to use a heavy-wheeled plow, which stirred the soil more deeply, and a three-field system that left fallow only one-third of the land. Utilizing a new horse-collar harness and horseshoes, they started to replace oxen with horse-teams which could plough more rapidly. The water mill, invented as early as the first century before Christ, began to be applied more extensively to the grinding of grain. Though the full effect of these measures would become apparent only with time, they were laying the foundation for a society of greater agricultural productivity.

Also, from the fifth to tenth centuries there developed within this agrarian society that seemed to be disintegrating a network of dependent relationships which proved tough and flexible in repelling Moslems, Norse, Slav, and Hungarian invaders in the ninth and tenth centuries. When the centralized Roman government proved no longer able to defend its citizens from invaders and brigands in the fourth and fifth centuries, the small, independent farmers in the west sought the protection of the local magnate. They surrendered their land to him in return for security and they became his tenants. By another process the slaves on the great agricultural estates were being freed and also becoming tenants. Thereafter, for many centuries, the reality of existence for most Europeans in the west was life in a village community on land which they neither owned outright nor controlled and for whose use they paid dues and services to a local lord. Meanwhile, from the fifth to the tenth centuries dependent relationships developed among the local lords. Lesser lords came to hold their villages of a greater lord as a fief and to do homage for them. They promised military service in return for protection. A greater lord in turn might hold his totality of villages and liegemen of a monarch. At all levels, the lords assumed the functions of government — taxation, justice, and coinage — and they warred with each other. In retrospect the decentralization of the exercise of governmental functions seems excessive. Yet by 955, in a forested area of poor communications, this network of local dependencies and defenses proved tough enough to secure for Europeans the upper hand over Moslem invaders from the south, Hungarian and Slav attackers from the east, and Norse pirates from the north. This achievement of European superiority over external attackers invites us to take a look at European society in the tenth century, on the eve of significant developments in intellectual and material growth.

In the late tenth century, Western Europe Christians occupied a restricted area bounded by the Mediterranean and Adriatic seas, the Oder river, and the Atlantic Ocean. This region included a strip of territory in northern Spain, its southern boundary running irregularly from the mouth of the Duero River to Barcelona; the Italian peninsula but not Corsica, Sardinia, or Sicily, which were controlled by the Moslems; Germany to a line running roughly from the northern tip of the Adriatic Sea to the mouth of the Oder River; Denmark; Scandinavia; France; the Low Countries; and the British Isles. The region was bordered by hostile peoples: to the south, by the Moslems, who controlled Spain, the western Mediterranean, and North Africa, and whose pirates ravaged Christian commerce; to the southeast, by the Balkan Slavs, only then in the process of being converted to Christianity; to the east of Vienna, by the Mongolian-blooded Magyars, masters of the Hungarian plain; and to the northeast, across the Oder, by the eastern Slavs.

After centuries of social disintegration, life was largely rural and agricultural. Although the population of the area was beginning to increase, it was still sparse, and wilderness covered huge tracts. It is tentatively estimated, for example, that England was inhabited by fewer than one million people, and the area of modern France by fewer than six million. The chief social groups, peasants, nobles, and clergy, were agricultural classes who lived on the products of the soil, whether they raised them by their labor or collected them from those who did.

The peasants lived in such a variety of agricultural arrangements that generalization is risky. The arrangements varied with the climate, soil, terrain, crops, and prevailing agricultural methods of a particular region. In the poorer parts of France, England, and the Mediterranean area, a peasant and his family often lived alone on a compact isolated farm cleared from the forest. Elsewhere, especially in much of northern Europe, the basic unit was the village, composed of fifteen to sixty peasant families, who lived in one-room thatched huts with dirt floors, no chimneys, and sparse furniture. The village, set in several square miles of clearing, was a largely self-supporting economic unit whose families made at home or raised on the land nearly everything they needed. From the double line of huts stretched the great arable fields, perhaps nine hundred to two thousand acres in extent, with that much more land in meadow, pasture, woodland, and waste. The arable fields were handled differently in different villages, depending on the contour of the land, the climate, the available implements, the crops, and local custom. Some villages steadily cultivated a field for several years and then left it fallow for an indefinite period. Other villages followed the Roman practice of dividing the arable land into two fields, which were tilled or left fallow in alternate years. This two-course alternation tended to predominate in the Mediterranean area, in France up to the Loire River, and in eastern Sweden and Finland. A more productive three-course rotation was coming to the fore in the villages of France north of the Loire, of Germany, of England, and of parts of the Netherlands. In the three-course system, during a given year winter wheat or rye was sown to one field in the autumn, oats or barley to a second field in the spring, and a third field would lie fallow. During the succeeding year the first field would be planted in the spring to oats or barley, the second field would lie fallow, and the third field would receive a winter grain. Each arable field was sub-divided into long strips usually about an acre in extent — the area that could be plowed in a single day. One family's holding of thirty acres would be scattered over the fields in thirty separate one-acre strips so that each family of the village had some of each kind of land.

All the peasants of a given village followed the same simple and laborious routines of the agricultural year. In the spring they plowed and harrowed for the sowing of the spring crops and in the early summer plowed the fallow. In June and July the sheep were washed and sheared and the hay made. At harvest the grain was reaped and bound into sheaves. Later, in autumn, there would be more sowing, harrowing, ditching, as well as threshing and winnowing, collection of wood, and repairing of utensils. Implements and methods of cultivation were being gradually improved and agricultural production was increasing, though crop yields were still slight. In northern Europe the Roman plow of shaped wood that was dragged across the ground had been generally replaced by the wheeled, fixed-mouldboard plow, which cut deeper. The improvement of harnessing through the invention and use of the head-collar was permitting the replacement of oxen with horses, which could plow more rapidly. The water mill was adding a source of power that could be applied to the grinding of grain into flour. However, the harrow was still a thorn branch or a thorn faggot weighted with a log. Grain was still cut with a sickle and threshed with a flail. The use of clover grasses to replenish the soil was unknown. Since hay was not intensively raised for fodder, but only gathered from the meadow, sufficient cattle could not be maintained to manure the land. The slender net yield of seven to eight bushels per acre, or threefold the seed, was considered normal. The yield was barely sufficient to carry the village through the winter to the next harvest.

Communication of the village with the outside world was slow and difficult though not impractical. Save for vestigial Roman highways, the roads through the encompassing forest were crude tracks or narrow trails. The villagers depended on themselves for their food; they wore the woolen clothes which the women spun and wove. They imported only salt, a little iron for tools and implements, and millstones, frequently brought in by itinerant peddlers. If exceptional cold, dampness, or hail brought crop failure, the village, unaided from the outside, sometimes starved. Contemporary accounts describe local famines in which peasants crawled on their bellies to the church door to die in the village road, as in India today.

The peasant was illiterate, superstitious, and religious. Perhaps because his customary procedures did not insure mastery of the mysterious forces of nature, he believed in evil spirits, devils, goblins, and witches and in charms to frustrate them. The clergy, in converting the heathen villagers, of necessity had accommodated themselves in part to existing superstitious practices, while the peasant had interfused superstition and Christian belief. His heathen ancestors for generations had believed, for example, that a pain in the side was caused by a worm in the marrow of the bone, and that if a knife were laid against a sore place and a charm uttered, the worm could be coaxed onto the blade. The peasant after his conversion to Christianity continued to utter the charm, but added "So be it, Lord." The peasant believed in God, Christ, and the Holy Ghost but especially in a ubiquitous Devil and in the power of the Mass, holy water, and relics to exorcise him.

The peasants, as we have noted, did not normally own their strips of land but held them as a grant from a lord and in return rendered him certain rents and services. The lord might be either a noble or a representative or the Catholic church, such as a bishop or the abbot of a monastery. From the standpoint of the peasants, the village was an organized community engaged in tillage and herding for subsistence; from the lord's standpoint the village or a part of it was his estate, termed a manor, which he operated with peasant labor.[a] He allowed the villagers to cultivate part of it for themselves in the strips of land which we have described. But he also retained for his own use the lord's demesne — that is, a part of the arable land, usually scattered in strips among the strips of the villagers, and also a part of the meadow, pasture, and woodland. A peasant, in return for his holdings, gave the lord a portion of the crop raised on it, worked the lord's strips, and performed other miscellaneous services.

The severity of the dues and services rendered by a peasant depended partly on whether he was a free or an unfree man. The majority of the peasants under the manorial system were probably unfree men, bound to the soil and to their lord's will, and called serfs. By manorial custom a serf paid a portion of the crop from his own holding to the lord. He worked on the lord's demesne three days a week usually, but four or five days during a pressure season such as harvesting. He had to wash and shear the lord's sheep, mow and make his hay, reap, shock, and carry his grain, and then thresh and winnow it. He plowed and harrowed the demesne of the lord with his own oxen or horses week after week at the great plowing seasons of autumn and spring. He must use the lord's mill, oven, and wine press and pay for the privileges. He must respect the lord's monopoly of hunting game and maintaining pigeons. The serf could not legally bequeath or sell his holding since it was not his. If he died without children or grandchildren, the holding reverted to the lord. A serf might not marry outside the manor for fear that

[a]In the simplest case of the unitary manor, the boundaries of the village and of the manor coincided, and all the peasants of the village held their farms of the same lord and owed him dues and obligations. In other instances, all the farms of a given manor were in the same village, but some of the farms were held of other lords. In yet other instances, the farms of a given manor (lord's estate) were scattered in several villages, in which other farms were held of other lords. However, in all instances, the village was a co-operative agricultural unit, even though the peasants might owe obligations to different lords.

his offspring and their labor might be lost to the lord, or if he did he must pay the lord an indemnity. He could not leave the manor without the lord's permission, but must live and die on it. In civil actions involving controversy with the lord or his fellow villagers and in minor police cases, the serf was tried by the manorial court conducted by the lord's agent. On the other hand, the serf was allowed the use of his holding as long as he faithfully rendered the lord his dues, and he could transmit it to his children. The free peasant likewise rendered dues and services for his holding, but these generally were lighter than those of the serf. The free peasant might sell his right to cultivate a plot of land and leave the manor after giving a percentage of the sale price to the lord. He might bequeath the holding to an individual of his choice, although his heirs might be required to pay a fee to enter upon their inheritance.

The complex whereby a lord cultivated his estate through the labor of free and unfree villagers and exercised judicial authority over them was known as the manorial system. It prevailed in most of France north of the Loire River and in northern Italy in the late tenth century, was established in central England after the Norman conquest in 1066, and expanded into Germany, Denmark, and southern Sweden, and much later into Poland and Russia. On the fringe of this area there were the stock-raising farms of Norway and Sweden, the isolated farmsteads of Normandy and Brittany, the free peasant farmers of Provence and Castile, and the great latifundia, or landed estates, of southern Italy.

The fundamental unit of life in much of northern Europe was thus the agricultural village. Each village was held and governed by a noble lord, of varying gradations of rank. There were noble lords who were simple knights; others were barons, counts, dukes, kings, or emperors. The peasant worked the land of his local lord, whatever the lord's title, and paid a part of his own crop in return for protection and the use of the land granted to him. Both the peasants and the lord were usually illiterate and superstitious. The lord's castle was merely a wooden blockhouse surrounded by a ditch and a stockade. The lord's military equipment consisted only of a sword, a lance, an iron casque, a buckler, and a suit of buckram. Only the wealthiest knights possessed a coat of mail. Nevertheless, there was a distinct social gulf between the peasant and his lord. The peasant, free or unfree, was a commoner; the lord was a noble, with a rank that was becoming hereditary. The peasant was a grubber of the soil; the lord was a professional fighting man who had learned to ride as soon as he could mount a horse. The peasant was a subject; the lord exercised many of the functions of government. He coined money, regulated weights and measures, levied tolls on the few traveling merchants, administered justice at least in lesser cases, and contended with other lords for the possession of agricultural villages.

The nobles differed among themselves in wealth and rank, the essential power of each noble depending largely on the number of manors he held. A simple knight might live off the produce of one manor. He did not own it outright, but held it by the grace of a higher lord, perhaps a baron. The knight swore to the baron to be "his man," promised usually an annual military service which in later centuries was defined as forty days, and agreed to offer counsel at the baron's court and to submit to its decisions — all this in return for the manor and the baron's promise of protection. The baron, in turn, might hold a number of manors and knights of a higher lord, perhaps a count or duke, to whom he rendered loyalty, counsel, and military aid. The duke or count usually held his possessions of the king or emperor, although he might hold a manor or two from one of his own barons. The dukes and counts, such as the French Duke of Normandy or the Count of Toulouse, were the great magnates of their time. The duke had a court, modeled on that of the king, with a chancellor, marshal, seneschal, and cupbearer. He had a few administrative agents to aid him in coining money, levying tolls, regulating weights and measures, as well as collecting taxes and enforcing justice. He tried to keep his restless barons and knights at peace with each other, while he fought with neighboring nobles to protect his own barons, knights, and manors and to acquire those of his enemies. Western society was rent by private wars among the nobility. This network of dependence in which nobles held land of other nobles and eventually of the king, performed many governmental functions, and fought each other for land, is known as the feudal system. It prevailed in France north of the Loire River, spread into England, Germany, Sicily, and southern Italy, and existed in modified form in southern France, Spain, and northern Italy.

The power of the kings in the latter half of the tenth century was either weak or precarious. In 987 the great nobles and prelates of France elected as their king Hugh Capet, the Duke of Paris. He was the first of a dynasty which was to reign over France for eight hundred years and was to achieve hegemony in Europe. But in 987 there was nothing to suggest this illustrious future. Hugh Capet, as Duke of Paris, had a few knights and manors huddled around Paris in the Île-de-France. His own knights often flouted his authority and descended from their castles to pillage travelers, pilgrims, peasants, merchants, churchmen, and even the king's retinue. Around the Île-de-France towered the domains of great nobles, the dukes of Normandy, Brittany, Aquitaine, and Burgundy, and the counts of Flanders, Anjou, Toulouse, and Champagne. Each one was as strong as or stronger than the king. They had sworn to be "his men" and owed him counsel and military service for their possessions. But they were virtually independent and often rebellious. They fought with each other as well as with Hugh Capet. And Hugh's power was restricted in other ways. France was then only a thin strip of land that reached from the mouths of the Scheldt in Flanders to the mouths of Llobregat in Catalonia and was confined to the east by the Meuse and the Saône Rivers. It included Bruges and Barcelona, but not Metz, Lyons, or Marseilles. The authority of the English king, likewise circumscribed, extended then only over England and not over Wales, Scotland, or Ireland. King Ethelred (987-1016) the Unready was a weakling who shared power with the English nobles, chiefly the great earls. The Christian Spanish kings of Leon, Castile, Navarre, and Aragon were border chieftains on the southern slopes of the Pyrenees who quarreled with each other, with their nobles, and with the Moors.

The Italian peninsula was desolated until 962 by the feuds of a crowd of petty princes. The Moslems controlled Sicily and fought to establish themselves on the Italian mainland. The dukes of Naples, Gaeta, and Amalfi in southern Italy owed allegiance to the emperor of the Eastern Roman Empire, whose capital was Constantinople. The pope attempted to govern the Papal States across the center of Italy. The marquis of Ivrea and of Tuscany in the north stood out from the horde of lesser nobles, while the north Italian towns under the leadership of their bishops struggled to be free of the rural nobility. Only Germany had the good fortune to be governed from 919 to 1024 by a series of outstanding rulers who held the state together by will and personal ability. Germany, which then spread from the North Sea to the Oder River, was divided into the five duchies of Saxony, Lorraine, Franconia, Swabia, and Bavaria. The German kings, notably Otto I (936-973), controlled the great dukes. Otto was Duke of Saxony and retained Franconia, thus reserving to himself the crown domains of two of the great duchies, and he placed his appointees over the other three. His success in bringing peace to Germany tempted him to dream of the loftier dignity of emperor. He claimed a protectorate over Poland, Bohemia, and Hungary. He crossed the Alps, was crowned king of Italy, and in 962 was anointed and consecrated as Holy Roman Emperor by the pope. He proclaimed Latin, the language of the Roman empire, to be the official language of his empire. He married his son to the niece of the emperor of the Eastern Roman Empire. He selected and deposed popes and pretended to a supreme secular authority over all the Christians of Western Europe. Otto and his immediate successors maintained substantial peace in Germany and Italy and were the strongest European monarchs. But their power was precarious even in Germany and Italy, while their pretentions to universal dominion were elsewhere ignored. The great German dukes and the lesser Italian princes obeyed Otto and his successors as monarchs of individual force. They would have successfully defied any ruler of lesser caliber.

Nearly everyone in Western Europe belonged to the Catholic church, and thus shared a common outlook upon the world and upon man's destiny in it.

In this world-view the contemporary theories of science and theology fitted together. The earth, it was believed, was the immovable center of the universe. Around it revolved every twenty-four hours the moon, the sun, and the planets. Beyond them was a firmament with fixed stars. Outside of the stars was Heaven, and underneath the earth was Hell. On the earth's surface was being enacted the drama of salvation. It was a simple, sublime, and heart-rending story. God had created the universe in six days, and man originally had been created in a state of perfection along with the sun, moon, stars, plants, and animals. But man had yielded to temptation, transgressed God's commands, been driven from the Garden of Eden, and ever since men had been tainted with original sin. In time the wickedness of men increased, until by God's grace Christ was sent to save the world by restoring to men the power of pleasing God. That power, now sleeping in mankind, must be re-invigorated in each individual by membership in the Catholic church and participation in its sacraments of Baptism, Confirmation, Holy Eucharist, Penance, and Extreme Unction. Central to Catholic theory was the Eucharist, which re-enacted Christ's sacrifice and restored to the individual the power of leading a life of holiness and righteousness. Since the death of Christ the struggle between the kingdom of God and that of the Devil was the supreme conflict in history. It was to culminate soon in the Last Judgment when the world would come to an end. The good who had loved God and their neighbor as themselves and who had belonged to the church and participated sincerely in its sacraments would ascend to Heaven; the wicked would sink to Hell. History was thus conceived in terms of the conflict between two spirits, two moralities, two parties, or as Saint Augustine called them, two cities. "Two loves have made two cities, love of self unto contempt of God the earthly city, love of God, unto contempt of self, the heavenly city."

The church, in a general sense, was the community of all faithful believers on earth and the angels and saints in heaven. The church, in a special sense, was the corporative hierarchy of ordained clergy. The Catholic clergy were divided into the regular clergy (monks and nuns who followed in monasteries and convents a rule of life usually enjoining poverty, obedience, and chastity) and the secular clergy (parish priests, bishops, archbishops, and pope). The lowest unit of organization was the parish, which usually corresponded to the village. The villagers who worked together also worshiped together at the village church. The parish priests were supervised by the bishop, who was the executive and responsible head of a diocese and who was then the central figure of clerical life. Neither the archbishops, whose administrative unit (the province) comprised several dioceses, nor the pope, the titular ecclesiastical head of Christendom, enjoyed great authority as yet. The medieval church thus had the elements of an administrative organization, from the parish priest to the pope, and indeed in many other respects resembled a state. It had its own official language, Latin, in which its correspondence was conducted. It levied its own tax, the tithe, supplemented by fees and by income from the vast clerical estates. It had its own law courts which asserted jurisdiction over all cases involving clergymen, the property and property rights of the church, the sacraments including marriage, and wills, vows, pledges, and contracts which rested on good faith. The bishops as judges applied in these cases the law of the church, that is decrees of its councils and of the popes. The church had the embryo of an educational system — the schools of the monasteries and cathedrals and, very occasionally, of the parish.

Intricately intertwined with the society of its time, the medieval church was contaminated at every level of its administration by association with the world. The parish priests were deep in the husbandry of the village. They were supported by tithes which were meant to take one-tenth of the gross yearly income of every villager — one tenth of his harvested grain, one-tenth of the increase of his cattle, one-tenth of his garden produce. The priests added to these tithes the products of certain parcels of land which belonged to the village church and which the priest cultivated himself and the fees paid for special ceremonies such as burial. Usually the priest was a peasant's son, as often as not an ill-educated, undistinguished man who could barely read the Latin of the services and who shared or acquiesced in the superstitions of his parishioners. Occasionally a poor priest climbed the clerical ladder to become bishop or abbot. But it was then infinitely easier to step across, from a secular noble rank to a bishopric, from one high rung to another, than to mount any ladder. So the younger sons of the nobility just stepped across, and as bishops and abbots they shared in the prejudices, the vivacity, and the politics of their noble kinsmen. The church was accumulating, largely through the gifts of the faithful, nearly one-third of the land of western Europe. In northern Italy, for example, the Bishop of Florence possessed 200 castles and the Abbey of Farfa, 192, while the Bishop of Bologna had 2,000 manors. The church exacted, like any secular lord, dues and services from the serfs in its villages. The church owned some of its land outright for the service of God; it held the rest as fief to a noble or the king and performed military service for it. There were fighting bishops and, less frequently, abbots, who led their knights into battle, had their cupbearers and seneschals, and sat on the king's council. The papacy itself was a prize for which Roman nobles squabbled. Christianity taught the fundamental equality and brotherhood of men, but some bishops and abbots were devising a social theory which corresponded more closely to the group interests and ideas of the nobility from which they sprang. Divine Providence, so ran the theory, had divided society into three orders or estates each of which had its proper function: the clergy, who were charged with prayer and conducting mankind to salvation; the nobles, who were to fight for the protection of all; and the peasants, who by their labor were to nourish and clothe themselves and the other two classes. Each individual was to labor contentedly in that field where God had placed him. "God forbid," wrote one medieval clergyman, "that the peasants, whose proper lot is daily toil, should abandon themselves to sloth and indolently spend their time in laughter and idle merriment."

Nevertheless, the teaching of Christ ("Be ye therefore perfect, even as your Father which is in heaven is perfect") exerted a continuing pressure and set up tensions within each individual believer between worldly and spiritual impulses, within the church between worldly clergy and spiritual reformers, and within society between the laity and the church. In the church there were periodical periods of spiritual renewal and reform. In society the clergy often tried to win the laity to a finer Christian life. Reforming and innovating spiritual leaders were frequently monks. Though the monasteries themselves often needed reform, yet at their best they held up the Christian ideal of spiritual perfection. At their best they also preached by example the ethos of work, the concept that a job well done was one way of serving God. The monks worked at many tasks. They cleared or supervised the clearing of the encompassing forests. Where a monastery was placed, fields were reclaimed and the wilderness was transformed into an agricultural estate that sometimes served as a model farm. The monks were the physicians to whom the sick were brought, they were the librarians who copied by hand the manuscripts of classical antiquity, and they were often the school-teachers. The monastic and cathedral schools together kept alive the surviving remnants of classical learning — a little grammar, rhetoric, and logic, a bit of arithmetic, geometry, astronomy, and music taught from the threadbare handbooks. The knowledge offered in these textbooks was meager, but already it was beginning to be enlarged through contact with Arab scholars in Spain.

Though Latin was the official language of the church, the inhabitants of Western Europe spoke varied vernacular tongues. In most of the area formerly controlled by the Roman Empire the Romance languages, Italian, French, Spanish, Roumanian, and later Portuguese, were crudely evolving from the colloquial Latin that had once been spoken. Along the left bank of the Rhine and in Germany, the Netherlands, Scandinavia, and England, Germanic tongues, including German proper, Danish, Swedish, Norwegian, Dutch, Flemish, and Anglo-Saxon, prevailed. A given language, such as French, was fragmented in turn into hundreds of dialects imperceptibly merging one into the other but over a distance so different that natives of southern and northern France could scarcely understand each other. Western Europe was a vast linguistic tapestry.

Western Europe toward the close of the tenth century is not easy to describe briefly. But if the reader will imagine the area west of the Oder River covered by immense forests, dotted here and there by isolated homesteads and village clearings between which crude tracks struggle, if he will see these villages — the rude manor house surrounded by a wooden stockade, the thatched peasant huts with dirt floors, the superstititious peasants tilling the arable fields and knowing of the outside world only by the intermittent arrival of an occasional peddler, if he will observe the vigorous nobles engaged in recurrent warfare with each other, and the kings attempting to wield their little power, and if he will bear in mind the presence of the parish priests, monks and nuns, abbots and abbesses, bishops and archbishops, and pope of the universal Christian church — if the reader does this he will not be seriously misled. Essentially, it was a rural, military, and religious culture operating at a fairly simple technological level.

An Invitation to Further Inquiry and Reflection

The transformation of society from the second century to the tenth in lands that constituted the western half of the Roman empire has long attracted the attention of historians. Indeed, what happened then and why are still subjects of historical controversy. Obviously, we need some method of thinking about the subject. Perhaps the following approach would serve, at least as a guide to inquiry and reflection. Let us make a multi-columned table. At the head of the vertical columns, let us write categories of social existence, such as boundaries and axis of the civilization; population; family; technology; economy — agriculture, manufacturing, commerce, labor; diet and health; society — urban/rural, classes; government and administration; military constitution; view of the world as expressed in art, philosophy, law, and religion. On the left-hand side of the table, let us set down a series of column heads, one for each century from the second to the tenth. Then in each block we enter the data; for example, what happened to the population in the second century, the third, the fourth, and so on for each century and for each category of social existence. Such a table immediately provokes comparisons and questions. We can compare the tenth century with the second. The differences immediately leap to view, and so, after some thought, do the resemblances. What had happened and how and why? Or we can follow one category through the centuries, and develop a sense of tendency. We can follow population, for example, and watch its decline for centuries, its recovery towards the end of the period, and query why the decline and why the upturn. Or we can note relationships to explore. Is there a relationship between diet, energy, and world-view? Will an energy-producing diet yield a more optimistic world-view? Is the adoption of the stirrup related to the predominance of cavalry over infantry and the triumph of the feudal system? And so on.

People, if undisturbed, tend to do the same thing in the same way day after day, season after season, year after year. In any society there are continuities of habit, persistence, and inertia. At the same time there are also circumstances provoking people to change, and if successive changes are in the same direction there will be tendencies of movement. A static cross-section, as of tenth-century Europe, by eliminating time tends to eliminate movement and to make the society appear more conservative than it actually was. To be sure, in tenth-century Europe there were imposing tendencies of continuity. Certain phrases, "the simple and laborious routines of agriculture," for example, were introduced to convey a sense of continuous living. Do you think such tendencies of continuity were more persuasive and stronger in the tenth century than in the twentieth? Why or why not? However, there was movement in tenth-century society, and certain phrases were intended to suggest where change was occurring or was apt to occur. Did you notice those phrases? And in what sectors of social existence they appeared? Can we anticipate what effects these alterations will have?

Suggestions for Further Reading

(For general reading, arranged alphabetically by author)

Philip Bagby, *Culture and History: Prolegomena to the Comparative Study of Civilization* (1958)

William C. Bark, *Origins of the Medieval World* (1958)

Frank Barlow, *Edward the Confessor* (1970)

Geoffrey Barraclough, *Origins of Modern Germany* (1947)

M. W. Beresford and J. K. S. St. Joseph, *Medieval England: An Aerial Survey* (1958)

Marc Bloch, *Feudal Society* (1939-40-, trans. 1961)

————, *French Rural History: An Essay on its Basic Characteristics* (1970)

P. Boissonade, *Life and Work in Medieval Europe* (1927)

Lowrie J. Daly, *Benedictine Monasticism: Its Formation and Development Through the 12th Century* (1965)

Christopher Dawson, *The Making of Europe: An Introduction to the History of European Unity* (1937)

Eleanor Duckett, *Death and Life in the Tenth Century* (1967)

Leopold Genicot, *Contours of the Middle Ages* (1967)

David Knowles, *The Evolution of Medieval Thought* (1962)

Robert S. Lopez, *The Birth of Europe* (1962; translated 1966)

Robert L. Reynolds, *Europe Emerges: Transition Toward an Industrial World-Wide Society 600-1750* (1960)

C. T. Smith, *An Historical Geography of Western Europe Before 1800* (1967)

R. W. Southern, *Making of the Middle Ages* (1953)

James Westfall Thompson and Edgar Thompson, *An Introduction to Medieval Europe* (1937)

David M. Wilson, *The Vikings and Their Origins: Scandinavia in the First Millennium* (1970)

(For advanced study)

John Morris, "The Later Roman Empire," *Past and Present*, No. 29 (December, 1964), 98-104.

A. H. M. Jones, *The Decline of the Ancient World* (1966)

A. H. M. Jones, *The Later Roman Empire, 284-602. A Social Economic and Administrative Survey*. 3 vols. (1964)

Marc Bloch, *French Rural History: An Essay on its Basic Characteristics*
——, *Land and Work in Medieval Europe* (1967)
The Cambridge Economic History of Europe. Volume I: *The Agrarian Life of the Middle Ages* (2nd ed.; 1966)
Robert S. Hoyt, *Life and Thought in the Early Middle Ages*. Articles by Robert S. Lopez ("Of Towns and Trade"), Joseph R. Strayer ("The Two Levels of Feudalism"), and Lynn White, Jr. ("The Life of the Silent Majority") (1967)
Henri Pirenne, *Mohammed and Charlemagne* (1939)
A. F. Havighurst (ed.), *The Pirenne Thesis: Analysis, Criticism, and Revision* (1958). Heath Problems Series.
Phillip Grierson, "Commerce in the Dark Ages: a Critique of the Evidence," *Transactions of the Royal Historical Society* 5th series, volume 9 (1959), 123-140.
W. H. C. Friend, "North Africa and Europe in the Early Middle Ages," *T. R. H. S., 5th Series, volume 5 (1955), 61-80.*
Lynn White, Jr., *Medieval Technology and Social Change* (1962)
R. H. Milton and P. H. Sawyer, "Technical Determinism: The Stirrup and the Plow," *Past and Present*, No. 24 (April, 1963), 90-100.
Joan Thirsk, "The Common Field," *Past and Present*, No. 29 (December, 1964), 3-25.
Keith Thomas, "Work and Leisure in Pre-industrial Society," *Past and Present*, No. 29 (December, 1964), 50-66.
B. H. Slicher van Bath, *The American History of Western Europe, 500-1850 A.D.* (1963) [i.e. 1964]
M. L. Laistner, *Thought and Letters in Western Europe, A.D. 500 to 900* (rev. 1957)
R. R. Bolgar, *The Classical Heritage and its Beneficiaries* (1954)

CHAPTER II

THE RISE OF THE TOWNSMEN

In studying the new Western European civilization from the tenth century to the sixteenth, we should note that the eleventh, twelfth, and thirteenth centuries formed a period of material and cultural expansion. Population increased, huge tracts of wilderness were cleared and the land claimed for agriculture, local trade and interregional commerce grew in volume, along the trade routes towns were founded or expanded, and industrial production for local use as well as for export rose. The feudal monarchy in England and in France was developed and strengthened. A series of able popes built the Catholic church into a powerful organization. A reforming monastic order, the Cistercian, and popular mendicant orders of friars, the Franciscan and Dominican, were founded. Under the auspices of the church, the knowledge of classical Greece and Rome and of the Arabs was assimilated, universities were established, scholastic theology and philosophy were elaborated, scientific investigation was initiated, and the Romanesque and Gothic cathedrals were built. The cultural leader in these centuries was northern France, and specifically Paris and its environs.

There followed one hundred and fifty years, from about 1300 to 1450, of uneven development. Several epidemics, including the Black Death, cut the population of western Europe by at least one-third. Cultivated lands were abandoned. The expansion of commerce and industry was arrested, although technical and commercial practices were improved. England and France fought each other intermittently in a Hundred Years' War that ravaged France. In the fifteenth century the English government was thrown into disarray by the War of the Roses among competing claimants for the throne and their nobles supporting them. The Christian kings of the Iberian Peninsula quarreled with each other. Imperial authority in Germany decayed. The papacy fell into disrepute. For years (1305-1377) the popes lived in exile on French soil, virtual captives of the French kings, and then for another period (1378-1417) two rival popes competed for the allegiance of the faithful. Scholastic philosophy and Gothic architecture declined into a decadence of over-elaboration. Yet even in the midst of a prolonged economic recession there was in Italy in the fourteenth and fifteenth centuries a cultural flowering. Especially in the north Italian towns there developed a veritable cultural complex of interregional trade, export industries, complicated social structure, vivid town and inter-town politics, love of the Latin and Greek classics, and an ineffable art. In the latter half of the fifteenth century aspects of this complex, including admiration of the classics of antiquity, began to cross the Alps.

However, in seeking to understand certain themes, tendencies, and processes in modern history, there are advantages in proceeding in these early centuries not by chronological periods but by themes and tendencies that were appearing in this emerging civilization. For this reason we shall focus on the chief tendencies of this early period – the rise of the townsmen, the rise of the monarchs, and the assimilation and development of knowledge. Chapters on these subjects will enable us to find our way into other topics, such as the origins of capitalism, the beginning of the nation-state, and the basic faiths by which Western man has lived. We shall also begin to discern the fundamental historical processes at work in the movement of history.

The Rise of the Early Towns
(Eleventh to Thirteenth Centuries)

Towns grew with the expansion of trade. Even in western Europe of the tenth century there existed stray nuclei of settlement that were larger than a manorial village but not primarily commercial or industrial in function. In Italy, many old Roman towns continued to exist, considerably shrunken, as the seat of the bishop's church, the cathedral, and the headquarters for the administration of the diocese. These episcopal towns in Italy and elsewhere in Europe often included little except what was indispensable for the ceremonies of the church, the management of the diocese, and the support of the cathedral clergy: that is, a market, warehouses to store the produce of the bishop's manors, possibly a school, a few vassals of the bishop employed in an administrative and military capacity, servitors, and petty artisans. Also, the spread of monasticism had led here and there to the growth of large agricultural establishments, which needed the labor of artisans as well as of peasants. The fortification of a monastery here and there in the open country had made it the center of refuge in times of trouble. Here and there, also, peasants and artisans had clustered around the "castle" of a noble, then a rude, palisaded blockhouse, often erected in a hurry to meet some crisis of invasion.

Then, too, even in western Europe there existed in the midst of those who farmed, or fought, or prayed, a few who trafficked: a few merchants and artisans who lived from exchanges of goods. The manor was never entirely self-sufficient: it needed millstones to grind the grain, salt to preserve the meat, and iron tips for plowshares. These articles had to be purchased from

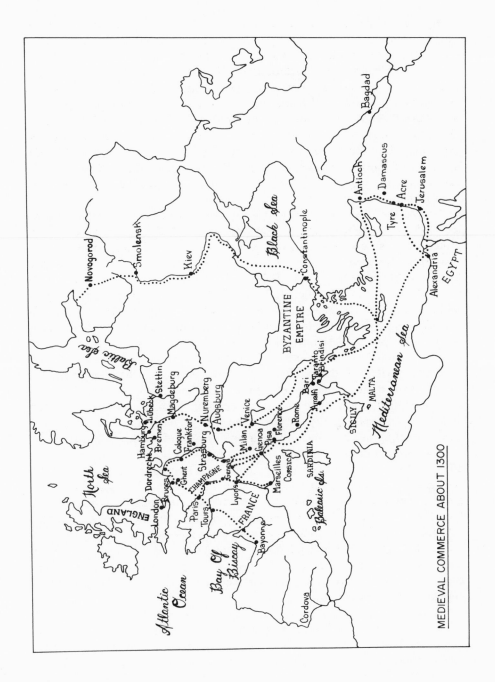

MEDIEVAL COMMERCE ABOUT 1300

other districts, perhaps through a merchant, with the surplus produce of the village. Meanwhile, a few peddlers trudged from village to village with packs of small wares. Other traders coasted along the shores of the northern seas. Normandy, Flanders, northeastern England, Ireland, the islands of Scotland, Iceland, Norway, Sweden, Denmark, and Russia formed a kind of economic unit around the North and Baltic seas. Scandinavian merchants, putting in and out along these shores, traded in the products of the area, such as timber, hides, furs, grain, fish, wine, salt, wool, and woolen cloth. Flemish craftsmen wove fine cloth from the wool of large flocks of sheep that grazed in the meadows of the Lys and Scheldt rivers. By the end of the tenth century the demand for the cloth was so considerable that raw wool had to be imported from England to supplement the local shearing.

Toward the close of the tenth century, a few merchants and artisans began to settle down about those stray nuclei of settlement and centers of protection — an enclosed cathedral area, a fortified monastery, or a castle — that were conveniently located with respect to trade. A striking instance was Bruges, where after 962 Count Baldwin Iron-Arm built a castle in a loop of the little river Lys. Outside of the castle there soon arose a new burg or suburb inhabited by traders, artisans, and tavern-keepers. One source tells us: "After this castle was built, certain traders began to flock to the place in front of the gate to the bridge of the castle; that is, merchants, tavernkeepers, then other outsiders (*hospitarii*) drifted in for the sake of [supplying] the food and shelter of those who might have business transactions with the count, who often came there. Houses and inns were erected for their accommodation, since there was not room for them in the chateau. These inhabitants increased so rapidly that soon a large ville came into being which is called Brugghe by the people from the word bridge." Elsewhere in northwestern Europe emerged other tiny islands of merchants and artisans: Paris, Cologne, Ghent, London — to mention those which became celebrated. In England, for example, Droitwich grew from local salt works, Dunwich from herring fisheries, Chester from the Irish-Scandinavian trade in furs, Gloucester from the iron industry, York, Lincoln, and Norwich from the Scandinavian trade, Dover and other southeastern ports from the cross-channel traffic. In each town handicraftsmen exchanged articles of their manufacture with each other and for supplies brought by peasants of the surrounding countryside. In a very few towns craftsmen and merchants from the start engaged in long-distance trade.

At the opposite end of western Europe, Venice and the South Italian ports of Bari, Brindisi, Taranto, and Amalfi had never lost contact with the "gorgeous East" of the Byzantine and Arabic-Moslem empires. The western half of the Roman Empire had gone under during the barbarian invasions of the fourth and fifth centuries. But Roman emperors in the East held out and withstood the barbarians' attacks. There a successor empire, the Byzantine, flowed out of the Roman. Continuity and internal peace, sustained by the bureaucracy and army, became the climate of a tree of culture with marvelous leaves. From the ninth to the eleventh centuries, when its manufacture, commerce, and towns were flourishing, this tree put forth a dazzling array of gems. Strangers in Constantinople marvelled at the imperial palaces, covering acres upon acres of ground. The churches sparkled with the glory of mosaics, gold, and silver, and the squares and streets were decorated with the masterpieces of ancient sculpture. Eastern wares, spices, drugs, precious stones, and silk fabrics, were carried there in great quantities. Byzantine scholars studied and copied the works of classical Greek authors. The clergy and laity continued a form of Christainity known as the Greek Orthodox. The Eastern Empire safeguarded the manufacturing techniques and the literary and philosophical heritage of the Greco-Roman world against the barbarian peoples to the north.

Meanwhile, to the south there had arisen a vast Arabian-Moslem state. This new state was the outgrowth of the preaching of a new religion by an early seventh-century Arabian prophet named Mohammed. Within a century after his death (632 A.D.), his inspired followers had united Arabia and had conquired the Tigris-Euphrates valley, Iran and Afghanistan from Persia; Syria, Egypt, Sicily, and Sardinia from the Byzantine Empire; North Africa, practically all of Spain, and later Corsica from the Western Christians. In this vast territory, stretching from the Indus River to the Atlantic Ocean, a great Arabian civilization began to thrive off three continents, unearthing and utilizing what it would find buried in the past. The Arabs, being excellent farmers, improved the production of cotton and sugar. Skilled artisans, they fabricated beautiful oriental rugs, the celebrated Damascus and Toledo swords, and Cordova leather. As expert caravan traders, they engaged in world commerce. They imported into western Asia and Europe precious stones from India, spices from the East Indies, and fine silks from China. The Arabs also wrote poetry, drama, and history and displayed a special talent for fiction. As translators of Greek philosophers and scholars, they mastered the Greek tradition which fascinated them, then interpreted and ramified it with their own explorations in mathematics and science. Their physicians became far better than any in the West. Their mathematics taught the world analytical geometry and much of trigonometry.

The Moslems were not averse to trading with Christians, but Moslem raiders and pirates made Mediterranean trade a risky matter. Nevertheless, even in the ninth and tenth centuries, merchants from Venice and south Italian ports, spurred by that avarice which their religion taught them was a cardinal sin, were trading with the Byzantine Empire and with Moslem Egypt and Syria. They carried off young Slavs from the Dalmatian coast and sold them to the

Moslem harems, and they brought iron and lumber to Egypt. The Italians returned from the Moslem lands and the Byzantine Empire laden with silks, spices, precious stones, and other exotic Oriental luxuries which took up little space and commanded high prices in northern Italy. Profits were fabulous and well worth the risk of piracy and shipwreck. It has been estimated that a round trip of a Venetian galley sometimes paid as much as 1,200 per cent of the initial investment.

Mediterranean commerce became large-scale with the advance of Christian military and naval power in the Mediterranean area during the eleventh century. We are still arguing why from the late tenth century population increased in western Europe, but we know it rapidly did. A manor could scarcely support a single knight, let alone a horde of children, and many younger sons of poor knights, without prospects at home, sought wealth and adventure abroad. Hundreds of French knights flocked to the richer provinces of southern Italy, which acknowledged the suzerainty of the Byzantine Empire. "Why live like a rat in a hole when you might rule these fertile plains?" one knight observed. An obscure knight of Normandy named Tancred of Hauteville had twelve sons, most of whom turned up in southern Italy. One son, Roger Guiscard the Sly (d. 1085) organized his fellow knights and brigands and wrenched the south Italian provinces from the Byzantine Empire. Whereupon he and his brother Robert (d. 1101), blessed by the pope, conquered from the infidel Moors the islands of Sicily (1060-1090) and Malta (1091). In other outposts French knights, exhorted by the pope and inflamed by tales of spoil and of Moslem women, aided the Spanish princes of León, Navarre, and Castile to recover the northern half of Spain from the Moors. The Christian advance was here signalized by the capture of Toledo (1085), the second city in Spain. Meanwhile, the Italian port towns of Pisa and Genoa, which the Moors periodically pillaged, were retaliating in commercial-religious crusades. Encouraged by the pope, they regained Sardinia (1050) and Corsica (1091) and assisted the Guiscards in conquering Sicily. By 1095 the Christian counterattack had largely freed the western Mediterranean of Moslem pirates.

In that year Pope Urban II persuaded tens of thousands of knights to seek adventure, spoil, land, and religious salvation in retrieving the Holy Places from the infidel Moslem Turks. The knights, in a massive offensive known as the First Crusade (1096-1099), traveled across Europe and the Mediterranean to Jerusalem, there set up Christian principalities in Palestine and Syria, and thus established a base in the heart of the Moslem country which it took the Moslems two centuries to whittle away. The merchants of Pisa, Genoa, and later Venice, stirred by the prospect of commercial gain, co-operated in the capture of the Syrian port towns. The successful First Crusade was followed by six other crusades, mass expeditions of Christian knights directed to an attack on Moslem possessions in Syria and Egypt.

Although one may debate their ultimate effects, the Christian expeditions in all corners of the Mediterranean did help to wake up Europe. During the eleventh, twelfth, and thirteenth centuries, they quickened the revival of commerce, industry, and town life that was already coming along with the growth of population. They cleared the entire Mediterranean Sea of Moslem pirates, so that it became a safe highway of exchange between Europe and the East. Now all the overland European trade routes to Venice, Genoa, and Pisa in Italy, to Marseilles in France, and to Barcelona in Spain were extended across the Mediterranean to the Levant and to Constantinople. Most of the caravans that came from India and from China, bringing spices and fine fabrics to the Syrian coast, now made for the Christian vessels which awaited them in the Levantine ports. At these ports the Italian merchant-cities had won a privileged position. When an Italian city aided the crusaders in a successful siege of a Syrian port, such as Tyre and Acre, it arranged that it be assigned a definite quarter in the captured place. There it established a trading post or "factory," which contained a market, docks, warehouses, churches, and all that was necessary for a commercial base. In their home cities, too, the Christian merchants had developed capital and shipping in transporting the crusading armies to Palestine and in forwarding supplies to the knights who remained there. Their galleys were enlarged from 200 tons to more than 500 tons and became more numerous. Efficiency was improved in the loading and unloading of ships. The famous Arsenal at Venice was described by a traveler as "like a great street on either hand with the sea in the middle." Warehouses, each with its special kind of materials and goods, lined the long waterfront. A galley making ready for sea was towed from warehouse to warehouse, from each of which stevedores handed out bales, cordage, arms, and food, until "when a galley reached the end of the pier she was equipped from end to end." An arriving galley was in like manner unloaded.

Christian conquest in the Middle East gradually enlarged the demand of western Europe for eastern luxuries. Christians were drawn out of their backwoods villages and introduced to the wonders of the Byzantine and Moslem empires. They experienced the softness of fine silk, the flavor of spiced wine and food, and the delight in jeweled ornament, and they took home the desire for those things. In consequence, when German merchants crossed the Alps to Venice with furs, twine, rosaries and metals (gold, silver, iron, copper, lead, tin), they brought back in exchange the pepper, cloves, cinnamon, nutmeg, mace, camphor, sugar, diamonds, emeralds, rubies, sapphires, and fine cottons and silks the German knights craved. Italian merchants also crossed the Alpine passes into France and southern Germany bringing spices, silks, and goldsmith's works. Long lines of pack-horses, with bales or baskets slung across their backs, made their way along paths often too narrow for two strings of loaded horses to pass one another. The merchants encountered, in addition to poor roads, robber knights and brigands, a motley of weights, measures, and coins since each noble could set his own standard, a multiplicity of tolls since each knight could levy his tax, and a confusion of dialects. Merchants on the road generally banded together into caravans armed for battle.

Italian merchants going north met at the fairs of Champagne in northern France merchants coming south from the North Sea-Baltic area with hides, flax, wool, and coarse woolen cloth. The North Sea-Baltic region was experiencing a revival of commerce parallel to that of the Mediterranean area. The merchants of the northern seas were usually from German towns, such as Hamburg, Bremen, Lübeck, and Stettin, which were united for protection into the Hanseatic League. Wheat from Prussia, furs and honey from Russia, timber, tar, salted fish from Scandinavia, wool from England, fine and coarse woolen cloth from Flanders, Brabant, and northern France, salt and French wines from the shores of the Bay of Biscay, and eastern luxuries that had been brought overland from Italy were the articles of the northern trade. The Italian merchants would return home from the Champagne fairs loaded with hides, flax, wool, and coarse woolen cloth. But there were other, stranger transactions at the Champagne fairs. The Italian merchants were brokers not only of goods but also of culture. Often unknown to those who carried them, hidden in the transfer of rich goods, like the ideas in the fabric of dreams, were the unmarked wares of thoughts, thought-patterns, customs, desires, needs, processes, inventions, languages. These also were being traded, but no one knew who carried them away, or in what combination, or where he would take and scatter them. The northern merchants took away, perhaps, new methods of bookkeeping and new technologies that Italians had invented. The Italian merchants themselves were altered. An Italian trader would return to northern Italy with raw materials and also with unsolved problems. He would stay awake at night and dream up solutions, schemes on how to change what he brought back that would make it worth more before selling it. Back home he would refine these raw products into superior leather, linen, and woolen goods and then, to close the circle of trade, ship these to the Near East. In thus changing things our Italian himself was being changed. He was ever widening the circle of trade in which he was moving. He was ever enlarging the scope of his activity. He was becoming a merchant-manufacturer, perhaps a little of a banker, even a bit of a politician, or scholar, or inventor. Or, maybe he remained only a bearer of ideas, like a bearer of germs innocent of his burden, and happy with his profit.

In conjunction with the overseas and overland commerce there arose in northern Italy, industries producing woolen, linen, silk, leather, and armor for export. Towns began to specialize in certain trades. Silk-weaving, introduced from the East, became concentrated at Lucca. Handicraftsmen in Venice imitated Byzantine and Moslem techniques in the manufacture of glass, paper, and fine weapons. Florence specialized in linen and wool weaving, Milan in armor- and leather-working. In the north the towns of Flanders became celebrated for the flexibility, softness, and beauty of their woolen cloth. To the strategic commerical and industrial centers flocked other artisans — butchers, tailors, blacksmiths, potters, cobblers — to supply the daily needs of the towns and the immediate countryside.

Old towns expanded and new ones appeared, chiefly along the trade routes. Venice, Pisa, and Genoa thrived. A host of lesser Italian towns clustered around Milan in Lombardy and Florence in Tuscany. Augsburg, Nuremburg, and Magdeburg in Germany became important, for they were situated on the line of trade between Italy and the North. Marseilles, Lyons, Dijon, and Troyes in France similarly were on the main land routes between the Mediterranean and northwestern Europe. Bruges, Ghent, Lille, Douai, Ypres, Arras, Cambrai, and other towns of Flanders, Brabant, and northern France were industrial textile centers at the focus of commercial routes leading from the Baltic and North seas and from the Mediterranean. Hamburg, Bremen, Lübeck, and Stettin, as we have noted, also participated in the Baltic traffic.

Let us not exaggerate either the volume of this early trade or the population of the early towns. The tonnage of a single twentieth-century steamship is equal to that of the total Venetian or Genoese merchant fleet in the thirteenth century. The English export of wool, a major interest, amounted in 1277-1278 to about 3,000 tons. Venice and Paris at the opening of the fourteenth century were populated respectively by about 200,000 and 100,000 inhabitants, but the other towns came trailing after: Florence, Genoa, and London with fewer than 100,000 apiece; Strasburg, Nuremburg, Frankfort, and Basel as late as 1450 with 26,000, 20,000, 8,700, and 8,000 individuals.

However, significance is not always proportionate to size. We are at the beginning of things. Individual merchants, with their minds on profit, were weaving, as it were, a fabric of trade that was to become world-wide. Townsmen started the freeing of the individual from external domination, a theme which until recently has been central in the history of Western culture. Of course these townsmen, initially, did not intend any revolutionary modification of the authority of the nobility, the clergy, and the monarch, but if they were to live by exchange, they needed freedom from serfdom and its entanglements. At first, individual merchants had simply assumed they were free. Later, inhabitants of a town usually purchased from the neighboring lord or monarch a charter that granted each town-dweller elementary privileges. A citizen under one of these charters could marry and give his children in marriage at will, could move away at his pleasure, come and go, dispose of his property as of his person, and acquire, possess, alienate, exchange, sell, will, and bequeath his goods, movable and immovable, without being subject to the lord's control. All feudal charges, such as the obligations to perform military service, to offer hospitality, and pay tolls to the lord, were either abolished or reduced to a fixed money payment. Many towns never secured more than these "elementary urban liberties." But the largest and wealthiest also obtained a degree of self-government: the right to elect a town council with the authority to look after the supply of water, to construct and repair the town walls, to regulate trade and industry, and to administer justice. Thus, as legal units, the town gradually struggled into life in the midst of the complexity of feudalism. The townsmen were proud of their freedom and power. When Ghent was warring with neighboring nobles and the king of France, its citizens took the city gates off their hinges for two years and dared their antagonists to enter. In northern Italy and in Germany, where the authority of the Holy Roman Empire had decayed, towns such as Venice and Florence, Hamburg, Lübeck, and Bremen became independent republics.

From the towns freedom began to spread through the countryside. A municipal charter customarily provided that if a serf successfully dwelt in a town for a year and a day, he became a free man. To hold his serfs on the manor, the lord was forced to moderate his exactions. Also, the revival of commerce had entailed the revival of a money (instead of a barter) economy. The Byzantines and Moslems used gold coins and expected to be paid in them. The kings of Sicily took the lead in minting gold coins, the Italian cities followed, and soon the ducats of Sicily, the florins of Florence, the sequins of Venice, and the coins of other towns and principalities were circulating throughout western Europe. Everywhere the local lord needed cash to purchase the luxuries he craved. At the same time, the lord and the peasants could now sell their surplus produce in the town market for cash. Out of this situation arose varying new adjustments between the lords and their peasants. Throughout western Europe both ecclesiastical and lay lords increased their agricultural production by bringing under cultivation the immense areas of waste and forest land. To attract peasants to the labor, they were offered a new set of terms: personal freedom and the inherited right to cultivate a plot of land in return for the annual payment of a fixed money rate. An immense work of clearance was thus accomplished, and the vast forest through which, in Germany for example, a traveler might journey for five days in complete solitude, began to disappear. On the older estates of France and western Germany the lord often relinquished administration of his manor. For a money payment he sold the peasants freedom to move away and to marry. He leased the demesne strips to prosperous peasants for a term of years for money. He also allowed the peasants of the village to retain the hereditary right to cultivate their strips of land as long as they rendered fixed and defined dues and services. These consisted of an annual money rent, payment for use of the lord's oven and mill, observance of his monopoly of game and hunting, offering in grain of one sheaf in either twelve or ten, and ten to twenty days of annual labor. The peasants were now hereditary tenants who could sell their right to cultivate their strips of land to other peasants and then leave. The more prosperous peasants were also long-term renters of the strips of the lord's demesne. A similar (and somewhat later) transformation of the manor in England, like the developing common law practice of jury trial, increased the practical freedom of Englishmen. The new type of manor freed the English peasant from a servile status and made possible several new kinds of status: independent yeoman farmers who owned their land, long-term renters of the lord's demesne, hereditary tenants (copyholders) who paid fixed annual quit-rent, and landless cottars who hired out as agricultural laborers. The lord of the manor had become a landlord. In general, though vestiges of service tenures persisted on many manors throughout Europe, many serfs had gained their personal freedom, while their remaining obligations in dues and services had been better defined and often changed into a single payment.

The Beginnings of Capitalism (Eleventh to Fifteenth Centuries)

A word, such as "capitalism," often appears only after the circumstances it denotes have led men to perceive the need for the term. And once the word is there, its meaning changes with changing circumstances and ideas. Its meaning is different in different centuries, in the same century among different peoples, and within the same people between different individuals.

Nevertheless, a word frequently has a central core of meaning that persists as long as the word is used. What is capitalism? Capital, we are told, is accumulated wealth, or an aggregation of (economic) goods which is used to promote the production of other goods instead of being valuable solely for purposes of immediate enjoyment. Capitalism is an economic arrangement in which individuals animated by a desire for gain use a respectable amount of capital as private property to obtain private profit through exchange in the market and through rational (that is, non-superstitious) employment of the available means. When Spanish explorers despoiled Montezuma and the Incas of treasure beyond the dreams of avarice, were they capitalists? No, they did not obtain the treasure through exchange in the market. When railroads were built in China, care was exercised that certain mountains, forests, rivers, and cemetery hills were avoided, for fear of disturbing the repose of the spirits. Was that a capitalist solution? No, it was not a rational, non-superstitious employment of the available means. Even the daydreams of a capitalist take shape as a calculus of profit and loss rationally computed. The symbol of capitalism is the account book: its center lies in its profit and loss account.

Were those handicraftsmen of the medieval towns who produced for the local market capitalists? No. They used a small amount of capital to secure a livelihood, not a considerable profit. Each master craftsman of this type had his own shop, owned the tools and raw materials that he used, and sold the finished article directly to the customer. Such craftsmen fashioned shoes or kettles or other articles for the townsmen and the inhabitants of the immediate countryside, in brief, for a market that was local, limited, and rather static. After all, in the days before advertising, only so many shoes could be worn and and worn out, and only so much clothing was needed. An exaggerated profit was unobtainable by these craftsmen and perhaps for this reason was not desired. They wanted security of livelihood. So the master craftsmen of each trade in each town, the shoemakers of Cologne for example, organized themselves into an association known as a guild. They agreed upon regulations that would assure them a monopoly of the local market and eliminate cutthroat competition among themselves. The regulations prescribed that only the products of master craftsmen of the guild might be sold in the town and the vicinity, that workers must pass through successive stages of apprentice and journeyman before becoming a master, and that there be only a limited number of apprentices. They determined wages, hours of work, prices, and the standards each product must obtain. The guild, like the village, monastery, or castle, both protected and restricted men. Perhaps these structures bear some resemblance, also, to the shapes of medieval consciousness, the vaguer edifice within experience, which cannot be seen with the naked eye.

The spirit of guild regulations was approved by the church theologians who taught that man's economic activity should not be all-absorbing but should be only supplementary to his attainment of salvation, and that an honest craftsman should produce an article of known merit and honest workmanship and charge for it just price. The economic-theological theory of "just price" was, like the guild regulations, adapted to a local market in which demand and technological methods changed slowly. The town councils, composed of merchants and craftsmen, enforced the craft regulations and added some of their own to protect the townspeople as a unit. To prevent peasants from exploiting the town, they were required to display their produce at the town market and compete among themselves. That all townspeople might have an equal chance, it was forbidden to buy goods on the way to market ("forestalling"); to buy larger quantities than were needed ("engrossing" or "cornering"); or to buy goods for re-sale before the ordinary consumers had supplied their needs ("regrating"). The same spirit of closure and self-protection which the town imposed on itself, it imposed on its relationship with the world. Revenue tariffs were levied at the town gates on many products. Merchants from other towns frequently had to sell through a local representative and pay a fee.

In every town in western Europe there were these craftsmen who produced in a small way, were organized into guilds, and were subject to local regulations, but in the major towns there were also merchants who engaged in export commerce on a capitalist scale. The Italian merchants led the way. Capitalism began in the north Italian cities in the eleventh century, first in commerce and later in industry and banking. The Italian merchants, as we have seen, were enabled by their geographical position to act as middlemen between the luxury traders and manufacturers of the Near East and the raw material producers of northwestern Europe. The problem and opportunity of this Mediterranean trade — the problem of assembling enough capital to equip an expedition to the Levant, the opportunity for fabulous profit — led individual Italians to associate themselves and their capital in various forms of partnership. A Venetian trader of the eleventh or twelfth centuries, for instance, might lack the capital to acquire a ship, pay the crew, and purchase the cargo. He therefore would find partners who would add their limited resources to his and share in the eventual profits in proportion to what they gave. Venetian partners, because of their city's near-monopoly position, could charge for their return cargo of Oriental luxuries what the traffic would bear. The standard of a "just price" could scarcely be applied to articles whose source of supply was distant and whose cost was indefinite, while the Venetian government was little interested in regulating the prices of goods that were to be sold to non-Venetians. The partnership formed for a single voyage, if successful, would be apt to be renewed. The partners would re-invest their profits and undertake another voyage and yet another, until working in partnership became a habit. With increased capital they would widen the scale of their operations. They would undertake several voyages simultaneously. They would discover new territories for exploitation and open branches along the routes of trade. They would admit to the firm members of their family — brothers and brothers-in-law, sons and sons-in-law. In this way, merchant companies grew great in activity and wealth. By 1300, one Genoese family-partnership firm operated alum works in Asia Minor, owned several galleys and leased others, and ran regular shipping services to the Black Sea, Syria, Tunis, the Balearic Islands, and Spain. Capitalists by then dominated Italian foreign commerce. By the beginning of the fifteenth century, Venice had replaced Constantinople as the greatest trading center in Europe, and the Venetians passed for the "lords of gold of Christendom."

Merchant capitalists branched out into industry. Wealth accumulated in commerce was invested in industries that produced for the export trade. The merchant of Florence, for example, who sold fine cloth that was consigned to the Near East, wished to assure a steady supply of quality cloth and also to appropriate the profits of its processing. He purchased raw wool from the north and then paid a succession of craftsmen — spinners, weavers, fullers, dyers, and finishers — to work it up in their rooms into the cloth which he required. Or he bought coarse woolen cloth from the north and paid fullers, dyers, and finishers to perfect it. The capitalist merchant retained ownership of the material throughout the processing; he frequently owned the tools that were used; and he paid the craftsmen a pittance wage that left them an industrial rabble. By the close of the thirteenth century capitalists of the north Italian cities dominated the export industries (linen, silk, and woolen cloth, leather and fur goods, and armor), and income from industry swelled the fortunes already gained from commerce.

Italian merchant capitalists also entered banking and lent money to popes, kings, nobles, towns, and commercial enterprises. The rates were 10 to 17 per cent for well-assured ventures; 50 to 150 per cent to risky accounts. Everywhere companies of merchant bankers multiplied, at Venice, Cremona, Bologna, Piacenza, Parma, Asti, Chiari, Genoa, Lucca, Siena, Pistoia, Rome, Pisa, and Florence. From the middle of the thirteenth century, Florence with its eighty banking firms was the financial capital of the West, as Venice was its commercial capital. These Italian banking firms had branches everywhere — at Acre, Alexandria, and Constantinople, in southern Italy and in northern France, in Flanders and in England — and they did almost everything. They collected the pope's revenue, paid kings' armies, bought and re-sold commodities, entered industry, organized transport by land and sea, accepted deposits, loaned money, and most of all grew rich. By the middle of the fifteenth century the capital of the Medici, the leading bankers of Florence and of Europe, was the equivalent of $7,500,000.

The peasants did the customary things in the customary way year after year, and the handicraftsmen, lulled by security, conscientious routines, and guild regulations, clung to old methods, but the capitalists were supple, ingenious, and quick to invent or adopt any device that would increase their chance for gain. The chief advances in business and technological methods during this period were invented or first extensively applied in capitalistic enterprises. Italians learned from the Moslems the use of the compass, the astrolabe (for determining latitude), paper, Arabic numerals, letters of credit, bills of exchange, joint-stock companies, the spinning wheel, and the windmill. The typical Mediterranean ship of the eleventh century was a slim galley of perhaps 200 tons, propelled by oars and a single sail, steered by an oar instead of a rudder, and cautiously kept within sight of land. In two or three centuries the Italian mariners enlarged the galley to 600 tons, replaced the oar with a rudder, tripled the sails while keeping the oars, mastered the compass and the astrolabe, drafted detailed, rational maps of the Mediterranean and

Atlantic coasts, and steered boldly out of the Straits of Gibraltar and across the Bay of Biscay to England.

Italian capitalists developed double-entry bookkeeping on paper instead of papyrus, and in Arabic instead of Roman numerals. They utilized (1) letters of credit (the prospective traveler deposited money at a bank and received a letter of credit which was honored when presented to the bank's branches and correspondents); (2) bills of exchange (an order to a partner or agent in another town to pay a designated person a specified amount of money at a future date in another currency); (3) bank deposits (individuals deposited money with the bank for safekeeping or the bank loaned money by creating a deposit on which the borrower could draw); (4) checks (the depositor ordered the bank to pay his creditor); (5) clearing-house procedures among banks of the same city; and (6) maritime insurance. Italian businessmen developed the partnership, which had, however, the weaknesses of not always assembling enough capital and of dissolving with the death of each partner. An early European joint-stock company, the Genoese Bank of St. George, founded in 1407, overcame these shortcomings. It gathered the savings of many individuals who purchased negotiable shares of stock which they might sell or bequeath without disrupting the life of the company.

The Venetians perfected the manufacture of glass until glass windows, a medieval innovation, were an accepted necessity in the houses of the well-to-do. In Italy and northern Europe old and new sources of power were applied to a variety of mechanical devices. The water wheel, long employed to grind grain, now furnished power for spinning silk, fulling cloth, and pulping rags for paper. It was used in south Germany in the capitalistic mining and metal-working industries to pump water out of mines, to crush ore and to drive more powerful bellows, and thus increase the capacity of blast furnaces. By the twelfth century windmills were adding another source of power, and within a hundred years were dotting the landscape of the plains of northern Europe. The crank, in the form of a rotary grindstone, had appeared in Europe as early as the ninth century. About 1420 the compound crank was known in the carpenter's bit-and-brace. By mid-fifteenth century the compound crank was being equipped with connecting rods and a flywheel, and by 1480 with a ball-and-chain governor, to secure continuous rotary motion. The foot treadle was applied to the hand loom in the twelfth century, to the lathe in the thirteenth, and to the organ in the fifteenth. The increased cloth output from the pedal looms pressed the spinners to produce more yarn. By the late thirteenth century, they were replacing the spindle and distaff with the spinning wheel, an interesting device that introduced the belt transmission of power. Mechanical clocks, driven by weights, appeared as early as 1250. As they came into use, they superseded the uncertain sundials and water clocks and brought a new regularity in the lives of merchants and craftsmen. Meanwhile, springs, which store energy, were employed to drive lathes by the mid-thirteenth century and were used in watches in the late fifteenth. These sources of power and their new application, a multiplicity of mechanical devices using a complexity of gearing and moving parts, imply a vivid technological curiosity greater than had ever existed in western Europe, whether in the tenth century or in classical antiquity.

The Italian capitalists, meanwhile, used the city governments which they controlled to protect their enterprises. Venice and Genoa each tried to make the Levantine trade a monopoly: only· Venetians, or only Genoese, might trade with the Near East. Other Italians and foreigners were in fact largely excluded while the Venetians and Genoese fought each other. The Venetian government acquired naval bases down the Dalmatian coast, across to Syria, and up to Constantinople, and also obtained trading "factories" in nearly every Near Eastern commercial town. It prescribed that Venetian merchant vessels must sail to the Near East only twice a year in two great fleets under convoy. The details of the semi-annual fleet were minutely regulated. Officers were required to take an oath to obey instructions. The size of anchors and quality of rope was scrutinized. The Venetian government determined the route. It also attempted to regulate its relations with western Europeans to Venice's advantage. German traders in Venice were disarmed and given a room; they were shadowed at every step; they were compelled to sell their entire stock in Venice, without the choice of withdrawing it and carrying it further. Venetian industries were encouraged and safeguarded. The government sought out markets and raw materials. It levied high protective tariffs on imports of foreign manufacturers. Special technical processes, such as glassmaking, were carefully guarded. Skilled workmen were forbidden to emigrate. Since the low prices of Venetian goods depended partly on low wages of its craftsmen and these in turn on the low price of foodstuffs, the import of food was encouraged, its export was prohibited, and new food-producing territory was conquered. Venice early insisted, furthermore, that an import by an individual Venetian merchant be balanced by an equivalent export. It was apparently felt that imports were harmful, perhaps because they caused a drain of gold and silver. Protective devices similar to the Venetian were enacted by other Italian cities.

In northern Europe early capitalism developed partly independently and partly in imitation of the Italian version. The North Sea-Baltic region, as we noted, experienced a commercial revival similar to that of the Mediterranean area. As in Italy, capitalists dominated the northern export trade and industries producing for export. Flemish and later English cloth merchants paid craftsmen to work up wool into fine cloth for a meager wage. Northern merchants formed partnerships. Northern capitalists sent their sons to Italy to study accounting and the most recent business methods. Northern capitalists also lent money to kings and nobles until the close of the thirteenth century, when the superiority of the Italian bankers temporarily put them out of business. The Italians had too many contacts, too many branches, and too many devices, and besides were too shrewd for northerners to match in money-lending. During the fifteenth century, however, great financiers appeared in France and southern Germany. Like their Italian counterparts, they did everything. The Frenchman Jacques Cœur owned several Mediterranean galleys and leased more. He handled silks, armor, feathers, spices, furs, and every class of merchandise, especially that required by the king, the dauphin, and the nobles. He lent money to the king, queen, and courtiers, became paymaster of the king's household, and was given a patent of nobility. The Fugger family of Augsburg engaged in commerce over all Europe, operated mines in the Tyrol and Bohemia, controlled half a dozen other industries, and conducted banking activities.

By the fifteenth century the new economy had created in the north Italian cities and in the major northern towns a complex array of new and old social classes. These classes included a patriciate of wealthy merchant families who had enjoyed their wealth for several generations; a rising class of new rich — first-generation merchants, industrial capitalists, and bankers on the rise; a middle class of small burghers — master craftsmen and shopkeepers whose interests centered in the local trade; and the industrial proletariat — the craftsmen who had sunk to the level of wage-earners. This was a rather complex social structure, quite different from that of the tenth century, when, outside of the clergy, there were only the nobles and the peasants. Also, unlike the society of the tenth century, that of the Italian and northern cities was fluid. Distinctions of birth, it is true, never disappeared, and the pride of the patriciate families was strong. Nevertheless, social distinction could be gained through the acquisition of wealth and culture, in other words through individual achievement. The townsmen were free to rise as well as to move about.

Again, it is well not to overestimate the volume of town life and of capitalistic endeavor in western Europe at the close of the fifteenth century, on the eve of the discovery of America. Nine-tenths, probably nineteen-twentieths, of the western Europeans were peasants, village-dwellers. Even in town the typical figure was the individual craftsmen who worked with one or two helpers, sold directly to the customer, and was not involved in the export trade. Even in the realm of capitalistic enterprise, the Medici bank, with seven and one-half million dollars, appears puny beside our multi-billion dollar corporations whose offices take up whole skyscrapers. Still, seven and one-half million appears immense against the background of the dirt floors and thatched huts of a tenth-century village. The Italians, moreover, had pioneered a complex of navigational, technological, business, and regulatory devices which later generations and other peoples would elaborate. The Italians had initiated a form of capitalism that was to prevail until the eighteenth century — "commercial capitalism" — so called because the greatest amount of capital was employed in commerce and the merchants usually dominated large-scale industry and banking. The Italians, also, had instilled in capitalism the fundamental motives of rivalry for wealth and economic power in which later generations of townsmen would be reared. Spurred by these motives, utilizing the urban freedom of persons and property and experimenting with new business techniques, the townsmen of the fifteenth century could achieve business careers as relatively independent, self-governing individuals. In technology, in the accumulation and organization of wealth, and in the individual drive for economic power, western Europe was far stronger on the eve of the discovery of America than it had been five centuries before. It was also far stronger in the organization of political power, as we shall discover in the next chapter.

An Invitation to Further Inquiry and Reflection

This chapter seems obvious, and so it is. Yet it embodies a theory of how history, that is life, moves at its simplest, a theory that the student may find valuable in all his later work. Reflecting upon the material of this chapter in response to a few questions may lead us innto this theory of explanation.

In the "Invitation" at the conclusion of chapter one we used a multi-columned table to discover certain historical tendencies in western Europe from the second to tenth centuries, without probing what we meant by "tendency." Now let us probe more deeply. From the tenth to fifteenth centuries there was a tendency in certain areas of western Europe toward commercial and capitalistic expansion. What *is* a historical tendency? Capitalism, we remark, is an institution. What is an institution? How does an institution originate? History moves, we say. Movement implies momentum. What gives momentum to history? History, as presented in the latter part of chapter one, was a cross-section in which time was largely eliminated. History in chapter two was a story in time, a narration. What were the elements utilized in this particular narrative to keep the story moving? From answers to these questions can we construct a theory of historical movement, of historical process, of historical explanation, and of historical presentation, at their simplest?

For Further Reading

(For general reading)

M. W. Beresford and J. K. S. St. Joseph, *Medieval England: An Aerial Survey* (1958)

Marc Bloch, *French Rural History: An Essay on its Basic Characteristics* (1970)

G. G. Coulton, *Medieval Panorama* (1938)

Joan Evans, *Life in Medieval France* (1958)

F. Heer, *The Medieval World: Europe 1100-1350* (1962)

Arthur Korn, *History Builds the Town* (1953)

Robert Lopez, *The Birth of Europe: A Reinterpretation of the Medieval World* (1962; translated 1966)

Achille Luchaire, *Social France at the Time of Philip Augustus* (1967; translated by Edward B . Krehbiel)

H. Pirenne, *Medieval Cities: Their Origins and the Revival of Trade* (1925, 1939)

Eileen Power, *Medieval People* (1924, 1930)

Fritz Rörig, *The Medieval Town* (1967)

Steven Runciman, *History of the Crusades* (1951-1954)
    Vol.I: *First Crusade and the Foundations of the Kingdom of Jerusalem*
    Vol. II: *Kingdom of Jerusalem and the Frankish East 1100-1187*
    Vol. III: *Kingdom of Acre and the Later Crusades*
Louis F. Salzman, *English Life in the Middle Ages* (1926)
R. W. Southern, *The Making of the Middle Ages* (1953)
C. T. Smith, *An Historical Geography of Western Europe Before 1800* (1967)
Urban Tigner, *Daily Living in the Twelfth Century: Based on the Observations of Alexander Neckam in London and Paris* (1964)
Charles Verlinden, *The Beginnings Of Modern Colonization: Eleven Essays with an Introduction* (1970)
Philip Ziegler, *The Black Death* (1969)

(For advanced study)

The Cambridge Economic History of Europe. Volume I: *The Agrarian Life of the Middle Ages* (2nd edition; 1966)
The Cambridge Economic History of Europe. Vol. III: *Economic Organization and Policies in the Middle Ages* (1963)
John V. Nef, *The Conquest of the Material World* (1964)
Alfred F. Havighurst (ed.), *The Pirenne Thesis: Analysis, Criticism, and Revision* (1958). Heath Problems Series
Carl Stephenson, "The Work of Henri Pirenne and Georg von Below with respect to the Origin of the Medieval Town," in S. A. Rice *Methods in Social Science* (Chicago, 1931), 368-82.
Ronald G. Witt, "The Landlord and the Economic Revival of the Middle Ages in Northern Europe, 1100-1250," *American Historical Review*, 76 (October, 1971), 965-988.
Claude Cohen, "An Introduction to the First Crusade," *Past and Present*, No. 6 (November, 1954), 6-30.
J. A. Brundage (ed.), *The Crusades: Motives and Achievements* (1964). Heath Problems Series.

CHAPTER III

THE RISE OF THE MONARCHS

Europe is a fabric of nations. We should begin to wonder what it is to be a nation, how it emerges and from where. To understand all this we need to look back nearly one thousand years, to the late tenth century, when the European kings were still virtually powerless and national consciousness did not exist. At that time real political authority — justice, coinage, tolls — was exercised by the great feudal vassals and by the lesser nobles. Loyalty was expressed either in a direct personal attachment to the local feudal magnate or, perhaps in a vague veneration for the ideal of a world empire. But gradually over the course of centuries the kings of England, France, Portugal, and Spain emerged. They began to develop their power and to extend and strengthen their control in a myriad of ways more or less devious. They sent out administrators who apply the king's law to areas hitherto only nominally subject to him. On the Continent they dug up the Roman law, whose basic principle was that the king's will *was* law. And they began to collect royal taxes in money to support a royal army as well as the royal administration. In all this the kings were aided by townsmen who had the same interest as the monarchs, namely, the elimination of feudal anarchy. The townsmen wanted relief from the private warfare in which the feudal nobility was chronically engaged. For reasons of good business they wanted peace over a large area and security for life and property. They furnished the kings with money, administrators, and lawyers. Gradually, as the king's administration and peace began to touch the people over a large area, loyalty to the monarch replaced loyalty to the feudal magnate. Even more gradually, by an even more complex process, the people of a given realm, say France, began to realize that they had the same king, the same history, and the same interests of defense. They began to form a society which we can think of in retrospect as one and which in its own time, was beginning to think of itself as one. Around that society as a unit men's emotions crystalized: they took pride in it, and we see developing what is called national feeling and a nation.

How far that process of the formation of a nation in any single country had gone by the end of the fifteenth century, how pervasive and how intense was the national feeling, is difficult to say. But it seems clear that from the eleventh to the late fifteenth centuries, the peoples in England, France, and Portugal, and to a later and lesser degree in Spain, were being gradually

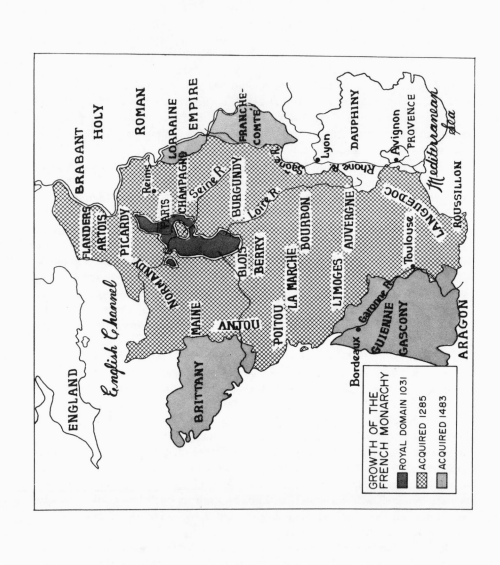

GROWTH OF THE
FRENCH MONARCHY

ROYAL DOMAIN 1031
ACQUIRED 1285
ACQUIRED 1483

ENGLAND

English Channel

BRABANT

HOLY

ROMAN

LORRAINE

EMPIRE

FLANDERS

ARTOIS

PICARDY

NORMANDY

Reims

PARIS

Seine R.

CHAMPAGNE

FRANCHE-
COMTÉ

BURGUNDY

Saône R.

Rhone R.

Lyon

DAUPHINY

Avignon

PROVENCE

Mediterranean Sea

Loire R.

BLOIS

BERRY

BOURBON

AUVERGNE

LANGUEDOC

ROUSSILLON

MAINE

ANJOU

POITOU

LA MARCHE

LIMOGES

Toulouse

Garonne R.

BRITTANY

Bordeaux

GUIENNE

GASCONY

ARAGON

brought by the activities of a royal administration to form a living whole which could not be forcibly divided and from which a section could not be sliced without cutting to the quick the feelings of the people. Italy and Germany each remained divided into a number of small states. There, the consolidation of royal authority did not occur, and the process of coalescence of a people was retarded, although educated Germans and Italians were becoming more and more aware of their common cultural heritage. To learn, if only in a somewhat schematic way, how the rise of the monarchs and of incipient national unity happened, let us turn first to the history of France.

France

When Hugh Capet became king of France in 987, he started with very little; in fact, the word "started" is a distortion. He was simply a duke in Paris who had recently been elected king of France by the great nobles and bishops. To be sure, with the title of king he received the major attributes of medieval kingship: he was feudal overlord and he was holy, when holiness was effective power. As feudal overlord of the great counts and dukes he possessed certain legal rights. He could summon his great vassals for counsel, or to make up a court of justice for the trial of other vassals. As guarantor of the feudal contract he could hear complaints from lesser vassals over the heads of their lords and interfere locally to maintain justice. He was legal guardian of minor heirs, and before they came of age he could enjoy the income from their duchy or county. His consent was necessary for the marriage of a widow of a great vassal or of daughters inheriting the fief. He could demand the payment of certain feudal aids, as when a vassal died his heir must redeem his inheritance. As king he might also demand that each year the great vassal perform with his knights forty days of military service. As a sacred person, anointed at his coronation with holy oil, Hugh Capet was the servant and minister of God, set apart by the sacred mystery of royalty from other mortals, even from the great vassals. He was also the protector of the church, a position which endowed him with considerable rights. In the center of France, four archbishoprics, twenty bishoprics, and a number of abbeys were at his disposal. On the death of the titleholder, the king seized the movable possessions of the deceased, enjoyed the income from the landed property of the benefice while it was vacant, and eventually imposed his candidate as successor.

The position of Hugh Capet, feudal overlord and sacred person, was in theory magnificent, but in actuality was unsubstantial. There was no assurance that he would be succeeded by his son; the nobles and bishops might choose the next king from another family. His personal domain as duke was not much larger than an average American county. It was surrounded by the holdings of the great barons, the counts or dukes of Flanders, Normandy, Brittany, Anjou, Aquitaine, Toulouse, Burgundy, and Champagne, who acknowledged the king's overlordship and rendered homage but who afterwards ignored the king when they were not fighting him. They governed their own territories and blocked the king from direct contact with their lesser knights and peasants. Within his own duchy around Paris, Hugh Capet let some of his villages to lesser knights, many of whom defied him and pillaged his followers, and he retained some of the villages for himself. A few royal agents, known as *prévôts*, collected dues from the knights, and grain, wine and chickens from the royal manors. They kept some of the dues as their remuneration and reserved the rest for the king. The *prévôts* also administered village justice. Hugh Capet, his wife and children, the chaplain, the chamberlain, the keeper of the stables and the grooms, and a few guests wandered from royal manor to royal manor in order to eat up the produce and thus to keep alive. Hugh Capet, living from day to day, just hung on *and* persuaded the great nobles and bishops to elect his son king while he (Hugh) was still alive. The measure worked and assured the succession. His immediate successors[1] imitated his example: while the monarch was still living he had the eldest son elected and crowned king until it was established in French custom that the throne should descend to the king's eldest son. By the time of Philip Augustus (1180-1223), the ceremony of prior election was no longer deemed necessary. This was the major achievement of the early Capetian kings: to solve the problem of the succession and to establish the kingship in a single family.

The rivals of Hugh Capet, the great counts and dukes, were scarcely better off than he. Their lesser knights defied them. But during the first decades of the eleventh century the dukes of Normandy got their duchy well in hand. Castles could be built only with the duke's permission and must be handed over to him on demand. Performance of military service owing the duke was systematically enforced. Private war was carefully restricted. The duke held the monopoly of coinage, and was able to collect a considerable part of his income in money. With the resources of a consolidated duchy, Duke William conquered England in 1066. The other French dukes and counts imitated the Norman dukes and during the twelfth century consolidated their governments. The inhabitants of each duchy and county, already differing from their neighbors in dialect, customs, and ruler, came to have a provincial pride. They thought of themselves, for example, as Normans, or Bretons, or Burgundians. The people of northern France regarded as foreigners the subjects of the southern duchy of Aquitaine and the county of Toulouse, so different were

---

[1] Robert the Pious (996-1031), Henry I (d. 1060), Philip I (d. 1108), Louis VI (d. 1137), Louis VII (d. 1180).

the latter in language, costume, and theatrical gestures.

From 1108 to 1328, the Capetian kings slowly asserted themselves in this feudal and provincial world. They had no pre-established plan. From king to king they profited from the occasions and met the needs of the hour. Louis VI, known as the Fat — but never too fat to fight — worked throughout his reign to subdue the lesser knights within his own domain around Paris. Louis the Fat's successors, using the resources of the duchy of Paris and their feudal rights as overlord, then enlarged this domain. They confiscated the fiefs of rebellious vassals, sustained rebellious sons of rebellious vassals, married heiresses, and acquired by forfeiture those fiefs whose rulers had died without direct heirs. They added to the royal domain Normandy, Maine, Touraine, Anjou, Poitou, Artois, Vermandois, Champagne, Carcassonne, Beaucaire-Nîmes, Toulouse, Auvergne — the list is long. By 1328 Flanders, Brittany, Guienne, and Burgundy were the only great semi-independent fiefs remaining, and the boundaries of the royal domain nearly coincided with the boundaries of the kingdom.

An enlarged domain required an enlarged administration. The king needed more officials, trustworthy individuals to do his business. The traditional royal agents, the *prévôts* having been rewarded with a fief and usually inheriting their posts, tended to escape his control. So the later Capetians, beginning with Philip Augustus, appointed a new type of local official, the *bailli*, who was responsible for a given district. A *bailli* supervised a number of *prévôts*, heard appeals from their judicial decisions, and received and passed on to the king the dues they collected. Usually lesser knights or townsmen without great social distinction, appointed by the king and removable by him, and paid by him in money, the *baillis* were completely dependent on the king for their position and advancement. To supervise the *baillis*, the king also developed a central administration at Paris. To audit the *baillis'* accounts, he set up a system of treasury officials, eventually forming a Chambre des comptes. To hear appeals from the *baillis'* decisions, a high court known in time as the Parlement of Paris, evolved. To support this more extensive, paid royal administration the king needed a more extensive, paid royal income. A couple of centuries before in a primitive barter economy, such increased revenue would have been impossible, an unheard of dream. But now with the revival of trade and a money economy, an increase was possible. The king began to collect feudal dues, to require legal fines and fees, and to extort forced loans from the Jews and the towns, all in money.

The authority of the king's agents began to touch every person and every class within the king's extended domain and even within the remaining great fiefs. The *baillis* and the treasury officials and judges at Paris were king's men, often university-trained men, ambitious for him and for themselves. They insinuated their jurisdiction everywhere. They heard appeals from the decisions of lesser knights, even those in the great fiefs; they took cognizance of cases involving clergymen if a temporal possession was at stake; they ordered the town governments to render an annual accounting of their funds. In the thirteenth century they forbade the bearing of arms and commanded that private warfare cease. By then every class was inclined to accept the royal jurisdiction. The nobility, decimated and impoverished by the Crusades, entered the king's service and began to attend his court. The townsmen, desiring peace and order that they might trade in security, welcomed his stronger authority. The French clergy, exploited by a papacy dominated by Italians, turned to the king for protection. Finally, the Capetians had the good fortune to have a saint, Louis IX (1226-1270), a just king who defended his own rights and those of others. The humblest peasant came to know that Louis himself sat under a tree in the forest of Vincennes, near Paris, and that anyone who had a grievance might come before him for judgment. Out of the veneration of this popular king there was born the religion of the monarchy. Meanwhile, the dialect of Paris was acquiring prestige as the dialect of the king's capital, of the royal administration, and of such medieval poetic masterpieces as the *Roman de Rose*. The Paris dialect was being carried to outlying regions of the kingdom by the king's administrators and by returning students of the University of Paris. In 1328 the Capetians were strong in their control of the enlarged royal domain, in their prestige as the supreme judge of the kingdom, and in the basic loyalty of the population.

The Hundred Years' War (1328-1453) with England severely tested the French monarchy. When the last Capetian, Charles IV, died in 1328 without leaving a son, the throne passed to his nearest heir in the male line, Philip VI (1328-1350) of Valois. King Edward III of England held the Duchy of Guienne of the French king. Angered already by the encroachments of French royal agents within his Duchy, he claimed for himself the French throne as the closest heir to Charles IV in the female line. There followed a century and more of intermittent war. Twice the French kings were near ruin: once when Edward forced his captive, King John (1350-1364), to cede to him outright in 1360 the western third of France, from the Pyrenees to the English Channel; again, from 1413 to 1422, when the English occupied all of northern France, and the French king retired south of the Loire River. Twice the French recovered, under Charles V (1364-1380) and under Charles VII (1422-1461).

Throughout the war the French kings struggled with the problem of maintaining an effective army. The later Capetians had enjoyed prestige but they had lacked an effective military force and were always short of money. As feudal overlord they could require their knights to serve only forty days, a term that scarcely permitted a sustained campaign. So the later Capetians, beginning with Philip Augustus, began to pay knights to serve for the duration of the campaign. But by feudal law the king could not levy a tax on his subjects that was not provided for in a feudal or manorial contract with knights or towns or peasants, unless he had the consent of his council of barons and prelates. The later Capetians, in search of money, resorted at first to expedients. They debased the coinage (coinage was becoming a royal monopoly and another unifying influence), borrowed from towns and Jews, and bargained with local assemblies of clergymen or nobles or townsmen for their consent to collect taxes locally. Meanwhile, Louis IX, Philip III (1270-1285), and Philip IV (1285-1314) occasionally summoned their bishops, barons, and representatives of the leading towns to sustain them in affairs of grave moment. They were called to Paris on the eve of the crusade to Egypt, and again to protest the arrogance of Pope Boniface VIII. In 1314 Philip IV asked this central assembly (whose members, incidentally, came only from northern and central France, the southernmost provinces having their separate assembly in the Estates of Languedoc) for its content to a tax for the support of a war with the Count of Flanders. The Valois kings continued during the Hundred Years' War to bring together this central assembly (which we shall call the Estates-General of the North), to obtain its consent for taxation. Little by little the French became accustomed to paying three types of royal taxes — the *gabelle*, by which the king's subjects must buy their salt from royal warehouses, in some regions at high prices; *aides*, originally a sales tax on every transaction but eventually only on the sale of meat, fish, and alcoholic beverages; and the *taille*, a property tax from which the clergy and nobility were exempt. Then, after Charles V and Charles VII were victorious they levied these taxes without summoning the central assembly and applied the proceeds to the support of a well-organized standing army.

No one gave the two kings permission to dispense with the Estates-General of the North. Yet the French people paid. Why? Partly because the need was obvious — the money and the army were indispensable to throw out the English —, partly because the king had divine prestige as a holy person and an honorable judge, and partly because the king was the only savior in sight. When the Estates-General of the North met, the three estates of clergy, nobles, and townsmen bickered with each other. The clergy detested the nobles, the nobles disdained the townsmen, and the townsmen in turn feared the nobles and disliked the clergy. Only the king was a symbol of unity. And finally, the war, in origin feudal and dynastic, came to engage the emotions of the French people. They came to hate the exactions, the depredations, and the *foreignness* in appearance and speech of the English soldiery. They came to realize that though they might, as Normans, or Bretons, or Poitevins, differ from each other in dialect and customs, yet as a group they resembled each other more and understood each other better than they resembled the "Goddamns," the English, whom they comprehended not at all. The French gained a sense of identity partly because of their common opposition to the English.

All these emotions were expressed by Joan of Arc, the popular heroine, who appeared in the reign of Charles VII. Joan, like many other peasant girls of her time, was devoted to the saints whose images stood in the village parish church, and she came to believe they in turn were devoted to her. She heard the voices of St. Michael, St. Catherine, and St. Margaret. What did the voices say? St. Michael told her that she must come to the aid of the king of France. The angel described the devastation that was the kingdom of France. Joan believed that the true sovereign of France was God and that the king held the throne of Him. She was exalted with pity for the kingdom of France that was so harshly trampled, and with worship for the royalty humiliated by the foreigner. Devotion to the king and to the kingdom and hatred of the enemy were fused in her spirit as in the spirit of other Frenchmen. Charles VII emerged from the war with a standing army, the right to levy the *gabelle*, the *aides*, and the *taille* without soliciting the consent of the Estates-General of the North, and the enhanced prestige of the savior of the realm, who had expelled the English from all of France except the port of Calais.

The achievements of the Capetians and of Charles V and Charles VII were continued and confirmed by Louis XI (1461-1483) and by his daughter Anne, who was regent until 1492 during the minority of Charles VIII. The throne passed without objection to the nearest heir in the male line. Louis and Anne added Picardy, Provence, Brittany, and the Duchy of Burgundy to the royal domain until it included nearly the entire kingdom. They retained the judicial hierarchy — the seigneur's agent administering village justice, the *prévot*, the *bailli*, and the high court, the Parlement. Louis levied the *gabelle* and the *aides* and increased the yield of the *taille* from 1,200,000 livres in 1462 to 4,600,000 in 1481, without recourse to an Estates-General. He perfected and doubled the standing army, recruited an expert corps of Swiss.pikemen, and developed the finest artillery to be had in Europe. He encouraged Italian silk weavers to settle in Lyons, tried to crack the Venetian monopoly of the Near Eastern trade by introducing French convoys to Egypt, and protected the Norman woolen weavers from foreign competition. He crushed one rebellion of nobles, and was not troubled thereafter. He appointed the French archbishops, bishops, and abbots and was impatient of papal interference in the French church. Louis was independent and brooked no opposition. "The King's Council," it was said, "rides on his mule."

Yet his power was not absolute. The authority of the French kings had grown within the feudal complexity. They had enlarged the royal domain by acquiring the domains of other lords. They had invented devices to administer and protect this enlarged domain. Among the populations loyalty to a local lord who offered protection was replaced by loyalty to the king who offered protection and justice and was also a sacred person. But in extending his authority through the feudal complexity he had left many customs unchanged and had entered into contracts with towns, provinces, and classes, all of which impeded the freedom and efficiency of his action. He could not tax most of the great wealth of the Catholic church nor levy the *taille* on the property of the nobility. He allowed recently acquired provinces, such as Brittany, to have assemblies (estates) and high courts (parlements) which could discuss his measures. The nobles were not permanently subdued but rebelled repeatedly in later reigns. The nobles' agents still administered village justice in courts of first instance. There was little law that was common to the entire kingdom. There were seven hundred local codes, by which even the king's judges decided. In southern France the code of the Roman Empire was the law, supplemented in each region by one of three hundred and forty local customs. In northern France three hundred and sixty local customs were the law, supplemented by the Roman code. Within each custom there was a different set of laws for the nobles and for the commoners. Nobles, for example, could not be brought before a *prévôt* but only before a *bailli* or parlement, and if convicted of a capital crime could not be hanged but only beheaded with a sword. Added to the customs and Roman law were the royal edicts, the decisions of the parlements, and the commentaries of the jurists. The clergy were tried in most cases in ecclesiastical courts which applied canon law. There was a motley of weights and measures and a host of provincial tariffs and local tolls which hampered trade. France was larger and more diverse than England. Its institutions were less coherent, and its people less cohesive. Nevertheless, there was in 1492 a populous society which was centered on a monarch who possessed authority.

England

Strangely, we shall learn a good deal about France and French history from studying English history. At the center of medieval English history were its kings. The English kings, like other medieval rulers, were engaged in the continuing adventure of acquiring and consolidating their power. The consolidation of royal power was made simpler for them by the smallness of their domain. England, without Wales, Scotland, or Ireland, comprised 50,874 square miles, less than one-third of the area of medieval France.

The establishment of a strong monarchy in England was promoted, furthermore, by the Norman Conquest and the procedures of the first Norman kings. William, Duke of Normandy and vassal of the king of France, known to contemporaries as a "stern and wrathful man," "greedy for gain," assembled in 1066 an army of approximately seven thousand Normans, Bretons, and Flemings, crossed the Channel, and at Hastings defeated the English king and took his kingdom. "Greedy," as well as "stern," William believed that he owned the country: that the boundaries of the royal domain coincided with those of the kingdom. This was a position which the French kings did not approach in France until 1328 nor attain until 1492. The French kings had to acquire their domain nibble by nibble; William secured his at a single bite.

England in 1066 was a thinly populated country with one to two million inhabitants scattered across the land in agricultural villages and differing from each other in dialects, customs, and laws. William, a foreigner at the head of a small band of alien adventurers, needed to consolidate his position among the English. He accepted most of the customs of the previous Anglo-Saxon monarchy. He continued the division of England into shires, which he renamed counties. He retained the king's agent in each county, the shire-reeve or sheriff. Over a century before the royal *baillis* in France, royal "shire-reeves," appointed and removed by the king, collected taxes in counties throughout England. They also assembled the local militia and presided over the semi-annual meeting of the county court, where the free landowners, obliged by the king to attend, judged civil and criminal cases by local law. Besides appointing the sheriff, William exercised other powers of the Anglo-Saxon monarchs. He collected tolls, took two-thirds of the fines imposed by the county court, and levied on occasion a general land tax known as the Danegeld.

He supplemented these powers with those derived from his position as feudal overlord of England. Thus he took from the great Anglo-Saxon landowners most of their property, keeping a fourth for himself, granting the church another fourth, and paying off 170 barons in his army with the manors and villages remaining. These were accorded to the barons upon the usual conditions of feudal tenure, William granting land, protection, and justice, the barons promising homage, knights for forty days annual military service, and attendance upon his court, there to offer counsel and to judge fellow barons. The monarchs, barons, and knights, no more than five thousand warriors in all, who were remnants of the band which had conquered England, were knit together by their mutual danger and need of one another among the more numerous conquered people.

At the same time William, to keep his barons and knights in hand, transferred from Normandy certain devices. Except for the two earldoms along the Welsh frontier, the manors of each of the barons were scattered over England and could not form consolidated fiefs. Castles were built only with the king's permission and were always his on demand. Sub-vassals swore homage directly to the king, an oath that took precedence over their oath to their immediate overlords. The king only could make war. The king only could make money. The king only appointed archbishops, bishops, and abbots. Bishops could not travel to Rome nor appeal to the pope nor receive communications from the pope without the king's consent. So William ruled.

The kings who came after him were lords of an extensive domain which they wished to "manage with as little trouble and as much profit as possible." They elaborated their government from day to day, year to year, as troublesome necessities intruded. During the medieval centuries, England was generally part of a larger empire. Under William's son, Henry I (1100-1135) this empire included Normandy, and under Henry II (1154-1189), the western half of medieval France from the English Channel to the Pyrenees. Henry I visited Normandy frequently, and Henry II, a red-haired, freckled-faced administrator of driving energy, spent more time in France than he did in England. For their continental expeditions the English kings needed a full-time army of experienced soldiery, which the feudal levy of knights serving forty days annually did not supply. Henry I allowed the ecclesiastical barons and Henry II the secular barons to pay a money fine, known as scutage, in place of sending knights and then used the money to hire mercenary troops who would serve continuously.

Both kings needed to leave behind in England a peaceful population and an administration that would go of itself in their absence. Both monarchs, but especially Henry II, experimented ingeniously. At the beginning of Henry I's reign the central administration was rudimentary. It was composed simply of men who were around the king and who usually journeyed with him – the chancellor who was chief royal chaplain, the chamberlain who took care of his bedroom, the steward who was in charge of the kitchen, the treasurer who was custodian of the king's strong box, and the constable in charge of the stables. They helped the king in royal living and in any business that came before him. They received letters and issued them authenticated by the king's seal, accepted the revenue and paid the bills, and helped the king to do justice. From day to day, under the press of unstable, shifting, and unforeseeable, yet to a degree repeatable situations, they shaped themselves roles which endured beyond their individual lives. Their duties, roles, tasks, their royal business, defined and crystalized, set them moving like planets around the king, in certain fixed and fated courses. They became councilors, they became treasurers, they became judges. They became part of what was permanent around the throne.

Thus the king turned for advice to his trusted servants who intimately lived with him – chancellor, steward, treasurer, and constable. They formed his permanent council and judicial court. Occasionally, the king enlarged the council by obliging his archbishops, bishops, and chief barons to attend when he wished to discuss with them the affairs of the realm, to commit them in advance to policy, or to share responsibility for judicial decisions. Gradually, as the volume and complexity of the king's business increased, some members of the permanent council were set apart to deal with segments of that business while yet remaining members of the council. In fiscal affairs the sheriffs collected the money due the king in their counties. Twice yearly the sheriffs brought to London a record of their receipts and disbursements and the surplus store of money. By the reign of Henry I, a permanent treasure hoard had been established near London, and a treasurer assigned as custodian. During the reigns of Henry I and Henry II, members of the king's council who became professional fiscal experts audited the sheriffs' accounts by well-tested procedures. They also heard, as justices of the king's court of the Exchequer, cases involving the royal revenue. It was difficult to cheat either king.

The two kings also elaborated the machinery for the administration of justice. Henry I, interested in securing peace and order in his kingdom, had an idea: why not send justices from his council on circuit to successive county courts? The measure seemed to work and so was repeated, occasionally under Henry I and regularly under Henry II, until it became a habit for the king to send justices on circuit each year. When the royal justices sat in a county court, their presence converted it for the time being from a popular into a royal court. The royal justices faced a problem: for the conduct and decision of cases what law should they apply, the local law or the law of the royal instructions? Being strangers to the county they probably did not know the local law, and on circuit they would have to get up the local laws of several counties. So they applied the law of the royal instructions. A good deal of civil litigation was brought before the court. An individual who felt that he had been illegally dispossessed of some property could purchase a royal writ or order commanding both the defendant and himself to appear before the royal judge for trial, or an heir who felt that he had been disinherited unjustly could do the same. The judge then summoned a jury of twelve representative freeholders from the county to decide what was the fact. Under Henry II there were fifty different kinds of writs, a century later four hundred and fifty, by which individuals or the king could bring cases before the royal court for impartial and expeditious judgment. Before the court also came criminal cases. The royal justices on circuit, strangers to the county, again faced the problem of discovering what crimes had been committed during the past year, since their last visit to that county. In answer to this problem Henry II in 1166 ordered twelve men from every hundred (a sub-division of the county) and four men from every village to come before his sheriffs and his justices to state on oath whom they believed to be murderers, robbers, thieves, and the harborers of such in their neighborhood. The measure seemed to work. It was repeated and elaborated, and became the germ of grand jury indictment. Later in the thirteenth century an individual so accused could purchase a trial by a jury of twelve men who would decide the fact of guilt. The new procedures (circuit judges, royal writs, grand jury indictment) so increased the press of business in the royal courts that Henry II delegated five advisers to serve as a full central court of appeal in London. All these measures augmented the fees and profits that the king derived from justice. They brought greater peace and order to England and thus won for the monarch popular confidence and gratitude.

The new administration of justice had the profound effect of bringing the freeholder into participation in justice and into a more intimate, continuing connection with the monarchy. The English already had two bonds of unity: They thought together in religion in terms of the beliefs of the Catholic church and in government in terms of a strong monarch. They now began to think together in terms of the common law and procedures of the king's courts, which replaced the diverse local laws of the counties and became a third bond of unity. They began to form group habits, which constitute part of the substance of group character. (The French did not fully possess the bond of legal unity until the first decade of the nineteenth century.)

A fourth bond was added with the evolution of Parliament. "Parliament" is another word like "capitalism" whose meaning changes through the centuries with the alteration of the institution to which it refers. It would be well if we forgot for the moment everything we thought we knew about Parliament and began over.

It long had been the practice of the English king, as we have seen, to meet with his trusted officials in the king's council. There he listened to advice, heard complaints and petitions, and dispensed justice. It also long had been his custom to add to the council on occasion leading bishops and barons. Toward the middle of the thirteenth century these enlarged councils, or parleys, of the king with his officials, archbishops, bishops, earls, and barons, came to be called parliaments.

At the same time, the practices of election and representation were developing in connection with the county. The county court was composed of knights, who were lesser independent landowners of gentle birth, and of townfolk. At the king's command they were electing, for example, a coroner. The kings began to order the counties to send representative knights to London. As early as 1213, King John, being in grave political difficulties, summoned knights from every shire "to speak with us regarding the affairs of our realm." In 1254 the regency summoned knights from all the shires to vote a financial aid to King Henry III. In 1275 Edward I, needing money, ordered each county to send two knights and each sizable town two burgesses to consent to a tax on movable property.

Gradually the kings introduced the innovation of having the representative knights and burgesses meet with the parliament of trusted officials, clerics, earls, and barons. At the beginning, the knights and burgesses were summoned to attend fewer than six of the fifty parliaments convoked between 1258 and 1286. But the innovation answered the needs of many individuals. Knights and burgesses could present to the king in Parliament petitions and complaints that the royal courts could not satisfy. The nobles also discovered in Parliament a means to restrain an incompetent or arbitrary king or administration. Above all, the king through Parliament kept in touch with local opinion, speeded up the machinery of justice, and won the consent of the knights and burgesses to new taxation. He thus tapped the wealth of those two classes who were profiting from the revival of trade. Not surprisingly, the innovation was repeated until it had become a habit. Edward I summoned the knights and burgesses to thirteen of his thirty-four parliaments between 1311 and 1327, and Edward III to all forty-eight parliaments of his fifty-year reign.

Once Parliament was in existence, its members began to define and elaborate its procedure and organization. During the fourteenth and fifteenth centuries the archbishops, bishops, earls, and barons reduced the king's trusted officials to advisers without a vote in Parliament, although the officials might still be members of the king's council outside of parliament. The archbishops, bishops, earls, and barons came to constitute a House of Lords in fact, if not in name. Meanwhile the representative knights and burgesses coalesced to form the Commons. Parliament came to be composed of three elements, the Crown, the Lords, and the Commons.

Individuals within and without Parliament began to use it for their own purposes. They gave Parliament things to do and thus strengthened and enlarged its powers without always intending to do so. It was used by the king, by individual commoners, and by factions of nobles. The king, needing money to carry on his wars in Wales, Scotland, or France, tried to get Parliament to help in collecting taxes. Almost every year he asked it to consent to a tax on property or (later) to import and export duties. Lords and Commons took advantage of his need and forced him to acknowledge in 1297 that no direct taxes, and in 1340 that no indirect taxes, might be levied without their consent. They compelled him to agree that the money granted must be spent for the project specified and that the accounts of his ministers be subject to a parliamentary audit. The monarch still enjoyed income from his estates and from fines, but in seeking the consent of Parliament to taxation he had led it to acquire the power to levy (with his consent) every variety of tax.

Or an individual subject would petition the king to rescue him, let us say, from the extortion of the king's sheriff. The subject would entrust the petition to the representative knight of the county or the burgess of the town to present to the king in Parliament. The knight or burgess would travel to London and discover that other knights and burgesses carried similar petitions against the extortion of a king's sheriff. The knights and burgesses of the Commons would combine their individual petition into a single common petition asking the king to order his sheriffs to desist. The Lords and the

Crown would assent to the common petition, and it would become statute law that it was illegal for sheriffs to do thus and so. Other petitions would be handled in the same way. The Commons with the Lords and the Crown began thus to participate in legislation. The king could still deny the petition and in effect veto the bill. He could still excuse an individual from the operation of the law. He could still legislate by a proclamation, an ordinance, or an order in council, that is, in other ways than by a statute passed in Parliament. But a new way of making law, by a country's representatives, had been hit upon. More important, a way had been discovered by which the inhabitants of a country through their representatives could alter the existing order, item by item.

Or a leading earl or duke, or a faction of nobles, feeling themselves unjustly treated or wishing to climb to power, would use Parliament to control the king or to dislodge his ministers. The nobles developed the procedure of impeachment by which the Commons could accuse the king's ministers before the Lords, who rendered judgment, usually of imprisonment or death. The nobles also persuaded Parliament to ratify their deposition of King Edward II in 1327, of Richard II in 1399, and of Henry VI in 1461.

Thus Parliament, as it was used by many individuals, slipped into the stream of English life. It participated in the levy of taxes, the initiation and passage of legislation, and the impeachment of ministers. It became an accepted, but by no means dominant, part of the English government.

Parliament probably did more than any other institution to unite the thriving classes of England. It met at least once a year nearly every year of the fourteenth and early fifteenth centuries. At the meetings the representative knights and burgesses would chat with each other and go over conditions in their localities, just as today congressmen in Washington ask each other, "Well, how is it in your district?" The knights and burgesses together discussed their common petitions and considered their common interests. If only because they voted taxes for the war with France, the Hundred Years' War became a common interest. England was a wool-raising country. As the prosperity of rural sheep-raisers depended on the ability of merchants to find foreign markets for wool and woolen cloth, the promotion and regulation of foreign trade was a subject for common exploration in Parliament. The attempts of the papacy to impose its appointees in English sees and to draw increasing sums of money from England were bitterly commented upon in Parliament. And when the representative knights and burgesses returned to their districts they carried to their constituents news of the papal extortion, the trade in wool, the war with France, the common petitions, and of conditions in other localities. Gradually, in various localities, people of the thriving classes began to realize that they shared with the rest of England a community of interest. In contrast, the Estates-General in France was a source of division. It became simply another place in which the French clergy, nobles, and townsmen could quarrel with each other. But in England Parliament and parliamentary discussions constituted a bond of unity.

A fifth bond of unity in England was the common language and literature. For years after the Norman conquest, the language of the conquering Normans, of the king's royal circle, and of the royal courts of law was French. The mass of conquered people spoke various dialects of Anglo-Saxon. But as the descendants of the Normans intermarried with the people, the conquerors also began to speak an Anglo-Saxon which was enriched by French, Latin, and technical terms, and came to be known as English. In 1362, in deference to this prevalent use of English, Edward III ruled that hereafter the proceedings of the royal courts should be in English. The opening speeches and sermons to Parliament also began to be made in English. Through the same centuries the differences of dialect were moderated among the prosperous town classes by the influence of travel, schools, and literature. The dialect of London, which was the idiom of the government, became the standard for English speech. In that dialect Chaucer wrote his *Canterbury Tales* and Wycliffe or his followers translated the Bible.

England was a small land. Its early history was a small population's history. At the close of the fifteenth century it still numbered less than five million persons. At the center of its early history were the kings. They had acquired England as a single royal domain (1066), utilized the sheriffs, developed the Chancery and Exchequer, dispatched the circuit judges, established central courts, invited knights and burgesses to attend their council, and engaged in wars with Scotland and France. Their activities and enterprises brought the inhabitants of the island together. In the history of France the provinces had come first in time and importance, and provincial customs, laws, and assemblies were entrenched before the king moved in. In England after 1066 the kings came first in importance, and the unity of law, the unity of a single parliament, and the unity of a small population naturally followed from the unity of the single royal authority.

From time to time, under a weak king the English government fell into disarray, and the great magnates fought each other for control of the realm. This happened under Stephen (1135-1154), Edward II (1307-1327), Richard II (1377-1399), and Henry VI (1422-1461). However, after the last debacle, royal authority recovered under the Yorkist kings, Edward IV (1461-1483) and Richard II (1483-1485), and under the first Tudor, Henry VII (1485-1509), who was a canny and skillful monarch. At the close of the fifteenth century, the king was still at the center of English institutional life. Henry VII exercised the powers inherent in the royal position within the limits that had developed over the centuries and that were generally understood by both the king and the people. He was the ruler of the nation.

He provided justice for his people. By him the justices of the three central courts of the common law (the King's Bench, Common Pleas, and Exchequer), the circuit judges, and the local justices of the peace were appointed and promoted; by him they might be dismissed. And yet, it was understood that the judges held office during good behavior, that the king could not meddle with the ordinary course of justice in common-law courts, and that the king hearkened to judges who told him that by law there were certain things he could not do — that he could not, for example, impose a tax without Parliament's consent.

The king was the source of much legislation. Parliament met upon his summons. The membership of Parliament was in part dependent on his will. He could create new peers — individuals who had the inheritable right to sit in the House of Lords; bishops and archbishops were his nominees; he granted to boroughs the right to send representatives; disputes over contested elections came before him and his council. He initiated legislation by introducing government bills that Parliament uniformly passed. He could fill in the gaps in parliamentary statute law by issuing proclamations and ordinances that had the force of law. He could veto bills introduced by members of Parliament. Since three-fourths of his revenue came from fines, confiscations, and customs duties granted by his first parliament for life, he needed to ask Parliament only for taxes to sustain extraordinary expeditions. He could suspend the sessions of Parliament, prorogue it, and dissolve it. And yet, once a parliamentary statute was passed with his assent, it was supreme law and he could neither violate nor repeal it. Nor could he levy a tax without Parliament's consent.

The executive power was his. The national treasure was his treasure, to spend as he thought best within a few general limits set by Parliament. He appointed the officers of the army and navy, the members of the council, which was the driving force of the administration, and the justices of the peace, who had replaced the sheriff as the representatives of the royal authority in the counties. The duties of these local justices were extensive. They were to keep the peace by putting down riots and arresting offenders; to try indicted persons; to fix the legal rate of wages; to punish those who used false weights and measures, and so on. The justices were checked by the circuit judges, supervised by the council, and kept well in hand by the king. And yet, since the justices of the peace, the members of the council, and the knights and burgesses of the Commons were almost all drawn from the class of well-to-do townsmen and country landowners, since the justices of peace received no salary but depended on fees and income from their estates, and since the king had no army of any size, he could not (for all his executive power) do anything that this middle group of country gentlemen and townsmen did not want him to do.

Likewise, in ecclesiastical affairs the boundaries of the king's authority were poorly defined. His nominees for archbishop and bishop invariably were accepted by the pope. And yet the king could not interfere too closely in the management of the English Catholic church. Not even a king nor an act of Parliament, for example, could ordain a parson.

This fluid situation, in which "the rules of government resembled rather the rules of conversation than those of bridge,"[1] required kings who were skilful and tactful managers. Henry VII and his two great successors, Henry VIII (1509-1547) and Queen Elizabeth (1558-1603) were just that. And because of the skill of these three monarchs and because of English history in which the monarchs had played so great a part, the English people in the sixteenth century were the most closely knit and best-governed in Europe. And as we shall see, during the reign of Queen Elizabeth the sensed community of interest which existed among the inhabitants of the island flamed in the crucible of war into passionate feeling. England, now Protestant, faced a hostile continental church, the Catholic, and a hostile continental empire, the Spanish, which were allied. The English resolved that though they might disagree with the government, though they might disagree with each other, yet against these foreign Spanish and papists they would stand together. England had become a living whole that could not be forcibly divided and from which a section could not be sliced without cutting to the quick the feelings of the people.

Spain

One peculiarity of the Spanish people today is the intensity of their "provincial and municipal feeling . . . Every village, every town, is the centre of an intense social and political life. As in classical times, a man's allegiance is first of all to his native place, or to his family or social group in it, and only secondly to his country and government."[2] In France and England we have watched and shall watch the slow growing together of peoples of different localities to form a nation. In Spain this process was delayed and never has been completed.

Through Spanish history from Carthaginian days runs this vein of separatism, of local peculiarities and local independence. Its existence can be explained by the circumstances of geography and the accidents of history. Topographically the Iberian Peninsula is an elevated plateau which extends as a rolling plain with an average elevation of about 2,500 feet above sea level. The plain is broken by several rugged mountain ranges, running in a generally

---

[1] Kenneth Pickthorn, *Early Tudor Government: Henry VII*, p. 1.
[2] Gerald Brenan, *The Spanish Labyrinth*, p. vii.

east-west direction, and by the gorges of mountain rivers, also running generally east-west. The gorges and mountain ranges cut the plateau into sharply-defined regions; there were awesome but limiting horizons. The inhabitants of each valley developed their local way of life, their local pride, and their local distrust of inhabitants who lived in the next valley.

The spirit of localism appeared in the campaign against the Moors. Toward the close of the tenth century, the Christians, as we noted, held only a strip of territory along the northern boundary of the Iberian Peninsula. They were divided into little border kingdoms and principalities, León, Castile, Navarre, and, later Aragon and Portugal. One would think that these kingdoms might have come together to fight their common enemy, the Moor. Instead, the inhabitants of each kingdom held fast to those ways which most separated them from the next, and their petty rulers bickered with and fought one another.

In the course of time Castile and León merged, and the enlarged Castile recovered central Spain from the Moors. At the same time, the eastern kingdom of Aragon extended its territory southward along the Mediterranean. By 1250 the Moslems were left with only the tiny kingdom of Granada. As Aragon, Castile, and Portugal, side by side, continued their expansion, they also continued their bickering. From 1250 to 1450 the relations between Portugal and Castile and between Castile and Aragon were a dreary chronicle of boundary disputes and inter-dynastic struggles in which Portuguese and Castilians as well as Castilians and Aragonese came mutually to dislike each other. The institutions of the three countries, the privileges of the social classes, and the governmental arrangements diverged. The ways of life differed and the ruts deepened: in Sunday dress, in the way of walking down the street, in the inflection of a curse. Here in the Iberian peninsula time had lent its hand to division not union. The original distrust of the neighboring valleys came to be loaded with apprehensions, fear, and arrogance.

But in 1469 the heir to Aragon, Ferdinand, and the heiress to Castile, Isabella, married. Isabella became queen of Castile in 1474 and Ferdinand king of Aragon in 1479. Henceforth, although the kingdoms were joined in only a personal union, the two monarchs called themselves king and queen of Spain. They were a remarkable couple who supplemented each other. Isabella, distinguished by piety, dignity, inflexible determination, and high courage, both moral and physical, as well as intolerance and excessive fondness for pomp, concerned herself primarily with internal affairs. Ferdinand, on the other hand, was a diplomat and devoted himself to foreign policy. He was cautious, calculating, unscrupulous, and persistent, a master at "playing the fox."

Ferdinand and Isabella, like their contemporaries Louis XI in France and Henry VII in England, entered in Castile and in Aragon complex legal and customary relationships which granted them certain powers and opportunities and also limited them. When Isabella came to the throne, the fortunes of the Castilian crown were at a low ebb. The royal revenues had been alienated. The nobles were rebellious and fighting each other. Lesser robbers infested the roads and waylaid travelers. There was no regular military force on which the crown could count. The towns were largely self-governing, having their own fortresses and electing their police, judges, and municipal councilors. The Cortes, a central assembly composed of representatives from the major towns, had to approve each new tax before it could be collected. In the kingdom of Aragon each province, Catalonia, Valencia, and Aragon itself, had its own Cortes with which the king must deal. The independent spirit of the Aragonese Cortes was expressed in the legendary oath of allegiance to a new monarch: "We who are as good as you," so it ran, "swear to you who are no better than we, to accept you as king and sovereign Lord, provided you observe all our liberties and laws; but if not, not." To political confusion was added religious diversity. The pope competed with the crown for the control of the Spanish Catholic church, which needed reform. In both Castile and Aragon there was a considerable number of Jews and Moors, and also Marranos and Moriscos (that is, respectively, Jews and Moors who had been converted to Christianity).

To a degree, Ferdinand and Isabella respected custom and the spirit of local separation. They did not try to merge Castile, Aragon, and their other possessions into a single unitary kingdom. They allowed Castile and Aragon, and within Aragon, the provinces and conquests of Catalonia, Valencia, Aragon, Navarre, the Balearic Islands, and Sicily, to retain their separate institutions.

Ferdinand and Isabella, however, tried to establish their monarchial authority within each of their possessions. They concentrated on Castile, for it constituted three-fourths of their Spanish territories. They allied themselves initially with the Castilian towns and Cortes to restore order, to subject the nobles, and to develop royal institutions. Isabella herself destroyed unlicensed castles of the nobility and summarily stopped private war. She organized an efficient mounted military police that exterminated brigandage in the country districts. The Cortes authorized the formation of a small Royal Council in which noble members were in a minority and lawyers predominated. Under the watchful regard of the two sovereigns, the council was the driving force of a developing bureaucracy which came into contact with every individual in the realm. The council purified and strengthened the administration of justice. It corrected abuses in the collection of taxes. Whereas the total annual yield of the Castilian imposts amounted to only 885,000 reals in 1474, thirty years later it stood at 26,283,334. Increased revenue enabled the two monarchs to support an effective mercenary army. As internal peace and order were restored, Ferdinand and Isabella began to encroach on the independence of the towns and the Cortes. They began to nominate the members of the town councils and to universalize the practice of having in each town a royal agent, the *corregidor*, to supervise the town government. In both Castile and Aragon they summoned the Cortes as infrequently as possible. The Castilian Cortes, for example, did not meet from 1482 to 1498.

The two sovereigns tried to weld the Spanish people together in a common devotion to the Catholic faith. "Isabella was a devout Christian; she did not divide religion from life; she did not regard church and state as separate bodies but as one, which (with the reservation of spiritual deference to the Pope) should be guided and governed by the sovereigns. Ferdinand concurred. He professed to believe that religion was to the state what the blood was to the human body, and as Machiavelli observed, gained great secular advantages from his pious professions."[3] Both sovereigns agreed that religious unity was a virtual necessity in order to secure political unity. Only through religious homogeneity, so they believed, would it be possible to establish order under a central government. They early established their control of the Spanish Catholic church by compelling the Pope to recognize their right to name the greater and lesser ecclesiastics. Their appointees were clergymen of distinguished caliber who were able to reform the Spanish church. Activity and zeal soon replaced idleness and corruption as the distinguishing marks of the Spanish priest.

The Catholic Sovereigns, as Ferdinand and Isabella came to be called, next moved to create religious unity and to arouse religious fervor among the Spanish laity. They received in 1478 papal authorization to name a religious court of ecclesiastical inquisitors. The court would try heretics, especially those converted Jews and Moors who professed Christianity but who secretly practiced Hebrew or Moslem rites. This Spanish Inquisition in nearly every respect was a royal institution. The inquisitors were appointed and dismissed by the monarch; they acted on royal instructions; their confiscations went into the royal treasury. There was only one Inquisition and one Inquisitor-General for Castile, Aragon, and the other Spanish possessions. It proceeded first against converted Jews whose sincerity was suspected. Meanwhile, the Catholic Sovereigns were undertaking a ten-year campaign against the kingdom of Granada, the last Moslem state on the Iberian Peninsula. They quite consciously utilized religious zeal to fuse their motley army. Throughout the campaign Ferdinand kept in his tent a huge silver cross, the gift of Pope Sixtus IX. After each victorious siege, the royal standard bearer placed the cross on the topmost pinnacle of the conquered town, and it was adored by the assembled army. After the conquest of Granada was

[3]Henry Dwight Sedgwick, *Spain*, p. 130.

completed, the Catholic Sovereigns issued in 1492 an ultimatum to the Spanish Jews: accept Christian baptism or leave the country. Many Jews fled, while those who remained and were outward converts fell under the surveillance of the Inquisition. Soon it was the turn of the Moslems. In 1502 the Moors of Castile and in 1525 those of Aragon were ordered to accept Christian baptism or leave the country. Those who accepted baptism now fell within the Inquisition's jurisdiction.

One effect of the attainment of religious unity by the conversion or expulsion from Spain of the Jews and Moors was to intensify religious sentiment in the realm. The religious unity of the people was fired at precisely the moment that they were attaining political unity under Ferdinand and Isabella. Religious and political unity became associated in their minds. A loyal Spaniard was a Catholic and an enemy of Catholicism was an enemy of Spain. By the close of the fifteenth century the Spanish, while still individualists of separatist tendencies who lived under separate institutions in Castile, Aragon, Valencia, and Catalonia, were governed by a common monarchy of growing power and were imbued with a common religious zeal.

Germany and Italy

With England and France we traced the evolution of the royal power; with Germany and Italy we have to note its dissolution. At the close of the tenth century the King of Germany was also emperor of the Holy Roman Empire, which included Germany and northern and central Italy. The emperors struggled through the succeeding centuries with shifting dynasties of great noble families, the German and Italian dukes, marquesses, and counts, and with the Italian towns. By 1075, a series of capable emperors had established their personal supremacy over the great feudal dukes. The way seemed prepared for the consolidation of imperial authority by the firm development of an imperial administration.

But instead, for various reasons, the imperial authority dissolved in the course of the next two centuries. The German kingship remained elective and passed from noble family to noble family. To purchase election from their fellow-nobles, the candidates frequently had to promise to surrender crown lands and crown rights. The German emperors frittered away too much time and energy in Italy. The emperor generally was too busy in Italy to keep the great German dukes in order and subjection, yet he was too busy in Germany to keep the rising Italian towns in subjugation. Also, the ambitions of the emperors in Italy brought them into conflict with the popes, who were trying to establish an independent papal state across the center of Italy. In Germany, the pope played the nobles against the emperor; in Italy, the pope used the towns.

As a consequence, by 1273, the German nobles had taken advantage of the elective character of the kingship, the distraction of the emperor in Italy, and his difficulties with the pope to despoil him of monarchical power. Germany by the fourteenth and fifteenth centuries was an anarchy in monarchical form. There were princes, great and small, knights, free cities, leagues of knights, and leagues of free cities. The great ecclesiastical and secular princes were consolidating their authority within their own domains. The princes included, among others, the archbishops of Cologne, Trier, and Mainz, the count of Württemberg, the landgrave of Hesse, the margrave of Baden, the elector of Saxony, the Wittelsbach duke of Bavaria, the Hohenzollern elector of Brandenburg, and the Habsburg archduke of Austria. Each prince subdued his knights, controlled his towns, convoked an assembly (estates) to grant taxes, and developed an administration and an army. Each prince turned his scattered, often broken, territories into a consolidated territorial state. Over this anarchy of greater and lesser territorial states, knights, and towns outside them presided an emperor – an emperor who was elected by seven of the great princes, an emperor unable to take any action without consent of all three houses of an imperial Reichstag dominated by the feudal magnates, an emperor without army, navy, administration, or taxes.

By the close of the fifteenth century the Holy Roman Empire was a field for foreign intrigue and was losing territory along its frontiers. Italy had been lost long ago. The Swiss Confederation and the Netherlands were drifting toward independence. The French kings were acquiring bits of German territory along Germany's western frontier. Holstein and Schleswig were falling under Danish influence. Poland and Hungary were severing their ties.

The Germans were a vital people. They spoke a common language, divided it is true into a number of dialects; they had a common literature; and they lived under a single emperor. Many Germans had traveled and knew of the common language, literature, and emperor. Many of them had a sense of being German and raged in frustration against French and papal intrigues and papal exactions. But for want of a strong central authority, the Germans had not been brought together into a cohesive unit nor could they act effectively in domestic or foreign affairs. There was no Germany in the sense that there was, intensely, an England.

A strong central government, likewise, failed to develop in Italy. The Holy Roman Empire was partly at fault. In Italy the emperors checked the rise of any native state to a sufficient strength to absorb the whole peninsula. To the influence of the empire must be added that of the papacy as an equally responsible cause. The position of the pope, as independent sovereign of a little state in central Italy, had forced him in self-defense to use all possible means to prevent the rise of any threatening power in Italy. Whenever such a power appeared to be forming the papacy would strive to arrange combinations against it until its strength was reduced below the danger point, and if one of the pope's allies gained too much strength, new combinations were immediately set afoot against the new danger.

Although no Italian central government was formed, in Italy, as in Germany, a number of territorial states came forward in the thirteenth, fourteenth, and fifteenth centuries. They absorbed their weaker neighbors and consolidated their administrations. By the close of the fifteenth century the Italian peninsula was largely divided among six territorial states: the Kingdom of Naples, an absolute monarchy in the south; the States of the Church, an ecclesiastical monarchy in the center; the Republic of Florence that was soon to become the Grand-Duchy of Tuscany; the Duchy of Milan; and the ancient, oligarchic republics of Venice and Genoa.

The Italians spoke a common language, divided to be sure into a number of dialects. They had a magnificent common literature, composed by authors such as Dante and Boccaccio in the Tuscan dialect. Many Italians had traveled and knew of the common language and literature. A few educated men, such as Dante and Machiavelli, thought of themselves as Italians and dreamed of Italian unity. But the majority of the people thought of themselves as Neapolitans, or Tuscans, or Milanese, or Venetians. For want of the nucleus of a common central administration, the Italians had failed to grow together into a cohesive nation. The Italian peninsula, like Germany, was a beckoning field for foreign interference.

An Invitation to Further Inquiry and Reflection

In chapter three we have data concerning the emerging nation-state, the characteristic political form of European civilization. We can institute comparisons between regions and then formulate hypotheses about how the nation-state emerged in this period. Before we do this we might decide first what we mean by "comparison," what conditions must exist before we can conduct a valid comparison, and how is the word "hypothesis" being used? We can then formulate hypotheses concerning the sequences and processes that apparently operated in the formation of both France and England. We can next check these hypotheses against the negative examples of Germany and Italy and the delayed consolidation of Spain. If we have time and resources for additional research, we can check our hypotheses against the positive example of Portugal, which by the sixteenth century was a nation-state, if there ever was one. By now, we should begin to wonder what is meant by "nation" and by "nation-state." Obviously, a nation-state is, among other things, a complex of institutions. From the economic phenomena of chapter two we developed a concept of "institutions" and a hypothesis about their origin. Now, we can test the concept and hypothesis against the political "institutions" of chapter three. Do the concept and hypothesis apply to both economic and political phenomena? Will they have to be modified? Hitherto, the resemblances between France and England have been stressed. At some point we should begin to note differences. What, thus far, were the distinctive features of the national tradition of France? England? Spain?

For Further Reading

(For general reading)

Americo Castro, *The Spaniards: An Introduction to Their History* (1971)
————, *The Structure of Spanish History* (1948)
Frederick Heer, *The Holy Roman Empire* (1968)
Amy Ruth Kelly, *Eleanor of Aquitaine and the Four Kings* (1950)
David Knowles, *Thomas Becket* (1971)
Achille Luchaire, *Social France at the Time of Philip Augustus* (1929)
Doris Stenton, *English Society in the Early Middle Ages* (1951)(4th edition 1965)
James Westfall Thompson and Edgar Johnson, *An Introduction to Medieval Europe* (1937)
J.B . Trend, *The Civilization of Spain* (1944, 1967)

(For advanced study)

Karl Deutsch and William Foltz (eds.), *Nation Building* (1963, 1966)

R. Fawtier, *The Capetian Kings of France* (1960)

Joseph R. Strayer, *The Albigensian Crusades* (1971)

J. O. Prestchurch, "Anglo-Norman Feudalism and the Problem of Continuity," *Past and Present*, No. 26 (November, 1963), 39-57.

C. R. Cheney, *Hubert Walter* (1967)

Charles R. Young, *Hubert Walter, Lord of Canterbury and Lord of England* (1968)

Geoffrey Templeman, "The History of Parliament to 1400 in the Light of Modern Research," *The Making of English History* (ed. R. L. Schuyler and Herman Ausubel, 1952), 109-127.

Stanley Chrimes, *English Constitutional History* (1965)

A. F. Pollard, *The Evolution of Parliament* (2nd revised edition; London, 1934)

J. E. A. Jolliffe, *The Constitutional History of Medieval England from the English Settlement to 1485* (1937)

William Holdsworth, *A History of English Law*. Volumes 1, 2

Kenneth Pickthorn, *Early Tudor Government: Henry VII* (1934, 1949)

Roger B. Merriman, *The Rise of the Spanish Empire*
    Volume I – *The Middle Ages* (1918)
    Volume II – *The Catholic Kings* (1918)

G[eoffrey] Barraclough, *Origins of Modern Germany* (2nd rev. ed., 1947)

James Bryce, *The Holy Roman Empire* (1864, many editions) (1873 ed.)

Chapter IV

The MOVEMENT OF THOUGHT
AND THE EXPANSION OF
KNOWLEDGE

Medieval Scholasticism and Science

The Odyssey of Western man, it has been observed, has carried him through three great configurations of fundamental assumptions. The first constituted the Graeco-Roman, or Classical, outlook, which flourished up to the fourth century AD. With the triumph of Christianity in the Roman Empire, the Graeco-Roman outlook was replaced by the Christian world view which proceeded to dominate Europe until the seventeenth century. The rise of modern science inaugurated a third important way of looking at things, a way that has come to be capsuled in the phrase "the modern mind."

The Europeans of the tenth century, from illiterate serfs to the educated clerics at the cathedral and monastic schools, were living within the assumptions of the Christian configuration of thought. They accepted the world view of the Christian epic of history, as presented by the Old Testament and the New Testament and as interpreted by the Church Fathers of the first five centuries of the Christian era. Into this world view the educated clerics of the tenth century fitted their sparse knowledge of the ancient world. Bits and pieces of this knowledge came to them in several different ways. Happily a few, original books had survived intact. Usually Latin classics, they included the works of Virgil, Ovid, Horace, Juvenal, Lucan, and Seneca, and the rhetorical and philosophical treatises of Cicero. Of the classical Greek authors, the tenth century knew only the simpler of Aristotle's logical treatises, *Categories* and *On Interpretation*, and part of Plato's dialogues, *Timaeus*. The classical heritage also reached the clerics through meager textboks in grammar, logic, rhetoric, geometry, astronomy, arithmetic, and music and through compendiums. In the seventh century, a Bishop Isidore of Seville had uncritically compiled from classical authorities an encyclopedia on all subjects from God to reptiles. For three centuries it was the main work of reference in monastic libraries. Another celebrated work was Priscian's Grammar, which contained ten thousand lines of quotations from Greek and Roman works. Finally, the heritage of classical thought was mediated by early Christian writers, notably by St. Augustine.

The influence of St. Augustine's great synthesis of Christian theology and classical philosophy was fateful for Western culture, and we might well begin our survey of the movement of Western thought with it. The nature of his philosophy was affected by his life. Born A. D. 354, in a closing century of the Roman Empire, of a pagan father and a pious Christian mother, Augustine drifted in adolescence into licentiousness and heresy. However, the Christian teachings of his mother continued to echo in his mind, and in his early thirties he was re-converted to a belief in the Hebraic-Christian God of the Old and New Testament, a personal, all-powerful Creator. Coincidentally, at the time of his conversion, he was reading neoplatonist writers. Plato, according to these authors, observed that an outstanding feature of everyday sense experience was its instability. Material objects and events revealed in the perceptions of eye, ear, touch, and the other senses were in constant change. Objects came to be, passed away, were always in flux and never real. A transient individual was feeling a transient table. How could a table be considered real, in any philosophic sense? True existence (reality) implied eternity and immutability. Where could such existence be found? The answer, said the neoplationists, was given in the platonic doctrines of Ideas. These universal, pure Ideas of Good, of Truth, of Beauty, of Love, or of a species went beyond what was given or presented in sense experience. Immutable, perfect, these Ideas have existed for eternity. Material things reflected them only in a corrupt, partial, and shadowy way.

After his conversion Augustine identified the universal Ideas of the neoplatonists with the all powerful Jehovah of the Hebrews. For Augustine, God was the Divine Mind in Whom the Ideas existed. The Divine Mind contained, or even was identical with, the totality of the Ideas. God was not only true but the Truth, not simply good but the Good, not merely rational but Reason in all its perfection. God was reached through intuition and faith, enlightened by reason. Chronologically and in importance faith came first. Put in possession of Truth by faith, St. Augustine then knew no rest till he had brought his reason into action in order to comprehend Truth. However, God was not to be reached through a study of His works in nature. Augustine admitted there was this subordinate region for investigation — a world of changing perceptions — but he was not interested in studying this unsubstantial realm. For him, the natural phenomena merely furnished the incidental scenery for the drama of salvation that was being enacted in each individual soul and in history. For centuries Augustine's views of God, man, and history (for he did much to formulate the Christian epic) were almost universally accepted in Western Christendom. Partly because of his writings, knowledge of nature was considered of secondary importance throughout the Dark Ages, from the fourth century through the tenth. The primary function of natural facts was to serve as symbolic illustrations for the truths of morality and religion. The moon was the image of the church reflecting the divine light, the wind was an image of the spirit, and so on.

However, with the eleventh and twelfth centuries there came a quickening of urban life and of intellectual inquiry as well as a reviving interest in the study of individual, particular, material objects for themselves and not for any moralizing purpose. Even during the Dark Ages, treatises had been prepared by practical mathematicians for the calculation of feast days, by doctors concerning the nature and use of herbs, and by craftsmen on the illumination of manuscripts. Apparently, during the eleventh and twelfth centuries treatises such as these increased. Also, during the same centuries the nominalist philosopher Roscellinus (fl. 1092-1119) and his pupil Peter Abelard (1079-1142) applied logic to theology and philosophy. They attacked the extreme platonist-Augustinian view that the individual, material object was merely the shadow of an eternal idea. Abelard, in his logical attack, put forth the notion of conceptualism. He maintained that through the study of individual objects, men for example, we can reach the general concept, Man. Neither the individual objects nor the general concepts (or general ideas) are shadows. Finally, in the twelfth century, as trading and military contacts with Islam increased, some Westerners sought to acquire the Greek, Hindu, and Arab mathematics, science, and learning amassed by the Arabians. In Sicily and Spain, teams of translators rendered Greek and Arabic texts into Latin. The West had had Aristotle's old logic, his *Categories* and *On Interpretation*. It now secured the new logic, his *Prior and Posterior Analytics, Topics, and Sophistical Refutations*, as well as the rest of his scientific and philosophic treatises, notably his *Physics, Metaphysics*, and *On Animals*. To these were added his *Ethics, Poetics,* and *Rhetoric*. Aristotle's works constituted a complete summary of Hellenic science and offered a philosophy that embraces all existence from "first matter" to God. Presenting his knowledge and ideas in a compact, clear-cut, and systematic style, he seemed "the master of those who know." (In the twelfth century, Plato offered him little competition since of Plato's *Dialogues* the West knew only *Meno, Phaedo* and part of *Timaeus*.) The translators also added the geometry of Euclid; the *Almagest* of Ptolemy, which gave a complete, detailed, and quantitative account of the motions of all the known celestial bodies; and the algebra and trigonometry of the great Arab mathematician Al-Khwari-mi. Arabic numerals, including the zero, were introduced. The whole corpus of Greek medicine, the works of Hippocrates and Galen, now became available. At the same time, Justinian's code of Roman law, the *Corpus Juris Civilis*, and the *Digest* of the opinions of the great Roman jurists were rediscovered.

These manuscripts presented a body of knowledge and theory whose dazzling range and power greatly exceeded anything known in the Latin West. Spread out before the educated clerics was most of the intellectual wealth of four great cultures, Hellenic, Hellenistic, Byzantine, and Arabic, and the law of a fifth, the Roman. Scholars, attempting to read the texts on their own, encountered innumerable problems. The problems were in part textual in origin. Some of the Greek masterpieces had been translated first into Syriac and then into Arabic before finally being rendered into a medieval Latin that did not always possess a vocabulary adequate to express an abstract subject matter. The successive translations by ignorant translators had deteriorated, and it was sometimes difficult for a Westerner to discover what Aristotle or Ptolemy had said. Then there were problems of comprehension. Aristotle, Ptolemy, Galen, and the Roman jurists operated at a high intellectual level, and they were not always easy to grasp. There also were problems of contradiction that needed to be resolved. Aristotle was not always consistent and contradicted himself. Furthermore, he was contradicted by other authors, such as Ptolemy and Galen. Also, his system often ran counter to platonized Augustinian Christian theology. In addition, the remarks of the revered authorities did not always jibe with observed facts. Students, baffled by the problems of reconstructing and comprehending a text and of resolving contradictions, flocked to teachers who could expound and explain: to doctors of medicine at Salerno who commented on Hippocrates and Galen, to the great legal scholar Irnerius of Bologna who glossed the *Corpus Juris Civilis* and the *Digest*, and to the theologians of Paris. Eventually these assemblages of students around celebrated teachers were formalized into universities.

Contradiction provoked discussion and investigation. Following the practice of Roscellinus and Abelard of applying logic to intellectual questions and using the powerful system of logic of the complete Aristotle, the university professors of Paris and elsewhere elaborated in the twelfth and thirteenth centuries a fine web of theological and philosophical reasoning that was known as scholasticism. They acutely defined and sharply debated grave questions, such as the nature of reality, the nature of God and of the Trinity, the interrelations of faith and reason, and the problem of sin and salvation. The glance of the majority of the professors was heavenward as they discussed things divine. However, a minority of the professors, few in number but important for the history of Western thought, observed the mundane works of God in nature. Submitting the scientific treatises of Aristotle to logical and empirical examination, they made discoveries in astronomy (the calculated position of the stars), optics (the explanation of the rainbow), terrestrial mechanics (the composition of movement, gravity, the lever, bodies on inclined plane, projectiles), magnetism (the properties of the lodestone), geology (tides, erosion, and fossils), biology, and human anatomy. Gropingly they began to devise an intricate method of logic, empirical observation, experiment, and mathematics by which new discoveries could be made.

The great synthesis of the age of scholasticism was constructed by St. Thomas Aquinas (1225-1274), who reconciled Aristotle and Augustine and at the same time offered a philosophy that was congenial to the scientific investigation of nature. A member of the Dominican order and a full professor of theology at the University of Paris at the age of twenty-five, Aquinas was inspired by a twofold passion, the love of truth and the love of prayer. Forgetful of personal considerations, he so neglected his physical wants that his ecclesiastical superiors felt themselves obliged to appoint another friar, Reginald of Piperno, to care for him. Aquinas lived at a time when belief in the Christian epic and in Augustine's interpretation of God was being menaced by the influx of the new knowledge, the recently recovered works of Aristotle and Hellenistic and Arabic science. Aquinas and his generation faced the problem that was presented to the Christians of the eighteenth century by the new science of Galileo and Newton, of the nineteenth century by the new science of Darwin and evolution, and of the twelfth century by the discovery of the Dead Sea Scrolls — the problem of establishing a comfortable relationship between an old belief and a new learning.

To Aquinas, Augustine was *the* Christian theologian, the Master whose doctrines had held sway for more than 800 years. However, to Aquinas, Aristotle was *the* philosopher, the Master of Those Who Know. He did not like to find his two masters in contradiction, and yet occasionally he did. Aristotle, for example, believed in the eternity of the world and did not believe in the immortality of the soul. In such instances of clear-cut opposition, Aristotle had to yield. More subtly, Aristotle differed from Plato and hence from Augustine at two important points. Like Plato, to be sure, he thought in terms of universal ideas or forms and of particular objects. However, for Aristotle the world of particular objects and of sense experience was not to be impugned as deceitful and shadowy; it was real and substantial. The changes which obviously went on in it were to be seriously studied and adequately explained rather than branded as corrupt and unreal. Furthermore, the changeless forms were not to be conceived as entities in a transcendent realm, separate from their imperfect copies in the world of particular objects; rather, for Aristotle, the universal forms were immanent principles and essential substance imbedded in the experienced objects, guiding the changes that occur and providing an explanation of their occurrence. It followed that knowledge could be built upon sense perceptions and the application of reason to them. Working from the perception of like particular objects, reason could induce the universal principle and essential substance imbedded in them. Then from that principle or essential substance, reason could deduce what changes in individual objects should occur in a particular instance.

In his reconciliation of Aristotle and Augustine, Aquinas believed with the latter in a Deity who was the Supreme Being, the all-powerful Creator, first cause and last end of the universe, the highest wisdom, the greatest good, the most perfect reason, a Supreme Providence who affected history in accord with His rational purposes. Also, Aquinas, like Augustine, placed the universal forms or principles in God. However, these were not Plato's transcendent entities, but Aristotle's universal forms which were imbedded in particular objects and controlled their changes. Through observation of like particular objects and then reasoning about them, a few educated men could conceptualize these universal forms that were in God's mind. Furthermore, reason, operating on sense experience, could know both that God is and something about His atrributes. However, according to Aquinas the knowledge about divine things which is reached by the reason of a few men must be reinforced by faith in the authoritative revelation of the Scripture as interpreted by the Catholic church, a faith strengthened by divine grace or energy infused by participation in the sacraments. Most men did not have the time, ability, industry, or early stability to apply reason to the attainment of divine knowledge: they needed to accept on faith what a few, trained in the use of logic, might gain by reason. Even the reason of the few men, though, could not reach toward the essence of God; only faith could do this and bring men into God's presence. And even with faith, men resembled nocturnal bats in the presence of the sun: they could feel the light, they could know the light was there, but they could not perceive its ultimate essence. In all this, faith determined what reason could and could not do. In an apparent conflict between reason and revelation interpreted by faith, revelation was to be accepted and reasoning subjugated.

In solving a particular problem, i.e., the reconciliation of Augustine and Aristotle, that was distressing him and his generation, Aquinas reached conclusions that were congenial to the scientific study of nature. He completed the construction of the view that God was a rational, intelligent Being who had created, in accord with His purposes, a rational universe and endowed man with faith and reason to understand it. Thereafter, medieval Christianity could impress into Western consciousness the basic theorems of the uniformity and knowability of nature, theorems which until recently formed the philosophical foundation of Western science. Also, Aquinas's reconciliation of Augustine and Aristotle encouraged medieval students of nature to believe that they were being good Christians in following Aristotle and observing natural phenomena. They could think that in proceeding by rational induction from particular objects to universal forms or principles and then by rational deduction to the changes which should flow from these principles they were tracing the operations of God's mind.

In astronomy and in terrestrial dynamics the medieval observers of nature set the problems for the scientists of the sixteenth and seventeenth centuries and even began to move toward their solution. Let us try to follow some of the roads they took. At first, in the thirteenth century, medieval students of astronomy, looking into the night sky, tended to accept Aristotle's and Ptolemy's view of the universe as wholly in keeping with Christian theology.

They accepted the Aristotlean and Ptolemaic view that the earth was the immobile center of the universe, and that around it revolved the moon, the sun, Mercury, Venus, Mars, Jupiter, Saturn, and the stars. They also accepted the Ptolemaic solution of the problems of the wandering planets. While the sun and the moon appeared to move steadily from east to west, the planets occasionally seemed to move eastward. To describe their normal westward motion and their occasional retrograde eastward motions, Ptolemy devised a set of *deferents, epicycles*, and *equants*. Today, for example, it is believed that the moon is traveling with the earth in a circle around the sun. This primary circle or orbit of about 365 days can be termed the moon's deferent. At the same time that it is traveling around the sun, the moon is also circling the earth approximately every twenty-seven days in a secondary circle that is called an *epicycle*. Then, while the geometric center of the moon's deferent is the sun, conceivably (though this is not the case) the deferent's rate of rotation might be uniform not with respect to the sun but with respect to an *equant* point several million miles distant from the sun. In Ptolemy's system the sun, moon, and planets were circling the earth, and by giving certain speeds and circumference to their deferents and epicycles and certain positions to their equant points, Ptolemy was able to describe their course and to predict their position on different days, months, and years over a long period of time.

Ptolemy's theory coincided with unaided sense perceptions (after all, the earth does seem immovable and the planets do seem to revolve around it); the mathematical descriptions, though seemingly complicated, offered an economical summary of multitudinous data concerning the successive positions of the planets evening after evening; the predictive success of the theory enabled common men to feel comfortably at home in a mysterious universe; at the same time, the theory enabled astronomers fruitfully to conduct further researches into the nature of the heavens. The theory also harmonized with non-astronomical views, with Aristotle's theory of motion and with Christian theology. To Christians of medieval times who believed that man was the center of God's attention, it seemed natural that man's home, the earth, was the center of God's universe. Coherent, psychologically satisfying, scientifically economical and fruitful, consonant with common sense and non-astronomical beliefs, sustained by authority, taught in the schools, believed by both the crowd and the experts, Aristotle's and Ptolemy's view of the physical universe seemed destined to reign forever.

However, even as it was accepted, it began to be undermined, notably in Aristotle's supporting theory of motion. Aristotle apparently derived his theory of motion from such observations as a horse drawing a cart. For Aristotle the normal position of the cart, or any inanimate object, was rest. However, the cart had the potentiality to move and when a horse, or motive power, was drawing the cart this potentiality was actualized as long as the motive power was in contact with the object. It moved at a velocity directly proportionate to the motive power and inversely proportionate to the resistance of the medium (air or water) in which the movement took place. When the motive power (the horse) was withdrawn, the movement stopped and the object (the cart) dropped suddenly to rest or fell straight to the ground.

The theory seemed plausible to medieval students of nature until they learned that some classical authorities had disagreed with Aristotle on this point and until they observed in the fourteenth century that the use of the longbow and arrows and of gunpowder, cannon, and cannonballs was presenting forms of motion that could not be easily explained by the Aristotelians. According to Aristotle's basic theory, the arrow (object) should fall to the ground as soon as it lost contact with the bow-string (motive power). Applying their reason to such contradictions of accepted theory with other authorities and with observed facts, university professors at Oxford and Paris began in the fourteenth and fifteenth centuries to suggest other hypotheses to describe and explain terrestrial motion. Jean Buridan (d. 1358), for example, suggested that a material object (an arrow) was carried forward by a persistent *impetus* implanted in it by the agent (the bow-string) that set it in motion. The impetus, or implanted motive power, would keep the body going indefinitely at uniform velocity were it not for the operation of external forces. One of these forces was gravity, which in projectiles gradually reduced the impetus while in falling bodies it operated to accelerate. Buridan accepted from Aristotle the principle that motion continued as long as there was a motive power, but he introduced notions, ideas, and questions that prepared the way for Copernicus, Galileo, and Newton. Implicit in Buridan's theory were the notions that a body in motion continued unless some force slowed, halted, or deflected it; that force was something which altered motion and did not merely maintain it; that an observer should devote most of his attention to discovering not the active mover but the forces which qualify the continuing movement; and that the measure of impetus or momentum is the quantity of the body multiplied by its velocity. Provoked by the activities of practical men with respect to projectiles, Buridan was imperceptibly moving toward a new mentality which concentrated not on the universal form embedded in a material object, but on the way the material object behaved.

The history of the changing theory of motion is an example of what was happening in nearly all fields of natural science during the later Middle Ages. During the twelfth and thirteenth centuries, medieval university professors assimilated the legacy of Greek and Arabic science. Then in the thirteenth, fourteenth, and fifteenth centuries, the professors, applying their reason to discrepancies between accepted classical theory and observed facts and using an intricate method that intertwined logic, empirical observation, experiment, and mathematics, began to revise and increase their inheritance.

Italian Humanism

The creative center of the civilization of the twelfth and thirteenth centuries was France, and especially a small region around Paris known as the Île-de-France.   In that small area, the Gothic style of architecture was invented, the greatest of medieval universities, that of Paris, developed, and at the university the medieval philosophy of scholasticism evolved. France as a whole, furthermore, was par excellence the land of feudalism, chivalry, crusading enterprises, and troubadour literature. But in the fourteenth and fifteenth centuries this medieval civilization in France and the rest of northern Europe waned and Italy assumed the cultural leadership of the Western world. In Italy there was a new, distinctive, upperclass civilization, marked by energy and individual activity; by unprecedented wealth and capitalism; by the growth of city-states and varied political experimentation within the city-state idea; by revival of interest in classical literature and devotion to scholarship; and by a memorable outburst of individual creation, notably in the fine arts. In spirit it was a freer and more secular age than that of medieval times. In the twelfth and thirteenth centuries Gothic architecture, universities, and scholasticism had developed in towns, to be sure, but they had done so under the auspices of the church. The university professors were educated clerics. In Italy, on the other hand the cultural innovators were educated laymen, expressing the needs and interests of a wealthy, urban, lay society.

Educated people of the Italian cities were attracted to the masterpieces of classical literature, finding in their beauty and secular moral counsel a liberalizing education. In the history of Western culture this was not the first revival of interest in classical literature. There had been a Carolingian revival of learning in the ninth century and another revival in the twelfth. The twelfth-century revival of Latin literature was associated with the cathedral schools of northern France, notably those of Chartres and Orleans. In these schools, the study of rhetoric and of logic was finely balanced, and great teachers, loving the classics, inspired students to write Latin of real distinction. But the cult of Aristotle in the thirteenth century upset this momentary equilibrum. Aristotle strengthened the propensity of thinking men to apply reason and logic to theology, philosophy, and natural science. The study of belles-lettres was disdained and neglected for a time in university circles, only to re-emerge among Italian lay scholars in the fourteenth and fifteenth centuries.

Why the third and most significant revival of interest in classical literature should have occurred in Italy is still debated by historians. In explanation one can point, tentatively, to certain general circumstances. The economic and social conditions in the Italian towns seemed to have been indispensable to a cultural revival. Prosperity was declining in Italy in the fourteenth and fifteenth centuries, but there was still more wealth in the Italian towns than elsewhere in Europe. The capitalistic organization of commerce and industry assured that although this wealth was to a degree diffused, much of it was in the hands of a few merchants and political despots. First-generation merchants and despots might be absorbed in their drive for profit and power, but their sons and grandsons had the leisure and wherewithal to subsidize men of letters and artists and to serve as their audience. The merchants were apt to do these things since they possessed a certain initial education: they had to know how to read and write. Also, town life was more exciting than village existence. News from the outside world came more frequently. The intricate politics and inter-class wars of the free republics, their struggles with domestic and foreign despots, and the inter-city wars caught up individuals in their turmoil and offered events for comment and reflection. There was a more rapid give and take among town citizens than among villagers and a greater absorption in life in this world for its own sake. Educated townsmen, absorbed in events of this life, would be apt to find uncongenial the writings of church theologians, with their stress on the other world and on how to live in this world so as to obtain happiness in the next. Italian townsmen might find more relevant the reflections of the poets, orators, historians, and moralists of the Roman and Greek city-states, who had lived in an urban environment roughly similar to that of the Italian towns. Italians were the more easily carried back to classical sources, since in a sense the history of Rome was part of their own and its remains lay around them.

Also, in Italian universities, the strongest suit had never been the study of theology but that of Roman law, which directed its devotees to practical everyday concerns and to Roman sources.

In explaining how the ancient world found its way into Italian thought, one can also point to an individual, Francesco Petrarch (1304-1374). A vital and enthusiastic person, he was a many-sided figure — a traveler, a mountain-climber, a scholar of talent, and an author of poignant Italian love sonnets. But the central fact about him that made him of historical importance was his contagious love for the classics, and especially for Cicero, whom he praised wherever he went. Before Petrarch, there had been a few isolated Italian classical scholars, but he was the first to win others to admire what he admired and to do what he was doing. He was reading Cicero with the conviction that his works were the noblest expression of a noble mind and with relish for their eloquence; he was seeking everywhere the scripts of Cicero's lost works and better versions of his known ones and was laboring to establish the best text, to the end of learning what his master had actually written; he was trying to write Latin as Cicero wrote it; he was taking Cicero's counsel on conduct; and as he went deeper and acquired a cause and mission for his own life, Petrarch urged Cicero on his friends as a guide for their lives and a pedagogue for the young, for he found in the eloquent old Roman something he felt absent in the present, something of forgotten beauty and goodness.

And so he traced paths and set roles that his humanist friends and successors followed for two or three centuries in Italy, and, after 1450, in Spain, Germany, France, and England. For the most part lay scholars who were outside the universities, they searched the monastic libraries for manuscripts of Latin and Greek authors, found them as often as not in dust and damp and darkness, and collected them or sold them to collectors. In this way were recovered for Western Christendom most of the works of Lucretius, Tacitus, and Manilius, of the Latins; and of the Greeks, Homer, Sophocles, Herodotus, Thucydides, Xenophon, Isocrates, Demosthenes, Plutarch, Lucian, Epicurus, and Plotinus. Many more works of Cicero as well as some notable works of Plato were also rediscovered. Humanist scholars had all these manuscripts copied and sent to friends and libraries. It was usual for humanists to have scribes copying manuscripts. Petrarch had had four; Pope Nicholas V (1397-1455), who spent most of the papal revenue on buildings and books, had an army of scribes working by shifts. After the invention of the printing press, works were disseminated in printed editions. The growing diffusion and popularity of the Latin classics would have been impossible without this systematic copying and later printing of classical texts. In comparing the different texts of the same book to establish the best text, the humanists acquired habits of exactitude, developed the techniques of textual and historical criticism, became expert in Latin orthography, grammar, and rhetoric, and learned ancient history and mythology. They prepared improved Latin grammars and composed essays and disquisitions after the Ciceronian model. The influence of the humanists caused the classical ideal — a sound mind in a sound body — to prevail in education. To train the mind they had their pupils study Latin and Greek literature, a course of study which existed in European schools well into the nineteenth century. In brief, the humanists recovered for Western Christendom Greek language and literature; extended the list of available Latin authors; purified the texts; achieved advances in critical method; and formulated an educational program that dominated Western Christendom for over four centuries.

The ardor of the humanists was very great. In 1397 when the magistrates of Florence invited a Greek scholar, Manuel Chrysoloras, to teach Greek, one of his pupils was Leonardo Bruni, later an eminent humanist. "I delivered myself over to Chrysoloras," wrote Bruni, "with such passion that what I received from him by day in hours of waking, occupied my mind at night in hours of sleep." Aside from the direct accomplishments of the humanists — the integration of classical literature into Western culture — their labors had wide-ranging implications for ideals of conduct, reform of Christianity, and science. Rejecting the persistent medieval Christian emphasis on man's innate depravity, they believed in the dignity of man. They preached that man might achieve nobility of spirit and a free and full development of his potentialities through association with classical literature. They presented the ideal of individual development in two versions: the contemplative life of a sage who has "a feeling for the vanity of all political concerns compared with the lasting significance of intellectual pursuits"[1] and who is devoted to personal culture and the advancement of knowledge; and the active life of the "civic humanist" who re-enters politics, serves his country in offices, applies rational analysis to its institutions and history, and strengthens its vernacular literature through the study of classical forms. Ever since Petrarch, the ideal of the development of human personality through self-culture has been that of many educated men.

Overtly and directly humanism was neither religious nor anti-religious, Christian nor anti-Christian. However, insofar as ardor for the classics drew men's attention from religious concerns, it tended to diminish men's religious interests. Also, a few humanists were converted by their reading to Epicureanism or Stoicism, agnosticism or even atheism. Most, though, remained Christians at heart and members of the Catholic church. Nevertheless, their Christianity and Catholicism differed in tone from that of Aquinas. They did not use logic to construct vast, intricate, abstract systems of theology. Rather, habituated by their own studies to return to classical sources, which presented the concrete experience of antiquity, some humanists returned to the Gospels and the early Church Fathers for the concrete experience of early Christianity. This return to the sources of Christianity, when combined in northern Europe with religious discontent, later had momentous consequences: it furnished the intellectual basis for the Protestant Reformation and the break-up of the Catholic church.

Toward the close of the fifteenth century and the opening of the sixteenth, several spiritually inclined humanists of Italy and northern Europe returned to Plato and to platonizing lines of thought and speculation. A leader in this direction was Marsilio Ficino (1433-1499), a Florentine who translated into Latin the complete works of Plato and of the neoplatonist Plotinus. He also founded at Florence a Platonic Academy, half learned society and half literary club, where for years he, his friends and associates, and northern visitors talked through the long afternoons about Platonic themes. The work of

---

[1] Hans Baron, *The Crisis of the Early Renaissance*, I, 291.

Ficino, too, had unanticipated results in many fields, in Catholic and Protestant theological speculation, in aesthetic theory, and, notably for us, in science. The humanists, for the most part, had not been interested in the scientific study of nature. Petrarch sounded almost like Augustine in his depreciation of natural science.

> Even if all these things were true, they help in no way toward a happy life, for what does it advantage us to be familiar with the nature of animals, birds, fishes, and reptiles, while we are ignorant of the nature of the race of man to which we belong, and do not know or care whence we come or whither we go.

Ficino and his associates were no more interested than Petrarch in the minute study of nature. For them, as for Plato, material things were only the corrupt, partial, and shadowy reflection of the eternal Ideas. However, Ficino now adopted the neoplatonist theory that numerical ratios and mathematical forms (the changeless circles and triangles of plane geometry) expressed the eternal forms and harmonies of nature. Partly because of what Ficino wrote, Copernicus and Kepler later sought mathematical regularities, simplicities, and harmonies in the multitudinous evidence of astronomy, and found an educated audience inclined to endorse their enterprise and its results. So, paradoxically, in the fifteenth century, two warring camps — the scholastic university professors engaged in revising Aristotle's theory of motion in the light of the mundane evidence of projectiles, and the spiritual, Platonizing humanists serenely soaring in the realm of eternal Ideas and mathematical harmonies — were preparing the ground for the growth of modern science.

Between the tenth century and the late fifteenth a distinctive European civilization had come into existence. It was based on a productive agriculture that, unlike the Roman, was not founded on slavery, did have livestock, and used effective equipment. Also unlike the Roman civilization, the new west European was not short of enterprising merchants, nor was it disdainful of those who engaged in trade and industry. Its merchants were learning to assemble capital for large-scale enterprises through partnerships and joint-stock companies. Its active-minded sailors and craftsmen were inventing, borrowing, and extending the application of an array of mechanical devices largely unknown to classical antiquity. At sea, the stern rudder had displaced the older and less efficient lateral steering devices; the full-rigged, three-masted sailing ship had replaced the simpler single-masted; and navigators were now aided by the astrolabe and magnetic compass. The water mill was now employed more extensively and was used to create a draft in blast furnaces, thus making cast iron possible; the windmill was available; the spinning wheel, the treadle loom, the sawmill, improved glass-making and the paper mill had all raised the level of production in their industries; and the printing press had just been invented. The use of pikemen and of gunpowder, meanwhile, had raised the military strength of western and central Europe. The kings were learning how to organize in a rudimentary way their military, administrative, and money power in support of large, state-directed enterprises. It was becoming apparent that politically the characteristic culture form was to be not the city-state as in ancient Greece, nor the confederation of towns as in the Roman empire, but the nation-state. Educated Europeans had embarked upon intellectual discovery, first through assimilation of the intellectual culture of Greece, Rome, and the Byzantine and Arabian empires, and then through active thinking. In the first quarter of the twelfth century, Bernard of Chartres remarked that a scholar of his day, compared with the ancients, was a dwarf standing on the shoulders of a giant. The important point was, even then the dwarf could see a little farther than the giant. By the close of the fifteenth century Europeans were developing the scientific method that would enable them to become giants on their own. In religion the new civilization was Christian. Perhaps this should be mentioned first, since Christianity permeated the attitudes and views of everyone, even the skeptics. With the emergence of a new civilization, people became self-conscious of being a part of it. In earlier centuries, they had referred to themselves as living in Christendom. But in the fourteenth and fifteenth centuries, the word Europe came into use, and educated men began to think of themselves as being Europeans and as sharing a new distinctive European culture. Europe, in the last decade of the fifteenth century, on the verge of overseas expansion to America and the Far East, was quite different from the crude, poor, politically decentralized, and relatively ignorant Europe that had expanded into the Mediterranean four hundred years before.

An Invitation to Further Inquiry and Reflection

Someone has observed that there are "dandelion" questions and "crepe myrtle" questions. A dandelion has a single root, and if we pull it up and get it all that is the end of the matter. On the other hand, the far-ranging roots of the crepe myrtle lead us all over the yard. Similarly, with questions. When did Christopher Columbus discover America? is obviously a dandelion question. October 12, 1492, we reply, and that ends the matter. Other questions are more far-ranging. One such question would be on questioning itself. From our experience thus far, what are the qualities of a good historical question for further inquiry and reflection?

Not every question has an answer, especially when the evidence is inadequate, but attempting to answer unanswerable questions may reveal aspects of the situation hitherto ignored. Why did western clerics in the tenth and eleventh centuries begin to become interested in active thinking about intellectual matters? That question could lead us far. We can say, contact with the learning of Arab Spain, but we really do not know. That learning had been available for contact for several centuries. Apparently it takes two to make an influence. We can refer to a "native" appetite of the new European for knowledge, but what does that mean and why did it now appear? Or why did Aquinas formulate his reconciliation of Augustine and Aristotle? Was it solely because of the personally distressing spiritual problem presented by the contradiction between two revered authorities? Why did Buridan modify the Aristotlean theory of motion? Was it simply because of the problem presented by the contradiction between revered theory and observable fact? If so, did advance in knowledge arise from resolution of contradictions, from problem-solving, in brief? Is the origin of economic and political institutions and of philosophic ideas, then, basically the same? But, why do we have periods when men find classical literature congenial? In a sense the classical literature is always there, outside a closed door or a closed mind, waiting to be invited to come in. But why in certain centuries is it invited, and in other centuries it is not? Is it simply because it solved a problem, or were deeper levels of experience involved? Have you ever been affected by literature, great or small?

One way to review is to ask a question that forces us to reorganize the material and thus to have new insights. Chapters two, three, and four on the emerging European civilization were organized under the rise of the townsmen, the rise of the monarchs, and the expansion of knowledge. But suppose we ask once again the question, what is a civilization? One answer might be, it is a web of relationships of people with each other, with nature, and with material artifacts. Or a related reply, it is interlocking behavior patterns (behavior being defined to include both action and attitude-ideas), expectations, and legitimizing values. On Sunday, the peasant enters the parish church, he kneels, crosses himself, and prays, and he has certain ideas about what he is doing and what he expects others to be doing. At the same time the priest leaves his parsonage, enters the church, begins his duties, and has certain ideas about what he is doing and what he expects others to be doing. In a new civilization new patterns of behavior, expectation and values are emerging to give the civilization its distinctive character. Using the material in these early chapters and any other knowledge we may have, can we derive some of the important behavior patterns and expectations of the new emerging European civilization?

For Further Reading

(For general reading)

Henry Adams, *Mont Saint-Michel and Chartres* (1959 [c 1933])

Erich Auerbach, *Mimesis: The Representation of Reality in Western Literature* (1953)

F. C. Copleston, *Aquinas* (1963)

A. C. Crombie, *From Augustine to Galileo* (2nd ed., 1961)

Wallace K. Ferguson, *Europe in Transition, 1300-1520* (1962)

Leopold Genicot, *Contours of the Middle Ages* (1967)

J. R. Hale, *Machiavelli and Renaissance Italy* (Teach Yourself History Library, 1966)

Charles H. Haskins, *The Renaissance of the Twelfth Century* (1933)

────, *The Rise of the Universities* (1923)

J. Huizinga, *The Waning of the Middle Ages* (1924)

David Knowles, *The Evolution of Medieval Thought* (1962)

Thomas S. Kuhn, *The Structure of Scientific Revolutions* (2nd edition, 1968)

Robert S. Lopez, *The Three Ages of the Italian Renaissance* (1970)

──── *The Birth of Europe* (1962; translated 1966)

Michael Mallett, *The Borgias: The Rise and Fall of a Renaissance Dynasty* (1969)

M. M. Phillips, *Erasmus and the Northern Renaissance* (Teach Yourself History Series, 1950)

James Harvey Robinson, *Petrarch: The First Modern Scholar and Man of Letters; A Selection from his Correspondence* (1898)

George H. Sabine, *A History of Political Thought* (1937)

R. W. Southern, *The Making of the Middle Ages* (1953)

Henry Osborne Taylor, *The Medieval Mind*. 2 volumes (1927)

James Westfall Thompson and Edgar Johnson, *An Introduction to Medieval Europe* (1937)

Helen Waddell, *Wandering Scholars* (1927)

Rudolph Wittkower, *Architectural Principles in the Age of Humanism* (1949)
Alfred North Whitehead, *Science and the Modern World* (1925)

(For advanced study)

Ernest Knapton, *Europe 1450-1815* (1958)
Frederick Copleston, *History of Philosophy*. Vol. 2, *Medieval Philosophy* (1946)
Gordon Leff, "The Fourteenth Century and the Decline of Scholasticism," *Past and Present*, No. 9 (April, 1956), 30-39.
Marvin B. Becker, *Florence in Transition*: Vol. I.: *The Decline of the Commune*. Vol. II: *Studies in the Decline of the Territorial State* (1968)
Richard Goldthwaite, *Private Wealth in Renaissance Florence: A Study of Four Families* (1968)
R.R. Bolgar, *The Classical Heritage and its Beneficiaries* (1954)
Paul O. Kristeller, *The Classics and Renaissance Thought* (1955)
Jerrold E. Sergel, *Rhetoric and Philosophy in Renaissance Humanism: the Union of Eloquence and Wisdom, Petrarch to Valla* (1968)
Hans Baron, *Crisis of the Early Italian Renaissance: Civic Humanism and Republican Liberty in an Age of Classicism and Tyranny* (1966)
Wallace K. Ferguson, "The Interpretation of Italian Humanism: the Contribution of Hans Baron," *Journal of the History of Ideas*, XIX (1958), 14-25, with a reply by Hans Baron, 26-34.
William J. Bousma, *The Interpretation of Renaissance Humanism*. No. 18 of the Service Center for Teachers of History, American Historical Association (1959)
Articles on the problem of the Renaissance by Wallace K. Ferguson, Lynn Thorndike, and Ernst Cassirer in Shepard Clough, Peter Gay, and Charles Warner, *The European Past*, I (1964), 3-28.
Wallace K. Ferguson, *The Renaissance in Historical Thought: Five Centuries of Interpretation* (1948)
Tinsley Helton (ed.), *The Renaissance: A Reconsideration of the Theories and Reinterpretations of the Age* (1961)
P.O. Kristeller, "Studies on Renaissance Humanism During the Last Twenty Years," in *Studies in the Renaissance*, IX (1962), 7-30.
Harcourt Brown, "The Renaissance and Historians of Science," *Studies in the Renaissance*, Vol. VII (1960), 27-42.
J. H. Hexter, "The Renaissance Again — And Again," *The Journal of Modern History*, XXIII (September, 1951), 257-261.

PART II — THE SIXTEENTH CENTURY:
EXPANSION, RIVALRIES,
AND RELIGIOUS UPHEAVAL

Introduction to Part II

To the thoughtful scholar the sixteenth century, or more broadly the period 1494 to 1659, is the most complex we shall study until we reach the nineteenth and twentieth centuries. During those years European powers expanded across the Atlantic Ocean to the Americas and around Africa to the Far East and began to build overseas empires of trade and settlement; the focus of the European economy shifted from the Mediterranean to the Atlantic; France and Spain, and then Austria, England, Portugal, Holland, Denmark, and Sweden, initiated the modern phase of the rivalries among the great powers; the Catholic church was both disrupted and reformed, while new Christian sects, "ineradicable as the dandelion," sprang up and flourished; and the foundations of modern science were laid. As they happened, these changes became interwined with each other, the building of colonial empires with the rivalries of the powers, the rivalries among the powers with the disruption of the Catholic church, and the disruption of the Church with the contest for colonial empire, to mention three relatively simple examples. Leaving for later discussion the foundation of modern science, we shall consider this period in two segments, the expansion of Europe overseas and the interrelations of the rivalries of the powers with religious reform. We shall be interested in the story of a complicated series of events, but as always we shall also look for continuing and fundamental processes of change that lie within events.

CHAPTER V

THE EXPANSION OF EUROPE OVERSEAS –
THE FIRST COLONIAL EMPIRES

A central theme of modern world history, perhaps *the* central theme, is the expansion of Europe. European techniques, institutions, and ideas have been exported to the rest of the world. Most of Asia is still listening to two Germans, Karl Marx and Friedrich Engels; listening, and sending back its own message. Asians trade through cities – Bombay, Calcutta, and Singapore – that are built on Western models. Most of the world is interested in going modern, which means going European.

The interaction of world cultures is an old theme. What is new after 1500 is the temporary dominance of one. One center of driving, shaping, exploratory energy emerges; the others fade. Between 500 A.D. and 1500 A.D. the energies in mind, we might call it culture or originating, shaping power, were gathered around four main poles: the Chinese, the Indian, the Arab, and the Byzantine-Roman. Among these four there was a rough balance of power and inspiration. This balance was disrupted by the development and expansion of Western Europe, which gained dominance.

Let us take our stance in Europe and look outward, through space and time. What is most evident spatially is the widening and deepening horizon, leading always out of sight, over the sea. Temporally we notice four chronological stages of expansion. The first stage was the expansion of Western Christendom southward against the Moslems in the Iberian Peninsula, the western Mediterranean, and the Levant. It opened, let us say, in 1022 when Genoa and Pisa seized Sardinia; it closed about 1291 when the Christians lost Acre, their last stronghold in Palestine. The loss of the Holy Land, however, did not interrupt the trade of the Italian merchants with the Moslems. The second stage was the period of the Old Colonial Empires of Portugal, Spain, Holland, England and France. It began in 1415 with the Portuguese capture of the Moslem fortress of Ceuta, at the northwest tip of Africa. The conquest initiated the Portuguese creep southward along the African coast and around the Cape of Good Hope to India. The period can be divided in half, about 1607-1608, when Portugal lost the wealthiest portions of its possessions, the East Indies, to Holland. The period closed with the French cession of their colonial empire to England in 1763, the English loss of their American seaboard colonies in 1783, and the expulsion of the Spanish and Portuguese from their mainland American colonies by 1825. The third stage was the period of modern imperialism, from 1871 to 1914, when England, France, Germany, Belgium, Italy, Russia, Japan, and the United States scrambled for the remaining unclaimed portions of the globe in Africa, the Near, Middle, and Far East, and the Pacific. Recently, two world wars have initiated a fourth stage: the retraction of European power from the outlying areas of the world.

We have used the term "expansion" rather glibly. It has many implications, and we want to make full use of them. What does the term mean? What did expand? First, European expansion meant simply discovery and exploration, and the consequent expanding knowledge of what was not European — what was formerly out of the minds of Europeans, unsuspected. Second, there is an expansion of the area settled by Europeans and by their descendants. This is the story of the colonies, another kind of discovery, the exploration of new ways of life in the formation of quasi-European societies in new environments. Here it is well to keep in mind that as Europe was expanding, its civilization was also developing, so that it was always a different Europe that was reaching other shores. It is also well to remember that at any given moment, European civilization varied in its expression from country to country. Settlers carried overseas some of the features of their own version of European civilization at the moment they migrated. In meeting the day-to-day problems of a new environment, settlers and their descendants sloughed off some features, modified others, and retained the rest. They developed new societies which were nevertheless variations of their mother country. Third, the expansion of Europe was an expansion of the areas affected by Europeans. Europe, then, as a message, heard, half-heard, variously misunderstood, translated into many languages and cultures, accompanied settlement and spread beyond into regions that Europeans did not colonize — into Japan, for example. Fourth, the expansion of Europe also involved the history of the rise, development, and decline of colonial empires, on the surface, so to speak, of the deep, underlying movement outward of European explorers, traders, missionaries, soldiers, administrators, and settlers. Lastly, the expansion of Europe included the return effects of the expansion on Europe itself — the rising standard of consumption, the complication of international rivalries, and the intangible, immeasurable freeing of thought which came with the vista of a new world and new opportunities. These five aspects were of course interrelated. Discovery and exploration generally preceded colonization, colonial empires and European civilization went along with both, and European civilization sometimes went beyond; and while one region was still in the exploration stage, a second already was being settled, and a third had not yet been discovered.

This chapter deals with the first half of the period of the Old Colonial Empires (1415-1608) and with two great types of empires: the trading empire

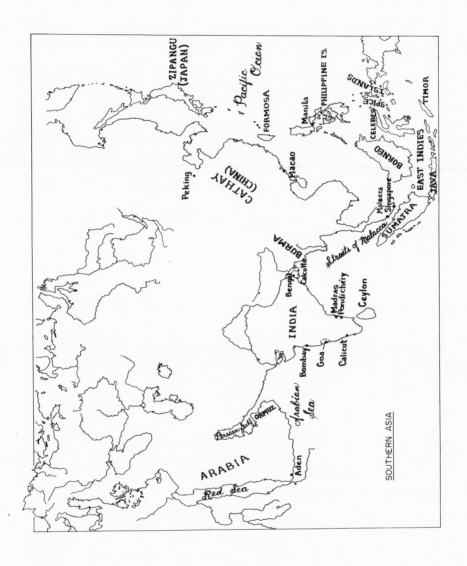

SOUTHERN ASIA

of Portugal in the Far East and the settlement empires of Spain and Portugal in the Americas.

The Trading Empire of Portugal in the Far East

Columbus's discovery of America in 1492 and Vasco da Gama's voyage around the Cape of Good Hope in 1497-1498 have often been picked out to mark the division between medieval and modern times. The two events heralded, it is said, the dawn of the modern age and are cited as revolutionary. Yet, never was the process of historical continuity more manifest than in these voyages. They were a part of the continuing flow of multiple European activities. Behind them lay a deep background of achievement and culture.

For nearly two centuries after the First Crusade the Italian merchant did not know where the drugs, spices, perfumes, and precious stones in which he traded were produced, or over what routes they traveled. He only knew that they came to Egypt or Syria from Far Eastern lands. As a matter of fact, nutmeg and mace, cloves and allspice were the native products of a small group of islands, the Moluccas (Spice Islands), which lay just under the equator in the midst of the Malay Archipelago. Pepper had a scarcely wider field of production. The forests that clothed a stretch of the Malabar (western) coast of India were filled with pepper vines, which also grew in Ceylon and Sumatra. Diamonds were found only in certain districts in the central part of India, especially in the kingdom of Golconda. Rubies also were found to some extent in India, but more largely on the island of Ceylon and in the highlands of Persia. Pearls were sought principally in the straits between Ceylon and the mainland of India. Drugs, perfumes, dyes, and fragrant woods came from the same general Far Eastern region. Fine fabrics were manufactured in China, Japan, and India. India, in a sense, was *the* manufacturing country of the Eurasian world. Fine silks and cotton cloth, woven by Indian artisans, were carried along established routes of trade to China, Japan, Burma, Arabia, Persia, and parts of Africa, as well as to Europe.

By the fifteenth century, Eastern goods regularly reached the West by two general routes, which ran somewhat as follows. Chinese and Japanese junks and Malaysian ships (proas) gathered goods from the coasts of China and Japan and the islands of the vast Malay Archipelago and brought them to Malacca. This port was one of the great trading centers of the East, occupied during the annual fair, it was said, by over a million people. Few Chinese traders passed beyond it, although for the Malays it was the center rather than the western limit of their commerce. At Malacca they were met by Indian and Arab traders who exchanged Indian and Arab products for wares and supplies from the farther East. The Indian and Arab traders brought their purchases to

Calicut and other ports of the Malabar coast. To these ports were also brought the products of Ceylon and of the interior of India. Then from the Malabar coast stretched two great highways of commerce. One led directly across the Arabian Sea to the western coast of the Red Sea, where the goods were landed and carried by caravan to Kus in Egypt, and thence either by caravan or boat down the line of the Nile to Alexandria. The second route led from the Malabar ports to the head of the Persian Gulf at Basra. Thence the goods were transported by trains of camels to the Mediterranean ports of Jaffa, Acre, and others. The routes were long. They were insecure. Storms and pirates took their toll. Sheiks, kings, and rajahs levied heavy dues. Successive middlemen exacted their profits. And at the end of the line the Italian merchants, in control of the Mediterranean situation, charged their fellow Europeans fantastic, monopoly prices.

For many years no Italian merchant could have told anything of the "isles where the spices grow" or of the countries which produced the rich fabrics in which he trafficked. During the thirteenth century, however, several European travelers, notably the Polo family, Maffeo, Niccolo, and Niccolo's son, Marco, journeyed through Asia. The Polos lived with the Great Khan at Peking for twenty years, from 1273 to 1293, and returned from China by the great sea route along southern Asia. The European travelers returned with tales of the old, thriving civilizations of China and India. They told of innumerable populous cities and great rivers, of industry, thrift, and glutted markets. On a single river in China, the greatest in the world, "there is more wealth and merchandise than on all the rivers and all the seas of Christendom put together." Of that great wealth very little, indeed, ever comes to the Levant: "for one shipload of pepper that goes to Alexandria or elsewhere, destined for Christendom, there comes a hundred, aye and more, too, to this haven of Zaition"; while the diamonds "that are brought our part of the world are only the refuse of the finer and larger stones." And above all the travelers told of treasure — of cities with "walles of silver and bulwarkes or towers of golde," palaces "entirely roofed with fine gold," and lakes full of pearls. This vision of the golden East beckoned to western Europeans for centuries thereafter.

Men began to wonder whether the Far East, the source of supply, could not be reached by another route that would avoid the middlemen and tribute-levying governments. Long before the fifteenth century, even in ancient times, many men had thought it possible to sail around Africa. In 1351 an Italian map represented Africa "with the point of the continent fore-shortened, with the Atlantic and Indian oceans joined off the tip, holding out the hope that one might sail from Gibraltar and end up in Calicut." Improvements in ships (their hulls and sails) and in navigational instruments (the compass, the astrolabe, and a timepiece) were beginning to make the voyage practical. As early as 1281 or 1291 two Genoese, the Vivaldi brothers, sailed through the Straits of Gibraltar to seek India by sailing round Africa. They were never heard of again, but the memory of their venture remained. The Italian cities, however, did not follow up the idea. Their merchants continued in the old and familiar way of reaching the East by going east. Of the other countries who might undertake the voyage, Germany was disunited and landlocked to the south and west, England and France were preoccupied with wars, and Spain was not yet united. Occupied with internal problems, these countries had not yet opened their minds on the sea. At first only Portugal, a tiny nation with half its frontier exposed to the uncharted ocean, responded to the lure of the East and ventured alone from the Mediterranean world.

The Portuguese, basically a peasant folk, were led into maritime exploration and trade by their geographical location and by their kings and other princes of the royal family. Their chief port, Lisbon, was on the sea route from the Mediterranean to northwest Europe, and it became a way station where Italian ships refitted and Italian sea lore was communicated. Soon King Diniz (1270-1325) was attracting Genoese shipbuilders to Portugal and employing an Italian as admiral. Succeeding monarchs, following his example, granted numerous privileges to shipbuilders and sailors. And in the fifteenth century, the brother of the king, Prince Henry the Navigator, undertook, after the Portuguese capture of the Moorish stronghold of Ceuta in 1415, to direct the systematic exploration of the African coast. Prince Henry was one of the decisive characters in history. Though the king's brother, he withdrew from the royal court at Lisbon to the southwesternmost corner of Portugal, Cape St. Vincent. On this rock promontory he constructed a palace which was also a chapel, a library of geographical and nautical works, and a laboratory. His time, until his death in 1460, was mainly spent "in thinking out his plans of discovery, drawing his maps, adjusting his instruments," sending out his ships year after year to grope ever farther down the African coast, and receiving the reports of his captains.

His motives for exploration were several and probably grew in number and shifted in emphasis as his activity developed. His immediate desire was to discover the source of the gold, ivory, and pepper that caravans brought to Ceuta from the African hinterland. But he also shared the mystic ideals of his age. He was a Christian who wished to ascertain the extent of Moslem dominion in North Africa. He accepted the medieval belief in a flourishing African Christian kingdom, and he hoped that if discovered, it would aid him against the infidel. In addition he would serve the Lord Jesus Christ by converting the heathen. At the same time he was a student, absorbed by an overpowering desire "to find out by incessant and unvarying search what the world was really like." As his captains discovered and acquired for Portugal the Cape Verde and Madeira Islands and the Azores and also engaged in the profitable gold, ivory, and slave trade of West Africa, he came to crave the extension of the wealth and possessions of Portugal. Toward the close of his life he probably was caught by the lure of the Golden East, and he pressed toward the discovery of a water route around Africa to India. His mind and spirit contained nearly all the motives, religious, intellectual, political, and commercial, of his civilization. A man with a cause, and a problem, the exploration of Africa, he utilized the best geographical knowledge and navigational devices of his time and improved upon them. Initially his expeditions were for the most part made under Italian captains, with Italian crews, and in vessels built by Italian shipwrights. Italian mathematicians constructed the charts and instruments by which they sailed, and Italian bankers furnished the funds with which they were equipped. In technical skill and capitalistic resources as well as (to a degree) in motive, the second expansion of Europe, over the oceans, grew out of the first, across the Mediterranean.

By the time Henry died in 1460, his captains had sailed south more than two thousand miles to Sierra Leone, and he had established the tradition of systematic, profit-bearing exploration in the minds of Portuguese monarchs and explorers. The succeeding generations of Portuguese kings and seamen continued his work with the deliberate intent of rounding Africa to reach the spices and alleged Christians of India. In 1486 Bartholomew Diaz rounded the Cape of Good Hope and then returned. In 1497 Vasco da Gama sailed from Lisbon around the Cape of Good Hope and anchored at Calicut on the Malabar coast. He was at a chief source of supply of Far Eastern luxuries. He loaded his ships with cinnamon, cloves, ginger, nutmeg, pepper, and precious stones and returned to Lisbon with a cargo which, valued at high European prices, paid for the costs of the expedition sixty times over. His achievement ended the Italian monopoly of the Far Eastern luxury trade.

The Portuguese, in exploiting the opportunities for profit which the discovery opened, entered a complex Far Eastern situation which they never entirely mastered. In India the Portuguese came into contact with one of the great world civilizations, which had passed its creative peak but still carried on at a high level. In physical power, the Portuguese had a slight military and naval advantage, sufficient at any rate to enable them to maintain military and trading posts in India, as the crusaders had not been able to do in Palestine. Otherwise, the Europeans, representatives of a rising but youthful civilization, were still rather uncouth. In craft techniques India was still far ahead. The Indian cities in the fifteenth century were more populous and wealthy than those of Italy, which were then the most populous and wealthy in Europe. In response to man's everlasting philosophical and spiritual questioning, Indian scholars and mystics had elaborated answers as subtle and profound as those of any medieval theologian or Italian neoplatonist.

As civilizers the Portuguese had little to offer, and their relations with the Indians were largely those of trade, huckstering, and bargaining. But even as traders, the Portuguese were entering a tangle of motives and relationships which was unknown to them. They understood Indian society as little as it understood them. India at that time was split into a number of states, some of them Hindu, some of them Moslem, some of them well governed, some not. Wars were frequent between the states. Sometimes a Moslem state fought a Hindu state, sometimes a Moslem and a Hindu state jointly fought another Moslem. The intrigues of the states, the varying inefficiency of their police, and general misunderstanding led to insecurity of Portuguese life and property on land. The Portuguese, for example, early gained permission of the Hindu Rajah who governed the Malabar port of Cochin to put there a factory, a warehouse-store where the Portuguese could trade. But even in Cochin, which remained friendly, there were difficulties. If a Portuguese refused to pay a full market price in the bazaar or touched a Moslem woman, as sailors will, the factory was besieged. Then if some Portuguese were left behind by the fleet to tend the factory, they were subject to the caprice of the local ruler and in peril of torture and death from the moment the friendly sails passed under the horizon. Security ashore was evanescent as long as the Portuguese possessed no permanent base.

There was also danger on the high seas. The carrying trade in the vast region from the Straits of Malacca to the Suez was almost entirely in the hands of Moslems, for the most part Arabs, though a few were Persians, Turks, or Egyptians. They had money at stake and religious zeal, and they would fight before they would permit the Portuguese to dispossess them of their traditional monopoly. Two Moslem powers, Egypt, which was still supreme in the Red Sea, and the Ottoman Empire, which had access to the Persian Gulf at Basra, had fleets that seemed strong enough to challenge any European rival. They were ready to sink Portuguese ships in the Arabian Sea and Indian Ocean on sight. Against the powerful Turkish and Egyptian fleets, how could the Portuguese protect their commerce in the Far East from a base, Portugal, that was five thousand miles distant? How could the ships be refitted and resupplied after even one combat?

The Portuguese, in facing their problems, and even in *seeing* them in a clear light, were instructed by the solutions that already had been worked out by the Venetians in the Mediterranean and by the Portuguese themselves in connection with the gold, ivory, and slave trade of the West Africa. In all three instances (the Levant, West Africa, and India), the goods which the Venetians and Portuguese desired already were being produced and then transported along established trade routes. The problems of the Venetians and Portuguese centered on how to break into the established trade and assure a steady source of supply, how to defend their intrusion against European rivals, Moorish enemies, and native hostility, and how to do all this in areas where climate or density of population or both did not permit extensive European settlement. The Venetian answer was monopoly — the ruthless exclusion of foreign merchants; semi-annual fleets under armed convoy; factories where a few Europeans could live and products could be assembled and exchange arranged; key naval bases where combat and merchant ships could refit; minute regulation for the benefit of the home state (Venice); and secrecy.

The Portuguese, profiting from the Venetian example, had developed a similar policy with respect to West Africa. A monopoly of the West African trade had been given to Prince Henry, and after his death it was assumed by the crown. Individual Portuguese might trade only upon royal license. Foreign ships visiting the African coast were sunk or captured without inquiry, and if captured their officers and men were thrown to the sharks. Information that might serve competitors was suppressed. A fort was established on the Arguin peninsula, strategically located to tap the mainland trade routes, to minimize irritating daily contact with the natives, and to be easily defensible from native attack. This island and other factories and forts later erected became naval bases at which ships could be repaired and resupplied.

When da Gama returned to Lisbon in 1499, King Manuel naturally applied to India the policy in which he had been reared. He wrote Ferdinand and Isabella of Spain: "We hope, with the help of God, that the great trade [of the Indian and Arabian oceans] which now enriches the Moors ... shall be diverted to the natives and ships of our own realm." Non-Portuguese Europeans might come to Lisbon for their precious stones and spices, but they were to go no further. The Portuguese king was merchant-in-chief of his kingdom — all commerce in pepper, cloves, and cinnamon was reserved to him. His subjects were admitted on royal license to other branches of the Far Eastern trade, but only on payment of 30 per cent tribute. Vessels sailed out to India and returned in annual fleets that traveled under convoy at least to and from the Azores. The secrets of the passage were guarded with increasing vigilance. The sale of maps of the region south of the Congo River and the service of Portuguese seamen in foreign navies were early prohibited.

At the same time, the Portuguese obtained naval supremacy in Indian waters. A large part of their navy was concentrated there after 1502, to protect Portuguese business. Armed with superior ordnance and manned by sailors made reckless by national pride and hatred of the Moor, it destroyed the Egyptian fleet at the Battle of Dir on February 3, 1509, and thus gained undisputed mastery of the Arabian Sea and Indian Ocean. King Manuel sent out as viceroy Alfonso Albuquerque, the first of a long roll of ruthless European administrators in the Far East, a roll that includes John Coen, Joseph Dupleix, Robert Clive, Warren Hastings, and Thomas Raffles, men of force and genius, half military, half civil, in policy imperial. (We shall examine later the meaning of imperial. For working purposes let us call to mind Clive's own description of his business: "fighting, tricks, chicanery, intrigue, politics, and Lord knows what.") Albuquerque decided to affirm the Portuguese naval and commercial position by seizing a few strategic points. In 1510 he besieged and took the island town of Goa, from which he was able to control the entire trade of the Malabar coast. Goa, he developed as a military base, where Portuguese agents were reasonably secure from the whims of local rulers; as a naval base, where merchant and combat vessels could be repaired and supplied; and as an emporium of trade, where cargo could be assembled, for the ships returning home. In 1511 he led an expedition that took Malacca, the great entrepot of Far Eastern trade, destined to remain in Portuguese possession for about one hundred years. In 1515 the Viceroy captured Ormuz, which commanded the entrance to the Persian Gulf. An attack on Aden, the key to the Red Sea route, failed, but at least the viceroy controlled the Far Eastern supplies for that route. After taking Malacca, Albuquerque sent an expedition to explore the Moluccas (1511), "the isles where the spices grow." Portugal's agents were placed in the islands, and in 1564 Portuguese suzerainty was acknowledged.

Portugal's navy and her possession of Goa, Malacca, and Ormuz enabled her to dominate the trade routes of southern Asia and to hold the region commercially by the throat. She was able to divert the export trade in spices, precious stones, and fine fabrics from the Red Sea-Persian Gulf routes to the Cape of Good Hope and Lisbon. Her king and the subjects he licensed enjoyed a monopoly of that Far Eastern-European traffic until the close of the sixteenth century and exacted monopoly prices. Albuquerque, to single out one man, had created for Portugal the first great type of European overseas empire: the purely commercial, nonsettlement empire, founded in this instance on naval supremacy and the possession of a few key bases.

Yet the duration of the Portuguese Empire was always in doubt. The resources of the home country were too small to support even a trading empire. A population of barely 1,500,000 people did not supply enough men to staff an empire that extended (as we shall see) from Brazil to the Moluccas. Also, the Portuguese tended to carry their crusading fervor into their mercantile dealings with the Moslems — these were infidels to be killed, not. traders to be negotiated with. In fact, the Portuguese as a group never learned tact in dealing with Asiatics. Offenses against native customs, prejudices, and superstitions persisted and raised up natives who would willingly aid any other Europeans who promised to destroy the Portuguese Empire. As this empire relied, furthermore, on naval supremacy and the possession of a few key stations, it would collapse whenever the navy was defeated and the stations were captured by a more powerful country. Portugal, indeed, had stopped at the surface of discoveries, halted by the impenetrable mask of coastline — dissipating its energies there, diverted by first impressions and the easy satisfaction of immediate needs. An additional weakness, the difficulty in distributing Oriental goods to the European markets, was dealt with haphazardly. Lisbon's land connections with the rest of Europe were poor. The Portuguese government developed at Lisbon a huge warehouse and administrative establishment known as the House of India. It supervised the unloading and storing of Oriental goods, rigorously inspected the imports, collected dues on them, and arranged for the supplying and equipping of Portuguese fleets outward bound for India. But no Portuguese organization was created to arrange the distribution of the products. Northern merchants were allowed to come to Lisbon to buy the Far Eastern luxuries and to carry them to re-sell in northern Europe. As a consequence, the Portuguese lost part of the profit that might have been theirs. Moreover, in time, northern Europeans were apt to sail past Lisbon and attempt to tap the Eastern sources of supply directly. A final weakness was the economic and spiritual decline of Portugal through the sixteenth century. The well-to-do squandered the new wealth in luxuries or in purchases of vast landed estates, cultivated by imported Negro slaves. The solid Portuguese peasantry flocked to the cities to live in idleness and dependence, to India to get rich quick, or to Brazil to exploit opportunities there. There ensued a decline in morale. Zeal was succeeded by apathy. The Portuguese, not a numerous people, had been carried by a sense of greatness into the great deeds of exploration .and conquest of the fifteenth and early sixteenth centuries. By the close of the sixteenth century the spirit of greatness had faded, and the Portuguese were less than they might have been. They accepted reluctantly but apathetically — where their ancestors would have defied — the acquisition of Portugal by King Philip II of Spain in 1580. Philip thus brought under a single command the two greatest empires of his day: the Portuguese Empire of Brazil and the Far East, and the Spanish Empire of the Philippines and the Americas.

The Settlement Empires of Spain and Portugal in America

In all justice, America should have been discovered under the auspices of Portugal, for Columbus's voyage was the outgrowth of Portuguese policy and experience. Born in Genoa sometime between August 25 and the end of October, 1451, Christopher Columbus found his way to the thriving port of Lisbon in 1477. Soon after, he married the daughter (and the pair lived with the widow) of one of Prince Henry the Navigator's captains, and he listened to his mother-in-law's tales of her husband's voyages. He lived for a time on the Madeira Islands and sailed down the African coast with Portuguese mariners, then the finest in the world. He learned from them "how to handle a caravel in head wind and sea, how to claw off a lee shore, what kind of sea stores to take on a long voyage and how to stow them properly."[1] — in brief, how to be one of the best practical voyagers history has seen.

At that time, the idea was in the air in Lisbon that one could reach the spices of Asia by sailing west. Aristotle reputedly had said the project could be accomplished, and Strabo, a Greek geographer who died about A. D. 25, even had reported that it had been attempted and the mariners had returned only because of the endless sea. King Alfonso V (1438-1481) of Portugal had wondered whether the passage to the Indies via the western ocean route would be shorter and less dangerous than the one sought around Africa. A Florentine scholar, Paolo Toscanelli, had assured him it would be. There were also the ancient and medieval myths of islands to be discovered in the Atlantic Ocean. The novelty of Columbus was not that he had these ideas, but that he acted upon them. Since he believed with Marco Polo that Asia extended farther eastward than the ancients had supposed and since he underestimated the length of a degree of longitude, he calculated that Asia could be reached by a relatively short sail westward from Lisbon. "He expected to get gold, pearls, and spices by trade or conquest when he reached 'The Indies.' He expected to find one or more islands on the way, which might prove convenient as ports of call, if not profitable in themselves."[2] He was sustained by a belief in the correctness of his calculation, and also by an unquenchable faith in himself as an instrument of God to bring Christianity to the Asiatics.

He attempted in 1484 to secure the support of King John of Portugal, but the Portuguese experts turned him down. He then persuaded Portugal's rival, Queen Isabella of Castile, to authorize and largely finance the venture. Columbus sailed from the Castilian harbor of Palos on August 3, 1492, with three ships of the type that had been developed and tested chiefly by the Portuguese in African exploration. The flagship, the *Santa Maria*, was somewhat cumbersome, but the *Nina* and *Pinta* were "sweet little vessels, seaworthy and sea-kindly, the sort that seamen became attached to."[3] He dropped down to the Canary Islands, which the Portuguese had early discovered only to yield possession thereof in 1479 to Spain, and refitted. From thence, on September 6, he sailed west, ever west, until he fell upon Watlings Island in the Bahama group on October 12 and thought he had reached an island off the Asiatic coast. Secure in this belief, he sailed in these

[1] Samuel Eliot Morison, *Admiral of the Ocean Sea: A Life of Christopher Columbus*, I, 55.
[2] *Ibid.*, p. 76.
[3] *Ibid.*, p. 168.

waters for two and a half months, discovering Cuba and Haiti, and then set out for home, reaching Palos February 15, 1493. The following year, Spain and Portugal agreed by the Treaty of Tordesillas upon a Demarcation Line that reserved to Portugal, for exploration and discovery, the regions lying east, and to Spain the regions lying west, of a meridian three hundred and seventy leagues west of the Cape Verde Islands. The Demarcation Line, as it turned out, granted Portugal the easternmost tip of South America.

Columbus's discovery brought the Spanish and later the Portuguese into contact with the American Indians, who seemed to the Europeans culturally backward. The Indians in Central and South America lived at three cultural levels, determined largely by the environment. The barrenness and cold of the southernmost section of South America were so rigorous and exacting that there the Indians lived in nomadic or semi-nomadic tribes of hunters and fishers. They practiced a primitive food-gathering economy such as had prevailed among mankind throughout the world before 8,000 B. C. The easier conditions that were found along the tropical coasts of Mexico and Central America, in all parts of the Caribbean islands, all along the northern and eastern coasts of South America down to the Rio de la Plata, and, finally, all through the great interior river basins of South America (the Orinoco, the Amazon, and the Paraguay-Plata) led the Indians there into a more sedentary, food-producing economy. Their tribes were simple kinship or semi-kinship groups, governed by a chief and perhaps a council of elders. They engaged in a little hunting, a little fishing, a little agriculture (sowing, perhaps corn, manioc, or beans), and a little basketwork and pottery-making. But in a tropical climate which enervated energy and offered food so easily, these Indians were not inured to hard and continuous labor, any more than were the hunters and fishers. Those Indians, however, who inhabited the temperate highlands that form the backbone of the Americas from northern Chile to central Mexico achieved a level of culture approximately equal to that attained by Egypt and Sumer in 4,000 B. C. They practiced division of labor, built magnificent edifices, and on occasion mobilized armies by rather sophisticated political systems. The majority were skilful hoe-culture farmers, who lived in villages, terraced and irrigated their lands, and cultivated corn, beans, potatoes, squash, cotton, and other crops, but there were also deft craftsmen who worked in stone, wood, potters clay, and gold. They were all trained to regular industry and were inured to pay tribute in work and in products to support priestly and military rulers. Many of them were incorporated in the territorial empires of the Incas of Peru, the Chibchas of Columbia, and the Aztecs of Mexico. The Incas had begun to work in copper and bronze; the Aztecs had devised a pictograph system of writing; all three empires had accumulated stores of gold and precious stones.

In the Far East the Portuguese were entering a thickly populated region and old civilizations whose craftsmen and plantations already produced the luxury commodities Europeans desired and whose merchants transported these products along well-established routes of trade. There Europeans did not need to settle in great numbers in order to get many of the things they wanted. But in the Americas there was more to be done between the wanting and the getting. Once the gold and silver ornaments were skimmed off, even the Indians of the temperate highlands had few ready-made commodities that Europeans desired. In the experience of the Spanish and Portuguese there was little to prepare them for the problem thus presented, that of profitably organizing the resources and labor of a relatively backward continental domain for the production of commodities Europeans would want to buy. The Spanish and Portuguese kings, administrators, explorers, missionaries, and settlers started, of necessity, with what they had — the Spanish or Portuguese practices, customs, ideas, and ideals, of that moment, used them in connection with the New World more or less consciously and more or less intelligently, and then modified them in the struggle with daily circumstance. Gradually through the sixteenth century, policies and practices that seemed to work were developed. Gradually, also, a new society began to evolve in the temperate highlands of Central and South America, a fusion of Indian and Spanish culture that no one could have predicted.

The historical accident that America was discovered in 1492, the year Granada was taken and Spain was finally reconquered from the Moor, meant that the ideals and attitudes of the closing decade of the Reconquest (intense national zeal *fused* with intense Catholic fervor, plus acquisitive desire for the possession of unbelievers) would animate any Spaniards who went overseas. Then, too, Spain had been cut open by the Moorish invasion. In the Middle Ages, a frontier had been opened *within* the Spanish mainland. After conquering this first frontier of Moors, she discovered another beyond her, overseas. Her administrators tended to see the new frontier in the light of the old. Problems which had been solved before were read into the new situation. Solutions which had worked before were tried again. The motives and activities have a certain persistent structure; they reflect, we are tempted to say, a certain national character.

The king of Castile had thus developed during their warfare against the Moors certain practices with respect to the acquisition and organization of conquered lands and peoples. A customary way of recovering land from the Moors was for the king to grant privileges to a group that would undertake its reconquest. The privileges included the right to establish a town, to fortify and maintain it. The property owners of the town would usually enjoy the privilege of self-government. Partly by virtue of this custom, the urban tradition was stronger in Castile than in England. Castilian kings also had frequently put frontier districts under governors, men known as *adelantados*.

They were direct representatives of the king, and as such had his power: military, executive, and judicial. In addition, Castilian monarchs gave huge chunks of conquered land to the military orders, the leading nobles, and the Catholic clergy. The same groups were rewarded with grants (*encomiendas*) of jurisdiction and manorial rights over the Moorish peasantry. The peasants presumably were crown tenants, but life rights to their services were given to the *encomenderos*. The common soldiers, most of the Christian army, received little. In the fifteenth century the same practices had been employed in the Castilian conquest of the Canary Islands. The army leaders or *adelantados* and their chief followers were rewarded with large estates. Of the natives, a few were permitted to retain small and generally undesirable portions of land, while others remained as tenants on the territories that had been handed over to the invaders.

Since Queen Isabella had authorized and financed Columbus's voyage, the new domain overseas was understood to belong solely to the sovereigns of Castile. Naturally, the Queen applied to it those measures her ancestors had used successfully after other conquests. Columbus was an *adelantado* in everything but name, and later conquerors such as Bartholomew Columbus, Ponce de León, Hernando Cortez, and Francisco Pizarro bore the title. They were sent out to advance (the verb *adelantar* means to advance) the cause of Castile on its latest frontier. Columbus saw the need to cultivate some of the newly discovered land, if only to build up a few supply bases for further exploration. He took with him on his second voyage horses, cattle, sheep, goats, pigs, chickens, seeds of vegetables, oranges, lemons, melons, rice, and sugar cane, as well as fifteen hundred men — twelve missionaries, two hundred soldiers, and a huddle of artisans, field laborers, knights, and young courtiers. In the Spanish penetration of America, the explorers and missionaries went into an area first, but they usually soon were followed by soldiers, settlers, and administrators. The motives for all five groups taken together included a desire for gold and other forms of easy wealth, a dream of glory, a devotion to the Christian faith, loyalty to the sovereign, and also, no doubt, an appetite for adventure, for novel sights and sounds and an escape for humdrum existence. Columbus, following Queen Isabella's authorization, distributed land in Haiti among his followers according "to their rank, their service to the Sovereigns, and the condition and quality of their person and estates."

Land without labor, however, was useless. Crops required cultivation, and even gold could not be plucked from trees. But the Spanish adventurers were averse to severe manual toil (as one of them remarked, if they had wanted to plow they would have stayed at home), while the Indians of the Caribbean, used to the relatively easy life of intermediate culture, were not interested in working even for wages and, when chased, took to the hills. Native labor could be had only under compulsion. Columbus' successor as governor of

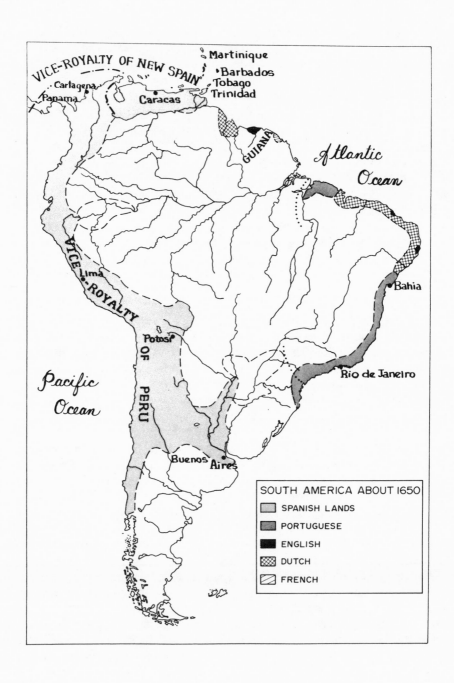

VICE-ROYALTY OF NEW SPAIN

Martinique
Barbados
Tobago
Trinidad

Cartagena
Panama
Caracas

GUIANA

Atlantic Ocean

VICE-ROYALTY
Lima

OF

PERU

Potosí

Bahia

Rio de Janeiro

Pacific Ocean

Buenos Aires

SOUTH AMERICA ABOUT 1650

SPANISH LANDS
PORTUGUESE
ENGLISH
DUTCH
FRENCH

Haiti was Fray Nicolas de Ovando, who had been *commendador mayor* of the military order of Alcantara and was experienced in the government of the conquered provinces of Granada. With Queen Isabella's permission, he called into operation in Haiti the *encomienda* system with which he had been familiar in Granada. He allotted to the leading Spanish landholders, including the priests, groups of Indians under their chiefs. These assignments were accompanied with a patent reading: "To you, so-and-so, are given in trust ("se ... encomiendan") under chief so-and-so, fifty or one hundred Indians, with the chief, for you to make use of them in your farms and mines." The Indians were to dwell in villages near their place of work; they were to be instructed in Christianity; and they were to labor for the *encomendero*. Under the system of large estates worked by compulsory labor, agriculture flourished in Haiti, Puerto Rico, Cuba, and Jamaica. Cattle multiplied until they "roamed by the thousands, ownerless, through the woods and fields." The woods were "full of cotton ... and fields of sugar cane were really marvelous, the cane as thick as a man's wrist and as tall as two men of medium stature." Hides and sugar, the products of Indian labor on large ranches or plantations under Spanish supervision, became commodities that could be profitably exported to Europe. However, the Indians, unaccustomed to continuous toil in a humid, tropical climate and falling victim to the European diseases of smallpox, typhoid, and measles, died by the tens of thousands. In 1492 the Indians of Haiti numbered over 200,000. By 1508, they had declined to 60,000; by 1514 to 14,000; by 1570, to only two villages. They were replaced on the sugar cane plantations by Negro slaves.

Within twenty years after Columbus's first voyage, the larger Caribbean islands had the resources, provisions, and manpower to outfit expeditions for the exploration of the mainland. Vasco Nuñez de Balboa crossed the isthmus of Panama with a few men in 1513 and ceremonially took possession of the Pacific Ocean for the king of Spain. From Panama later explorers turned north to the Yucatan and Mexico and south to Colombia and Peru. Cortez forced his way to Mexico City and compelled the ruler of the Aztecs, Montezuma II, to yield gold spoil valued at twelve and a half million dollars. Pizarro ordered the Inca (ruler) of Peru to fill a room 35 by 17 feet and as high as a man could reach with gold plate in exchange for his freedom. The gold spoil of this single expedition was equivalent, it is estimated, to seventeen and one-half million dollars and enriched the commonest footsoldier beyond the dreams of avarice. From Peru Spanish explorers spread north to Ecuador and south to Bolivia, Chile, and Argentina. From Mexico individuals, lured by the dream of riches, roamed north to Nebraska and California. By 1550 Spain had staked out her claims in the Americas from California to Patagonia and had secured certain strategic points of vantage, which might serve as foundations for the colonial Spanish America yet to be constructed.

The Spanish conquerors, notably Cortez in Mexico, Pizarro in Peru, and Gonzalo Jimenez de Quesada in Columbia, encountered the same problems as had faced the kings of Castile — how to reward their followers and how to organize the conquered natives profitably and securely. The Spanish were entering in Mexico, Peru, and to a lesser degree, Colombia, societies which resembled their own in several respects. Both the Indian and Spanish societies had distinct gradations of rank. Both had nobles who held large estates and exacted dues in labor and products from ignorant, non-literate villagers. Thus peasants in Mexico and Peru raised corn, beans, and squash on a plot of village land for their own subsistence, cultivated another plot for the support of the local chief, the upper nobility, the priesthood, and the Inca or Aztec emperor, and labored on roads, mines, and other public works for the state. Both Indian and Spanish societies felt religion to be a matter of life and death. Like their conquerors, the Indians had a well-organized priesthood, endowed with wealth and numerous influence. There were even affinities of ritual and religious doctrine; both societies had forms of baptism, confession, penance, and communion as well as belief in the immortality of the soul, in an intermediary place of judgment, and in resurrection after death.

Cortez, Pizarro, and Quesada and their aides, who had served their apprenticeship in Haiti and Cuba and were aware of the employment of the *encomienda* there, now applied it to the mainland conquests. Cortez, as an example, distributed large estates of land and villages to his leading followers. He told the Indians that "they were to be taught in the Holy Catholic Faith, that they were to provide food for the Spaniards to whom they had been assigned, that they were to work on the Spaniards' farms [and mines], and serve them." The *encomenderos* were charged "to do away with idolatry in their villages and to build churches in their *encomiendas* within six months . . . and to bring all male children to the monasteries for religious instruction . . . or to hire a priest."[4] However, the royal government began to have second thoughts about the power it had granted. *Encomenderos* able to command the land and labor to many Indian villages might become independent semi-feudal magnates. Also, other problems developed. As the Indian population in Spanish America fell dramatically from perhaps 50 million in 1500 to 4 million in the seventeenth century while the number of whites increased to two or three million during the same period, a new means of rationing Indian labor among white employers was needed. After 1550 the government began to hand out fewer *encomiendas* and devised instead the *repartimiento* (or *mita*), a system of forced labor. Under it each Indian village had to supply as tribute up to 4 per cent of its laborers to work "for the good of the state" in mines, on roads and other public works, or on private

[4]Lesley Simpson, *The Encomienda in New Spain*, pp. 67-68.

estates producing food. A few men of each village would work for several weeks, to be then replaced by another consignment from the same village. Managers of private estates applied to royal labor exchanges for successive batches of Indian laborers from neighboring villages. This system remained intact until the eighteenth century. But from the standpoint of the estate-owner the *repartimiento* had certain disadvantages. It made him dependent on the state for labor. Also, as the number of Indians dwindled and there was competition for their labor, white employers needed to pin down their Indians. Increasingly, many estate owners turned to debt peonage. They invited Indians to settle on their estates. The owner paid the Indians' tribute to the state, gave them a slight wage usually in kind, and advanced them a credit. Once the Indians accepted credit, they had to keep working to pay off the debt, which they never could discharge. As the Indian population began once again to increase in the eighteenth century, from approximately 4 million to about 7.5, more Indians were incorporated within the peonage system.

By 1574, about four thousand Spaniards owned in the temperate highlands of Central and South America large estates, ranches, and mines on which several million Indians worked. The Spanish owners ran their enterprises for profit. By means already mentioned (*encomienda, repartimiento*, and debt peonage) they mobilized Indian laborers to produce food for sustenance, wheat, meat, and other provisions for sale in neighboring colonial towns, and hides, sugar cane, tobacco, dyewoods, and a marvelous flow of gold and silver for export to Europe. The Spanish owners and friars also persuaded the Indian labor force to accept Christianity, at least outwardly. Meanwhile, the *adelantados* and other settlers were founding towns on Haiti, Cuba, and the American mainland, until by the close of the sixteenth century there were two hundred chartered municipalities. They were located at strategic commercial centers, political or military capitals, and mining camps. Most of the 160,000 Spanish living in America in 1574 resided on the temperate highlands, and most of these were concentrated in towns, leaving the countryside to the Indians and a few overseers. Several towns attained moderate size: Potosi, the site of the great silver mines, numbered 114,000 people in 1611; Mexico City approached that figure. The municipalities tended to repeat features of Spanish urban life — the Spanish square; the great Spanish Cathedral, of baroque architecture; the Spanish university — twelve universities were established in Spanish America before Harvard was founded in 1636; the town council dealing with such matters as garbage removal and street repair; and the leisurely Spanish social existence.

In the countryside of the temperate highlands, the Spanish ownership and Catholic Christianity formed from one standpoint a superstructure, below which the inner life of the non-literate Indian village went on much as before.

Perhaps the Indians had only changed their masters. Landholding Indian peasant households still raised corn, beans, and squash on a plot of village land for their own subsistence; cultivated other plots for the local chief, the (now Spanish) priesthood, and the (now Spanish) owner, who often resided in town; labored on the roads for the good of the state and in the mines for the profit of the owners; and permitted themselves to be baptized into the religion of their new masters, while retaining many of their old religious concepts of the cult of nature and its forces.

From another viewpoint the elements of Spanish culture that were brought over[a] and the Indian culture were blending into a new Indo-Spanish fusion. In the realm of material objects and techniques, the Indian continued and the Spanish accepted the use of the turkey, guinea fowl, and llama as domestic animals, the cultivation of certain crops peculiar to America — corn, squash, "Irish" potatoes, yams, cocoa, pineapples, peanuts, tomatoes, sarsaparilla, tobacco, and several commercial varieties of cotton — and the mining of gold and silver. The Spanish in turn introduced certain products and devices, which the Indian accepted when he found them useful, within his means, and compatible with his way of doing things. He accepted from the Spanish the use of horses, cattle, sheep, pigs, bees, and chickens as domestic animals; the cultivation of wheat, barley, sugar cane, and many vegetables and fruits; and the application of such devices as the wheel for both pottery and transportation, the quicksilver process for separating gold and silver from the ore, the plow and other iron implements, the flat-bed loom, Spanish-type fishing devices, and Spanish carpenter tools. At the same time the Indian often rejected Spanish material objects that did not appeal or were too

[a]Of course, much of the culture of Spain was not brought to America. Many of the very early settlers came from the provinces of Andalusia and Estremadura, that is, from southern and west-central Spain, and brought the customs, for example, a type of plow or fishing net, that prevailed in their provinces. When later in the sixteenth century settlers from other Spanish regions arrived in America with different customs, they discovered that the Andalusian plow or net had already solved the technological problem in question, had entered a crystalized Spanish-Indian fusion, and was in possession. Many, though not all, the cultural practices of eastern and northern Spain remained in Spain. Also, certain Spanish practices were dropped because they were not applicable in America. The lack of sufficient streams of water and of regular winds in the American temperate highlands ruled out the water mill and the windmill. Finally, Spanish and royal and ecclesiastical authorities screened out certain elements of Spanish civilization. For example, Spanish towns had been noted for centuries for their political independence and individualistic diversity. Only a few new towns had been constructed along a standard grid-plan of rectangular city blocks. However, in America the royal government kept the towns under a close surveillance and insisted that they all be built on a grid-plan of rectangular city blocks, with a central plaza bordered by the church and governmental buildings. The Catholic missionaries likewise presented to the Indian an essential, purified Christianity stripped of popular superstitious practices that had accrued over the centuries in Spain.

expensive. Indian women sometimes refused to wear sandals, because they liked to go barefoot. Indians declined to eat eggs and drink milk, because they did not like the taste. They persisted in sleeping on mats because bedsteads were not in keeping with an entire complex of sitting, eating, and sleeping habits. They continued the use of pottery since porcelain and metal wares were too costly.

In the realm of social organization, religion, and folk culture, the Indians often replaced indigenous practices with similar Spanish ones. They accepted the hierarchical organization of society and the yielding of forced labor and tribute to the Spanish more readily because they had always lived in a hierarchical society and yielded forced labor and tribute. Their acceptance of Christianity was eased by the resemblance of many Christian practices and beliefs to their own. They learned the catechism by rote; they marveled at the ceremonies of the Catholic church; and they also took on little by little the Spanish language in which religious instruction was eventually couched. However, in approaching Christianity, they often altered it, the alteration varying subtly from one Indian culture to the next. They might, for example, follow the ritual of Passion Week, without believing in the Resurrection. Also, in the realm of folk culture, they might continue intact the intimate practices of family life — the preparation of food or the delivery of children from a kneeling position — partly because they had never come into contact with the Spanish customs and partly because they were comfortable with their own. In the durations of simple, daily things, the objects man uses, or the animals he befriends or chooses to kill, the Indians kept much of the past intact, and delivered it whole into the common Spanish-Indian life. Thus out of the personal decisions of many individuals, both Spanish and Indian, by 1580 in the countryside of the temperate highlands a culture crystalized that was neither entirely Spanish nor entirely Indian, but was Indo-Spanish, a fusion no one had intended or anticipated.

Likewise, the towns were affected by the Indian presence. These were not Spanish towns in Spain, but Spanish towns in America, and their social structure was influenced by that circumstance. The occupation and hence social position of an individual came to hinge on the purity of his blood and the place of his birth. Since few Spanish women migrated to America, marriages between Spaniards and Indian women were early established and gave rise to offspring known as mestizos. Most people in the towns were mestizos or Indians — about nine out of ten in the major cities. The Indians of the towns usually were in domestic service, although a few might follow a trade or a handicraft. A few mestizos filled the humble positions of servants in parishes and convents, but the vast majority were town artisans. Although the poorer creoles (pure whites who were born in America) might learn a craft, as a rule they entered law or medicine, owned the plantations, ranches, and mines, as well as much of the town property, and pursued the avocation of learning and literature. Peninsular Spaniards (pure whites who had been born in Spain) were occasionally poor but usually they were the leaders – in commerce, government, and the Catholic church. In most respects, the white Peninsular Spaniards and creoles aped the customs of Spain – the siesta, the late afternoon stroll around the plaza of the town, and the dilettante interest in literature, and to a degree the mestizos and town Indians aped the whites. The Indo-Spanish culture of the towns, unlike that of the countryside, was more Spanish than Indian.

The Spanish-American colonies were in theory and to a degree in practice governed from Spain. While conquest and settlement were progressing in America, the Spanish monarchs were developing the colonial administration. From the start, Ferdinand and Isabella were interested in the revenues that the new discovery might yield and in the maintenance of their authority over the new possessions. Queen Isabella governed Castile through and with the advice of the supreme and royal Council of Castile. Initially she deputed a member of that Council, Bishop Fonseca, to take charge of all matters relating to the newly discovered lands. He was in effect colonial minister from 1493-1503. As the press of colonial business became too great for a single man, however, his supervision of economic affairs was handed in 1503 to a House of Trade modeled upon the Portuguese India House. The personnel of the House of Trade came to consist of a president, a treasurer, a comptroller or bookkeeper-secretary, a factor or business manager, and a secretarial staff. It supervised all traffic to and from America – licensed the ships, inspected and recorded the cargoes, approved the captains, prepared the maps, and in general administered the economic regulations of the crown. As the complexity of colonial affairs continued to increase, other men were joined to Fonseca to form a committee, which in 1524 was established as the supreme and royal Council of the Indies, equal to and coordinate with the Council of Castile.

Thereafter, the Spanish kings dealt with the New World through the Council of the Indies. It resided at court. Its members met twice daily. They prepared for royal approval all laws relating to the administration, taxation, and police of the American dominions. The council proposed to the king the names of individuals who might be appointed to colonial posts. As the Spanish monarch controlled the Catholic church in Spain, so he controlled the church in America, and the council nominated for his ratification the American bishops and archbishops. It corresponded with colonial officials, lay and ecclesiastical, and supervised their conduct. The House of Trade was under its superintendence. As a judicial body, the council sat as a court of final appeal for all cases concerning American affairs which were of sufficient importance to be carried to it. Throughout the sixteenth century its members were hardworking and capable.

Ferdinand and Isabella and their successors, Charles V (1516-1556) and Philip II (1556-1598), gradually brought the towns, nobles, and the Cortes of Castile under royal control. In America they tried to prevent the rise of similar challengers. The towns of Haiti early petitioned and received the privileges of self-government of the Castilian towns and began to choose their own local officials. Then representatives from several towns in Haiti began to meet in a single common assembly. Cuba followed the lead of Haiti, and at least as early as 1540 representatives from towns on that island met annually in an embryo cortes. But Charles V frowned on this development of representative government. He declared: "Without our command it is not our intention or will that the cities and towns of the Indies meet in convention," and he never issued the command. The island assemblies ceased to exist. Eventually even the town council became a closed corporation whose creole aldermen inherited or purchased their position and accepted the surveillance of crown officials.

The early *adelantados* and governors, inventive and daring, also displayed disquieting tendencies toward independence and threatened to assume the power and position of a feudal nobility. The Spanish kings, haunted by the old nightmare of a disobedient nobility, moved against them. The king in 1511 appointed a board of judges known as the *audiencia* to check the governor of Haiti and in 1526 one to check Cortez, now governor of Mexico. In Spain an *audiencia* was a court of law; in America it was that and more too. It heard appeals from the decisions of the governor and worked with him in opening the king's letters and preparing replies. The *audiencia* proving inadequate to restrain Cortez, the king appointed in addition a viceroy to govern in his name in America. During the sixteenth century Spanish America was divided into two viceroyalties: that of New Spain (1535) with its capital at Mexico and a jurisdiction extending over the West Indies, northern Venezuela, the Spanish mainland possessions in North America, and the Philippine Islands; that of Peru (1542) with its seat of government at Lima and a territory that included all of South America except northern Venezuela and Portuguese Brazil. Each viceroyalty was divided into three or four subordinate provinces, known as *audiencias* from the fact that an *audiencia*, a board of judges, exercised judicial and administrative power over it. A captain-general might serve as president of the board in its administrative capacity. All the viceroys, judges, and captains-general as well as the archbishops were appointed by the crown. Usually they were Spaniards who were sent out. The powers of the viceroy were vast, corresponding to those of his royal master. He was commander-in-chief of the army, comptroller of the revenue, and special guardian of the Indians. He issued ordinances having the force of law and in general was responsible for the well-being and development of the colony. He, the *audiencias*, the captains-general, the archbishops, and bishops received instructions from the king and the Council of the Indies. The Spanish government of its overseas dominions was in spirit a royal autocracy.

But there were limits upon this concentration of power. Even while the centralized governmental structure was being built, immunities, privileges, and in effect public authority were being accorded to various corporate groups and private individuals in the New World. "Both the secular and regular clergy emerged as powerful elements in colonial society, claiming tax exemptions, special trial by ecclesiastical courts, and extensive rights over the labor and tithes of the Indians. Spanish and creole merchants of the colonial guilds obtained a monopoly (with the Seville merchants) over trade, jurisdiction in special commercial cases, and the tax farm. Mine owners and the mining guild gained the right to use forced labor in the mines, jurisdiction over mining cases, and the privilege of minting coins."[5] The owners of large estates became virtually independent in them. Royal officials at various levels in the administrative hierarchy often treated their public office as a private independent patrimony, and extorted produce and money from the Indians and accepted bribes. The viceroy himself, in theory the agent of the king, sometimes simply did not enforce the laws against privileged colonials. The operation of the royal autocracy was tempered and in a sense made workable by this dispersion of public authority among privileged corporate groups and individuals.

For a moment Ferdinand and Isabella apparently considered imitating Portuguese practice and making the American plantations, mines, and trade a royal monopoly, which they would exploit with salaried royal agents. But to cultivate a whole continent of wilderness was finally beyond their means. Even they could not reach that far. So making the best of the situation, they opened the American trade to the Catholics of Castile and (later) Aragon. Of course, they regulated this trade very closely, for the expected enrichment of the crown and of Spain. Only Spaniards might trade with the Spanish-American possessions. And these Spaniards must leave for America in Spanish ships with Spanish crews and only by the single port of Seville. There the House of Trade could conveniently register their names and their cargoes and inspect their ships. At first the ships went out singly or in small companies, but as French pirates began to swarm around the bullion like flies on honey, the ships were permitted to sail only with an annual fleet that left Seville under army convoy in the spring or summer. It sailed to the Caribbean

---

[5] J. J. TePaske, "Constitutional Tensions in the Eighteenth-Century Spanish Empire," (paper read at the San Francisco meeting of the American Historical Association, 1965), p. 3.

Islands where it divided, one section going to Vera Cruz for the Mexican trade, the second to Portobello on the Isthmus of Panama for the Central American and Peruvian commerce. On the return the two sections reunited at Havana and then proceeded to Seville. Although annual sailings were not the invariable rule, they were the ideal striven after and sometimes achieved. In any case, single ships had to await in Seville or in America the formation of a fleet, even if it consumed two or three years. The fleet carried to America manufactured wares and some foods, the major articles being textiles, clothes, hats, shoes, glass, china, paper, mercury, flour, dried fish, wine, and olive oil. It returned with bullion (gold or silver), sugar, hides, and dyewoods, and with lesser quantities of precious stones, cacao, drugs, spices, and indigo. The House of Trade thus tried to canalize or to squeeze the entire Spanish-American trade between the European continent and the two American continents through the neck of an hour-glass, the single port of Seville. As the ships were shepherded to and fro across the Atlantic by armed convoys, "the supplying of a great kingdom [Spain] was carried on like the provisioning of a blockaded fortress."

Who benefited from the traffic? In all the trading, who really got the Spanish gold? The merchants of Seville got some, by extorting monopoly prices. And foreign manufacturers got some, because Spain's industry was dying. By the close of the sixteenth century, non-Spanish manufacturers, using Seville merchants as middleman, furnished five-sixths of the cargo of the outbound fleets and received two-thirds of the incoming bullion. Then, the crown benefited, at least in the short run. It taxed the traffic as it passed through the control ports. It levied a sales tax of 2 per cent on each transaction; another 2 per cent tax on the cargo to pay for the armed convey; and a customs duty of about 7.5 per cent on all goods imported into or exported from the colonies. It also took one-fifth of all gold, silver, and precious stones. A little over 50 per cent of this revenue defrayed the expenses of colonial administration and defense, but the rest was clear profit and amounted in Philip II's reign to 10 to 25 per cent of the crown's total income.[b] Lastly, the smugglers thrived, the people underground, who received with open hands what could not be strained and squeezed through the legal channels. They broke into the system and obtained the prevailing monopoly prices. The towering edifice of legal Spanish commerce was combed with secret passages of underground activity.

In Brazil the Portuguese faced the same problem of securing reliable labor as did the Spanish in the Caribbean islands. The Portuguese were entering a

---

[b]The net revenue from the colonies was 445 cuentos in 1577, 700 in 1585, and 945 in 1598. This amounted to 10, 25, and 22 per cent of Philip II's total income in the respective years.

tropical wilderness where Indians largely subsisted by hunting, fishing, and cannibalism, although a few groups added a little agriculture. One Indian expressed surprise that the Portuguese killed men "and did not eat them." From 1500 to 1532 the Portuguese came as traders and exchanged trinkets and tools with the Indians for quantities of a dyewood called brazilwood. In accord with their customary commercial practices, they founded two or three trading "factories" to accumulate brazilwood between the ships' visits. Since the Indians felled the trees, trimmed and cut them up, and transported the logs to the factory, the system of barter purchased both product and Indian labor.

The Portuguese moved with deliberation, inching forward in America. In 1532, King John III, to protect his holding against the French and to develop Brazil as a colony, decided to send settlers. He, his advisers, and eventually the settlers drew on Portuguese experience. One of Prince Henry the Navigator's methods, perfected along the African coast, had been used to exploit India. Another of his methods, pioneered in the Azores and Madeira islands, was now taken to Brazil. It was simplicity itself. He had granted large sections of each island or sometimes an entire island to an aide, on condition that he colonize, settle, and administer it. Soon the Madeira settlers were exporting wood, wax, honey, and above all, sugar. Following in Prince Henry's wake, King John III in 1532 granted to twelve great nobles "captaincies," which extended in most cases fifty leagues along the Brazilian shore and stretched indefinitely into the interior. The twelve "donataries" were to be feudal lords, empowered to charter cities, to apportion land among the colonists, and to administer justice. Several "donataries" sunk their fortune to equip an expedition, bring over several hundred settlers, build a fort, and found a town on the coast. The settlers imported sugar cane from the Madeira islands as a potential export crop. They needed reliable labor to raise food and sugar cane. Drawing on experience, they at first bartered trinkets and tools for Indian labor. But the Indians were soon satiated with European beads and bangles. The settlers then enslaved unfriendly Indians taken in war. After the Indians, both friendly and unfriendly, were nearly exterminated by two smallpox epidemics, the settlers imported Negro slaves to raise the imported cane. Inevitably, great plantations emerged, each with its big house, its single master, its single crop, its many cabins, and its swarm of slaves. The propinquity of white master and Indian and Negro slave women on each isolated plantation led to offspring of mixed blood, mamelukes (mestizos) and mulattoes. Like Charles V of Spain, King John III grew apprehensive of the authority he had given away, and proceeded to draw it in. In 1548 he deprived the "donatarios" of their political power and dispatched a captain-general (viceroy) to give Brazil administrative cohesion. But the power was never held tightly. Portugal, in contrast to Spain, did not closely regulate its colony. Brazil's economic growth was gradual in the sixteenth and seventeenth centuries, rather than flashy. Its white population in 1574 was less than 17,000, located mostly along the coast. The basis of its economy was large-estate monoculture. "The conditions were a patriarchal stability of family life; the regularization of labor by means of slavery; and the union of the Portuguese male with the Indian [and Negro] woman, who were thus incorporated into the economic and social culture of the invader."[6]

Some Leading Ideas

This chapter is a long one, and apparently it only tells a story. Yet embedded in the story are four major interpretive ideas. The first idea is that of historical continuity — that the expansion of Europe overseas was neither sudden nor abrupt, that each event grew out of a preceding one, and hence that the total movement was a flow outward of European complexity, technological, economic, social, and political. The second major idea is that individuals often built up, bit by bit, economic, social, and political institutions at home and overseas in the process of solving practical problems and of repeating the solutions until they became habitual. The way individuals perceived the problems and the solutions they devised were affected, of course, by the ideas and attitudes they had at the moment. The third major idea is that the Portuguese in the Far East and the Portuguese and Spanish in America developed two major types of European overseas empire — the commercial and the settlement empires, each a distinctive answer to distinctive problems. Both the problems and the answers of the two types of empire might be compared. The fourth major idea is that Spanish settlers carried to the temperate highlands of Central and South America some of the ideas, customs, and practices that prevailed in Spain at the time of their migration, that these ideas, practices, and customs were acquiring new content in the new environment, and that there was evolving an Indo-Spanish culture with definite characteristics, which might be reviewed. If the chapter is re-read with these ideas in mind, the story will take on deeper meanings.

The second stage of European expansion, like the first, reacted on European society. The chief trade shifted from the Mediterranean Sea to the Atlantic Ocean. With the shift came not the immediate but the eventual commercial decline of Italy and south Germany and the rise, momentarily of Spain and Portugal, and, later, of France, the Netherlands, and England. Just as important as the change in routes was the change in goods brought to European markets and the consequent rise in the standards of consumption of

---

[6] Gilberto Freyre, *The Masters and the Slaves: A Study in the Development of Brazilian Civilization*, p. 3.

the upper and middle classes. What Europe had previously imported from the Far East, spices, precious stones, silk, and other fine fabrics, had been essentially luxuries small in bulk and for the few. But when a direct sea route was opened to India and the Malay Archipelago, it became possible to import such quantities of spices that their reduced price brought them within the reach of the middle class. At the same time, it was possible to carry bulky goods like rice, tea, and coffee, and, from America, tobacco and sugar, which became part of the ordinary middle-class diet.

With the influx of American gold and silver, prices rose. It is estimated that in 1500 the amount of coinage in circulation in Europe was the equivalent of $170,000,000 to $200,000,000. Shortly after 1520, the Spaniards got in large lump sums the Aztec and Inca treasures, and then developed a steady supply of precious metals from the mines of Peru, Bolivia, and Mexico. The amount that was mined and shipped to Europe in the sixteenth century is still obscure, but it exceeded $600,000,000. As the supply of gold and silver coins increased, their value declined and it took more pesos to buy goods — in brief, prices of commodities rose. The European price level doubled or tripled in this century, some commodities rising more than others. This great increase in prices, coupled as it was with the accumulation of capital, stimulated trade and speculation. It increased the profits of the industrial and merchant classes and hence their social importance.

Increase in the sheer volume of trade and in the money in circulation was accompanied by the wider use of bills of exchange and credit and the growth of larger enterprises. The old family partnership method of organizing a capitalistic undertaking was no longer sufficient for an increased volume and continuity of enterprise, and it was replaced more and more by the joint-stock company, already invented in Genoa. The joint-stock company was based on negotiable shares — shares that could be bought and sold in the open market. The negotiability of shares gave rise in Antwerp to the first stock exchange (1531), an event of the first order in the history of European capitalism. In general, the focus of European economy was shifting to the Atlantic seaboard, and the economy was becoming more powerful and complex.

Finally, the colonial empires of Portugal and Spain, as possessions of the Portuguese and Spanish kings, became entangled in those rivalries and wars for power in which the kings of Europe were engaged. The expansion of Europe overseas thus extended the area involved in the rivalries among the great powers.

An Invitation to Further Inquiry and Reflection

In North America the Indians were virtually exterminated, their few remnants were isolated on reservations, and their culture had little effect on the dispossessing whites. In much of Central and South America, on the contrary, they survived in considerable, if diminished numbers, and they and the Spanish entered into cultural relations which modified the culture of both groups and from which a new culture emerged. Why was the Indian experience different in the two segments of the western hemisphere?

What was happening in the highlands of Central and South America between the Spanish and Indians was "acculturation," which has been defined as "those phenomena that result when groups of individuals having different cultures come into continuous first hand contact, with subsequent changes in the original culture patterns of either or both groups." Acculturation may be viewed as a process (the series of actions that bring an adoption of cultural elements) or in terms of results (the cultural changes produced). Acculturation is widespread and significant in history; it has been going on for millenniums and it is going on today, all over the world. The *results* of acculturation have been catalogued and studied in many historical situations yet, strangely, the *process* of acculturation — what actually happens and why in the moment of cultural transmission — remains relatively unexplored, and to a degree, a mystery. Consider an Indian village in the Central American highlands upon the arrival of a Spanish missionary. Who were the innovators in the village? In what situation did the innovators find themselves? How did they perceive the situation, what were their ideas about it, and what were their attitudes toward it? What elements of the Spanish culture did they select and why? Which kinds of people in the village were inclined to follow and which ones were inclined to resist? What modifications, if any, were made in the form of the borrowed element and why? What modifications were made in the meaning of borrowed object, in terms of its relations with other elements of the village's culture? When was the borrowed element adopted by the first innovator? How long before it was fully integrated into the village culture? What adjustment in the preexisting culture pattern resulted by the acceptance of the new element? How were these adjustments accomplished and again why? Similarly, in the Spanish group, who were the innovators? In what situation were they placed? How did they perceive the situation, and what were their attitudes toward it? And so on. And then, what were the interrelations between the Spanish Indians and the Spanish, the questions of rapport and of hostility, of submissiveness and dominance, of admiration and disdain, and of interlocking and interacting personalities and personality roles? Such queries with respect to underlying relationships are still a subject for inquiry and reflection.

For Further Reading

(For general reading)

C. R. Beazley, *Prince Henry the Navigator* (1895)
Herbert Bolton, *Coronado, Knight of Pueblos and Plains* (1949)
Edward G. Bourne, *Spain in America* (1904)
Cottie A. Burland, *The Exotic White Man* (1969)
C. W. Ceram, *Gods, Graves, and Scholars: The Story of Archaeology* (1952)
    2nd edition
Bernard Diaz Del Castillo, *The Discovery and Conquest of Mexico* (1956)
Bailey W. Diffie, *Latin-American Civilization: Colonial Period* (1945)
J. H. Elliott *Imperial Spain, 1469-1716* (1963)
——————, *The Old World and the New, 1492-1716* (1970)
Gilberto Freyre, *Brazil: An Interpretation* (1945)
——, *Masters and the Slaves: A Study in the Development of Brazilian
    Civilization* (1946)
Charles Gibson, *Spain in America* (1966)
Lewis Hanke, *The Spanish Struggle for Justice in the Conquest of America*
    (1959)
C. H. Haring, *The Spanish Empire in America* (1947)
John Hemming, *The Conquest of the Incas* (1970)
John Tate Lanning, *Academic Culture in the Spanish Colonies* (1940)
Ralph Linton, editor, *Acculturation in Seven American Indian Tribes* (1963)
James Lockhart, *Spanish Peru, 1532-1560: A Colonial Society* (1968)
Samuel Eliot Morison, *Admiral of the Ocean Sea: A Life of Christopher
    Columbus*, 2 volumes (1942)
——, *The European Discovery of America: the Northern Voyages, A.D.
    500-1600* (1971)
J. H. Parry, *The Age of Reconnaissance* (1963)
——, *The Spanish Seaborne Empire* (1966)
Elsie Clews Parsons, *Mitla: Town of Souls* (1936)
C. H. Phillips, *India* (1949)
Marco Polo, *Travels* (several translations)
Edgar Prestage, *The Portuguese Pioneers* (1933)
E. Sanceau, *Indies Adventure* (1936)
William L. Schurz, *The Manila Galleon* (1939)
C. T. Smith, *An Historical Geography of Western Europe before 1800* (1967)
John J. TePaske, editor, *Three American Empires* (1967)
George Thomson, *Sir Francis Drake* (1972)
Hugh Trevor-Roper, editor, *The Age of Expansion: Europe and the World
    1559-1660* (1968)

Charles Verlinden, *The Beginnings of Modern Colonization*

J. A. Williamson, *The Age of Drake* (1938, 1946)(1960)

James A. Williamson, *Hawkins of Plymouth: A New History of Sir John Hawkins and of the Other Members of His Family Prominent in Tudor England* (1949)

J. A. Williamson, *Sir Francis Drake* (1951)

(For advanced study)

Charles Bishko, "The Iberian B ackground of Latin American History, Recent Progress and Continuing Problems," *Hispanic American Historical Review*, XXVI (1956), 50-80.

George M. Foster, *Culture and Conquest* (1960)

Charles Gibson and Benjamin Keen, "Trends of United States Studies in Latin American History," *American Historical Review*, 62 (July, 1957), 855-877.

Charles E. Nowell, "The Columbus Q uestion: A Survey of Recent Literature and Present Opinions," *American Historical Review*, 44 (1938-1939), 802-822.

Alan Manchester, "Columbus: An Historical Note on the Literature," *South Atlantic Quarterly*, LIX (Spring, 1960), 278-283.

Herbert Bolton, "The Epic of Greater America," *American Historical Review*, 38 (1932-1933), 448-474.

"Have the Americans a Common History?", *Canadian Historical Review*, XXIII (June, 1942), 125-156.

Silvio Zavala, "A General View of the Colonial History of the New World," *American Historical Review* 66 (1960-1961), 913-929.

Charles R. Boxer, *The Portuguese Seaborne Empire, 1415-1825* (1969)

E. Bradford Burns, *A History of Brazil* (1970)

Alexander Marchant, *From Barter to Slavery: the Economic Relations of Portuguese and Indians in the Settlement of Brazil, 1500-1580*. The Johns Hopkins University Studies in Historical and Political Science, Series LX, Number 1,(1942).

Ward Barrett, *The Sugar Hacienda of the Margueses del Valle* (1970)

P. J. Bakewell, *Silver Mining and Society in Colonial Mexico: Zacatecas, 1546-1700* (1971)

Ibero-American monographs:

No. 29 — Carl Sauer, *Colima of New Spain in the Sixteenth Century* (1948)

No. 30 — Robert West, *The Mining Community in Northern New Spain: the Parral Mining District* (1949)

No. 31 — Sherburne Cook and Lesley Simpson, *The Population of Central Mexico in the Sixteenth Century* (1948)

No. 32 – James Parsons, *Antioqueno Colonization in Western Colombia* (1949)

No. 33 – Sherburne Cook, *The Historical Demography and Ecology of the Teotlalpan* (1949)

No. 34 – Sherburne Cook, *Soil Erosion and Population in Central Mexico* (1949)

No. 35 – Woodrow Borah, *New Spain's Century of Depression* (1951)

No. 36 – Lesley Simpson – *Exploitation of Land in Central Mexico in the Sixteenth Century* (1952)

No. 39 – B. Le Roy Gordon, *Human Geography and Ecology in Sinu Country of Colombia* (1957)

Chapter VI

THE GREAT POWER RIVALRIES AND THE PROTESTANT
CHALLENGE (1494-1564)

The Contest for Power

The modern phase of the contest for power among the states began in Italy in the fifteenth century. At that time there was a continual contest for power and a jockeying for position among the larger states of Florence, Milan, Venice, the Papal states, and the Kingdom of Naples. Occasionally, one of these states and then another tried to dominate the Italian peninsula while other states (usually Florence) attempted to maintain an even balance of power, just as later one state or another would try to dominate Europe while other states (usually England) would attempt to maintain an equilibrium. In Italy too there were a few smaller states which struggled to survive and to remain neutral. There were alliances, ultimatums, threats, and wars; and diplomats who "fenced with nice weapons of cunning and deceit, aiming rather to thrust through the weak point of their foe's armour than to beat him down in strength, seeking always to catch him unawares, to trick him by fair promises, and betray him by false hopes."[1] A former diplomat of the Florentine staff, Niccolo Machiavelli, described in his classic manual *The Prince* (1513) these methods of securing power at home and abroad that were being used by Italians and by foreigners who intrigued in Italy. Perhaps unintentionally, he held up for the emulation of later generations of European statemen the Italian methods and their underlying philosophy that the end (power) justifies the means.

One year in the 1490's Ludovico Sforza, the powerful ruler of Milan, associated himself with the discontented subjects of King Ferrante of Naples and appealed to King Charles VIII of France to revive the old claim of the French kings to the throne of Naples. Charles had been left by his father, the crafty and niggardly Louis XI, a compact kingdom in which all the great fiefs had been absorbed and a formidable mercenary army strengthened by Swiss pikemen, Gascon crossbowmen, and a train of light, quick-firing artillery. Charles was just coming of age. He was a young and licentious hunchback of

---

[1] Conyers Read, *Mr. Secretary Walsingham and the Policy of Queen Elizabeth*, I, 24.

doubtful sanity. He was surrounded by a group of madcap nobility and courtiers to whom an adventure in Italy seemed alluring. So Charles decided to invade Italy and assert his claim in Naples. The expedition was a breeze. Unopposed, Charles and his army marched "with blare and glitter" from France to Naples and took possession in 1494-1495. To win this piece of territory proved easy — to hold it was different. The astute and shifty Italians, fearful of Charles's preponderance and not quite willing to believe the French had beaten them, began to weave intrigues for the destruction of the invaders. Just across the straits from Naples, Ferdinand of Aragon, the husband of Isabella of Castile, ruled Sicily. He himself had certain old dynastic claims to the mainland Kingdom of Naples. As he feared that from Naples Charles would attack Sicily, Ferdinand aided the Italians. Charles, warned of the league that was forming, beat a retreat. He and his army reached France without a mishap, but also without possession of a single yard of territory. Jules Michelet, the great French historian, observed that the French were then the best marchers in Europe: they had marched right into Italy, and they had marched right out again. Thus lightly and rather foolishly was initiated the European phase of the modern contest for power among the states.

Since Charles's escapade of 1494-1495 there have been many continuing aspects of this contest, four of which may be mentioned now. First, the area involved in the contest for power has constantly increased during the last five centuries, as country after country, continent after continent, has been drawn in, as into a widening whirlpool. France and Spain, as we have seen, were sucked in during the last decade of the fifteenth century. The Ottoman Empire, Austria, Germany, the Netherlands, and Tudor England became involved in the sixteenth. The Scandinavian countries entered by taking part in the Thirty Years' War (1618-1648). Toward the close of the seventeenth century, Russia became a factor. During the eighteenth century, the French and English colonies in America and India actively participated. During the nineteenth century no new major areas were added, although two recently united countries — Germany and Italy — entered the field to upset old relationships. However, the United States re-entered power politics in the Spanish-American War and during the presidency of Theodore Roosevelt. At approximately the same time, China and Japan became important in the calculations of world diplomacy, and shortly after, World War I swept in the Union of South Africa, India, Australia, New Zealand, Canada, and most of the Latin-American states. The contest for power which had begun among the small city-states and principalities of Italy now had spread to include and involve virtually the entire world. Today, no state is untouched by its operation.

Secondly, during these four centuries of strife, different sets of rivalries and different patterns of enmities have flourished for a time, only to be replaced by others. From 1494 to 1659 the central rivalry was between France and the combined power of Spain and Austria, France eventually winning. From 1689 to 1815 the central contest was between England and France, England winning. From 1871 to 1945, probably the central quarrel was between Germany and her changing allies and a French and English combination that was supported by Russia and the United States, Germany losing. Since 1945 the central struggle has been between the United States and Russia, a contest which is yet undecided.

Thirdly, during the course of these rivalries it sometimes happened that a single country became so strong that its power cast a shadow over all Europe. The Habsburg power of Spain and Austria was predominant in Europe from 1519 to 1635 before its power declined as a result of internal weakness and the combined assaults of France, England, Holland, and Sweden. From 1661 to 1713 France under Louis XIV occupied a similar dominant position until the combined attacks of England, Holland, and Austria brought Louis to terms. After that, from 1713 to 1794, a balance of power prevailed among the various states. But then from 1794 to 1815 during the French Revolution and under Napoleon, France again dominated Europe, until the combined efforts of England, Russia, Prussia, and Austria finally brought her down. From 1815 to 1871 ensued another period when a balance of power existed. From 1871 to 1943, however, Germany was repeatedly the most powerful European country and at times dominated the European continent as thoroughly as the Habsburgs, Louis XIV, and Napoleon had done in their day.

A fourth aspect of this strife may be noted. Sometimes the contest for power became intermingled with internal affairs, complexities, and ideas of the time. Thus, the struggle between the Habsburgs and the kings of France became mixed with the religious fanaticism of the wars of the Reformation and Counter-Reformation. The struggle between England and France eventually became entangled with the wars to defend and spread revolutionary principles, and on the other side were in part wars to check their diffusion. More recently, into the rivalry of France, England, and the United States with Germany was woven the antagonism between democracy and autocracy or dictatorship, and into the enmity between the United States and Russia the hostility between capitalism and communism. This projection of essentially domestic issues into the realm of foreign affairs immensely complicated diplomacy and war. It increased the intricacy of human motivation. Men did not always fight simply to enlarge their country at the expense of other countries. An individual diplomat or an individual citizen when he considered foreign problems might be swayed by a number of motives — desire for personal reward, loyalty to a dynasty, loyalty to a country, loyalty to a rank or class, loyalty even to an order of chivalry or a religious belief, or devotion to a secular cause. The number of motives as well as their relative intensities

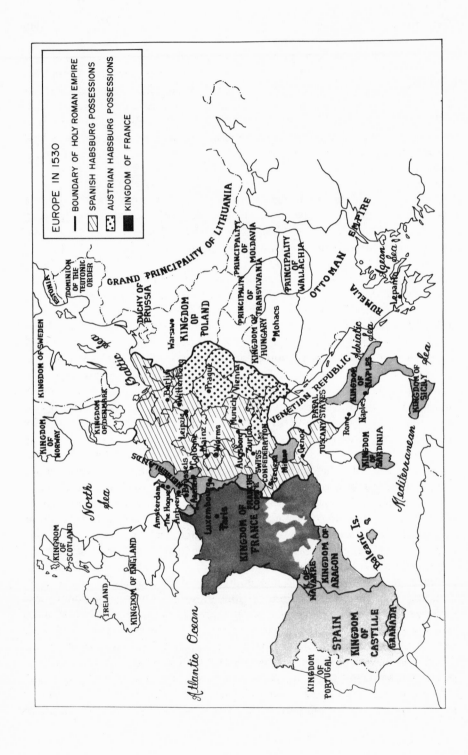

EUROPE IN 1530

—— BOUNDARY OF HOLY ROMAN EMPIRE
▨ SPANISH HABSBURG POSSESSIONS
⣿ AUSTRIAN HABSBURG POSSESSIONS
■ KINGDOM OF FRANCE

Atlantic Ocean

KINGDOM OF SCOTLAND

IRELAND

KINGDOM OF ENGLAND

North Sea

KINGDOM OF NORWAY

KINGDOM OF SWEDEN

KINGDOM OF DENMARK

Baltic Sea

ESTONIA

DOMINION OF THE TEUTONIC ORDER

GRAND PRINCIPALITY OF LITHUANIA

DUCHY OF PRUSSIA

Warsaw

KINGDOM OF POLAND

NETHERLANDS

Amsterdam
The Hague
Antwerp
Brussels
Ghent

Cologne

Berlin
Wittenberg
Leipzig
Prague

Mainz

Munich Vienna

Worms

Augsburg
Zurich

SWISS CONFEDERATION

Belgrade
Milan

Genoa

VENETIAN REPUBLIC

Adriatic Sea

PAPAL STATES
TUSCANY

Rome

Naples

KINGDOM OF NAPLES

KINGDOM OF SICILY

KINGDOM OF SARDINIA

PRINCIPALITY OF MOLDAVIA

PRINCIPALITY OF TRANSYLVANIA

KINGDOM OF HUNGARY

Mohacs

PRINCIPALITY OF WALLACHIA

OTTOMAN EMPIRE

RUMELIA

Aegean Sea

Lepanto Sea

Luxembourg
Paris

FRANCHE COMTE

KINGDOM OF FRANCE

KINGDOM OF NAVARRE

KINGDOM OF ARAGON

Balearic Is.

Mediterranean Sea

KINGDOM OF PORTUGAL

SPAIN
KINGDOM OF CASTILE

GRANADA

varied from individual to individual, and within each individual from time to time. Domestic issues often aroused emotional fervor, which astute rulers could cultivate and use. Domestic issues gave rise to fifth columns, which able governors repressed at home and encouraged abroad, so that an international war often became an international civil war. Yet, through this moving maze of motives and circumstances, in which domestic issues came and went, ran the continuing desire of the larger states for security and power, and of the smaller for existence and survival.

The Emergence of Spain from Isolation (1479-1519)

Two European wars, which merged, were being fought during the sixteenth and early seventeenth centuries. One war between Spain and France was secular in nature and was for power; the other between Catholicism and the Protestant churches was ideological. What we have to catch, among other things, is the intertwining of the two wars and the effect the intertwining had on each. Such a theme has for us both intrinsic interest and contemporary relevance.

The power struggle between Spain and France started first; the war over beliefs, not long after. During the Middle Ages, Spain was off the main current of European endeavor, preoccupied with the Moors and her own inner divisions, but during the first twenty years of the reigns of Ferdinand and Isabella, those problems that had held her back were removed. During the Middle Ages she had been divided — now she was united; she had struggled against the Moors — now she was free; she had suffered from disorder under the feudal nobility — now a more powerful crown maintained order. Spain now had a population of nine million people, second only to that of France, her agriculture still produced enough food to feed them, and her merino wool gave her a raw material to sell abroad for cash. At the same time that Spain was united and her energy was released, Ferdinand drew her along the old Aragonese possessions of the Balearic Isles, Sardinia, and Sicily to intervention in North Africa and Italy, where he met an expanding France.

We have to remember that foreign policy was still in only a few hands — the king and his immediate relatives and advisers. The peasants, of course, took little note of negotiations between monarchs — or any other matters of state as long as they did not occur in their immediate neighborhood. The townsmen were better informed on most public issues, but they too were largely helpless in the realm of diplomacy and war. The king and his circle thought of foreign policy mostly in terms of the power of the royal family or dynasty. Here, following Machiavelli, we have as the end, the power and perpetuation of the dynasty; and as the means, diplomacy, marriage, and war. The king's own personal policy sometimes made him blind to the best interests of his country. His dynasty might seem to thrive in a degenerating atmosphere: this happened more than once in Spain.

The foreign policy of the royal pair of Isabella of Castile and Ferdinand of Aragon was directed largely by the latter. Ferdinand was cautious, calculating, and unscrupulous. "Machiavelli held him as a model for princes in his skill at 'playing the fox.' Ferdinand himself was quite aware of his abilities in this regard and gloried in them. It is said that on learning that Louis XII of France had complained that he had deceived him for the second time, he promptly replied, "He lies, it's the tenth.' "[2]

Ferdinand, having already extended the possessions of Isabella and himself by the conquest of Granada, now hoped to extend them farther. He aspired to recover Cerdagne and Roussillon, border counties which spilled north of the Pyrenees and which Louis XI had acquired for France; to annex that segment of the Kingdom of Navarre which intruded south of the Pyrenees — Navarre was ruled by a French family; and to conquer the mainland Kingdom of Naples, already coveted by the French kings. But France, with an approximate population of fifteen million, a developing central administration, and an able army, was substantially the strongest European country, and the Valois kings were as ambitious as Ferdinand. They had reigned over France since 1328. They had extended their power over the great feudatories through diplomacy and war to reach the Atlantic Ocean and the Mediterranean Sea, and they now proposed to extend their possessions into Italy. Charles VIII (1492-1498) desired the Kingdom of Naples, and Louis XII (1498-1515) and Francis I (1515-1547) wanted both Naples and the Duchy of Milan. Inevitably Ferdinand's chief enemy was the Valois dynasty.

Ferdinand looked to his army and to his diplomacy. His great captains, Gonsalvo de Ayoraba and Gonsalvo de Cordoba, reorganized the Spanish soldiers into well-disciplined infantry units of 3,000 men (one-half pikemen, one-third short-sword javelin men, and one sixth arquebusiers). The superb Spanish infantry never was defeated in a pitched battle for over a century, from 1515 to 1643. Ferdinand also sought to encircle France through marriage alliances. He and Isabella had one son, John, and four daughters, Isabella, Joanna, Maria, and Catherine. To safeguard his flank, he married Isabella to Alfonso, the son of King John II of Portugal (1490), and after Alfonso's death to his cousin King Emanuel (1495). When Isabella and then her baby boy died, Emanuel married Maria (1500). To win England, France's hereditary enemy, Ferdinand married Catherine to Arthur (1501) the eldest son of Henry VII. When Arthur died in 1503, Catherine was betrothed to his brother, who ascended the English throne in 1509 as Henry VIII.

Ferdinand married John and Joanna into the Habsburg house of Austria

[2] Merriman, *The Rise of the Spanish Empire*, II, 43.

GENEALOGICAL TABLE

THE PATRIMONY OF CHARLES V, SHOWING THE ANCESTORS FROM WHOM HE INHERITED HIS LANDS

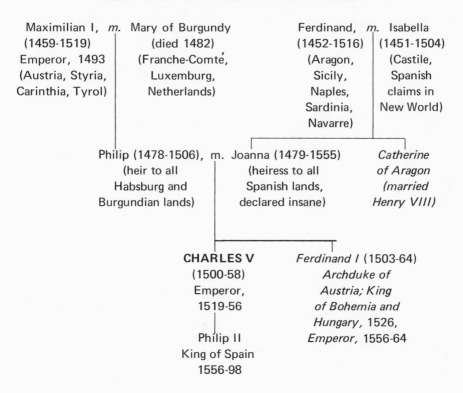

Maximilian I, *m.* Mary of Burgundy
(1459-1519)   (died 1482)
Emperor, 1493   (Franche-Comté,
(Austria, Styria,   Luxemburg,
Carinthia, Tyrol)   Netherlands)

Ferdinand, *m.* Isabella
(1452-1516) (1451-1504)
(Aragon,   (Castile,
Sicily,   Spanish
Naples,   claims in
Sardinia,   New World)
Navarre)

Philip (1478-1506), m. Joanna (1479-1555)
(heir to all   (heiress to all
Habsburg and   Spanish lands,
Burgundian lands)   declared insane)

Catherine
of Aragon
(married
Henry VIII)

CHARLES V
(1500-58)
Emperor,
1519-56

Philip II
King of Spain
1556-98

Ferdinand I (1503-64)
Archduke of
Austria; King
of Bohemia and
Hungary, 1526,
Emperor, 1556-64

and Burgundy. The Habsburg dynasty was one of the more powerful German families. From their ancestral castle of Habichtsburg in Switzerland they had fought and married their way down the Rhine into Alsace and also had acquired in southeastern Germany the following holdings: Austria, Styria, Carinthia, Carniola, and the Tyrol. Several Habsburgs had been elected Holy Roman Emperor: Frederick III, a Habsburg, was emperor from 1440 to 1493, and his son and heir, Maximilian, from 1493 to 1519. In 1482 Maximilian had married Duchess Mary of Burgundy, who brought him the Free County of Burgundy, Flanders, and the provinces of the Netherlands that were part of the Holy Roman Empire, all of these situated along the frontiers of France. By his acquisition of the Burgundian heritage Maximilian was exposed to Valois aggression either in Germany or Italy. Maximilian and Ferdinand of Aragon thus had a common enemy, the Valois kings of France. It was natural that Ferdinand's son, John, should marry Maximilian's daughter, Margaret (1497), and that Ferdinand's daughter, Joanna, should marry Maximilian's eldest son, Philip (1496).

Ferdinand, assured of Habsburg friendship, pursued his intrigues and repeated wars in Italy against the Valois dynasty. As a result of diplomacy and war, Ferdinand and Spain had acquired by his death in 1516 the added possessions and responsibilities of Cerdagne and Roussillon, Spanish Navarre, fortresses along the North African coast, and the mainland Kingdom of Naples, although the Valois king Francis I was in possession of the Duchy of Milan. Spain had been drawn by Ferdinand from isolation into the complexities of Italian affairs and a continuing conflict with France.

Spain was drawn by Ferdinand's successor, his grandson Charles V, still farther afield — into the war and intrigues of northern Europe. This was because Ferdinand's marriage dealings had yielded an unintended consequence: the Spanish scepter passed to a grandson who was not even a Spaniard, much less an Aragonese. Circumstances — John's death and the death of John's son, the deaths of Isabella and her son, and Joanna's mental derangement — brought the transmission of Ferdinand and Isabella's heritage to Joanna's son, Charles, a foreigner born in 1500, in the Netherlands and reared there.

Charles had inherited by 1519 the multitudinous possessions of Burgundy, the Habsburgs, and Aragon-Castile (see map) and had been elected Holy Roman Emperor. His empire was the largest European collection of territory from the time of the Roman Empire until Napoleon. It included the commercial wealth of the Netherlands; the manpower of Italy and Spain; and the gold and silver of America. But the possessions were scattered. In days when communication went at the pace of a man on horseback, it was difficult to hold the empire together, to gather its resources for a single blow, or to defend it from attack. The possessions were also heterogeneous. They were so diversified in climate, language, economic, religious, and cultural interests that no single consistent policy could be applied throughout, no central administration was feasible. Each major dominion — Spain, Italy, the Netherlands, the Holy Roman Empire — retained its peculiar institutions. And each one of the major dominions lacked within itself political unity and administrative uniformity. Each fraction (the seventeen individual provinces of the Netherlands, the eight cortes of Castile, Aragon, Valencia, Catalonia, Navarre, Sardinia, Sicily, and Naples, for example) had to be dealt with separately. With his possessions Charles also inherited enemies. As heir to Burgundy and Aragon, he was committed to war against France. As Holy Roman Emperor he had to deal with the German territorial princes, who did not really want his or any rule, and with Lutheranism, a troublesome movement of religious protest beyond the grasp of his understanding. The Moslem Ottoman Turks had captured Constantinople in 1453 and were now moving across the Balkans to attack Hungary and menace Vienna. Charles, as Holy Roman Emperor, was committed to repel their advance. The Turks were also seizing Venetian outposts in the eastern Mediterranean and supporting the Algerian pirates in the western. The pirates pillaged the coasts of Naples, Sicily, and Spain, ravaged Christian commerce, and carried Christians into slavery. Charles, as heir to the Spanish-Italian empire, had to handle them.

Charles slowly matured in meeting his responsibilities and reached a mutual accommodation with his Spanish subjects. He was, to quote one of his biographers, "not quite a great man, nor quite a good man, but all deductions made, an honorable Christian gentleman, striving, in spite of physical defects, moral temptations, and political impossibilities, to do his duty in that state of life to which an unkind Providence had called him."[3] He had the pride and the longing for honor and glory of a Burgundian nobleman: he was imbued with a sense of dynasty, of the obligation to leave his hereditary lands undiminished or enlarged; and he was a devout and conscientious Catholic. He came to have a strong sense of responsibility toward God, his lands, and the yet unborn princes of his transcendent line. He grew more fond of the Spaniards, and they of him, as he learned Spanish, married the Iberian princess, Isabella of Portugal, and spent sixteen years of his forty-year reign in Spain. The Spaniards gave him steady support as he conscientiously wore himself out wandering through Europe from one of his possessions to another, never quite at home, even in Spain, never quite solving one problem before he had to turn to the next.

[3] Edward Armstrong, *The Emperor Charles V*, II, 387.

The German Lutheran Revolt

After being crowned Holy Roman Emperor on October 23, 1520, Charles faced the problems of restoring imperial authority over the German princes and of dealing with the Lutheran movement. The latter was in large part a product of growing dissatisfaction with conditions in the Roman Catholic church. During the tenth and eleventh centuries, as we have seen, most individuals in western Europe were members of this church and had, in most instances, an attitude of obedience and heartfelt attachment toward it. But through the succeeding centuries both the church and the society of which it was a part altered, so that attachment was oftentimes replaced by discontent. For one thing, the doctrines of the church were becoming more rigid. As late as the eleventh century, much of Catholic doctrine still was fluid and indefinite, and could accommodate many varieties of belief and life. Scholastic theologians still argued over the number of sacraments and whether or not in the central sacrament, the Eucharist, the bread and wine really were transformed (transubstantiated) into the actual flesh and blood of Christ. But gradually as theologians debated, popes regulated, and general councils decreed, the doctrines became more fixed and definite. It became more difficult for the church to interpret her doctrine so as to include a wide variety of belief, more difficult for a reformer not to become and to be considered a heretic. The doctrines, moreover, were usually defined in a manner calculated to enhance the authority of the clergy, of the pope, and of the rites they administered. The Fourth Council of the Lateran, for example, decreed in 1215 that every adult believer must confess at least once a year to a priest, receive absolution, and then participate in the Eucharist in which the miracle of transubstantiation, it was now believed, occurred. This decree delivered the soul of every living person in Europe into the hands of the parish priest. This interpretation of the sacraments also could render salvation for ordinary men as a mechanical thing: participate in the sacraments of the church as they are administered by a consecrated priesthood and you will be saved.

Then, too, the Catholic clergy was becoming increasingly worldly and corrupt. The popes had developed since the tenth century a large, centralized bureaucracy to handle the increased business that was being brought to Rome. To support this bureaucracy and the papacy itself in grandeur and magnificence, the popes drew more and more money from all of western Christendom to central Italy. During the fourteenth and fifteenth centuries commercialism and corruption entered this administrative and pecuniary machine. Members of the papal administration would reserve to themselves or their favorites, to the inner circle of Italians who were "in," the more valuable northern benefices under papal control. They sometimes granted several benefices to one Italian, who stayed in Italy and drew the revenue, but performed none of the duties attached to the office. The common people in northern dioceses often supported absentee prelates in luxurious living and then paid a second time in order to maintain local church edifices and resident clergymen. With benefices so valuable and the papal administration so corrupt, clergymen were willing to buy and the pope to sell appointments to these lucrative offices. This abuse was called simony. Pope Leo X (1513-1521), the pope of Martin Luther, made 500,000 ducats, the equivalent of about $1,125,000, annually from the sale of more than two thousand offices. As the traffic continued, the price became stabilized at about ten times the income of the benefice. The purchaser's dividend, that is, would be 10 per cent annually. These abuses of the papal administration infected in time the entire church. There were good prelates here and there, of course, but inordinate wealth of the higher clergy, simony, immorality, neglect of pastoral duties, ignorance, and departure from monastic rules were common charges brought against the bishops, parish priests, monks, and nuns of Western Christendom during the fifteenth and early sixteenth centuries. The administration of salvation, it seems, became more materialistic and routine than it had once been. The church, in effect, was regarded as "keeping the books" for individual souls.

Many of the Christain laity, especially in northern Europe, hungered for a more personal religion. Northern Europe, especially the Netherlands, northern France, the Rhineland, Germany, and Switzerland, was experiencing a religious revival during the late fourteenth century and all of the fifteenth century. Both burghers and prosperous peasants were returning to a simpler Christianity, to individual prayer, to imitation of the life of Christ, and to the simple evangelical piety of apostolic days. We need only read their favorite hymns to feel the change in the air. People were singing in the vernacular, and not only in the parish church but at home and in the field. Friedrick Myconius, a humanist of some repute, tells us that his father, a substantial burgher of upper Franconia, was accustomed to expound the Apostles' Creed to him in his boyhood, saying that God had bestowed salvation on man as a free gift for the sake of what Christ had done. This old burgher was thus dismissing the church as the agency of salvation and putting his trust in individual prayer.

Members of the learned class, the northern humanists, shared this popular piety. Humanism, that is, interest in Latin and Greek classics, was imported from Italy into northern Europe during the fifteenth century by young northern scholars who made the trip to Italy. As they traveled to Italy, they caught from personal observation the enthusiasm of the Italians for the classics, and returned home with it. Their ardor was very great. Thomas Platter, a Swiss humanist, tells in his autobiography of how, when young, he had supported himself through manual labor by day and at night studied the ancient tongues with sand in his mouth that the gritting against his teeth might keep him awake. At first the northern humanists did no more than their Italian counterparts. They returned to the sources of classical antiquity. They collected manuscripts of Latin and Greek classics, compared texts and edited them, taught Latin and Greek and discussed the classics, and wrote letters and compositions in classical Latin. But many northern European families were experiencing a new devotion to religious life. They were turning away from a purely formal religion to a simple, evangelical faith of praying and living after the example of Christ. The northern humanists were reared in that society. So it was natural for several second-generation northern humanists to turn to the Latin and Greek sources of Christianity and to apply to them their skill in editing manuscripts. In effect they became cultural brokers between their Italian schools and their northern homes, between the Renaissance of learning and the Reformation of religion. Jacques Lefèvre, an eminent French scholar, published a revised Latin version of the Psalms (1509) and of St. Paul's Epistles (1512); John Colet, a noted English scholar, commented on the Epistles (1497-1498); and Desiderius Erasmus, the most distinguished humanist of all, published the Greek text of the New Testament (1516). These works were disseminated by printing, which served in this way as a factor in the diffusion of reform ideas. Those who studied the new publications discovered that much that was characteristic of the contemporary church had little support in the Bible. There was, in the Gospels, as one man put it, "little about the Pope, but much more about Christ." Just as the literary humanists were homesick for the unadorned, original nobility of Greece and Rome, so the northern humanists longed for the old, simple purity of apostolic Christianity as portrayed in New Testament sources. Northern humanism laid in large part the intellectual basis of the Reformation.

To these new conditions of life that favored an interest in reform — an awakening piety, northern humanism, and the printing press — may be added a fourth, the rise of the monarchs of England, France, and Spain, and of the German territorial princes. For centuries the popes had engaged in a running fight with kings, emperors, princes, and parliaments. The grievances of the secular governors were usually the same: the exemption of church property from taxation, the exemption of clergymen from the jurisdiction of civil courts, the appeal of ecclesiastical cases to Rome, and the appointment of foreigners to local benefices. Sometimes the kings, sometimes the popes, had been successful in these struggles, but by the close of the fifteenth century the monarchs were stronger and they were supported by the antipapal, national sentiments of their populations. Ferdinand and Isabella gained virtual control of the Spanish church. Appointments to the important benefices were in their hands; the Inquisition, it may be recalled, was a royal instrument.

Francis I of France struck a bargain with Pope Leo X in the Concordat of Bologna (1516), whereby the king named the appointees to the highest positions in the French church, while the pope continued to collect annates, about half the first year's income from a benefice immediately after the appointment of a new bishop to a diocese. Henry VII of England in effect nominated his own bishops. The weakness of the Holy Roman Emperor exposed Germany, more than any other region, to papal exactions, and the Imperial Diet referred in 1510 to the Roman papacy as the "hound of hell." Nevertheless, the German territorial princes struggled to control the church within their own principalities. Outside Italy the transformation of the universal Roman Catholic church into local royal or princely churches already had begun. A king or prince would be apt to support any reform that promised him the opportunity to increase his power over the local church, to curb its privileges, and to seize its wealth.

All these tendencies — dissatisfaction with a materialistic, mechanistic salvation and a corrupt, worldly clergy, desire for a more personal religion, return to the sources of Christian faith, and German hatred of the Italian papacy — flowed into Martin Luther and were transformed by his personality and profound religious experience into a vital doctrine. Luther was born in 1483 of prosperous peasants in Eisleben, which lies in central Germany. He attended elementary schools in Mansfeld and Madgeburg and entered Erfurt University. In his adolescence, taking himself quite seriously, he became obsessed with his own unworthiness in the eyes of a stern, awful God, and with the problem of winning the favor of an angry God and attaining salvation. He broke off a promising university career to become a friar in the Augustinian order. Surely a monastic life devoted to religion and observing the rules of poverty, obedience, and chastity would satisfy God. But after a year the evil passions of jealousy, envy, and lust returned. Luther fasted, sometimes going for three days without a crumb. He cast off the blankets permitted him and nearly froze to death. The passions and his sense of sin remained. He confessed frequently, often daily, and for six hours at a time. But how could he be sure that he had remembered to confess each evil moment of the soul and to secure its absolution? He came to hate the angry God who gave no surcease. To divert Luther from self-absorption, his superior, Johann Staupitz, commissioned him in 1513 to lecture on the Bible at the University of Wittenberg. He commenced his lectures with Psalms, using Lefèvre's edition, and continued in 1515-1517 with Paul's Epistles to the Romans and the Galatians. One evening, as Luther was studying, he put together two verses "the righteousness of God revealed in the Gospel" and "the just shall live by faith." A new light flooded his soul: God is not an angry judge but a merciful Heavenly Father; all He asks of the individual is that he have faith in His mercy and in the redemptive power of Jesus Christ, and He will forgive all trespasses. This insight was for Luther a wonderful experience. He was left with a sense of release and of overflowing power.

In the next five years (1516-1521) he developed in lectures, in sermons, and eventually in print the implications of this experience. He expressed the basic theoretical tenets of the Lutheran view. *Priesthood of the believer*: each individual stands in a living, personal relationship to God, without need for the mediation of a priesthood. *Scripture Alone*: each individual will read and study the Scripture; it alone is the sole ultimate authority in matters of faith; popes and church councils may err, but not the Scripture. *Justification by faith alone*: through study and interpretation of the Scripture each individual comes to have faith not in his own prayers or merits or works; "for we are not saved by our own exertions," but in the saving mercy of God as expressed in the life and death of Jesus Christ. *A simplified church*: no longer a formal institution, the church is a body of believers who are living in a vital, personal relationship with God; they each serve God in their own calling; they appoint one of their number to serve as pastor, but they are all of the spiritual estate; they dispense with monasticism, pilgrimages, and the sacraments of ordination, confirmation, extreme unction, marriage, and priestly absolution of sins, for these are not needed by a contrite believer; they retain only the sacraments of baptism and the Lord's Supper, as instituted by Christ himself and as outward signs of a divine promise of inward regeneration to all who receive the sacraments in true faith. Luther thus broke with the Catholic emphasis on the sacraments and the consecrated priesthood, with the papal-monarchical organization, and with much of the Roman Catholic ritual. He had been driven by his inner experience to a different center of assurance and belief: the ultimate guide of the soul was to be found not in a divinely-blessed institution but in a voice which the soul hears in the Word of God and which comes to the soul from within. He also exhorted the Germans to undertake measures of immediate reform litigation in church courts involving Germans should be tried in Germany under a German primate; the income of the church should be curtailed — no more annates, fees, and crusading taxes by which Germans were fleeced by cunning Italians; communities should choose their own ministers; temporal concerns should belong to temporal rulers; and so on.

Luther's pamphlets, his debates with the theologians, and his condemnation by Pope Leo X became the talk of Germany. Luther, to his astonishment, became a national hero. His biographer compares him to a man who was "climbing in the darkness a winding staircase in the steeple of an ancient cathedral. In the blackness he reached out to steady himself, and his hand lay hold of a rope. He was startled to hear the clanging of a bell."[4] He appealed

---

[4]Roland H. Bainton, *Here I Stand: A Life of Martin Luther*, p. 83.

to many German groups. To the Christian, he appeared to promise a purer faith; to the patriotic German, freedom from foreign exploitation; to the humanists, a return to apostolic simplicity; to the princes, an end to the pope's meddling; and to the lower classes, a millennium of universal brotherhood. Luther expressed the many longings of discontented Germans, and they rallied around him.

Pope Leo X excommunicated Luther, and asked Emperor Charles V to impose the imperial ban of outlawry upon him. Charles, a loyal Catholic, had already burned Luther's books in his hereditary Austrian dominions, but he feared to flout German national sentiment and he allowed the Imperial Diet to give Luther a hearing. Luther traveled from Wittenberg to Worms and appeared before the Diet on April 17 and 18, 1521. Few scenes have been as dramatic, or so dense with converging lines of history. The son of peasants stood before the son of Caesars; a poor and, until lately, obscure, monk before an august imperial assembly. Luther's books were on a small table; after preliminary skirmishing, Luther was asked: "Do you or do you not repudiate your books and the errors they contain?" He answered:

Unless I am convicted by Scripture or by right reason (for I trust neither in popes nor in councils, since they have often erred and contradicted themselves) — unless I am thus convinced, I am bound by the texts of the Bible, my conscience is captive to the Word of God, I neither can nor will recant anything, since it is neither right nor safe to act against conscience. God help me. Amen.

The answer expressed the Protestant theory of the right of private judgment as applied to the Bible, and it has echoed through the centuries. Scarcely less notable, though no longer remembered, was Charles's reply, which affirmed his sense of and devotion to the continuity of the Catholic tradition. Charles said to the German princes the next day:

My predecessors, the most Christian Emperors of the German race, the Austrian archdukes, and dukes of Burgundy were until death the truest sons of the Catholic Church, defending and extending their belief to the glory of God, the propagation of the faith, the salvation of their souls. They have left behind them the holy Catholic rites that I should live and die therein, and so until now with God's aid I have lived, as becomes a Christian Emperor. What my forefathers established at Constance and other Councils, it is my privilege to uphold. A single monk, led astray by private judgment, has set himself against the faith held by all Christians for a thousand years and more, and impudently concludes that all Christians up till now have erred. I have therefore resolved to stake upon this cause all my dominions, my friends, my body and my blood, my life and soul.

The continuity of a thousand years of history was here challenged by a moment of private judgment: a tragic meeting and intersection, if only for the blood that flowed from it. The Spanish people came solemnly to accept Charles's religious commitment. If he was to use the power of his empire to suppress heresy as well as to attack the infidel Turk, they as earnest Catholics would support him. Charles issued the Edict of Worms, which placed Luther under the ban of the empire. It forbade anyone to shelter him and commanded all to give him up to the authorities. It also forbade the printing, selling, and reading of his books.

The Imperial Distractions of Charles V and, Specifically, the Duel with France Permit the Consolidation of Lutheranism

Charles hoped to deal with Luther and his followers at once, but he was diverted for twenty-four years by his worsening troubles with France, whose King Francis I already held the Duchy of Milan and now coveted the Kingdom of Naples and domination of Italy; with the Turks, who captured Belgrade in 1521, defeated and killed the King of Hungary at the battle of Mohács in 1526, and in 1529 besieged Vienna and threatened southern Germany; with the Algerian corsairs; and with the popes at Rome. Charles came to desire a general council of the leading Catholic ecclesiastics that would meet certain Lutheran criticisms by reforming abuses in the Catholic church and defining its doctrine. But the popes feared that the reform would cut off the more lucrative sources of their revenue and that a council might declare itself superior to the papacy. Also, as an Italian territorial power the papacy opposed Charles's dominance in Italy and tried to extend the papal domains. The enemies of Charles frequently leagued against him. When Pope Clement VII, for example, conspired in 1533 at Marseilles with Francis against Charles, an emissary from the Moslem Algerian corsairs was also present.

In his first war against France (1521-1526), Charles appeared in the beginning to be the weaker power, and Henry VIII of England and the pope rallied to his side to counter-balance the apparent French preponderance. But Charles's troops defeated the French army at the Battle of Pavia (1525) and took Francis captive. Charles released Francis upon his promise to abandon all claims to Milan and to persuade the French Estates-General to assent to the cession of the Duchy of Burgundy to Charles. Once he was free, Francis took back his promise. He, the Pope, Florence, Venice, and Francesco Sforza (the claimant Duke of Milan) formed under the benevolent protectorship of Henry

VIII a league against Charles. In this second war (1526-1529), Charles fought his adversaries to a draw that was reflected in the concluding Treaty of Cambrai. In effect, Charles gave up the Duchy of Burgundy, but finally got hold of Milan. Now for a moment he could turn his attention to the Lutherans, only to be almost immediately distracted again, this time by the Turks, who were marching up the Danube. From 1532 to 1535 he was engaged with the Turks and then with the Algerian corsairs. But before he could solve the Algerian corsair problem, he had to fight with France a third war (1536-1538), which affirmed the Treaty of Cambrai. The war finished, he returned to the Algerian corsairs, only to be interrupted by a fourth war with France (1542-1544), which reaffirmed the Treaty of Cambrai. At last Charles was free to deal with the Lutherans. The Sultan was busy after 1545 with Persia; Pope Paul III called as Charles wished a general council to consider church reform, and it held its first meeting at Trent on December 13, 1545; and Francis I had secretly promised Charles to help him suppress heresy. In addition, Charles had, as always, the resources of Spain. Spanish soldiers and Spanish gold had been used in nearly every expedition he undertook, and the Spanish pikeman was now a familiar figure throughout Europe.

But while Charles had been moving along the periphery of his empire, the Lutherans in the center had not been idle. The Germany to which Charles returned in 1545 was quite different from that of 1521. He was no longer dealing with a renegade monk applauded by an undisciplined crowd of malcontents. The opposition to Charles of His Most Christian King of France, His Holiness the Pope, and the infidel Sultan had given Luther and the Lutherans time to consolidate their position. Luther in his early writings had implied that each person should read the Bible alone and judge for himself its meaning. This teaching might lead to as many sects as there were readers. Also, the early Luther had opposed subordination of the church to the state. But after the Edict of Worms Luther, like many another rebel, soon had to cope with the chaos following hard upon his revolt. Each village which had embraced Luther's doctrine had its own ritual, and sometimes the same village would follow diverse rituals on different occasions. Pastors who knew nothing of Lutheran theology preached to congregations who knew nothing of it either. The blind were leading the blind, and in every direction. The monasteries and convents were emptying, and ex-monks were living as Lutheran pastors with ex-nuns in "wild wedlock." Fanatics in congregations, taking the Old Testament literally, rejected images and music and adopted a rigid observance of the Sabbath. Luther felt he needed some organizing authority. He could not turn to the Emperor for he was hostile, nor to the bishops for they had remained Catholic. But he found an ally in his own territorial prince, the Elector of Saxony, and he asked him to serve as an emergency bishop in his own possessions. Agreeing, the Elector took over the property of the monasteries and dioceses, enforced a uniform ritual devised by Luther, set standards of learning for the pastors, and inspected their performance. Soon other secular princes and town governments of northern, central, and southwestern Germany as well as the kings of Denmark and Sweden were following suit. These worldly powers embraced the other-worldly Lutheran faith, and in the conversion found new sources of worldly power. They excluded the authority of the Catholic archbishops and bishops, seized church property and revenues, and supervised the administration of the Lutheran church in their territory. They were now controlling, as they had longed to do for centuries, the church in their domains. We have stumbled, as did Luther, on the problem at the heart of this chapter: the dreamlike mingling of human motives. By 1545 the German Lutheran princes formed a strong vested interest and were allied with each other in a defensive Schmalkaldic League able to defy Charles on the battlefield.

Charles enjoyed a moment of victory in his war to restore imperial authority over the princes and to suppress Lutheranism (for his motives were mixed too): he beat the Lutherans badly at the Battle of Mühlberg in 1547 and led the Lutheran electors of Saxony and Brandenburg into captivity "between the files of Spanish arquebusiers." But in 1552 the Schmalkaldic League signed a pact with Henry II of France. The Catholic Henry agreed to aid the Lutheran heretic princes against their Catholic emperor; the German Lutheran princes agreed that Henry might occupy the German bishoprics of Metz, Toul, and Verdun as Imperial vicar. The alliance caught Charles napping, and in 1552 every one of his projects crumbled. The Protestant forces in Germany forced him to flee for his life over the Alps. His army failed to re-take Metz from a French garrison. The pope prorogued the Council of Trent. The Algerian corsairs were again on a rampage. Weary of human affairs, Charles divided his possessions between his son, Philip II, and his brother, Ferdinand, abdicated his multifarious titles in 1555-1556, and retired to a Spanish monastery. There he died in 1558.

Philip II, who received Spain and its colonies, Sicily, Naples, Milan, the north African posts, the Free County of Burgundy, Luxembourg, and the Netherlands, came to terms with France in the Treaty of Cateau-Cambrésis (1559). France again renounced her Italian claims but was allowed to retain her imperial vicariate over Metz, Toul, and Verdun. Ferdinand, who had inherited the Habsburg lands in Germany and was king of Hungary and Bohemia in his own right, came to terms with the German Lutheran princes and towns in the Treaty of Augsburg (1555). The treaty granted each prince and imperial town government the right to decide whether the religion of their subjects should be Lutheran or Catholic. If a subject disliked the religion of his prince or town, he was free to sell his property and move. Church lands confiscated prior to 1552 were retained by the present owners. The treaty thus gave legal recognition to the Lutheran confession and rent "the seamless robe of Christ." The quarrel between the Catholic dynasties of Valois and Habsburg had given Lutheranism the time to consolidate in Germany and Scandinavia and had insured the break-up of the Roman Catholic church.

The Extension of Religious Reform: Calvinism
and the Anglican Church

While Lutheranism was being consolidated in Germany and Scandinavia, the general dissatisfaction with conditions in the Catholic church was giving rise to other reform movements, both Protestant and Catholic. Luther in his early days had felt that if people read more deeply into the Bible, their major differences would dissolve in the clear light of the Word. The essential doctrines seemed written there, as in red print, for everyone to read. But when leaders with other backgrounds, temperaments, and motives – Ulrich Zwingli and John Calvin in Switzerland, Henry VIII and Archbishop Cranmer in England, Ignatius Loyola in Spain and the Spanish theologians at the Council of Trent, for example – reconsidered the Bible, they emerged with a variety of different interpretations which also won adherents. From their interpretations and those of Luther grew the major Protestant sects (Lutheran, Reformed, and Anglican) of the sixteenth century, as well as the renewal of the Roman Catholic Church.

Protestants agreed among themselves on certain points on which they also agreed, without always realizing it, with Catholics. Both Catholics and Protestants believed in God; in the God of wrath and love of the Old and New Testaments; in the divine inspiration of the Bible and in the epic story of salvation which it related; in the redemptive power of Jesus Christ, the Son of God; and in the immortality of both reward and punishment. Protestants also agreed among themselves on the major points upon which they disagreed with Catholics. The Protestants asserted the supremacy of the Bible. The supreme authority, they said, was not the church, or tradition, or the priesthood, but the Holy Scripture. The Catholics placed the tradition of the Catholic church on an equality with the Bible. There were, they maintained, certain important teachings, institutions, and ceremonies, not expressly mentioned in the Scripture, that had been handed down orally from Christ and his apostles as a sacred heritage to the church. They, as well as the Bible, were divinely inspired. Early Protestant theory, but not Protestant practice, asserted the right of the individual believer to apply his individual judgment to the Bible, to discover for himself the principles of Christianity and to apply them to his life, and thus be saved directly without mediation of the priesthood. The Catholic Church consistently rejected both in theory and in practice the right of private judgment in matters of faith and morals. The church is the depository of truth, infallible and the sole expounder. The Catholic church also denied that the priesthood of the believer is generally possible. The Catholic priesthood must mediate between the believer and God. In church organization, the Protestants denied the headship of the pope and admitted laymen to participation. In ritual, the Protestants stressed a simpler ceremony and laid greater emphasis on the sermon than did the Catholics.

But Protestants differed among themselves on details of dogma, ritual, church organization, and the relation of the church to the state. Religion was for Luther profoundly emotional, and the central emotional tone of Lutheranism was gratitude for the love and mercy of God as revealed in Christ. Luther wanted people to be able to read the Bible, worship, sing hymns, and hear a good sermon, all not in Latin but in the daily language. He wished to reduce the number of the sacraments to baptism and the Last Supper. But once he had reached these goals, he tended, in ritual as in politics, to become conservative. Vestments, candles, crucifixes, and pictures were to him unimportant, to be used if not superstitiously abused. He would allow in the worship of God nearly everything that the Bible did not expressly forbid. In church organization he initially favored congregationalism but was drawn as we have seen into an arrangement whereby the German territorial prince defined doctrine with the advice of university theologians, appointed superintendents to supervise individual churches in a given district, and appointed pastors.

Religion for John Calvin, the founder of the Reformed churches, was more a steady intellectual fervor than a tempestuous spiritual experience. He was born in 1509 at Noyon, France, of substantial, middle-class parentage. A student of theology, law, and the Latin and Greek classics in three major French universities, he developed an intellectual power that was rare among religious reformers. Study of Erasmus' Greek Testament and Luther's sermons persuaded Calvin by 1533 that the Catholic church had strayed from the Gospel story, and he began to develop his own doctrine of which the essence first appeared in his *Institutes of the Christian Religion* (1536). His characteristic doctrines were four. *Predestination*: Calvin was impressed with the overwhelming sovereign power of God. Since God is absolutely sovereign, He is all-powerful, and all-knowing: He knew in advance what would happen, He had made it to happen so. He predestined those believers who would have faith in Christ and be saved, and those in whom belief would fail and who would be damned. For Calvin this was no cause for the believer to fear. To have faith in Christ indicated certainty of salvation. Belief in predestination nerved Calvin and his followers to be a race of heroes, for "if God is for us who can be against us." *An austere morality and worship*: Calvin, an austere man himself, required an austere morality and an unadorned, intellectual form of worship. An individual who has faith is capable of doing good works. He will lead a frugal, industrious, and upright life and will attend church regularly to strengthen his faith. The church service will exclude everything, such as candles and images, not specifically prescribed by Scripture and will center on the intellectual exposition of the Word of God in the sermon. *A democratic church organization*: The congregation will elect deacons to care for the poor and sick, elders to maintain discipline, doctors to teach the doctrine to the young, and a pastor to preach the Gospel and administer the two sacraments of baptism and the Last Supper. The elections will proceed under the watchful eye of other ministers. *Alliance of church and state*: Both church and state derive their lawful authority from God and each will work in its own sphere to create a holy community. While ecclesiastical authorities will deal with the life of the "soul or the inner man," the magistrates are concerned with "setting up of civil and external justice of morals." However, subjects may rebel against an "uprising power which overrides conscience."

Calvin had the opportunity to apply his ideas in the Swiss town of Geneva. An earlier Swiss Reformed movement, which had been started by Ulrich Zwingli in 1519 at the canton of Zurich, had spread to Berne, Basel, and then to Geneva where its adherents were fighting the Catholics. Invited by the reformers to stay, Calvin remained in Geneva from 1536 to 1538 and again from 1541 to his death in 1564 and made it what we today might call a sixteenth-century Moscow — the disciplined, militant center for the international diffusion of Calvinism. The city council accepted his doctrines and set out to make Geneva a rigidly puritan city, a showcase of virtue in which gambling, swearing, dancing, drinking, and lesser misdemeanors were banned. Pilgrims came from the far corners of Europe, were trained and toughened in Calvin's theology, and were sent out to establish cells of Calvinists in France, the Netherlands, Scotland, England, Hungary, Poland, and Transylvania. Calvinist congregations, strong and dynamic, sprouted throughout northwestern Europe, as prolific and ineradicable as the dandelion.

The Anglican Revolution, unlike the Calvinist movement, is difficult to define, partly because it never completely defined itself. The kings of England, like other kings in their own countries, had long shared with the papacy the government of the Catholic church in England. In the sixteenth century Henry VIII (1509-1547), unable to persuade Pope Clement VII to grant him a "divorce" from his wife Catherine that he might marry Anne Boleyn and have a male heir, moved to withdraw the church in England from papal jurisdiction and to assume greater control over it himself. He played on the ancient English suspicion of the pope to coax Parliament into passing a succession of anti-papal laws. The Act in Restraint of Appeals (1533) eradicated the pope's jurisdiction in England and made the courts of the Archbishop of Canterbury the ecclesiastical court of last resort — under this act Archbishop Cranmer declared Henry's marriage to his brother's widow Catherine null and void. The

Act against Papal Dispensations and Peter's Pence (1534) forbade the payment of any papal impositions. The Act of Supremacy (1534) confirmed the king's right to be "the only supreme head on earth of the Church in England." An act of 1536 extinguished "the authority of the Bishop of Rome" in England.

As a result of these measures, the church *in* England was becoming a separate Church *of* England. The English king stood at its head. At the king's right hand was Parliament. The English king, the English Parliament, and the English church moved forward together in the minds of Englishmen. The pope, always a foreigner, was becoming to them the leader of a foreign enemy church. But the measures opened several questions. They greatly extended the king's authority over the English church. What were the new limits of that authority? The monarch could appoint bishops. Could he also say Mass? Henry had worked with Parliament in order to get the well-to-do classes behind him against the pope and thus to strengthen his position. But in the process he strengthened Parliament also by leading it to acquire the practice of legislating more extensively on ecclesiastical affairs. What were the limits of Parliament's ecclesiastical legislation? Could a member of Parliament introduce a bill to alter the doctrine of the Church of England?

The mass of people and Henry were attached to the traditional Catholic ritual and dogmas. But once the moorings with the papacy had been severed, and English leaders and people began to drift out of Catholic channels, what was to be the doctrine and form of worship of the Church of England? Archbishop Cranmer was being persuaded by his reading of the Scripture and of Lutheran tracts to adopt a more Lutheran view of Christian ritual. Lutheran and Calvinist exiles affected the opinions of English townsmen, while some Englishmen visited Wittenberg and Geneva. The English government zigged under Edward VI (1547-1553) toward Lutheran and Calvinist worship and then zagged under Queen Mary (1553-1558) toward Catholicism before stabilizing its course for a time under Queen Elizabeth (1558-1603). Elizabeth appears to have possessed little or no religious enthusiasm herself. She was concerned primarily with the unity, tranquility, and prosperity of her people and with the preservation of her power. She insisted that the national church be administered by bishops supervised by herself as supreme governor of the Church of England, but she tried to make her church broad enough to satisfy all moderate Christian believers. An Act of Uniformity (1559) passed by the first parliament of her reign reflected her views. It prescribed worship in a parish church according to a Book of Common Prayer phrased vaguely enough so that Protestants and even moderate Catholics could sincerely participate. A Second Act of Uniformity (1571) was a bit stiffer, and narrower. It required adherence to the doctrinal Thirty-Nine Articles (1563), which affirmed the general Protestant theories of supremacy of the Bible, predestination, justification by faith, the existence of only two sacraments, and the marriage of the clergy, but these tenets were so ambiguously worded that a Lutheran, Zwinglian, or Calvinist might all loyally subscribe. Elizabeth cared less for what her subjects thought than for the way they acted. As long as they were quiet, she was willing to leave them alone. Under her relatively mild ministrations the great majority of Englishmen came to be bound together in a national church less by a common doctrine than by a common Protestant worship. The powers of the monarch and of Parliament over that church were still ill-defined.

By 1564, the year of Calvin's death, the tide of Protestantism had almost reached its flood. The Swiss cantons long ago had agreed by the Peace of Kappel (1529, 1531) that the government of each canton was free to choose its religion, an agreement that allowed the cantons of Zurich, Berne, and Basel to remain Protestant. Denmark and Norway, under a single monarch, and Sweden had been Lutheran for decades. Germany was divided, but in the main was Protestant. Her secular princes were mostly Lutheran or Calvinist, and even in the territories of the Catholic duke of Bavaria, the Habsburg archduke of Austria, and the archbishops of Cologne, Trier, and Mainz the greater part of the nobles and many of the towns had deserted Catholicism. Lutheranism, Calvinism, and Socinianism (Unitarianism) had spread among the nobility and in the towns of Poland, Transylvania, and Hungary, the number of converts compelling the authorities to allow widespread toleration. French Protestants, known as Huguenots (most of them artisans and lesser nobles but a few from the great noble families), formed about one-tenth of the French population. Although small in number they were a determined, tightly organized minority whose national synod had just adopted in 1559 a Calvinistic confession of faith. Through others like them Calvinism was moving down the Rhine and across the North Sea. It was replacing Lutheranism as the chief dissenting sect in the Netherlands. It was also bearing down on Scotland where John Knox and others were getting the Scottish parliament to abolish in 1560 the pope's authority in Scotland and to proclaim a confession of faith along extreme Calvinistic lines. The accession of Queen Elizabeth to the throne of England in 1558 gave the Protestants an upper hand there. To the Venetian ambassador at Rome it seemed that all of Europe north of the Alps and the Pyrenees was being lost by the pope.

An Invitation to Further Reflection and Inquiry

Discussion of historical periods can often be fruitful. A familiar periodization is the division of European history into ancient, medieval, and modern. If we inquire when did modern European history begin, we are led to analyze the fundamental characteristics (ideas, institutions, and affective tone) of contemporary Europe, the fundamental characteristics of medieval Europe, and the characteristics of European culture at various points in between. One characteristic of modern Europe is a strong international commerce and the prevalence of towns and cities. Shall we then start modern European history with the eleventh and twelfth centuries, with "the revival of commerce" and "the rise of towns"? Another aspect of modern Europe is its secular temper, which began to permeate the mentality of educated Europeans in nearly every country in the eighteenth century. Shall we then delay the start of modern European history until then? Or should we choose some intermediate century or date? And if we select a date, what shall it be and why? Shall it be 1415? or 1492? or 1494? or 1517? or another year, of your choice? As we discuss these questions, we shall notice that a period is a conceptual tool that forces us to look backwards and forward and provides us with a useful framework for assessing the pace and direction of change.

Actually, a historian is always comparing the present with the past and the past with the present, and seeing more in the present by reason of his knowledge of the past, and vice versa. A comparison, for example, of the intertwining of religious ideology with power politics in the sixteenth century with a similar intertwining in the capitalist-communist conflict in the twentieth century may yield insights into the twentieth that have been overlooked. Can we notice, in both instances, stages in the intertwining? At first power politics and ideology are running their separate courses; then for decades they are intertwined; and then they draw apart. During the period of intertwining, what effects do ideas of an ideology have upon power politics? And what effects do power politics have on ideas? Would it help to compare in each instance, the stage of intertwining with the stages before and after, as well as to compare the past with the present? Once again we are seeking relations and interrelations, and once again comparison is a valuable instrument. In what stage is the current capitalist-communist conflict?

Another procedure for the discovery of relations is to imagine the historical situation with one element removed and then to ask, would its absence have changed the course of events and, if so, how? At its most sophisticated, this procedure is known as counterfactual analysis. Suppose Martin Luther had never lived, would the German Protestant Revolt have occurred? Would it have occurred at the same time? Would it have occurred in the same way? Were conditions in Germany so overriding, did they offer so few alternatives, that no matter what Luther did or did not do, the Revolt would have come at approximately the same time and would have followed approximately the same course? Was the preparation of the Protestant Revolt so advanced that it required a relatively simple act — a posting of 95 theses — to set it off? The powder had been accumulated, all Luther did was to light the fuse? Was the onset of the Reformation as inevitable as the onset of a depression used to be? And then once the German Revolt had broken out, what effect did Luther have on its nature and course? Did the German situation in 1517 resemble circumstances in France in 1799, Russia in 1917, and the United States in 1933, when a despairing, disillusioned population was hungry for leadership? And then did Luther, like Napoleon, Lenin, and perhaps Franklin D. Roosevelt, decisively send his people in one direction when they might have taken another? What is the role of the individual in history?

For Further Reading

(For general reading)

Roland H. Bainton, *Erasmus of Christendom* (1969)
————, *Here I Stand — A Life of Martin Luther* (1959)
K. Brandi, *The Emperor Charles V: The Growth and Destiny of a Man of a World Empire* (1939)
Cottie A. Burland, *The Exotic White Man* (1969)
R. Trevor Davies, *The Golden Century of Spain 1505-1621* (1937)
A. G. Dickens, *The Counter Reformation* (1969)
————, *The English Reformation* (1969)
————, *Martin Luther and the Reformation* (1967)
————, *Thomas Cromwell and the English Reformation* (Teach Yourself History Library, 1967)
Edward M. Earle *et al.* eds., *Makers of Modern Strategy: Military Thought From Machiavelli to Hitler* (1961)
John H. Elliott, *Europe Divided, 1559-1598* (1969)
Erik Erikson, *Young Man Luther* (1958)
Pleter Geyl, *The Revolt of the Netherlands, 1555-1609* (1932)
Georgia Harkness, *John Calvin* (1931)
Hans J. Hillerbrand, *Men and Ideas in the Sixteenth Century* (1969)
Hajo Holborn, *A History of Modern Germany*, Vol. I (1959)
John Huizinga, *Erasmus and the Age of Reformation* (1957)
P. Hughes, *A Popular History of the Reformation* (1957)
F. E. Hutchinson, *Cranmer and the English Reformation* (Teach Yourself History Library, 1951)
P. Janelle, *The Catholic Reformation* (1949)

B. J. Kidd, *The Counter-Reformation, 1550-1600* (1933)

H. G. Koenigsberger, *The Habsburgs and Europe, 1516-1660* (1971)

Garrett Mattingly, *Renaissance Diplomacy*, (1955)

————, *The Armada* (1959)

Roger B. Merriman, *The Rise of the Spanish Empire* (1918)

Kenneth B. McFarlane, *John Wycliffe and the Beginnings of English Nonconformity* (Teach Yourself History Library, 1953)

Conyers Read, *Mr. Secretary Walsingham* (3 vols., 1925)

Gerhard Ritter, *Luther: His Life and Work* (translated by John Riches) (1963)

Michael Roberts, "Gustav Adolf and the Art of War: The Political Objectives of Gustav Adolf in Germany, 1630-1632," *Essays in Swedish History* (1967)

Nancy Lyman Roelker, *Queen of Navarre: Jeanne d'Albret, 1528-1572* (1968)

Theodore Ropp, *War in the Modern World* (1959)

Matthew Spinka, *John Hus: A Biography* (1968)

David C. Steinmetz *Reformers in the Wings* (1971)

R. H. Tawney, *Religion and the Rise of Capitalism* (1927)

J. B. Trend, *The Civilization of Spain* (1944, 1967)

Hugh Trevor-Roper, editor, *The Age of Expansion: Europe and the World 1550-1660* (1968)

Williston Walker, *The Reformation* (1900)

Max Weber, *The Protestant Ethic and the Spirit of Capitalism* (translation: 1930)

Cicely Wedgwood, *The Thirty Years' War* (1938)

————, *William the Silent* (1944)

(For advanced study):

Pieter Geyl, *The Netherlands in the Seventeenth Century* (1961-64) Part I, 1609-1648; Part II, 1648-1715

Roland Bainton, "Interpretations of the Reformation," *American Historical Review*, 66 (October, 1960), 78-84.

Wilhelm Pauck, "The Historiography of the German Reformation During the Past Twenty Years," *Church History*, IX (December, 1940), 305-340.

Articles on the interpretation of the Reformation by Wilhelm Pauck, Jacques Maritain, Philip Hughes, and E. G. Schweibert in Clough, Gay, and Warner, *The European Past*, I, 29-55.

Gordon Rupp, *The Righteousness of God: Luther Studies* (1953) Part I: The Historians Luther

Donald B. Meyer, "A Review of Young Man Luther: A Study in Psychoanalysis and History," in *Psychoanalysis and History*, edited by Bruce Mazlish (1963)

Norman Brown, *Life Against Death* (1959)

Edgar M. Carlson, *The Reinterpretation of Luther* (1948)

H. L. Grimm, *The Reformation in Recent Historical Thought* (1964)

J. Lynch, *Spain under the Habsburgs.* Vol. I: *Empire and Absolutism, 1516-1598* (1964)

Ephraim Fischoff, "The Protestant Ethic and the Spirit of Capitalism: The History of a Controversy," *Social Research* XI (1944), 61-77.

John V. Nef, *The Conquest of the Material World* (1964)

S. N. Eisenstadt, editor, *The Protestant Ethic and Modernization: A Comparative View* (1968)

W. Fred Graham, *The Constructive Revolutionary: John Calvin and His Socio-Economic Impact* (1971)

Peter Heath, *The English Parish Clergy on the Eve of the Reformation* (1969)

J. V. Polisensky, "The Thirty Years' War," *Past and Present*, No. 6 (November, 1954), 31-43.

J. W. Smith, "The Present Position of Studies Regarding the Revolt of the Netherlands," in S. J. Bromley and E. H. Kossman, *Britain and the Netherlands: Papers Delivered to the Oxford-Netherlands Historical Conference* (1960)

Charles Wilson, *Queen Elizabeth and the Revolt of the Netherlands* (1970)

Roderic H. Dawson, *Turkey* (1968)

Chapter VII

THE GREAT POWER RIVALRIES AND THE CATHOLIC COUNTER OFFENSIVE (1555-1659)

Catholic Reform

By 1564, the Catholic church had undertaken to reform itself and had forged the weapons of a counter-offensive. The Catholic Reformation started in Spain, actually several decades before Luther. Many devout Spanish Catholics had been appalled by the prevalent worldliness and corruption of the clergy at the close of the fifteenth century. Queen Isabella and her confessor, Cardinal Ximenes, a man of austere power, undertook after 1494 the renewal of the Spanish church. They imposed new standards, and found new men to match them. Devoted and rigorous churchmen replaced the easygoing and licentious. Under the close watch of the queen the Spanish Inquisition plucked out heresy. The universities were generously endowed to foster the education of the clergy and the study of the theology of Thomas Aquinas. These measures, which were essentially conservative, deepened the religious life of the Spanish clergy and laity. They also enhanced the power of the Crown. For among the Spanish (as we have already noticed) political and religious loyalties were fused. When one loyalty was strengthened, so was the other, in a powerful fusion of motives.

One fruit of the Spanish spiritual awakening was the career of Ignatius Loyola, a Spanish soldier who was sidelined by a wound in 1521 and decided to spend the rest of his life battling for Christ. Thus changing wars, he gathered a small band of followers and was authorized in 1540 by Pope Paul III to form a Society of Jesus that would combat the heathen and the heretic. The Jesuits took the usual vows of chastity, poverty, and obedience and added a fourth of absolute submission to the pope, who might send them wheresoever he chose. As of a soldier, obedience was the first duty of a Jesuit, obedience to the superiors of the society and to the pope. The inferior must train his will to become identical with that of his superior. "He must let himself be carried and ruled by his superior, as if he were a dead body that lets itself be carried anywhere and carried anyhow, or like an old man's staff, which he who holds it in his hand, may use to help himself wheresoever and howsoever he may wish," all to the greater glory and honor of God.

A second fruit of the Spanish awakening was the activity of the Italian Cardinal Caraffa. As onetime papal nuncio in Spain, he had been impressed by the efficacy of the Spanish Inquisition. He persuaded Pope Paul III to establish in 1542 at Rome a similar Inquisition, which imprisoned, burned, or drove into exile the few Lutherans and Calvinists to be found in Italy. A third fruit was the work of two great theologians, Domingo de Soto and Melchior Cano, who with their Italian counterparts helped to formulate at the Council of Trent (1547-1549, 1551-1552, 1561-1563) a systematic expression of Catholic doctrine. Every Catholic could now know precisely what the Catholic church believed. Out of the spiritual awakening of Spain and now of Italy grew also a succession of reforming popes — Paul IV (1555-1559), Pius V (1566-1572), Gregory XIII (1572-1585), and Sixtus V (1585-1590). These men of earnest, even saintly life, burned the dross – both the unnecessary and the impure — out of the papal administration and appointed a pious and competent clergy.

From the two southern peninsulas, Italy and Spain, now solidly Catholic, the Jesuits, the other regular orders, and the bishops sallied north to reclaim the peoples lost to Protestantism. They had the basic advantage that they were seeking to recover what had once been universally acknowledged to be theirs. Fundamentally, they wanted to restore an image buried in men's minds, the once sacred image of the universal church. They had other advantages too. They were operating under the unified command and central will of the pope, whereas the Protestants were bitterly divided (Luther, for example, had considered the Swiss reformer Zwingli so little a Christian that at one interview he had refused to shake his hand). The Catholics also had the loyalty of the peasants of Hungary, Poland, Bavaria, and France, who had remained Catholic. The Jesuits (to single out the chief agency of reconversion) swarmed into France, the Rhineland, Bavaria, Austria, Hungary, Bohemia, and Poland. They preached sermons "charitably, gravely, soberly, sedately" — it was noted that the number of communicants increased after the Jesuits had passed through. They founded or took over colleges (one hundred and fifty-five in the Holy Roman Empire alone before 1650), brought into them order, hierarchy, and methodical organization, and captured for Catholicism the sons of the well-to-do and powerful. Wherever possible they sought to win the support of the temporal princes. Albert V of Bavaria, who had been forced to tolerate his Protestant nobles, welcomed the Jesuits. Using them as a kind of royal guard, and special forces, he made Bavaria a Catholic stronghold and a political and religious base for the further Catholic recovery of Germany. The Habsburg Ferdinand admitted the Jesuits to Vienna in Austria and then to Prague in Bohemia. From Prague they passed to Hungary and reclaimed the local pastors. Simultaneously they entered Poland and, aided by their former pupil, King Sigismund (1587-1632), eventually reduced the Polish Protestants to a small and persecuted minority.

Philip II of Spain, the Catholic Counteroffensive, and
the Consolidation of Calvinism in the Northernmost
Provinces of the Netherlands

The Catholic recovery, which involved both a spiritual revival of the
Catholic clergy and laity and an outgoing effort to recover the lands lost to
heresy, was sustained by the sword and diplomacy of Philip II (1556-1598) of
Spain. Philip was a careful man, the "Prudent King" his subjects called him,
who tried to superintend his empire from his residence in Castile. Day after
day, night after night, he sat at his worktable, reading and annotating reports,
apart from men, distant, meditative, imperturbable. "It is well to consider
everything," was a phrase that frequently occurred in his writings. But
unfortunately Philip was unable to separate the essentials from the details or
to persuade himself ever to delegate the details to subordinates. The
unanswered dispatches piled up by his desk. Philip fell months behind in his
annotations and orders, until his viceroys and ambassadors, it is said, began to
express the hope that death would come to them by way of Spain, for then
they would be certain to live to a ripe old age. Philip was devoted to Spain
and the Catholic church, two causes that were fused in his mind. What was
good for Spain was good for the Catholic church, and what was good for the
Catholic church was unusually good for Spain. He felt that his churchly zeal
and Catholic orthodoxy were so beyond question that he could afford to
oppose the papacy in many things and occasionally to fight the Jesuits. Sure
of the essential integrity of his intention to serve the two causes of Spain and
God, he could be entirely unscrupulous in the means he used to promote
them.

To his contemporaries Philip appeared to "bestride the world like a
Colossus." His territories in Europe included the Spanish kingdoms, the
Netherlands, Franche-Comté, the Balearic Isles, Sardinia, Sicily, Naples, and
Milan, as well as indirect control of every other Italian state except Venice
and the Papal States. To these were added scattered posts along the North
African coast, the growing domain and treasure in the Americas, and in Asian
waters the Philippines. As a Spanish historian proudly remarked, "the Sun
never set on the dominions of the King of Spain and at the slightest
movement of that nation the whole earth trembled."

Philip was, on the whole, successful during the first thirty years of his
reign, when Spain reached the apex of its glory. His chief enemy, France, was
paralyzed by internal strife as the fanatical Huguenots fought extremist
Catholics under the presiding auspices of three weak kings, Francis II
(1559-1560), Charles IX (1560-1574), and Henry III (1574-1589). France was
torn by eight wars (1562-1563, 1567-1568, 1568-1570, 1572-1573,
1574-1576, 1577, 1580, and 1585-1589) to determine whether the Huguenots

might worship freely or not. France was unable to compete effectively during these years for the political mastery of Europe. It followed that Philip's second enemy, the Turkish Sultan, was now unsupported in the Mediterranean area. The Spanish fleet aided by Venetian and papal vessels nearly destroyed the Turkish navy at the battle of Lepanto on October 5, 1571. This emptied the western Mediterranean of Turks, although Algerian corsairs still lurked here and there. Then in 1580 Philip took advantage of a dynastic claim to annex Portugal and her far-flung colonies. He thus brought the entire Iberian peninsula under a single scepter. He added Brazil to his colonial holdings, thus eliminating his only competitor on the two American continents, and the string of African and Far Eastern posts that had assured the Portuguese a monopoly of the Far Eastern trade in pearls, spices, and other precious merchandise. Philip's empire girdled the earth. Never had one man ruled so extensive a domain as his.

In a few years began a decline, precipitated in large part by the struggle with the third enemy, the Protestant heresy. Since the beginning of his reign, Philip had been in trouble with the inhabitants of the seventeen provinces of the Netherlands. Philip was trying to apply to the Netherlands the same policy that he was using with respect to his Italian dependencies — he was trying to increase his monarchical authority at the expense of local customs or institutions that ran counter to it, to reform the Catholic church according to the principles of the Catholic Reformation, and to repress the Protestant heresy. He tried to proceed from 1559 to 1567 gradually and stealthily. The Society of Jesus was introduced in the Low Countries. Spanish appointees and officials were placed in influential positions in the central government while native Netherlanders were elbowed aside. New bishoprics were created and filled with Spanish appointees of learning and character who formed a royal party in the States-General (the parliament). An increasingly active Inquisition executed heretics. When these measures provoked protest and riots, Philip threw off the mask and with a heavy hand sent in the Duke of Alva and a strong detachment of Spanish infantry, 12,000 in number and superbly equipped. The Duke judged that the quickest way to get peace was to kill the critics of "the best of kings." He appointed a special court, dominated by three Spaniards, to supersede all traditional courts and jurisdictions. Methodically it singled out the ringleaders of disaffection and executed them, 84 persons on January 4, 1568, 108 on February 20-21, 55 on March 20, and so on. The bishops were encouraged to hunt out Lutherans and Calvinists. In all, perhaps six thousand heretics lost their lives during Alva's reign of terror. Finally, in defiance of constitutional tradition, Alva levied a sales tax of 10 per cent without consent of the States-General, a measure intended to render the Spanish administration financially independent of local control.

Those who dwelt in the Netherlands were used to self-government and a certain freedom. The region was pre-eminently a region of self-governing towns, which elected representatives to the local provincial assemblies, which in turn chose delegates to the central States-General, whose consent was necessary to the levy of taxes. Most of the people were casual Catholics of pre-Counter-Reformation temper who were averse to fanaticism and persecution. They knew also that a 10 per cent sales tax would wreck their complex commercial system. They always had disliked Philip as a cold, haughty, austere foreigner, and now they suddenly hated him and his agents. Still most people of the Netherlands were not prepared to give their lives for political or economic grievances. On the whole only the Calvinists, who hated priests and papists and who believed that they were the elect of God and that a private citizen might legitimately rebel against a usurping sovereign, were prepared to fight the Spaniards. The Calvinists, only a few devout burghers to begin with, were scattered in towns throughout the seventeen provinces. A few of them took to the sea during the dark night of Alva's repression and raised the flag of William of Orange, a great noble who had refused to submit to Alva. On April 1, 1572, these Sea Beggars, as they called themselves, seized the coastal town of The Brill in the province of Zealand. In May, June, and July they brought most of the towns of the provinces of Zealand and Holland under the authority of Orange. As they occupied a town they set up a Calvinist Reformed church and discouraged the public exercise of Catholic worship. Gradually the casual Catholic majority in the two provinces joined the Reformed sect. (Very gradually, in fact, for as late as 1587, 90 per cent of the people of Holland were still Catholic).

The war of Holland and Zealand against Philip ebbed and flowed. Dominated by a small band of Calvinist zealots and aided by their water defenses, the two provinces stood off the attacks of Alva and his successor, Requesens, from 1572 to 1576. For a few amazing years after 1576 the two provinces were joined by the other fifteen in a common uprising against Spanish tyranny. At length in 1578 Philip appointed as governor Alexander of Parma, probably the finest soldier-diplomat of the sixteenth century. Parma restored to the towns and provinces their constitutional privileges. He did not levy the sales tax, nor did he actively press the Inquisition. When he captured a town, he gave the Calvinist citizens two years to decide whether to migrate or to conform to Catholicism and remain. Many of them migrated with their property and zeal to Holland and Zealand, thus making these more Calvinist and the southern provinces more Catholic than before. William of Orange was assassinated at Philip's instigation on June 10, 1584 and Parma seemed on the verge of a complete triumph. Town after town surrendered to his soldiers and charm, until by August, 1585, he had recovered for Philip all the provinces except Holland, Zealand, and Utrecht, and he was poised for an invasion of these. With the religious zeal of the Jesuits balanced by the religious zeal of the Calvinists, the dividing line between Catholics and Protestants was being determined in the Netherlands by the power of force and not by the power of ideas.

In their moment of greatest danger the three provinces were saved by their water defenses, by their commercial wealth, and by the intricacies of power politics which diverted Philip's attention and resources from the Netherlands to England and France. Although neither Philip nor Queen Elizabeth of England wanted war with the other, a series of incidents had bred suspicion and bitter feelings on both sides. Elizabeth permitted English privateers to plunder the Spanish-American colonies, and secretly (but not too secretly) pocketed a share of the booty. Philip, in turn, kept captive English sailors languishing in the prisons of the Inquisition. The Jesuits were encouraged to invade England in force, while Philip's agents plotted with English Roman Catholics the assassination of their queen. Elizabeth disliked Calvinists, but after the death of William of Orange, whom she considered the keystone of the Dutch effort, she began to feel that she had better resist Spain now while one ally, the Dutch, was still standing than face the encircling Spanish and Catholic power later alone. Accordingly she dispatched her favorite, the Earl of Leicester, with 6,000 men to the aid of the Dutch in 1585, and released Sir Francis Drake for a plundering foray along the Spanish Main. Philip felt that he had been patient long enough with Elizabeth; these last measures were past endurance. The annexation of Portugal had given him several Atlantic harbors, the Portuguese shipyards, and an Atlantic fleet. He ordered the preparation of an armada of naval vessels that would protect the transport of Parma's troops from the Netherlands across the English Channel to England. The armada of 130 rather large and ungainly vessels was constructed for the type of naval warfare practiced in the Mediterranean and at the battle of Lepanto, in which one grappled with enemy vessels and boarded them. One hundred ninety-seven English vessels, smaller, more nimble, and heavily gunned, refused to play that game. They fell in behind the Spanish Armada as it sailed up the English Channel in August, 1588, darted in, fired their broadsides, made off; gradually nudged the Spanish vessels past Parma's army at Dunkirk, and forced them to return to Spain via the storm-laden route around Scotland and Ireland. Only 57 of the 130 Spanish ships limped into port. The repulse of the Armada prevented Parma from invading and saved England and the Anglican church. In that sense Philip lost out in England. But the repulse did not cripple irretrievably the Spanish navy. In these years Philip, imperturbable as always, rebuilt the Spanish fleet along English lines. He sent armada after armada against the English and Irish coasts, while the English continued their plundering forays against Spanish and Spanish-American ports.

In the midst of the naval war with England, Philip was drawn into France.

The assassination of the last Valois king, Henry III, in 1589, left the French throne to the Bourbon Henry IV, who was a Huguenot and an enemy of Spain. Philip dispatched Parma and Spanish soldiers to join the League of extremist French Catholics against Henry. Philip also put forward the claims of his daughter to the French throne. When Henry discovered that he could not make headway against the combined forces of the League and Spain and the hostility of most French Catholics to his religion, he announced his conversion to Catholicism in 1593. He then rather easily chased out the Spanish soldiers, subdued the remnants of the League, and granted toleration to the Huguenots in the Edict of Nantes (1598). By the edict Huguenots could worship everywhere in private, and publicly in about two hundred towns. They had all other legal rights of Catholics, including eligibility to all offices. To guarantee them in these rights, separate courts of justice were instituted in each parlement for the trial of all cases touching their interests. As further security, the Huguenots were allowed to hold a number of fortified towns in which they kept garrisons and paid the governors. Philip thus lost influence in France for Spain but not for the Catholic church. Since his intervention had forced Henry's conversion, he had assured that the French monarchy and hence France would remain Catholic.

Meanwhile, the three Dutch provinces of Zealand, Holland, and Utrecht had taken advantage of Parma's absence and subsequent death in 1592 to conquer and hold the four provinces of Friesland, Groningen, Overijssel, and Guelderland north of the Rhine River and a small slice of territory south of that stream. In all towns that fell into the hands of the Dutch armies, the Dutch authorities at once suppressed the public exercise of the Catholic religion and introduced the Reformed church organization. Just as the international preoccupations of Charles V had favored the consolidation of Lutheranism in Germany, so the concern of Philip with England and France had assured the consolidation of Calvinism in the seven northernmost provinces of the Netherlands.

The Decline of Spain under Philip III and Philip IV and the Religious Deadlock, or How the Return of Catholic France to the Wars Won the Protestants a Draw (1598-1659)

The line of Spanish grandeur, during the closing years of Philip's reign, was subtly falling. He lost in England, but kept fighting her on the sea. He lost in France, but left her in Catholic hands. He lost seven provinces in the Netherlands, but kept ten. Spanish fortunes waned, though at any moment it was hard to see the line go down.

The decline of the Spanish empire continued under Philip III (1598-1621) and Philip IV (1621-1665). It was accelerated by the decay of the Spanish economy. The Spaniards were discovering that a world-wide empire was a luxury a nation pays for, first with bullion, then with blood. The wars of Charles V left a debt estimated at $300,000,000. The war against the rebellious inhabitants of the Netherlands cost an estimated $1,650,000,000 by 1598 and was to absorb another $600,000,000 before 1609. The governments of the impoverished southern Netherlands, Milan, and Naples by 1598 all ran deficits which Spain made up. The Spanish kings tried to cover their expenses by taxing Spaniards. But most of the land was owned by the privileged clergy and nobility, and largely escaped taxation. An increasing tax burden here fell on commerce and industry. The *alcabala*, a tax of 10 per cent later increased to 14, was levied on the sale value of everything that changed hands by purchase. An excise tax, called the "millions," weighed on wine, vinegar, meat, and oil, the principal food of the people. These taxes were rather wretchedly administered. Spanish rule was personal either by the king himself, as under Philip II, or by his favorites, as under Philip III and Philip IV, and was exercised through a growing bureaucracy. Though there was a growing loyalty to monarchs who were sincere, devout Catholics, separatist feeling and institutions still existed. The monarchs still ruled over a bundle of realms and dominions with more-or-less diverse institutions. It was hard to organize them for finance or war. Growing corruption, moreover, invaded the bureaucracy. Much of the money that was collected never reached the king. Revenue lagged behind expenses, and by the close of his reign Philip II owed an estimated $1,500,000,000.

Most of this debt was owed to German and Italian bankers, who charged 15 to 30 per cent and sometimes more. Most of the gold and silver imported from America did not remain in Spain but passed to foreign merchants in payment for goods and to foreign bankers. But all this bullion helped to raise prices. The cost of commodities in Spain went up 200 or 300 per cent over the century. The separate provincial governments and the king himself tried by various laws to protect the consumer. These laws were well-meaning but usually misguided. They forbade, for example, the export of foodstuffs and forced down the price of wheat to its former level, though costs of production had doubled. Or they set a maximum price above which manufactured goods might not be sold, thus making it not worthwhile to produce them at all. Or they opened the Spanish market to foreign imports, thus suddenly ruining Spanish manufactures. Clumsy legislation and heavy taxation helped to ruin Spanish industry and agriculture during the sixteenth and early seventeenth centuries. By the mid-seventeenth century, many industries had deserted Spain, and many an agricultural field was idle, prey to thistles and nettles, War, expenditures, administrative inefficiency and corruption, inequitable taxation, unwise economic legislation, and the impoverishment of a country whose population of nine million was slightly declining brought the kings to their wit's end. In 1601 royal officers went from door to door accompanied by the priests of each parish, to beg alms for the King. The master of the treasures of the New World lacked money to pay his household servants, or to set forth the meals for his own table. The enterprises of Philip II had been kept going largely by the one-fifth which he claimed of American gold and silver. This supplied about 20 per cent of his total income. But after 1598, the better-paying lodes in America were worked out, and the amount of bullion imported into Spain steadily shrank from an annual average of $19,664,532 in 1591-1595 to $7,692,213 per year in 1641-1645.

Even when collapsing, however, an aging empire may hold off a younger one that is rising. The Spanish government still had a navy that was not to be ignored, a base in Flanders for the reconquest of the Dutch, and a general — the Genoese genius, Ambrogio Spinola — to attempt it. The Spaniards had gained a breathing space by making peace with the English in 1604 and negotiating a Twelve-Year Truce with the seven northern provinces of the Netherlands in 1609. The Spanish Habsburg kings also had reached an understanding with their Catholic cousins, the Austrian Habsburgs. The two branches of the family would now move together to recover the seven Dutch provinces and Germany for the Habsburg dynasty and Catholicism. Success in the Netherlands depended on success in Germany. The old supply route from Spain to the Netherlands by sea was jeopardized by Dutch privateers. The land route, which led from Genoa to Milan, over the Alps by the Val Telline pass, and then down the Rhine, was crossed for fifty miles by the Rhineland Calvinist state of the Palatinate. Its ruler had to be removed.

The Habsburg offensive in Germany began in 1618. The Catholic recovery of German believers, spearheaded by the Jesuits, had been proceeding apace. By the early years of the seventeenth century, the inhabitants of Bavaria, Baden-Baden, and Fulda, and the Austrian Habsburg emperors had been won to the Catholic cause. The Habsburg Emperor Ferdinand (1619-1637) and his Spanish cousins resolved to extend the Catholic reform to Bohemia, of which he was the elective king. The majority of Bohemians were Protestants of four sects, Lutherans, Calvinists, Utraquists, and Bohemian Brethren. The Bohemian Estates had wrung from one of Ferdinand's predecessors, Rudolph, a Letter of Majesty (1609) which guaranteed the right of Lutherans to worship freely. But an imperial decree of March, 1618, now prohibited meetings. When the Bohemians, rebelling, chose the Calvinist Elector Palatine their king, the imperial army (paid with Spanish money) crushed the rebels at the Battle of White Mountain (November 8, 1620). The Spanish general Spinola occupied the Palatinate in 1620, thus securing the land supply route from Italy. He resumed the war against the Dutch in 1621, and re-took the strong fortress of

Breda in 1625. Meanwhile, Ferdinand made the Bohemian crown hereditary in the Habsburg family, transferred the estates of the Protestant nobility to Catholic families, and so maltreated the Protestant subjects that they were forced to turn Catholic. Rarely had persecution been so effective in changing the religion of a majority of the people. Ferdinand was ready to pursue further gains for the dynasty and Catholicism in northern Germany.

At this point, when the Habsburg dynasty and the Catholic church seemed to be carrying everything before them in central Europe, France intervened. Except for a few years under Henry IV, France had been immobilized since 1559 by internal religious or factional strife. But in 1624 the young Louis XIII appointed as his chief minister Cardinal Richelieu, a skilful diplomat of iron will. Richelieu coordinated French inner and outer policies by giving them a stable political center. He wanted two things: to check internal disunion in France and to stop the sweeping drive of the Habsburgs in Europe. By doing these he would strengthen his king and his country. It did not bother this Cardinal of the Church that, to be consistent in his politics, he must be sometimes inconsistent in his religion.

Richelieu began at home by dealing firmly with the French Huguenots, who had revolted in 1625. While allowing them to worship freely, he deprived them of their political privileges — their law courts, fortresses, and fortified towns — that had made them a state within a state. Abroad he organized against the Habsburg rulers their scattered and dispirited opponents — the Dutch, the Protestant German princes, the Swiss Confederation, the Republic of Venice, and the kings of Sweden and Denmark. He negotiated a treaty of alliance with the Dutch in 1624. The Lutheran King Christian IV of Denmark feared Habsburg expansion in north Germany and desired several north German bishoprics. Richelieu subsidized his declaration of war against the Habsburg emperor in 1626. When the imperial-Catholic armies crushed Christian's armies, swept north to the Baltic Sea, and forced Christian out of the war in 1629, Richelieu subsidized the entrance of King Gustavus Adolphus of Sweden into the conflict against the Austrian Habsburgs. Gustavus Adolphus, a warrior-king who was devoted to the expansion of Protestantism and of Sweden, smashed the imperial-Catholic forces at the Battle of Breitenfeld on March 31, 1631, and thus secured north Germany for Protestantism. When Gustavus Adolphus was killed at the battle of Lützen on March 30, 1632, and the Swedish army was defeated by a Spanish-imperial force at Nördlingen on March 30, 1634, Richelieu took the Swedish and German mercenary armies into his pay, declared war on Spain in May, 1635, and began seriously to organize the French army and navy. The war which had started in 1618 as a secular-religious crusade to expand Catholicism and Habsburg authority was becoming solely a secular conflict between Catholic Spain and Catholic France for power. At the Battle of White Mountain in

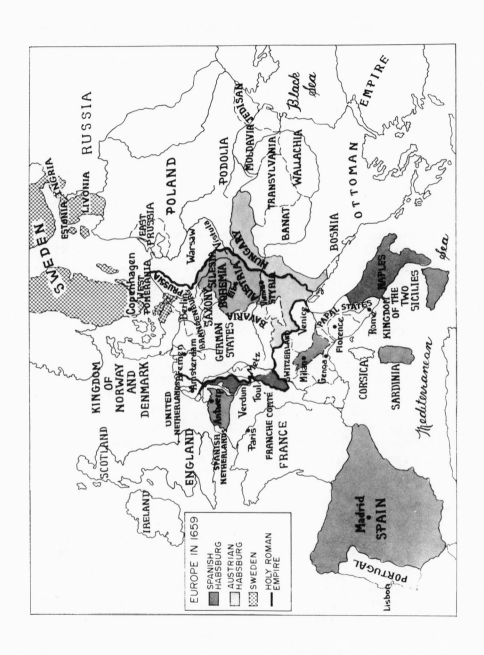

EUROPE IN 1659

SPANISH HABSBURG

AUSTRIAN HABSBURG

SWEDEN

HOLY ROMAN EMPIRE

SWEDEN

RUSSIA

ESTONIA
INGRIA
LIVONIA

POLAND

PODOLIA

MOLDAVIA
BUDJAK

TRANSYLVANIA

WALLACHIA

BANAT

Black Sea

OTTOMAN EMPIRE

BOSNIA

KINGDOM OF NORWAY AND DENMARK

SCOTLAND

IRELAND

ENGLAND

UNITED NETHERLANDS

SPANISH NETHERLANDS

Copenhagen
WEST POMERANIA
EAST PRUSSIA
PRUSSIA
Warsaw
Vistula
Berlin
BRANDENBURG
SAXONY
SILESIA
BOHEMIA
GERMAN STATES
BAVARIA
AUSTRIA
HUNGARY
TYROL
STYRIA

Amsterdam
Antwerp
Metz
Verdun
Toul
Paris
FRANCHE COMTÉ
SWITZERLAND
FRANCE
Milan
Genoa
Venice
Florence
PAPAL STATES
Rome

CORSICA

SARDINIA

NAPLES
KINGDOM OF THE TWO SICILIES

Mediterranean Sea

SPAIN
Madrid

PORTUGAL
Lisbon

1620, the Spanish-imperial troops shouted "Sancta Maria"; at Nördlingen in 1634, "Viva Espana."

In time, the efforts of Richelieu began to tell upon the declining Spanish monarchy. In 1638 one of his mercenary captains, Bernard of Saxe-Weimar, occupied the town of Breisach and the provinces of Alsace along the Rhine, thus cutting the Spanish land route to the Netherlands. In 1639 the Dutch Admiral De Tromp sank in the Battle of the Downs 70 out of 77 Spanish warships, thus putting a quietus to Spanish sea power and cutting the sea route. The Spanish effort in the Netherlands began to wither, like fruit on a severed vine. Spain itself began to break up. Portugal broke away in 1640, carrying its remaining colonies with it. Catalonia, the separatist northeastern province, revolted and with French support held out for years. For the first time in over a century, the Spanish began to lose on the battlefield. The French army defeated the Spanish forces at the Battle of Rocroi in 1643; the auxiliary Flemish and German troops of the Spanish army fled the field, but the splendid Spanish infantry was slaughtered where it stood. The dominion of the seas no longer belonged to Spain, but to the Dutch; the finest European army was no longer the Spanish, but the French; and the outstanding diplomats were now French and not Spanish. After Rocroi, Spain could not longer help the Austrian Habsburgs nor defend herself. The French and Swedish armies together invaded Catholic Bavaria in 1646, and the Swedes alone occupied Bohemia; French armies invaded the southern Netherlands and Catalonia, until the Habsburgs were ready to sue for peace.

The treaties of Westphalia (1648) for Germany and of the Pyrenees (1659) for Spain and France reflected the decline of Spain and the success of France and its allies. By the Treaty of Westphalia the independence of the seven Dutch provinces from both Spain and the Holy Roman Empire was recognized. France was confirmed in the possession of the three fortress towns of Metz, Toul, and Verdun, plus Moyenvic, Breisach, and Philipsburg on the Rhine, and Pinerolo on the frontier of Savoy and France; Alsace, except for Strasburg, also became French. France's ally, Sweden, received as imperial fiefs western Pomerania, Bremen, and Verden, Wismar, and Stettin, together with some territory at the mouth of the Oder River. The religious clauses of the treaty admitted Calvinism to an equality with Lutheranism and Catholicism. A German prince might decide to be a Calvinist, a Lutheran, or a Catholic and force his subjects to follow suit. In effect, the Catholics kept by treaty what they had gained by the Counter-Reformation and the early years of the war: Austria, Bohemia, Bavaria, Württemberg, Baden-Baden, and the ecclesiastical territories of south Germany and the Rhineland. The Protestants retained north Germany. French and Swedish money and men had won the German Protestants a draw, and the demarcation of Catholicism and Protestantism was established in continental Europe on the general lines which it still exhibits. Almost as a postscript to the general settlement, the purely secular Treaty of the Pyrenees (1659) between France and Spain provided for the marriage of the Spanish princess, Maria Theresa, to Louis XIV and the Spanish cession of Cerdagne, Roussillon, Artois, and a number of Flemish towns to France.

European Rivalries Overseas

Spain's decline was reflected in the colonial field. The waning of her naval power enabled the English, Dutch, and French to crack the Spanish-Portuguese colonial monopoly in the Far Eastern and Atlantic areas. In the Far East the Dutch took the lead, the English and French trailing after. By the seventeenth century Zealand and Holland had developed into the principal commercial power of Europe. The Dutch fished in the North Sea, dominated the carrying trade of the Baltic, and trafficked even in wartime with their enemies in Portuguese, Spanish, and Mediterranean ports. The money brought in by this enterprise was supplemented by the wealth of Calvinist businessmen migrating from the southern Netherlands. Dutch-capital, thus increased, financed trading expeditions to the four corners of the world. The Dutch long had sailed to Lisbon to pick up for European distribution the spices, precious stones, and other luxuries the Portuguese had brought from Asia. Several Dutch adventurers had sailed to the Far East on Portuguese ships and had returned to tell of the route. After enemy Spain had annexed Portugal in 1580, the Portuguese colonial empire was legitimate prey for the Dutch merchants. At first, individual Dutch merchant adventurers voyaged into Asiatic waters in competition with one another and at their own risk. But as this led to disorder, the Dutch government brought together the various existing enterprises under the name of the Dutch East India Company (1601) and granted it a monopoly for all Dutch trade east of the Cape of Good Hope and west of the Magellan Strait.

The Dutch were entering the easternmost sector of the Portuguese commercial empire. The Portuguese empire focused on Goa on the Indian coast and extended from Ormuz off the Persian Gulf to Malacca on the Malay peninsula with a few fringe outposts in the Moluccas (the spice islands) and on the island of Macao off the China shore. The activities of the Dutch East India Company centered in the East Indies and the Moluccas themselves. The company was mainly interested in making quick profits such as the spice trade afforded. It had no intention of building a colonial empire. The Dutch agents of the company sought at first merely to establish trading connections with the native princes and to cajole them into giving the company exclusive delivery of the native products, pepper, rice, indigo, and spices. But as the Dutch agents delved deeper into the trading complexities of the East Indian archipelago, they came upon the same problems as had the Portuguese. The problems were security ashore in the midst of warring, poorly administered native states of different customs from the Dutch, organization of the sources of supply, and security on the high seas against native rivals and Portuguese, Spanish, English, and French fleets. The Dutch solution until the middle of the seventeenth century resembled the one the Portuguese had stumbled on: factories defended by forts at a few key strategic locations, warships, and the elimination of competitors. The great governors-general, John Coen (1618-1623, 1627-1629) and Anthony van Diemen (1636-1653), did for the Dutch East India Company what Alfonso Albuquerque had accomplished for Portugal. Coen acquired an overlordship over the key islands of the Moluccas group and founded in 1619 the fortified city of Batavia, which commanded the Straits of Sunda between Java and Sumatra. Van Diemen captured from the Portuguese the ports of Negombo and Gale (1640) on Ceylon and of Malacca (1641), drove the Spaniards out of northern Formosa (1642), and strengthened the Dutch trading post on the Island of Desima off the Japanese port of Nagasaki. By 1653, after sixty years of hectic trading and fighting, the Dutch East India Company controlled the sea lanes from the Gulf of Bengal and Ceylon to Nagasaki in Japan, had largely eliminated its rivals from the East Indian archipelago, and had monopolized the spice trade. In the solution of daily problems the Dutch had been drawn into the formation of a commercial, colonial empire almost in spite of themselves. The Spanish, meanwhile, had been confined, in Asiatic waters, to the Philippines. Except for the small islands of Macao and Timor, the Portuguese had been thrown back to the mainland of India. The English and French East India companies, founded respectively in 1600 and 1604, had been expelled from the East Indies and forced to compete with each other for the less valuable commerce of the Indian sub-continent.

Also in America the three intruders, England, France, and Holland, invaded the Spanish-Portuguese monopoly. England founded Jamestown in 1607; France, Quebec in 1608; and in 1609 Henry Hudson, an Englishman in the employ of Holland, sailed up the river which has since borne his name. After 1613 a blockhouse on the island of Manhattan flew the Dutch flag. In the succeeding decades the three newcomers expanded their settlements in North America and took scattered West Indian islands (St. Kitts, Barbados, and Jamaica to England, Guadeloupe and Martinique to the French, Curacao and St. Eustatius to the Dutch). In additon, the Dutch seized a segment of the Brazilian coast. The eventual outcome of the five-party fight among Spain, Portugal, Holland, England, and France for colonial spoil in America was a complicated arrangement that was less happy for the Dutch than the one reached in the Far East. Spain constructed great fortifications at Havana, Portobello, and the Pacific ports to protect the progress of her treasure fleets.

She was able to conserve a few important islands of the West Indies, California, Mexico, Central America, and all of South America other than Brazil. "Like a huge turtle basking in the sun, protected by its shell, and showing only here and there a tooth or claw" (the figure is Wilbur Abbott's), Spain in America lay before the onslaughts of her foes. Portugal expelled the Dutch administrators from Brazil by 1665, and the English shut them out of the Hudson River valley in 1664. By 1670, Dutch authority was reduced in America to the two Caribbean islands of Curaçao and St. Eustatius and a part of the coast of Guiana, including present British and Dutch Guiana. Meanwhile, England and France continued to expand their settlements in North America and the West Indies.

As a result of the Dutch, English, and French invasion of the Spanish-Portuguese colonial monopoly and of the limited ability of the Spanish to halt this invasion, an informal colonial compromise had been reached by 1689. Spain was left with the Philippine Islands, a long segment of territory from California to Chile, and a few of the West Indies; Portugal had Brazil and posts along the coasts of Africa and India; and the Dutch had gained a free hand to reap dividends in the East Indies. The chief colonial contest after 1689 would be between England and France over North America, portions of the West Indies, and India.

Epilogue

Two wars, which merged, were being fought during the sixteenth and early seventeenth centuries. One war between Spain and France was secular in nature and was for power; another between Catholicism and the Protestant sects, for belief. The war between Spain and France started first when Spain, in the reign of Ferdinand and Isabella, acquired possessions and responsibilities in North Africa and Italy, and there collided with an expanding France. The accession of Charles V to the throne of Spain in 1516 and his election as Holy Roman Emperor in 1519 added the responsibilities of defending his northern possessions and of repressing the Lutherans in the same year (1519) that Cortez' discovery of gold in Mexico was giving Spain the wherewithal to sustain the new responsibilities. In the succeeding wars the Spanish kings were fortunate in one respect. They could advance with good conscience onto the field. In the attempt of Charles V, Philip II, Philip III, and Philip IV to repress the Lutherans, Calvinists, and Anglicans, the political and dynastic interests of the rulers and of Spain coincided with the religious desire to defend and extend Catholicism. On the other side, the desire of the German Lutheran princes, of the Swedish King Gustavus Adolphus, of the Calvinist Dutch provinces, and of Queen Elizabeth's advisers to defend and extend the Protestant faith coincided with their wish to maintain and increase their power both at home and abroad. The only dissonance came in France. The French kings were caught between. Their political and dynastic interests collided with their duties as Catholic princes. Usually, either by diverting the attention of the Spanish rulers or by allying directly with Protestant princes, the French kings promoted the Protestant cause. The support of Spanish soldiers, treasure, and diplomacy helped the reformed Catholic church to hold Portugal, Spain, Italy, France, Ireland, and the southern Netherlands and to re-win southern Germany, the Rhineland, Hungary, Bohemia, and Poland. This success would seem to suggest that although ideas are good and zeal is fine, ideas and zeal plus arms and munitions are even better. French arms and diplomacy helped the Protestants keep Scotland, England, the northern Netherlands, northern Germany, Denmark, Norway, and Sweden; and eventually French power humbled Spain.

One effect of these one hundred and fifty bitter and twisted years was the division of Christendom (and possibly the consequent division of European consciousness) into believers who adhered to the papal-monarchical Catholic tradition and those who accepted the private-judgment and salvation-by-faith theories of Protestantism. A second result of the Protestant Reformation was the increase in the power of the secular rulers. In Protestant countries, the king, as in England and Sweden, or the territorial princes, as in Germany, used the revolt to get a better hold on the church and church lands. The ruler now appointed church officials and shared in the definition of doctrine. In Catholic states, the rulers took advantage of the pope's distress to acquire added authority, at his expense, over the local Catholic church.

A third *long-range* consequence of the Protestant movement was increased freedom for the individual. Looking to the future, we can notice many reasons for this change. The Protestant Reformation, for one thing, started a process by which men were freed from obligatory allegiance and obedience to one church, and eventually to any church. It eventually led in the seventeenth, eighteenth, and nineteenth centuries to religious toleration. Minority sects, such as the Anabaptists, Unitarians, and Quakers, built up a theory of toleration. Protestants in Catholic countries and Catholics in Protestant countries came to demand freedom of worship. As people became more indifferent to the minutiae of religious belief, governments discovered that toleration was not necessarily destructive of the unity of the state. Nor was the everlasting influence of the gentleness of Christ without effect in bringing an end to cruel religious persecutions. Also, the Protestant Reformation increased the authority of the individual in matters of religion. The Protestants emphasized, in their better moments, that the individual must interpret the Bible for himself and attain salvation by individual prayer and faith. In the government of the Calvinistic churches, the individual member of the congregation was consulted. It is possible that the Protestant emphasis on the individual, especially in the activist, Calvinistic churches, was congenial with the individualistic, aggressive capitalism that was arising in northwestern Europe. If this was true, then the spirit of rising capitalism and of an activist, individualistic faith mutually reinforced each other. Finally, the Protestant Reformation indirectly and in the long run helped the cause of free-ranging intellectual speculation. Formerly, the Catholic church had imposed its opinions in intellectual and spiritual matters. But the great divisions in Christendom weakened ecclesiastical authority in general. The Reformation, by asserting the right of private judgment in religion, probably encouraged its exercise in other fields. Religious toleration was an important step toward complete freedom of opinion. In addition, Bible worship led to close examination of the Bible and eventually to perception of its factual discrepancies, which undermined the quality of its authority and its hold on men's minds.

PART III

THE CONSOLIDATION OF THE
GREAT STATES
1492-1763

Introduction to Part III

During the sixteenth, seventeenth, and eighteenth centuries the governments of the great European states grew stronger. In England the parliamentary monarchy came into being. On the European continent the typical state form came to be the administrative monarchy. After Spain declined, and Holland had her day of glory, the most powerful states were France, Austria, Prussia, and Russia. To a degree the histories of these major continental states resembled each other. In each instance, the state was largely the creation of a dynasty — the Capetian in France, the Habsburg in Austria, the Hohenzollern in Prussia, and the Romanov in Russia. In each case, members of the dynasty gradually accumulated a ragged, conglomerate mosaic of territories. Almost daily they faced the difficulties of securing obedience and of territorial defense, and they were allured by the possibilities of territorial expansion. Although their perception of situations and of possible courses of action was affected by what they saw in other countries and by religious and political theories which exalted the authority of the monarchy, their decisions were primarily the responses of matter-of-fact, practical men to the shifting responsibilities, necessities, temptations, and problems of the moment. In their responses they reached compromises with the leading families of their kingdoms which preserved many old usages, while they gradually built up institutions (army, taxes, and bureaucracy) of the central government that were new, so that each state was an ever-changing mingling of the old and the new. States differed from each other, to be sure, in many features of their development (the character of each state varied, for example, with the relationship of the leading families to the government), but by the eighteenth century the continental states were all *tending* toward the administrative monarchy. It can be argued, indeed, that the central administration which the monarchies of the European continent created was their greatest and most enduring achievement.

France, England, Spain, and also Holland, whose European eminence was of relatively short duration, expanded overseas, to the Americas and to Asia, transmitting their institutions to non-European lands. Austria, Prussia, and Russia expanded eastward overland. Through the direction of their expansion and their repeated wars with each other, the actions of the great states were determining which forms of European civilization would influence which areas of the world.

Chapter VIII

FRANCE: THE EMERGENCE OF THE
ADMINISTRATIVE MONARCHY
(1492-1774)

As we have seen, the French kings gradually gave their authority a longer reach: they came to control situations remote from them in space. They were able to work their authority deeper, too, insinuating it into the lives of their subjects. This extension of their power did not happen overnight. Since Hugh Capet the French kings had been laying the foundations of their rule, but they had followed no blueprint at first, no formula. Animated by the desire to extend their power and to make it secure, the more capable rulers had simply answered the needs of daily circumstances by creating from time to time agents and precendents. Those that were found useful had been continued.

Thus, as the royal domain had been extended, the king has sent out his *baillis*, to collect his revenues. As their accounts came to need checking, the king appointed auditors, who came to form a central Chambre des comptes. When the revenues of the royal domain were no longer enough, the king started levying taxes, — the *taille*, the *aides*, the *gabelle* — first with, then without the approval of the Estates-General. In all this, much of feudal society was left untouched.

This process of pragmatic, piecemeal expansion of royal institutions continued from 1492 to 1661. It was interrupted only here and there, by weak kings (during the religious wars), and by kings too young to rule (the minorities of Louis XIII and Louis XIV). After 1661, Louis XIV tried to introduce for the sake of efficiency a degree of planned order among institutions that had beforetime simply grown.

The Society and Government of France at
the Close of the Fifteenth Century

For centuries one problem of the French monarchs was to get themselves obeyed. In the struggle to secure obedience they had enlarged the royal domain by acquiring bit by bit the domains of their feudal vassals. They had retained the obedience of the inhabitants of their enlarged possessions by agreeing to a series of individual bargains, contracts, and understandings with the provinces, towns, and leading classes, and by inventing devices to administer and protect their subjects. By the close of the fifteenth century the

French monarch had come far since the days of Hugh Capet. He had a royal army, a royal justice, and a royal revenue derived from his domain and royal taxes. The royal authority, under the influence of Roman law, was coming to be considered in theory absolute. As the president of the Parlement of Paris declared to Francis I in 1527: "You are above the law, and laws and ordinances cannot constrain you." Yet at this time the king did not perform many more functions of protection, justice, and finance than a feudal chief, nor did he have a much more extensive administrative staff to execute them. The exercise of the absolute authority of the monarch was tempered in practice by the concessions he had granted to the provinces, towns, and leading classes to retain their obedience as well as by the smallness of the army, the inadequacy of the administrative staff, the objections of the Estates-General and parlements, and the habits of unruliness and resistance inherited from medieval times.

The king had usually conceded to the people of each locality permission to keep parts of their lives intact. They were allowed to retain many of their local customs and privileges. There had resulted for France an infinite diversity of weights and measures, tolls, and laws. The king had also permitted seven outlying provinces to have representative assemblies, known as provincial estates.[a] These assemblies, usually composed of delegates from the clergy, the nobility, and the towns, managed to hold on to some very tangible powers. They were able to discuss, sometimes even to supervise the assessment of the land tax (the *taille*). They could haggle with royal agents over the amount of any new, extraordinary levies. They thus secured for their provinces a far lower tax rate than was imposed elsewhere in France. Many towns also had received royal charters. Under these charters townsmen with property governed themselves in part. Town officers (not agents picked by nobles or by the king but representatives elected by other townsmen) served as courts of first instance, regulated prices, collected town taxes, and reconstructed town walls.

The kings, in bartering for obedience, had let the leading classes retain many privileges. The French people were divided by now into three legal classes, called estates. The First Estate was the Catholic clergy, who as the top legal class possessed a number of privileges. They were free of most taxes: they paid neither the *taille* nor the principal indirect taxes. They were free of the civil law: they could as a rule be tried only in church courts by canon law. They were free economically: they depended materially neither on the state nor on the generosity of the faithful. The church collected the tithe on

[a]The provinces were Auvergne, Burgundy, Brittany, Dauphiny, Languedoc, Normandy, and Provence.

all products of the soil. In theory the tithe was one-tenth, in practice about one-fifteenth, of every peasant's harvest. The church was still the largest single proprietor in the kingdom. It held perhaps one-fifteenth, of every peasant's harvest. The church was still the largest single proprietor in the kingdom. It held perhaps one-fifth of the land of the kingdom — thousands of scattered manors, from whose peasants the church collected manorial dues. The income derived from the tithe and the property, however, was distributed unequally among the clergy. Parish priests — those in daily contact with the faithful — received a bare subsistence. Archbishops, bishops, and abbots, many of them younger sons of noble families, feasted on large revenues.

The Second Estate was the nobility. The nobles had lost the sovereign powers to coin money, levy tolls, and wage war, but still had much to keep them from complaining. They were still exempt from the land tax, the *taille*. In judicial proceedings they could be compelled to appear only before a royal *bailli*, an intermediate court, and if accused of a crime they could be tried only by a parlement, a superior court. They could wear a sword, display a coat of arms, and hunt game. If they were lord of a manor (commoners could now be lords of manors as well), they could collect manorial dues from the peasants and administer manorial justice.

The Third Estate was everyone else. It included the townsmen, who formed perhaps one-fifteenth of the population. Except for a few lawyers and doctors, most townsmen were traders and artisans. Their wealth and prosperity varied, just as it does today, among individuals. There were well-to-do merchants who traded with distant regions. There were shopkeepers and craftsmen whose scope was the town, "butchers, bakers, and candlestick makers," some of whom had a journeyman, some not. Below them were apprentices, peddlers, drifters, the unemployed. To be a citizen of a town and possess the right of bourgeoisie was itself a privilege and carried advantages. A townsman was free from manorial dues and was outside the jurisdiction of manorial justice. He was generally exempt from the *taille*. Often he was eligible for municipal office and for officerships in the town militia. The Third Estate also included the peasants, who still formed over eleven-twelfths of the French population. They still pursued with primitive implements the immemorial routines of open-field village agriculture. They usually inherited the right to cultivate certain strips of land, but this was the right to labor from dawn to dark and from childhood until death. Most of them were not serfs — they could sell their hereditary right of cultivation and leave — but as long as they remained they owed obligations to three masters: the *taille* to the king, the tithe to the priest, and manorial dues and services to the manorial lord. The manorial obligations usually included an annual money-rent (an offering in grain of one sheaf in twelve or ten), payment for use of the lord's oven and mill, observance of his monopoly of game and hunting, several days of annual labor, and if the right of cultivation changed hands, payment by the purchaser to the lord of 5 to 12 per cent of the purchase price.

Royal agencies were still sketchy. The army at the close of the fifteenth century was heterogeneous in composition and, for a population of twelve million, small in size. The peacetime guard consisted of a few regiments of infantry and cavalry, while the wartime expeditions across the mountains into Italy rarely exceeded 25,000 men. In each frontier province, a personal representative of the king, a governor, commanded the local troops and in wartime took charge of the area's defense. The royal administration of justice and finance was rudimentary. A peasant accused of civil or criminal wrongdoing usually would be arrested by a sergeant of the local manorial lord and summarily tried by the lord's agent. A non-privileged townsman would be brought to trial before elected town magistrates. If an individual felt wronged by a decision, he might appeal — first to the local royal *prévôt*, then to the lieutenant of the royal *bailli*, and finally to one of the seven superior courts of the kingdom, known as parlements. If he were a member of the privileged classes, he might then carry the case to the king's council. But unless an individual appealed, he usually did not come into contact with a royal officer. Likewise, in finance. A peasant paid the land tax, the *taille*, to an amateur assessor, who had been elected by the chiefs of the village parish and who assessed and collected the local tax. An individual paid the indirect taxes, the *aides* and the gabelles, to private citizens known as tax-farmers who had paid the king a lump sum for the right to collect these taxes and make a profit. France was divided into eighty-five fiscal districts called *élections*, which were grouped into four larger *généralités*. The local assessors and tax-farmers passed their collections to royal collectors in each *élection*. These paid the local royal expenses and passed the surplus on to the royal collector general for each *généralité*, who in turn paid the local royal expenses and passed on the remainder to Paris. But unless an individual Frenchman appealed his tax, he did not see a royal fiscal officer. Michel de Montaigne, the sixteenth-century essayist, noted with satisfaction that rarely did a French subject come into contact with the authority of the King more than once or twice in a lifetime. Over the rudimentary royal agencies was the king and a rather informal, non-specialized council of five or six advisers who helped him consider everything that might come before him.

In many respects this was a feudal situation: feudal in that many of its features were inherited from feudal times; feudal in the legal division and separation of classes; feudal in the existence of manorial dues and of the privileges of the clergy and nobility; feudal also in that the great bulk of the population, the peasants, nobility, and clergy, lived off the land and the two privileged classes lived off the peasants. Yet there were significant non-feudal elements. The revival of commerce, of a money economy, of towns and townsmen, had introduced an element of social fluidity. A peasant might sell his rights of cultivation and move to town. He might start as an apprentice, become a journeyman, and eventually qualify as a master craftsman. If he and his descendants prospered, they could become great merchants. With money in hand, much more was possible. They could buy a fief by paying a year's revenue to the royal treasury, or they could buy a high judicial office: either way they could buy themselves an accompanying patent of nobility. The French aristocracy was thus almost entirely renewed during the sixteenth century. A second non-feudal element was the royal administration, which continued to grow in power and activity during the succeeding centuries.

The Growth of the Activity and Power of
the French Monarchy from 1492 to 1661

Without a far-flung administrative staff, the firmness, power, and prestige of the monarchy depended on a single variable, the monarch himself. Under weak kings the gains of centuries of royal effort nearly dissolved. Even the strongest kings had their troubles. As we saw, the French monarchs became involved in the long, costly duel with Spain, lasting from 1494 to 1659. They also began squandering money on the theatrical aspect of the monarchy. Anne of Brittany, the wife first of Charles VIII (1483-1498) and then of Louis XII (1498-1515), revived the gaiety of the French court after the mean penury of Louis XI. Francis I (1515-1547) greatly enlarged the court and attracted to it young nobles with the promise of pensions and offices and the dream of social success. The court was useful — it fascinated and domesticated nobles who might be rebellious; it was also expensive. The twin extravagancies of war and the court exhausted the royal revenue. Francis and his successors, to meet recurring deficits and a mounting debt, increased taxes, forced the rich to lend them money, and sold offices and segments of the royal domain. They sold the position of *bailli*, the fiscal post of royal tax collector, and the office of justice in the parlements. As these positions became hereditary in the family of the purchaser, their owners escaped royal control and could oppose the monarch. The *baillis*, the fiscal officials, and the justices had been established to control the population; now they themselves needed to be controlled. During the reigns of three degenerate kings, Francis II (1559-1560), Charles IX (1560-1574), and Henry III (1574-1589), France was devastated by religious wars. These were years of insecurity, when there was no center in France, no forceful king, no centrifugal will. France seemed to be regressing to the disorder and local independence of medieval times. The nobility in local assemblies, the Catholic clergy in their general assemblies, the provinces under their governors, and the towns under their magistrates asserted their semi-independence. Henry IV (1589-1610), a rollicking and popular but shrewd soldier-king, restored internal peace and monarchical prestige but was assassinated before he could affirm his work. Most of the ground gained under Henry was lost during the minority and early manhood of Louis XIII (1610-1643) until the somber Cardinal Richelieu became chief minister in 1624 and intimidated the nobles and Huguenots until his death in 1642. Cardinal Mazarin (1643-1661), the chief minister during the youth of Louis XIV, had to subdue the last rebellion of the nobility and of Paris against the monarchy before he could govern securely. Even the best of kings, Henry IV, and the most authoritarian of ministers, Richelieu, frequently had to improvise measures and expedients to keep the monarchy operating.

Nevertheless, some of the measures that were taken by kings and royal administrators during these troubled years were maintained and entered the stream of French institutional life. Francis I and Henry II clarified somewhat the fiscal administration. A central coffer to receive all receipts was set up in Paris, seventeen *généralités* were added to the original four, and a single royal treasurer, endowed with fiscal responsibility, was placed in each one. After 1560 the fiscal immunity of the Catholic clergy was infringed by constraining their periodical representative assemblies to vote "voluntary" gifts to the king. These measures brought results. In the century following the death of Francis I in 1547 the amount of money taken in each year by the government increased tenfold, from eight million livres to eighty million. Louis XIII succeeded in claiming a total revenue ten times as large as that of his contemporary Charles I of England, and a per capita income four times as great. As even these sums were not enough to pay wartime expenses, the French kings began to sell government securities.

Now and then, here and there, the government began taking measures to increase the wealth, prosperity, and strength of the French economy and thereby the yield of taxes. Gold and silver, which the early Middle Ages had viewed as sterile, were coming to be considered during the sixteenth and early seventeenth centuries a valuable form of wealth. This was understandable. The kings and royal administrators lived at that time in a money-poor, credit-poor continent. There were few gold and silver mines in Europe; paper money was a device not yet invented; there were no government banks, and few private ones. In that situation, a store of bullion *was* a convenience to have ready, to pay the army and to stimulate business. And bullion was flowing from Spanish-American gold and silver mines to Spain, and then in the course of trade throughout Europe. Naturally, French administrators as well as those of other countries tried, somewhat unsystematically at first, to acquire and retain some of this specie. Since the only public economic policy which they knew was the medieval one of regulation, they resorted to that policy on a national scale. Behind each regulation often lay a variety of motives — desire for economic self-sufficiency, hatred of the foreigner, need for revenue, pleasure in uniformity — but the simple wish for a store of precious metal was always there. But foreign manufactured goods and other luxuries coming in drained France of bullion. To check this drain French kings started levying import duties on costly incoming products — spices, drugs, and luxury fabrics such as silk and velvet. They issued regulations setting high standards for the domestic manufacture of woolen cloth, so that it might surpass the foreign product. These regulations went into great detail, prescribing the length and width of the cloth along with the number of threads per square inch and the ingredients of the dye. The kings also aided manufacturers of such bullion-attracting products as silk, tapestry, and glassware, by granting them a nation-wide or local monopoly, exemption from taxation, and government orders. We must continually bear in mind how the king was a little better off with every profitable enterprise which came along; how the king's income and those of newly-rich entrepreneurs were advancing step by step together. Commercial companies, too, were chartered in the seventeenth century and accorded monopolies to develop French commerce with the East Indies, Canada, the Baltic, and the West Indies. Though many of these government-supported enterprises failed, sentiment grew among royal administrators that the state by regulation and encouragement could correct all that was wrong in the economy and create all that was needed.

The activity of the royal administration became more extensive in other ways. Richelieu began to build a navy. The peacetime army of a few regiments increased to 10,000 men by Henry IV and grew under Richelieu to a wartime force of 147,000. Military affairs became so voluminous as to require the specialized attention of a secretary of state for war. Royal judges continued to encroach on the jurisdiction of the manorial lord by claiming that certain classes of cases were royal cases (counterfeiting or crime on the highway, for instance), or by taking hold of a case before the agent of a manorial lord had seized it. They also progressively narrowed the jurisdiction of the ecclesiastical courts, for example by bringing clergymen under royal judges in non-spiritual cases. Unification of the law was promoted when the Parlement of Paris began to apply the local customary law of Paris in cases where other local customs were silent, and when two great ordinances (1499, 1539) prescribed the uniform procedure to be followed in all criminal cases throughout the realm.

As the volume of business considered by the royal government grew, the council of the king was transformed. At the beginning of the sixteenth century, it was a single organism, endowed with a universal competence. In time, it divided into specialized sections, which acquired a degree of independent action but continued to form, in theory, the parts of a single whole. By the beginning of the seventeenth century, there were four councils: the Conseil d'en Haut (High Council), composed of five or six intimates and leading men with whom the king daily conversed about the general affairs and policy of the realm; the Conseil d'Etat (Council of State) which met four days a week to consider administrative business, particularly the general supervision of finance; the Conseil des Parties (Council of Disputes), of the same membership as the Conseil d'État but meeting only twice weekly to settle high level judicial controversies, especially those between privileged persons; and the Conseil des Finances, assembling once a week, to check rather closely the operations of the fiscal bureaucracy. At the beginning of the sixteenth century, four clerks called *secrétaires d'état* put in good form and dispatched the council's decisions. As business increased, these secretaries of state each acquired a staff of clerks and began to specialize. By 1600 there was a secretary of state for war and a secretary of state for foreign affairs, men who were masters of their specialty, who headed bureaus and expedited orders, and who needed but little to become ministers of state. About the middle of the sixteenth century the king began to send out special, temporary commissioners to check on the éxecution of his orders by the *baillis,* royal treasurers, and justices who had purchased or inherited their office and were escaping royal control. Originally, these commissioners, called intendants, were trouble-shooting investigators dispatched to clear up a situation in a difficult *généralité.* They were equipped only with resolution, cunning, a thick skin, and a bit of royal parchment, and they were expected to check, spur, and supplement the existing officials and then return. But these emissaries proved so ruthless and so effective in enforcing the royal will that they were sent out again, and again. By 1661 there was an intendant in nearly every *généralité,* a certain number resided permanently at their posts, and, instead of supplementing the *bailli* and treasurer, they were supplanting them in the trial of cases and the assessment and collection of taxes.

As the kings were putting together a kingdom, building it up beneath them in the forms of an army, navy, bureaucracy, mercantilistic system, a splendid court, a staff of middle-class administrative technicians, a diplomatic corps, they became more impatient with people who were not wholly on their side. They were less and less inclined to listen to groups which might wish to discuss and delay the execution of their acts. The kings were allowing the Estates-General to perish from inactivity. It was summoned only five times, 1560, 1576, 1588, 1593, and 1614, and met vainly each time for only six weeks to three months. The Parlement of Paris, which claimed the right of refusing to register a royal decree and then of submitting only by the king's express command, was increasingly browbeaten by capable rulers such as Henry IV or Richelieu. The quinquennial Assembly of the Clergy was directed more and more by royal agents. Indeed, the French Catholic church, which was losing the right to try its own members and to be immune from taxes, also was losing to the king the right to chose its own chiefs. Francis I had gained by his Concordat of 1516 with the pope the right to appoint the archbishops, bishops, and abbots. The French Catholic church was thus settling down under the royal will. Meanwhile, the danger from the Protestant side, that the French Huguenots might form a state within a state, was reduced when Richelieu in 1625 took away their fortified towns. Richelieu also deprived Burgundy, Dauphiny, and Provence of their provincial estates, while carefully restricting the activity of those of Normandy, Brittany, and Languedoc. He began even to intervene in the selection of town officials. Amid the disorder and turmoil of civil discord and foreign war there were forming, almost imperceptibly, the institutions and power of an administrative monarchy.

The Administrative Monarchy of Louis XIV

A great institution does not begin at a definite moment. It comes into being slowly, from many sources, long before it is recognized. It "emerges rather than being born, and what is meant by emergence is the process by which during a given period its outlines become visible at all, like a whale coming to the surface of the sea."[1] The great Leviathan, the French administrative monarchy, had long been in the making. It emerged in the reign of Louis XIV and was given a distinctive individuality by that monarch.

Louis XIV, who was born in 1638 and came to the throne at the age of five, had the longest reign in modern history, from 1643 to 1715. His youth of relative idleness and play deceived many observers, but the do-nothing boy did not become, as many expected, a do-nothing king. When Cardinal Mazarin died in 1661, Louis began to govern as firmly and maturely as though he had never done nothing else. Universally considered to be handsome, Louis was at once charming, serious, polite, calm, and irresistibly gracious. Mme de Motteville described him as he appeared to her in 1661: "He was agreeable personally, civil, and easy of approach to all; but with a lofty and serious air which impressed everyone with respect and awe and prevented even his confidential advisers from forgetting his position when they engaged in private conversation with him." His courtesy, at once natural and measured, was

a masterpiece in itself and a method of government. It was charming, it was also useful. Everybody knows that 'he never passed the humblest woman without raising his hat, even to waiting-women, I say, and whom he knew to be such . . . To ladies he lifted his hat right off his head, but from a greater or lesser distance; to men of title he half lifted it, and held it up, or over his ear, for a few moments, more or less markedly: to

[1]Carl Friedrich, *The Age of the Baroque, 1610-1660*, p. 1.

gentlemen — who were really such — he contented himself with raising his hand to his hat. He took it off to the Princes of Blood just as he did to ladies.' His words, like his salutations, were measured, graduated according to the quality of the persons to whom they were addressed. He spoke little, and gravely, saying what it was necessary to say, and to the person to whom it was proper to say it . . . 'No man [indeed] ever sold his words, his smiles, and his glances to better advantage.'[2]

He was a certain kind of artist, we must remember, laboring always on his own pedestal, which he himself did so much to construct. He was not brilliant, but "he was judicious, thoughtful, hard-working, practical, master of himself."[3] He had a natural sense of justice and order and abhorred the world of improvisation of his father and grandfather, Louis XIII and Henry IV. Haunted by memories of the rebellion of the nobles and of Paris during his minority, he maneuvered endlessly to secure ever great obedience. Passionately devoted to his calling (to be the monarch was in his words "a great, noble, delightful" thing) and animated by dreams of glory, he worked steadily, regularly, unfailingly for fifty-four years at the creation of a glorious reign.

Louis XIV continued to do what Capetian monarchs had been doing since 987 — to insinuate and assert royal authority through and over the French community and to continue to develop royal administrative institutions, while leaving the social arrangements among the classes largely undisturbed. Louis continued and greatly enlarged the court. As late as the reign of Louis XIII, there had still been great nobles who lived in the provinces, surrounded by serving men, soldiers, and other retainers, and brooding on rebellion. Louis XIV attracted these nobles to court. He amused them with a constant round of festivities and showered them with favors — pensions, dowries, lands confiscated from others, lucrative ecclesiastical posts. To accommodate them he built the great palace and grounds of Versailles, to the west of Paris.

After 1682, Louis resided at Versailles with the princes and princesses of his family, many nobles of his realm, and his ministers, his life governed by a perpetual and resplendent ceremonial. His ceremonial included regular hours of work in his study. Having a few original ideas himself, he liked to hear those of others. He liked to sit in the great chair in his study, listen to his ministers talk well, talk well himself, assemble the pertinent information, consider all the angles, then gather the opinions of those present and render a measured decision, usually according to the majority of votes. In the course of these daily discussions, Louis and his ministers took the indefinite, confused administrative institutions which they had inherited and gradually ordered

[2] Jacques Boulenger, *The Seventeenth Century*, p. 176.
[3] *Ibid.*, p. 177.

them for smoother and more efficient operation. Through the preceding decades the secretaries of state had been tending toward specialization, the Council toward sub-division and regularity, and the intendants toward residence and omnipotence. Louis accentuated these tendencies and made them explicit. By 1669 he had appointed an administrator for each aspect of government: a chancellor for justice; a controller-general to take care of finances, and also agriculture, commerce, industries, and the colonies; a secretary of state for war; one for foreign affairs; another for the household of the king, which illogically included the Catholic church and the navy; and a fourth, for the Huguenot "reformed religion."

Louis consulted these officials regularly in four councils which together canvassed all questions relating to the state. On Sundays, Wednesdays, Thursdays, and alternate Mondays he met with the Conseil d'en Haut, consisting of his closest and most important advisers. Together they went over the broad perspectives of general policy. On alternate Mondays he met with the Conseil des Dépêches (Council of Dispatches), composed of the secretaries of state. Here questions of administration were considered. On Tuesdays and Saturdays it was the turn of the Conseil des Finances. It customarily included the controller-general as well as two assistants and the king, and dealt with fiscal matters, such as taxation and tariffs. Over the fourth council, the Conseil des Parties, which heard appeals from the royal courts, the chancellor usually presided.

From the discussion of these councils would emerge Louis' choices. For Louis reigned. The apex of the whole administrative structure, including the vast groundwork at its base, was his royal eye and his royal will. His decisions would be formulated into orders and ordinances and transmitted to outlying subordinate officials. No type of official was abolished. The old hierarchies of judges (manorial lord, *prévôt, bailli*, and parlement) and of fiscal officers (amateur parish assessor, collector of taxes for the *élection*, collector general for the *généralité*) were retained. But an intendant was now settled in the capital of each *généralité* to (in the words of the royal instructions) "watch over the enforcement of edicts, the administration of civil and criminal justice and economic legislation, and in general over all the affairs concerning the well-being and repose of our subjects." The intendant was further charged to keep an eye on "all those whose dignity, office, or fortune assured them a personal influence, which they might abuse: the ecclesiastics, the nobles, the royal officers. He was to seek out abuses which were being committed...and propose the remedy."[4] He was to watch the parlement, preside if he wished over lesser courts, attract cases to himself and decide them; verify the

[4]George Pagès, *La Monarchie d' ancien regime en France*, p. 161.

accounts of the collectors of taxes, correct the distribution of taxes among parishes and individuals, and issue fiscal regulations; serve as inspector of manufactures with power to regulate industry; direct the levy and victualling of troops and provide for the payment of garrisons; deliver an opening address to the provincial estates (where these existed), propose the amount of money they should grant, and manage and menace them until he got it; appoint the mayors and other officials of the town and village communities, verify their accounts, approve their expenditures, and liquidate their debts. The intendant, in brief, was the king in the *généralité*. To aid him in the performance of his duties, he could depute his powers to sub-intendants, each one responsible for a group of parishes. The sub-intendant brought the royal authority right into the parish and into the life of each individual. The sub-intendant assessed the taxes, regulated the commerce in grain, and in effect selected the town and village officials. No town or village could spend any money or make any repair to its church or roads without the authorization of the intendant, upon the recommendation of the sub-intendant. As the sub-intendants corresponded with the intendant and often referred problems to him for decision, and the intendants corresponded with the controller-general and the relevant secretaries of state and often referred to them for decision, nearly all the business of the kingdom was supervised from Versailles and all important decisions (and many that were unimportant) came before the king for his signature. The king, through his administrators, was looking and reaching down to the social foundations of his kingdom. As his reach was extended, his grasp was strengthened.

His administration was far-flung, and reasonably efficient for its time. Louis had inherited from Cardinal Mazarin several able organizers and administrators of bourgeois origin: Michel Letellier and his son François Louvois in military affairs, Hugues de Lionne in foreign affairs, and Jean-Baptiste Colbert in finance, the navy, and economic life. Their action was regular and incessant, and they tried to settle matters as they came along. Their achievements, besides the elaboration of an administration, were chiefly in the fields of finance, economic legislation, law, and the army and navy.

The finances of the French government in 1661, after twenty-five years of war, were in confusion, and the treasury was on the verge of bankruptcy. Colbert, who was controller-general and one of the most successful administrators in history, introduced regular accounting methods, checked fraud, and in six years doubled the revenue available to the king without greatly increasing the tax burden on the people.[b] A practical opportunistic statesman, Colbert shared the economic notions that had been developed

[b]From 1661 to 1667 Colbert increased the gross revenue from 85 to 95 million *livres* and the net revenue available to the king (after subtracting the expenses of collection) from 31 to 63 million *livres*.

during the sixteenth and early seventeenth centuries. He believed that any additional increase in revenue must come from an increase in the amount of gold and silver circulating in France. With this belief was another: that the state might intervene in the economy to attract specie from abroad and to promote its free, internal circulation. With these purposes in mind, he brought together and amplified the scattered economic measures of his predecessors. He regulated very carefully the quality of the products of the great exporting industries, such as woolen cloth, silk, linen, stockings, and paper, that they might capture foreign markets. He encouraged new industries, which would either produce for export thus bringing in bullion, or free France from dependence on foreign sources of supply, thus preventing a drain. For this purpose, manufacturers of fine glassware (formerly bought from Venice) and of fine lace (formerly purchased from the Netherlands), for example, were granted special privileges. The state would accord them interest-free loans for the first establishment, or give them shops, or at least pay for the first machinery. Their workers would be exempted from the *taille* and from service in the militia. The new industries were protected by import tariffs, which were then considered high. Colonies were fostered in order to supply raw materials and a market for French industry. Commercial companies were again chartered for the East Indies, the West Indies, the Baltic, and the Levant to encourage French overseas commerce. A navy of considerable size was constructed to protect French commerce and to damage that of its rivals.

Colbert's vision of things to explore and to accomplish led him from one activity to another, from finance to economic legislation to the navy and eventually to the codification of segments of French law. Under his supervision codes of civil procedure (1667), criminal procedure (1670), commerce (1673), and maritime law (1681) were prepared by a committee of jurists. The code for criminal procedure, in accord with French and continental custom generally, denied the accused many safeguards that he enjoyed in England. Permission to have counsel, to abstain from self-incrimination, to confront and cross-examine witnesses, to have a jury trial, all were denied the accused, while torture was retained.

Meanwhile, Louvois, secretary of state for war and the great rival of Colbert, created for Louis an army of 280,000 men, the most powerful and best organized in Europe, suitable to conquer territory abroad or to subdue rebellion at home.

Compared with the other elements of government in the kingdom, Louis and his administration by 1685 were overwhelmingly powerful both in theory and in circumstances. The people and Louis believed that by feudal law he was owner of France and was free to manage his domain as he chose; that by Roman law sovereignty resided in the king alone and his will had the force of law; and that by the theory of Divine Right the king, "the earthly image of

God's majesty," received his authority from God. "If in the Chapel of Versailles, the courtiers turned their backs on the altar when the King appeared, there was at least a shadow of excuse for their undeniable servility: they were bowing, not merely to the power of the flesh, but to the vicar of God."[5] The king, in brief, was the sole earthly source of all authority in France, and everything had to be done in his name. Louis and the royal administration exercised his authority unhampered, on the whole, by a formal check. Although usually people were accused and tried by normal legal procedure, Louis as sole dispenser of justice might (and occasionally did) imprison anyone he chose for any length of time without trial.[c] No central representative assembly ever met to discuss or challenge the actions of the king or his agents. The old medieval assembly – the Estates-General – had not met since 1614 and was now a historical memory. The local provincial estates and the towns and the villages were kept in leading strings. The Parlement of Paris objected in 1665 to one of the king's edicts, but after being rebuked, it never objected to Louis again.

Nor was Louis greatly bothered by the leading classes of the kingdom. In the course of his daily conversations, he gradually had tamed them. They were now held to obedience by fear and even more by hope. The Catholic clergy, to be sure, were carefully excluded from positions of power in the civil administration where they might become dangerous. But they were allowed to retain their collective landed property, the tithe, the right to trial in ecclesiastical courts in spiritual cases not involving a layman, the practice of holding an assembly every five years, and the freedom from taxes upon payment of a "voluntary" gift that was never proportionate to their wealth. They were expected to think of the king as the earthly image of God's majesty and as the eldest son and protector of the church – a protector who would take measures against the Huguenots heretics. The archbishops, bishops, and abbots, dependent on the king for appointment and advancement, were

---

[5] Albert Guerard, *The Life and Death of an Ideal: France in the Classical Age*, pp. 151-152.

[c] The story is told of how Louis XIV brought to trial Fouquet, a finance minister who probably had embezzled government funds while Louis was still under the guidance of Mazarin. Fouquet was very popular in Paris, and Louis could not find a court that would not acquit him. So Louis interfered in the normal course of justice and appointed a special commission to try Fouquet. In the course of the trial, it became apparent that even the commission would acquit Fouquet. So in the midst of the trial, Louis dismissed some of the commissioners and appointed others who might be more subservient. But even this commission only condemned Fouquet to perpetual banishment from France. Louis stepped in, condemned Fouquet to perpetual imprisonment in France and banished some of the judges. The significant aspect of the affair was that no one was astonished – everyone took it as a matter of course that the king had the right to exercise this power of justice as he chose, arbitrarily if he wished.

encouraged to look to him for lucrative favors, a pleasant word, a smile, a glance.

The nobility likewise were prudently excluded from high administrative position (the Duc de Beauvilliers, son-in-law of Colbert, was the only gentleman ever admitted to the council), while in the army they were forced to compete with the commoners for officer commissions. At the beginning of the reign they had been intimidated by an initial display of royal power. A special commission of the Parlement of Paris had been set up in 1665 in Auvergne to repress "the murders, abductions, rapes, robberies, and extortions" perpetrated by robber knights. The commission did good and prompt justice: it tried and executed marquises, counts, viscounts for crimes they had committed — thirty to fifty condemnations a day. Most of the guilty were executed in effigy, since they had fled, but what examples were made repressed the audacity of the powerful, and no one (except the Chevalier de Rohan) dared to conspire against Louis. At the same time, Louis left the nobles their titles, their right to wear swords, their exemption from the *taille*, their manorial justice, and their manorial dues. He reminded them that as first gentleman of France, he was one of them. If they attended Versailles, he flattered them with a glance, a word, a smile, and gave them gifts, pensions, dowries, ecclesiastical preferments for their younger sons, and empty but impressive duties at court.

The bourgeoisie were not inclined to rebel against a king who brought internal order and encouragement to commerce and industry. Also, just as Louis bound the nobles to him by gifts and flattery, so he bound the bourgeoisie by the offering of offices. He employed them in the law courts and administration right down the line. Bourgeois administrators, being of lowly origin and owing their lofty positions entirely to him, were less likely than clergyman and nobles to become independent and rebellious.

The great administrator and financier who made the splendor of the reign possible, Colbert, was a bourgeois, a tradesman's son. Louvois, who drilled and equipped the armies (and was only too eager to have them put to use), was the son of Le Tellier, a bourgeois. Vauban, who girdled the realm with fortresses which are classical masterpieces, was a country squire, the descendant of a provincial lawyer. Bossuet, favorite preacher, tutor of the king's son, theorist of monarchy by divine right, mouthpiece of the Gallican clergy, was a bourgeois.[6]

Louis also attracted to his service poets, playwrights, painters, sculptors, and architects, who were often of bourgeois origin. "Boileau, the lawgiver of

[6] Albert Guerard, *France: A Short History*, p. 143.

Parnassus, to whom the king himself gracefully bowed in matters of literary taste, was the quintessence of the bourgeois spirit. Louis treated the bourgeois Racine as a friend. He upheld the bourgeois Molière even in his pitiless satires against vapid courtiers, and in his attacks on religious hypocrites."[7] Louis founded or took under government direction several cultural organizations: the Académie française (for language and literature) the Académie des sciences, the Académie de peinture et de sculpture, and the Académie d'architecture. These were to direct taste and thought along classical lines of dignity and restraint, to the glorification of the state. An author who deviated from this line or was critical of the government was silenced. Books had to be read and approved by a royal censor before they would be printed. With the leading classes (clergy, nobility, bourgeoisie, and intellectuals) in train behind him, Louis felt he could ignore the artisans and peasants.

Louis XIV's administrative and social policy was a consummation of eight centuries of French history. Since Hugh Capet, the nagging, perennial, and often overwhelming problem of French kings had been to get themselves obeyed. Louis, through the smooth employment and extension of the practices of his predecessors, had become the first king in French history not to face a serious armed rebellion.

Yet his reign lasted too long for his glory. There were always serious shortcomings to his character and his accomplishment, and as the reign progressed these became more apparent. Perhaps the chief weakness of this king, so courteous, graceful, and dignified and so industrious, was his vanity. For this perhaps, he was not to be blamed. From childhood he had been surrounded by flatterers telling him how intelligent he was, how excellent was his judgment. With only a few advisers, such as Colbert, daring to be direct and frank in speech, Louis's vanity grew throughout the reign until it finally became outrageous and caused errors of policy. He came to feel that "no one even approached him in military talents, in plans and enterprises, in government" (Saint-Simon), and that no will was needed except his own. As the brilliant servitors of his early years died (Lionne in 1671, Colbert in 1683, and Louvois in 1691), he replaced them with men of lesser ability.

Carried away by his dream of glory and his vanity, Louis made several mistakes. In 1685 he revoked the Edict of Nantes, which had granted religious toleration to the Huguenots. There were then only a million Huguenots in France — that is, about one in twenty Frenchmen. The bulk of them were loyal subjects, the very kind of subjects Louis needed. By and large, they were doing Louis more good than harm. On the whole they were industrious, frugal, and enterprising. Excluded in fact, but not in law, from government positions, they had forged ahead in commerce, industry, and the professions.

[7]*Ibid.*, pp. 143-144.

However, they often were regarded with suspicion, envy, and hostility by the Catholic laity, while the French Catholic clergy had never accepted the Edict of Nantes as permanent. Eventually the Catholics around Louis persuaded him that it would redound to his temporal glory and eternal salvation to make France unitary in faith once more. The document revoking the edict, signed by the King on October 18, ordered the demolition of all Huguenot churches, the stoppage of all Huguenot services, and the closure of all Huguenot schools. It required Catholic rebaptism of those baptised in the Huguenot faith. Huguenot laity caught attending Huguenot services were sent to the galleys, Huguenot ministers caught conducting services were executed. Over 200,000 Huguenots, it is estimated, renounced their country rather than deny their faith. They fled to England, Holland, Brandenburg, and other countries, taking their talents with them and their hard-earned money. In their new homes they built up new industries — paper, glass, silk, cotton prints, linen, woolens, playing cards — that competed with those of France. Many Huguenots who remained in France continued to worship secretly.

The economic losses which went with the revocation were aggravated by war. Louis was led by his desire for glory to dream of dominating Europe. Colbert was able to finance the first two wars, of Devolution (1667-1668) and against Holland (1672-1678), largely from current revenue. The last two wars, of the League of Augsburg (1689-1697) and of the Spanish Succession (1701-1714), however, were fought against the rest of western Europe and engaged the royal government in expenditures hitherto without parallel in European history. Although war spurred iron production, for munitions especially, it brought near-ruin to many textile areas. To the horrors of invasion and war were added those of famine in 1693, 1694, and 1709. France became, in the words of the good archbishop Fénélon, "a vast, desolate hospital without provisions." Local uprisings of peasants and artisans against heavy taxes had occurred sporadically throughout Louis' reign; now they began happening by the month and had to be suppressed with troops. Government deficits rose frighteningly. In 1706 expenses were 196 million livres, net revenue only 53 millions; in other words, for every four livres spent, one came in. By 1715 the government debt had reached 3,000,000,000 livres, an enormous sum for those days. The colossal baroque proportions of the palace at Versailles were matched by the equally baroque figures in the royal ledgers. All made up a whole, and a rather shaky whole by now, despite its magnificence.

Part of the trouble was that Louis' power was not yet absolute. He had perpetuated in the interests of assuring obedience too many bargains, contracts, and understandings with the localities, provinces, and leading classes to be able to mobilize France completely and effectively for peace or for war. He had, to be sure, sunk the groundwork of the centralized administration into every parish. He thus was able to draw on resources of manpower (his later armies totaled 400,000 men) and revenue his predecessors had never tapped. Also, the pressure of the royal administration for uniformity was moderating differences among towns and provinces and promoting the fusion of Frenchmen into a single nation. But weights and measures were still diverse. The procedure used in civil and criminal cases had been codified, but one still changed the substantive law applied in deciding a case as one changed post horses — every twenty miles. Tolls and provincial tariffs had been largely cleared out in the northern third of France but remained elsewhere. Tolls and diversity in weights, measures, and laws clogged the free movement of trade. The provinces with provincial estates still paid a much lighter *taille* than did the others. The property of the church (despite the "voluntary" gift) and of the nobility still largely escaped taxation. Those who had the least, the peasants, still paid the most. The division of the population into privileged and non-privileged and the incitement of envy and emulation among the privileged tended to separate Frenchmen rather than to draw them together. Both in its achievement and in its difficulties, the administrative monarchy of Louis XIV was a continuation of the previous eight centuries of French history.

The Deterioration of the Administrative Monarchy Under Louis XV

In the reign of Louis XIV's successor, Louis XV (1715-1774), the difficulties of the French royal government continued, without the steady drive of a Louis XIV to overcome them. At his accession Louis XV was a child of five. Since he was young, others had to govern for him, first his great-uncles, the Duke of Orleans (1715-1723) and the Duke of Bourbon (1723-1726), and then his tutor, Cardinal Fleury (1726-1743). The Duke of Orleans, as regent, tried the experiment of governing with the aristocracy. He set up a system of six administrative councils for war, navy, finance, royal household, foreign affairs, and religion, composed each of ten members, five of them nobles and five, bureaucrats. The nobles, though, were too ignorant, frivolous, and inattentive for the system to work. By 1718 the Duke's experiment had failed. The councils were suppressed, and the regent returned to government by heads of departments. These heads included, as under Louis XIV, the chancellor, the controller-general, the keeper of the seals, and the secretaries of state for war, navy, foreign affairs, and the royal household. As long as the Duke of Orleans and, later, Cardinal Fleury were there to coordinate the work of these chief ministers and to pursue a foreign policy of peace, the administration worked not too badly and the country recovered from the devastating wars of Louis XIV.

Upon the death of Fleury in 1743, however, Louis XV proclaimed himself his own prime minister. He did not serve himself successfully. The cause of his failure lay in the depths of his personality. He was intelligent and perceptive, but he was also timid and bored. He sought relief from boredom in hunting and in women. He lacked a persevering administrative will and simply did not do the endless reading of reports, conferring, and coordinating that Louis XIV's system required. The chief ministers went their own way, independently administering their own departments and maneuvering, thrusting, parrying, and feinting against each other. Major decisions in diplomacy, war, reform, and personnel — the whole deadly power game — became the sport of court factions, the royal confessor, and the royal mistresses. At the very center of the monarchy there was a void of authority.

In this situation, the nobles, whom Louis XIV had barred from positions of influence, invaded the government. We must remember there were two types of nobility, the nobility of the sword and the nobility of the robe. The nobility of the sword, comprising dukes, counts, and barons, was in turn divided into the great nobles, who were usually in attendance upon the king at Versailles, and the provincial nobles, who lived on their estates. The nobility of the robe were magistrates who had purchased, or inherited from ancestors who had purchased, the office of judge on one of the high courts of the kingdom, the Parlement of Paris or one of the provincial parlements. Through the manipulation of court intrigue, the great nobles of the sword and the nobles of the robe now secured their appointment to nearly all the best offices at the disposal of the royal government. The archbishoprics, bishoprics, and abbacies in the French Catholic church became havens for the younger sons of the nobility of the sword. They lived luxuriously on annual incomes of 40,000, 80,000 or 100,000 livres, while parish priests made do on a pittance of 300 livres. In the army of Louis XIV, the nobles had been forced to vie with commoners for commissions. But on December 25, 1718, the aristocratic council of war made it a rule of service that officer commissions were reserved for nobles, when such were available. To be sure, the temporary enlargement of the army during the wars of the Polish Succession (1733-1736) and the Austrian Succession (1740-1748) and of the Seven Years' War (1756-1763) forced the government to appoint commoners as officers, but with peace these were always the first to be dismissed. In the navy the same policy prevailed — the officers in command of the ships were nobles. The chief ministers of the administrative departments, with perhaps two exceptions, were drawn from the nobility of the sword or of the robe. The ambassadors, as might be expected, were nobles. The blunders of ministers of foreign affairs, ambassadors, and generals, who owed their positions to court favor rather than to ability, wasted the resources of France in the War of Austrian Succession and the Seven Years' War and lost her a colonial empire.

Meanwhile, the nobility of the robe, whom Louis XIV had silenced in the Parlement of Paris and the provincial parlements, recovered their voices. Primarily law courts, the parlements yet claimed political functions. Having a parlement register a royal decree was the normal method of promulgating a law. On occasion, a parlement would refuse to register a decree and would publish detailed remonstrances against it. The king could then compel registration by attending a session of parlement in person. During the reign of Louis XV, king and parlement quarreled frequently over ecclesiastical and fiscal decrees. In a running religious-political debate that went on for decades and involved the entire French community in its bitterness, the Parlement of Paris took the part of the Gallican defenders of the independence of the French Catholic church and of a Catholic sect known as Jansenists, on the one hand, while the king usually sided with the pope and the Jesuits on the other. Louis XV, timid, irresolute, and fundamentally indifferent ("No matter, things as they are will last as long as I do"), alternated between severity and pardon, repeatedly exiled the magistrates and then recalled them, and in the process showed that he could not make himself obeyed. Occasion by occasion, the parlements grew bolder. Growing hostile to absolutism, they developed the theory of a constitutional monarchy tempered by intermediary bodies such as themselves. Every kingdom, they argued, has fundamental laws; in France, in the absence of the Estates-General, the repositories, interpreters, and rightful defenders of the fundamental laws were the parlements; in the performance of their duty they might legitimately defy the king. They thus posed as the defenders of the nation against an arbitrary (law-less) monarchy and to the people gave an example of resistance. A climax of the quarrel came in 1762, when the Parlement of Paris expelled the Jesuits from France over the ineffectual opposition of Louis himself.

Not all royal administrators during this reign were inept nobles. In fact, several controllers-general and secretaries of state for war and the navy and their often able subordinates struggled intelligently and manfully to give France a sound administration. Simply from day-to-day consideration of administrative problems, they became aware of the perplexing difficulties of French government and society, and they proposed reforms. Occasionally, the idea for the reform came from outside the administration, but usually it arose inside, among the administrators themselves. If the reform did not challenge the security of a vested interest, it was sometimes, though not always, enacted. Thus varying the value of the coinage had for centuries been an annoying aspect of royal fiscality. In 1726 the controller-general fixed the value of the coinage at a rate that lasted until 1785. The stability of the coinage was one of the main factors in French commercial prosperity during the eighteenth century. French roads had suffered from neglect since Roman days and perhaps reached their lowest level of degradation in the seventeenth century. In 1747, the controller-general created in his department the great technical Corps of Bridges and Highways. Under the supervision of its engineers, peasant workmen build a network of fine roads, radiating from Paris and unsurpassed in Europe. At the same time the Bureau of Commerce, also in the controllers-general's department, gradually abolished or eased the enforcement of the more stringent mercantilistic regulations of industry.

When, however, the proposed reform threatened a vested interest, it was almost always blocked. Traffic still had to fight its way through a thicket of internal tariffs, tolls, and transit dues. Throughout the reign reforming officials prepared plans to unify France into a single customs unit. Each time they were thwarted by the provinces, cities, and tax farmers, in short by those who collected the internal dues and profited. Intermittently, the royal council discussed the abolition of the parlements and the total reorganization of the courts of law, only to draw back before the formidable antagonism of the members of the parlements. However, toward the end of his reign Louis asserted himself. In 1770 his keeper of the seals, Rene de Maupeou, abolished the Parlement of Paris and set up new courts of appeal. He then proposed a fundamental reform of the whole judicial system of France. He would unify and codify laws, reform the barbarous procedure, and reduce the number of intercessory jurisdictions. However, Louis XV died in 1774 before Maupeou could realize his plans, and Louis XVI (1774-1793) undid his achievement by recalling the Parlement of Paris and abolishing the new courts. Failure also dogged the successive controllers-general who sought to tax the wealth of privileged individuals and groups in French society. The key struggle occurred when in 1749 Jean-Baptiste Machault, a determined and able controller-general, persuaded the king to decree a tax of 5 per cent on the income of everyone, without exception. Opposition immediately appeared. The Parlement of Paris, always an opponent to fiscal reform, registered the decree only under compulsion. The provincial estates of Languedoc and Brittany resisted the tax. Each estates offered, as in the past, to subscribe a lump sun that it would apportion and collect. The French Catholic clergy, too, offered as before to pay a small lump sum that bore little relation to its taxable wealth. The nobles, in their tax declarations, dissimulated the size of their income. After two or three years of conflict, Louis, influenced by his confessor, his queen, and the pious factions at court, gave way. He accepted the subscriptions of the provincial estates and the clergy and transferred Machault to the ministry of the navy. After that the French monarchy, without firm leadership, still unable to tax much of the wealth of the country and involved in the ruinous Seven Years' War, drifted toward bankruptcy.

While the French monarchy coasted and inwardly deteriorated, and Louis XV was becoming the prisoner of his nobility, the rest of France was changing in a complex and uneven development. The population of France, like that of other European countries, steadily increased throughout the eighteenth century. Starting at 18 to 19 million in 1715, it rose to 22 million by mid-century and to 25 million by 1789. France's population was larger than that of any other European country, including Russia. The years 1733 to 1774 were also a period of gradually rising prices and, perhaps as a result, of commercial and industrial expansion. Colonial trade increased from 40 million livres a year in 1716 to 204 in 1756, and overseas commerce nearly quintupled in value from 1715 to 1789. Large capitalistic enterprises, aided by state subsidies, were founded in coal mining and in the manufacture of paper, glass, iron, and textiles. There was money around, to be acquired by several kinds of resourceful men. There was money for the financiers and bankers, who made huge sums loaning funds to the king, collecting his indirect taxes, participating in war contracts, and speculating on the exchanges. There was money for the great merchants of the port towns of Marseille (trade with Levant), Bordeaux (the sugar islands of the West Indies), Lorient (India), and Nantes (the slave trade). There was money as well for the few industrial capitalists and the horde of lawyers. Money, and comfort, too, trickled down to energetic, independent master craftsmen: they ate and dressed better and even, perhaps, purchased a piano for their daughters. Acquisition of wealth implied social mobility. A family might start at the level of artisan and within one or two generations belong to the great merchants and financiers. It might then intermarry with the nobility or purchase the office of judge and belong to the nobility of the robe. Wealth also implied a sense of frustration. Proud of their achievements, conscious of their value as resourceful individuals, many townsmen resented their exclusion from the best positions at the disposal of the government and the social snubbing by the nobility.

However, not all groups were well off in this expanding economy. French population, it seems, increased faster than did agricultural and industrial productivity. The slowness of the French peasant to change his ways and the shortage of fertilizer owing to a deficiency of livestock pervented the increase of agricultural production. Similarly, the conservatism of French craftsmen, restrictive guild regulations, shortage of capital, and the limitation of the internal market by internal tariffs and by the absence of good transverse roads retarded technological and capitalistic innovation. The small-scale operation — a craftsman, his family, and perhaps a journey man or two — was still the rule in industry. The returns to most craftsmen and the journeymen helpers were meager and were obtained only after an extraordinary day of labor of twelve to fourteen hours. In each village there were well-to-do peasants, but the majority, bound to poverty by the laborious routines of a simple agriculture and burdened by the payment of dues to the seigneur, taxes to the king, and the tithe to the church, eked out a bare living. Some of them, to secure a little cash, devoted their spare time to cottage industry, thus depressing the wages of urban handicraftsmen still more. With the growth of population, the number of landless proletariat and unattached vagabonds and beggars increased. The rising townsmen had their grievances; the poor had their smoldering resentments, the journeymen against masters who paid too little and the peasants against seigneurs who were extortionate, royal tax-collectors who were becoming more exacting, and the upper clergy who frequently diverted to themselves tithes meant for the parish priests. It was hard for Frenchmen, cut off from each other by a social order based on privilege and by the self-regarding emotions of contempt, envy, and hatred, to have a sense of community. The situation invited proposals for reform.

An Invitation to Further Inquiry and Reflection

We might continue with an idea expressed earlier, that a civilization or a single nation's culture may be viewed as a system of interlocking behavior patterns (behavior being defined to include both action and attitude-ideas), expectations, and legitimizing values. For example, on the simplest terms, the sheriff of my county may send me a notice that I should appear on April 1 at the Superior Court Room, to serve as juror. He is performing a role, he has certain attitudes and ideas about his role, and he expects me to appear. I recognize the legitimacy of the summons, I do appear, I assume the role of being a juryman, I have certain attitudes and ideas toward the role, and I have certain expectations of the solicitor, the defense attorney, and the judge, whose roles interlock with mine; they in turn have certain expectations of me. Much of our life is spent in these interlocking role arrangements. An institution can be conceived as a collectivity of roles that are legitimized in the minds of participants by the common acceptance of certain values. In the institution of jury trial we all believe, for example, in the rule of law. And these roles, institutions, and values have emerged in time — the sheriff or shire-reeve, for instance, antedates William the Conqueror; the juror and many procedures of common law courts date from the twelfth and thirteenth centuries. Why do we behave as we do? Partly because of roles, role expectations, and values that are already prepared for us.

Role theory is especially useful in interpreting social, economic, and political history. The history of the development of the central government and administration of France from 1492 through Louis XIV can be viewed as the story of the invention, regularization, and routinization of roles and role expectations, of the monarchs developing new roles for themselves, for their officials, and for their other subjects, and of persuading their subjects to accept the legitimacy of the new administration and of its demands. What were some of these new roles or patterns of behavior? What were some of the roles that were being dissolved? In this context what is meant by "legitimacy"? What arguments and material means did Louis XIV use to secure recognition of the legitimacy of his authority and his action? Why, from 1661 to 1685, would the overwhelming majority of Frenchmen probably accept the legitimacy of his authority and extended action? What were the bases of loyalty? What were the foundations of social order?

Though the French monarchs have been portrayed, for the most part, as practical men solving practical problems and bieng little influenced by formal ideas, their action was yet permeated and sustained by value orientations they shared with their subjects. What were some of these deeper and persuasive value orientations in French society of the sixteenth and seventeenth centuries? Consider, for example, a single episode: the king makes a marquis a duke, and the entiry population accepts the validity of the action as a matter of course. What do we see in that episode? We see acceptance of the hierarchical arrangement of Frenhcmen by formal rank. The French were legally divided by estate into clergy, nobility, and the rest of the population, and the nobility were ranked by title — prince of blood, duke, marquis, count, baron, chevalier. We see acceptance of the king's authority to denominate men of rank. And more deeply, we note acceptance of the values of a competitive, invidious culture whose members, despite Christian preachments, sought place, distinction, and formal rank and rated each other in terms of hierarchical success. What other value orientations permeated French society of these two centuries and sustained and directed action?

For Further Reading

(For general reading):

M. Ashley, *Louis XIV and the Greatness of France* (Teach Yourself History Library, 1948)

Jacques Boulenger, *The Seventeenth Century* (1920)

A. L. Guerard, *The Life and Death of an Ideal: France in the Classical Age* (1928)

E. E. Reynolds, *Bossuet* (1963)

Cicely Wedgwood, *Richelieu and the French Monarchy* (Teach Yourself History Library, 1950)

John B. Wolf, *Louis XIV* (1968)

(For advanced study):

Robert Mandrou, *Introduction a la France moderne (1500-1640); Essai de psychologie historique* (1961)

R. Doucet, *Les Institutions de la France au XVI e siecle* (1948)

Gaston Zeller, *Les Institutions de la France au XVIe siecle* (1948)

John B. Wolf, "The Reign of Louis XIV: A selected Bibliography of writings since the war of 1914-1918," *Journal of Modern History*, 45 (1973), 277-291.

C. W. Cole, *Colbert and a century of French Mercantilism* (2 vols., 1939)

John B. Wolf, *The Emergence of the Great Powers* (1685-1715) (1951)

Alfred Cobban, *The History of Modern France*. Volume 1, *1715-1799* (1959)

Franklin Ford, *Robe and Sword: The Regrouping of the French Aristocracy after Louis XIV* (1953)

Ragnhild M. Hatton, "Louis XIV: Recent Gain in Historical Knowledge," *Journal of Modern History*, 45 (1973), 277-91.

Vivian Gruder, *The Royal Provincial Intendants: A Governing Elite in Eighteenth-Century France* (1968)
Elinor C. Barber, *The Bourgeoisie in 18th Century France* (1955)

Chapter IX
THE KING AND PARLIAMENT (1485-1714)

Tudor Government

For centuries the kings of England were at the center of English history. The government of the monarchy, in many respects, was a personal one, and the relations of the king to his councilors, judges, bishops, members of Parliament, and justices of the peace varied with his character and with the circumstances he was called upon to meet. Of course, this was also true of France: for centuries its kings had been the center of French political history and the government of the monarchy had been a personal one. But whereas France emerged from the turmoil of the sixteenth and seventeenth centuries with an administrative monarchy that became the model for all other continental European states, England came out of the crises of the same period with a parliamentary monarchy whose institutions acquired world-wide importance. To discover how this parliamentary monarchy came into being, we have to go back to the government of the Tudor dynasty in the sixteenth century.

The monarchs of the Tudor line who reigned the longest were Henry VII (1485-1509), Henry VIII (1509-1547), and Elizabeth I (1558-1603). Canny and skilful, they each established the masterful rule of a strong royal personality. The rules of English government then resembled the rules of conversation rather than those of bridge. The constitutional understandings concerning the sources, nature, and extent of an English king's power had never been precisely defined in any one place. The great Tudors accepted, as did their subjects, these understandings and basic governmental arrangements. They acted now through one organ of government, now through another, as the necessities of situations and the conventions of English constitutional custom seemed to require. Operating in accord with constitutional custom and popular consent, they greatly expanded the activity and authority of the royal government.

For the day-to-day conduct of business, the Tudors took over and rendered more efficient the Privy Council. They chose for privy councilors usually not the great barons, but the most able, most ambitious commoners. These men learned to be wary, vigilant, and single-minded in their devotion to the monarch and the task of government. In executing the king's orders, they engaged in a vast range of activity. They supervised the kingdom's defense, conducted diplomatic negotiations, prepared proclamations regulating trade and industry, censored the press, and watched over a thousand sundry details. They attempted to manage Parliament by influencing elections, by sitting as members of both houses, and by initiating and debating government bills. They were effective and ruthless in the performance of their duties.

The Tudors also went to work on the central courts. By 1485 the king's power to do justice had been delegated largely to the judges and courts of the common law — the King's Bench, Common Pleas, and Exchequer. These three courts, each composed of a chief justice and three associate judges, held sessions in London. At regular intervals the justices of the first two courts also traveled on circuit through the country. In the course of the twelfth, thirteenth, fourteenth, and fifteenth centuries, the judges of the common law, borrowing a little from canon law, from Roman law, from the king's instructions, and from early statutes, developed in the actual decision of cases methods of only with the consent of the Lords and Commons in Parliament. Once a statute had been made he might, under certain circumstances, dispense with its penalties in a particular case, but he could not violate it. The king must move within the rules of the common and statute law when these had spoken.

The Tudors continued the administration of the common law as they had inherited it. However, common law was defective or silent in some areas and did not always allow the Tudor kings to solve all the problems susceptible of legal attack and settlement. Where necessary, the Tudors expanded the exercise of the royal judicial power by intervening in situations through the Privy Council or by setting up "prerogative" courts. Petitions of frustrated suitors who could not find an appropriate remedy or substantial justice in the courts of the common law were referred to the chancellor, who would render a decision in the Court of Chancery in accord with the principles of equity. To hear complaints of poor men involving restitution of property, fulfillment of contracts, and non-payment of debts, a Court of Requests was created. For cases involving sea matters, like the loss of ships and goods, piracy, contraband, and prize, a Court of Admiralty was established. Most important, to bring to book disorderly nobles who overawed local juries, witnesses, sheriffs, and even judges, Henry VII set up in London a court of the Star Chamber. Dispensing with the forms of the common law (there was no jury and torture might be used to compel testimony) and free from local prejudices and fears, the Star Chamber imposed prompt judgment on disturbers of the peace. These new courts made for the more effective administration of justice. At the same time, the common law judges resented the growth of business in the new courts, not least because they were being deprived of fees from cases which might have been theirs. Quarrels arose between competing courts, which the Privy Council usually tried to settle.

The law had not only to be made and judged; it had to be administered daily in each county and hamlet. Here most useful to the Tudors was the commission of the peace, composed of the local justices of the peace. The typical justice was a country squire of some property and of good standing in the neighborhood. He was a volunteer, amateur, unpaid man-of-all-work. The justices of the peace were charged with the execution of stacks of statutes as well as the Privy Council's administrative orders. They were responsible for upkeep of roads, dispersal of rioters, drilling of the militia, collection of fines for non-attendance at church, licensing of alehouses, appointment of overseers for the poor, enforcement of laws relating to industry, and so on. The king of England, unlike the king of France, did not have salaried officials in the localities. Nor did he have a sizeable standing army. He could therefore do little without the willing consent to his rule on the part of the volunteer justices. Their loyalty was necessary, and the great Tudors were able to get it. For the local justices and many of their friends — stable, solid landowners — a stronger monarchy still meant a more peaceble, more stable realm.

On particularly important affairs the Tudors sometimes consulted Parliament. Henry VIII and Elizabeth, especially, were skilful in working Parliament into their scheme of government, in getting Parliament to do their business. Henry VIII, indeed, has been called the greatest English parliamentarian ever to be king. To be sure, he summoned Parliament no more frequently than the kings just before him, assembling only nine in a reign of thirty-eight years. And when he did it was often for the same familiar reason: to ask its consent to extra taxes. The country squires and the merchants in the House of Commons were getting richer as time went on. He used Parliament to tap their wealth.

But where Henry VIII went further, and differed from past kings, was in asking Parliament to participate in the abolition of papal authority in England. By contemporary constitutional theory, he did not have to involve Parliament in this revolutionary step. By constitutional custom, Parliament could not even discuss issues involving the king's discretionary power, or prerogative, unless he so asked. It might not discuss on its own initiative foreign affairs, defense, succession to the throne, regulation of trade, censorship of the press, and governance of the church. Indeed, Henry VIII might have abolished papal authority by royal proclamation. But he chose to do it through Parliament — by initiating bills and getting them passed as statutes. He thus sounded the opinion of the leading groups of the kingdom — the great lords, the country squires, and the merchants — and carried them along with him in his rash enterprise. Also, he assured that the abolition of papal authority would be written into statute law, which took precedence over proclamations, ordinances, and common law. Thus it was by statute that King Henry VIII in

Parliament abolished the payment of annates to the pope (1532), forbade the appeal to Rome of cases in ecclesiastical courts (1533), declared the king to be the supreme head of the church of England (1534), dissolved the monasteries and seized their property (1536, 1539), and ordered adherence to six articles of belief (1539). Also it was by statute that Henry's son, Edward VI, in Parliament prescribed the use of the Book of Common Prayer (1549, 1552), and that Henry's daughter, Elizabeth, declared the monarch to be supreme governor of ecclesiastical matters (1559) and restored the Book of Common Prayer (1559).

These measures greatly enlarged the power and importance of the Crown. Henry VIII and his successors were head of both state and church, an unprecedented position in English history. They still lacked the authority to ordain a pastor, but they might prescribe the government, beliefs, and ritual of the Anglican church. They could effectively intrude into the religion of their subjects in many ways. At the same time, the way the measures had been enacted, in co-operation with Parliament, greatly enhanced the importance of that body. For a number of years Henry VIII had gone to the Lords and Commons, especially the latter, on matters involving the church. He also had consulted them about the royal power to issue proclamations and about the succession to the throne. They expected to be consulted in the future. Conscious of their growing significance, the members of the House of Commons began to acquire an *esprit de corps* and to insist on certain privileges. Under Henry VIII, the Lords and Commons asserted the immunity of their members from arrest on a civil process while Parliament was in session. The Commons began to request and to receive permission to speak freely in the House, withour fear of royal retaliation, about the measures the king laid before them. In the course of a few years, this request and grant became one for an undefined "freedom of speech." After 1547 the House of Commons began to keep a journal of its proceedings in which these privileges could be recorded and which would form a basis for later demands.

The Developing Controversy: Elizabeth I, James I, and the Issues

During the reign of Elizabeth, members of the House of Commons began slowly to adopt an amibguous position in regard to the monarch. They extended their claims and began to dispute some of her measures. After Elizabeth, the two parties, Crowns and Commons, entered the field of contest at opposite ends. Under her successor, James I (1603-1625), they took each other's measure. Under James's son Charles (1625-1649), the quarrel flared into open rebellion and revolution.

We must remember that the conflict between the Crown and the House of

Commons involved different members of one national society, and *may* have been related to changes in the ordering of that society. England was then a relatively small unit, its population in 1620 of five million people being approximately one-third that of France. Its society was still predominantly rural, though less rural than the French. In seventeenth-century France approximately fourteen-fifteenths or 93 per cent of the population lived in rural villages; in seventeenth century England, approximately four-fifths or 81 per cent. English society was also hierarchical, with prescribed legal ranks forming, as it were, a stairway on which men were climbing or descending or staying where they were. In France there were the three legal estates, and within each estate there were legal gradations and social quarrels over precedence. From our distance, the English stairway looks a bit different. At the top in England there were about a hundred great noble families. They were peers of the realm; they sat in the House of Lords, and they bore titles such as the Duke of Norfolk, the Marquis of Salisbury, and the Earl of Chester. They were expected to spend much of their time in London attending Parliament, waiting on the king at Whitehall Palace, and possibly serving as royal ministers. When not occupied with political affairs at the capital, they sojourned on their magnificent estates, mainly occupied with hospitality and hunting. Just beneath the Lords were the country gentlemen, constituting in 1603 about .3 per cent of the population. These did not bear titles of nobility but they were of gentle birth. They had the right to wear swords and to demand duelling satisfaction of an earl and could show a coat of arms. They were landowners who lived on their estates, leasing a portion to tenant farmers and cultivating the rest with agricultural laborers. They were important men in the community, frequently serving as local justices of the peace. Interspersed among the estates of the country gentlemen were the lands of independent small farmers (yeomen) who were not of gentle birth. To be counted among them a man had to receive an income of at least 40 shillings a year from his own freehold land. Though a yeoman had no coat of arms and could not aspire to become a justice of the peace, he served on juries and took his place in the ranks of the militia. The yeoman composed perhaps 17 per cent of the population. The tenant farmers, who rented land from the country gentlemen, were at 14 per cent of the population a little less numerous than the yeoman. The landless agricultural laborers made up the most numerous group of all, comprising nearly half of the total population of the kingdom. In the towns there were two main groups: the well-to-do merchants, larger shopkeepers, and lawyers, equalling perhaps 1 per cent of the population, and the artisans, the wage-earners, and the poorer shopkeepers, constituting another 18 per cent. In this society people were moving vertically, up or down and also horizontally, from country to town or from town to country, through travel and through intermarriage. An energetic landless laborer might move to town, become an apprentice, then skip up several steps and die a merchant prince. Or — what was more common — a hard-working yeoman might become a country gentleman. At the same time, since by law of primogeniture the eldest son of peers and country gentlemen inherited the estate, the younger sons often entered trade. Marriage also intertwined the country gentlemen-merchant-yeoman groups and even on occasion the great noble families.

This social structure was related to the political organization. The peers, of course, sat in the House of Lords. But who sat in the House of Commons? In 1603 the counties sent 92 members and the listed boroughs about 400. In the counties the country gentlemen and yeomen, as owners of freehold land yielding 40 shillings a year, could vote. The yeomen of each county usually chose one of the local country gentlemen, who on election days courted them hat in hand. In the boroughs, the franchise was usually restricted to propertied people. The large cities, such as London, Bristol, and Plymouth, generally chose merchant princes, an alderman or the mayor, and lawyers. The smaller boroughs, however, generally selected a local country gentleman, the shopkeepers considering that their interests would win more attention if presented by a man of gentle birth. Out of about 500 members of the houses of Commons of the early seventeenth century, then, twenty-five or so would be merchants, aldermen, mayors, and lawyers, and the remaining 450 would be country gentlemen — "baronets," "knights," and "gentlemen" — representing the yeomen in the counties and the shopkeepers in the lesser towns. These country gentlemen were substantial men. They generally owned and supervised the management of landed property; most often they had been educated at Oxford, Cambridge, or the Inns of Court at London; they were leaders in their locality and served as justices of the peace; and they represented and were intertwined with the other substantial classes of the English community.

There is some evidence that during the sixteenth century and the first four decades of the seventeenth, there were shifts in relative economic power and social importance between the various social groups that may have had political repercussions. The period was one of rapid demographic and economic change. Between 1500 and 1620 the population of England and Wales, it is estimated, "nearly doubled, from between 2½ and 3 million to 5 million." London grew from a middle-sized town (60,000) into a European city (350,000). As a result of demographic growth and also of the influx of bullion from America "prices rose by between 400 per cent and 650 per cent from 1500 to 1640. Food prices (and therefore agricultural profits) soared, wages . . . lagged behind." Foreign trade expanded in sudden bursts, particularly from 1508 to 1551 [and from] 1603 to 1620."[1] So did credit

[1] Lawrence Stone, "Social Mobility in England, 1500-1700," *Past and Present*, No. 33 (April, 1966), 40, 42, 43.

and transport facilities and market activity within the country. Familes who were making money in an expanding economy wanted an education for their children. There was an educational boom in the lower schools as well as in the Inns of Court, which prepared for the law, and by 1640 over half the male population of London was literate. About three-fourths of the members of parliament and of the justices of the peace had attended Oxford, Cambridge, or the Inns of Court.

English society, partly in response to these changes, underwent a complicated and uneven development. At the upper levels there was a striking though temporary decline of the prestige of the peers, manifested in a diminution of tenant loyalty, gentry deference, and electoral obedience, with a consequent reduction of the influence of the House of Lords. At the same time the country gentlemen as a group were gaining in wealth, through acquisition of monastic lands, better management of their estates, and speculation in rising prices. In 1628, someone bragged that the country gentlemen in the Commons could buy out the Lords three times over. The merchants, too, and the members of the professions, including the lawyers, rose in wealth, numbers, and social ambition. On the other hand, the poor, the wage earners in town and country, hit by prices that rose faster than wages, were getting poorer. Both those who were rising and those who were falling were apt to be unhappy with the establishment of King, Court, and Courtiers. One economically rising group, the merchants, felt themselves denied social prestige, and resented the affront. Other advancing groups, the successful lawyers and the greater squires, felt themselves excluded from power by the Court, and also were resentful. Those nearest London were most discontented, since they were most aware of the opportunities that were being denied them; they often joined the cause of revolt and revolution. Those most distant, poor backwoods gentry of the west and north, not knowing what they were missing, were more apt to be loyal to Church and King. Of the declining groups, the wage-earners were in a state of abject misery which found intermittent relief in rioting and mob violence. It is plausible to assume, though it had not been proven, that these social discontents, which often had an economic root, found expression in the mounting quarrel between Crown and Commons over religious and political issues.

The quarrels between the Crown and Commons, which arose in Elizabeth's reign, at first concerned religious issues. At the time, the overwhelming majority of Englishmen were "simply and sincerely religious. They did not doubt that their souls were immortal or that Christ had died to redeem them." Neither did they doubt that "good government must be founded on true religion," as taught by a single established (state) church.[2] However,

---

[2] Cicely Wedgwood, *The King's Peace, 1637-1641*, p. 76.

individuals, while united in love of God and Christ, could differ bitterly about what doctrines this state church should follow, and how and by whom it should be governed. The Anglican Church Settlement of Elizabeth defined doctrines so broadly and ambiguously as to enable Lutherans, Zwinglians, and Calvinists, indeed all Christians save Roman Catholics and extreme dissenters, to find shelter within its latitudinarian boundaries. The monarch, as supreme governor of the church, appointed a hierarchy of officials – archbishops, bishops, pastors, and deacons – to administer it.

But many members of the House of Commons wished to advance beyond the moderate religious settlement of Elizabeth. They wished to "purify" the Anglican church of what they considered to be "popish" remnants, and hence they came to be known as Puritans. They wished to dispense with the wearing of vestments by the clergy, the use of holy water, the sign of the cross, and other vestiges of the "popish" ritual. After the bishops began opposing their program in 1571, some Puritans wished to abolish the episcopacy and replace it with a representative organization of local church consistories, provincial conferences, and a national synod. Still more radical groups, later known as Separatists or Independents, cried for the end of any state church whatsoever and for allowing each congregation to seek God in complete freedom.

Accustomed by decades of ecclesiastical statute-making to discuss and pass measures concerning the Anglican church, the Puritan members in successive sessions of the House of Commons introduced bills of their own, embodying their ecclesiastical program. However, it was still recognized constitutional doctrine that members of the Commons could not discuss questions involving the royal prerogative except when the king asked them, and it was still clear that governance of the church was part of the prerogative. Elizabeth, wishing for a variety of reasons, mainly political, to keep to a broad middle way in religion, repeatedly warned off the Puritan members of the House from meddling with matters involving the church. The Puritans went right on talking. They rejoined that "freedom of speech" was one of the ancient liberties of the House. Any member, they said, might freely speak about any issue potentially profitable to the realm. Several times Elizabeth imprisoned the chief orators. Several Puritans, notably Peter Wentworth and James Morice, then examined the fundamental nature of the English constitution. In 1576 Wentworth quoted the great medieval legist, Bracton: "The King ought not to be under man but under God and under the law because the law maketh him a king." By law the king might levy extra taxes, but by law he might levy them only with popular assent as expressed in Parliament. By fundamental law then, and not by king's grace, Parliament existed. An essential quality of Parliament's operation, Wentworth continued, was freedom of speech. It too rested not on the grant of the monarch but on fundamental law. It was a necessary and ancient liberty of the House, embedded in the constitution. The Puritans also invaded in debate other areas of the royal prerogative. They debated foreign policy. In Parliament they urged the queen to accept the sovereignty of the Netherlands after the assassination of William the Silent in 1584. Fearful of a Catholic successor to the throne, they discussed the question of the succession, another royal preserve. Toward the close of her reign (1597-1598 and 1601), all members attacked the abusive use of the royal prerogative to grant trade and industrial monopolies. However, Queen Elizabeth was a national heroine and a master politician, and she knew how to lead. As long as she was there to cajole, to flatter, to discipline, and to yield gracefully, and always to fascinate, members of the House of Commons did not press their arguments to the point of rupture. They were apt to be more high-handed with her successor.

Elizabeth's successor was a distant relative, James VI of Scotland, who became James I of England and united the two kingdoms in a personal union. Not an old man – he was thirty-seven years old – he was yet an old king, having become king of Scotland at the age of six months. By the time he ascended the English throne in 1603 he had learned how to survive in the rough-and-tumble feuding of the Scottish nobles and pastors and even to enjoy a degree of authority. His appearance was pleasing, he was not without shrewdness, and he meant to govern his English subjects as a father governs his children. For the position of king of England, however, he had certain defects of experience and character. He knew Scottish ways and customs, but he was ignorant of English ones. This ignorance was compounded by his laziness. Even in Scotland, he never had liked to work steadily at the business of government. After entering upon his English inheritance, he cared even less. He preferred to loiter in his country houses, hunting and reveling and giving offhand decisions inspired not by study but by preconceived ideas and principles formed in the struggles of Scottish politics. Add to his ignorance and laziness his astounding vanity, which sometimes defied comprehension. He was learned in a miscellaneous sort of way. In his lifetime he published books on subjects ranging from predestination and the theory of kingship to tobacco. From the supposed heights of his learning, he liked to lecture in a father-knows-best tone. He particularly liked to lecture his English subjects on his theories of kingship and law. In his view the king as God's lieutenant on earth received his power from God, and in the exercise of this power was answerable only to God. While a good king would observe the laws and consult Parliament, yet law flowed from the king and he could make and unmake laws and ignore Parliament's advice if he chose. With his good intentions, shrewdness, laziness, vanity, ignorance of English ways, and theory of kingship, James blundered into persons and groups in England, provoked antagonism and fury, grew furious himself, and yet always remained puzzled as to what the fuss was all about.

He soon came into conflict with members of three rising and aggressive groups: the Puritans, judges of the common law, and the House of Commons. The Puritans hoped to obtain of James what Elizabeth had always denied them, a further reformation of the doctrine and ritual of the Anglican church. In 1604 they presented a petition to that effect to James. However, one of their spokesmen incautiously used the word "presbytery." Immediately James took this group of rather moderate Puritans for Presbyterian advocates of representative church organization. He had had some bitter moments with these in Scotland. Furiously he declared that if the Puritans were Presbyterians he would harry them out of the church and out of the land. And in fact, he and his bishops did drive the ministers of Puritan sympathies out of the church. This move had serious consequences. It headed the church not towards greater comprehension of all Englishmen but towards a narrow exclusiveness. The cause of the "deprived and silenced ministers" was taken up by the House of Commons and was transformed there into a starkly political issue: a grievance of Parliament against the king. The sense of grievance was aggravated by the toleration that James was extending to lay Catholics. He reasoned, quite plausibly, that they were loyal Englishmen, but to members of Parliament they were papists and collaborators with Spain and hence national enemies.

Under James I, as under the Tudors, the royal power to do justice generally was exercised by the judges of the various common law and prerogative courts. During the sixteenth century the royal Privy Council had taken a hand in distributing business among the courts and had decided disputes about jurisdiction between them. A precedent existed, thus, for its being the royal prerogative to settle disputes between courts. However, in the closing years of Elizabeth's reign, the judges of the common law began to question this precedent. They began to claim that they ought by right to determine their own jurisdiction and that of the other courts. Under Elizabeth and then under James they issued the writ of prohibition, to forbid another court from proceeding with a case, or the writ of habeas corpus, to hale before them parties to a case being considered in another court. When James protested that by right he and his Privy Council were the proper arbiters of jurisdictional issues, Sir Edward Coke, the intractable chief justice of Common Pleas, moved from particular defense of the writ of prohibition to the higher principles of English fundamental law, as he understood it. The right of issuing the writ, as an ancient and established custom, was part of the law, he said, and the king could not touch it. The king, to quote Bracton, was under no man, but was under God and the law. The power of the king was created, defended, and limited by law. Law was the common law and the customs of the realm, unless altered by a statute of Parliament, and the common law judges were its interpreters. Wrote Coke, in a case involving the royal power to issue proclamations: "It is a grand prerogative of the King to make proclamations . . . upon fine and imprisonment." But "the King by his proclamation, or other ways, cannot change any part of the common law, or statute law, or the customs of the realm . . . the King hath no prerogative but that which the law of the land allows him."

On several occasions, James furiously declared that such words were those of a traitor: the royal power created and defended the law, not the contrary. The quarrel climaxed in 1616, when James ordered the twelve common law judges to delay consideration of a case involving his prerogative until he could consult with them. The judges, under Coke's influence, considered the case anyway, asserting that by law the king had no right to interfere in this instance. James sent for the twelve judges, berated them like schoolboys until all twelve fell on their knees. All the judges apologized and promised thereafter to consult the king in cases involving the prerogative — all the judges except Coke, who remained silent during the upbraiding. At last James turned to him, "Well, Sir Edward, and you, how will you behave:" "I shall do what it befits an honest and just judge to do," was the reply. James dismissed Coke from the bench and appointed a more subservient judge. But James was much too late and in the wrong country for such action. Coke and the common law were popular in England. His cause, too, was taken up by Parliament.

James blundered again. Vain, and cocksure, with an exaggerated notion of his own authority, he blundered this time into the country gentlemen of the House of Commons, who had just as firm a notion of their own importance and rights as he of his. They had been sent up to London by the substantial elements of the English community. They began with James where they had left off with Elizabeth. In 1586, the Commons had momentarily gained the right to judge who had won a disputed election. Although they abandoned this right for a few years, they asserted it again in 1604 under James, forced him in practice to recognize it, and thereafter maintained it. In the same year (the year of their first confrontation with a Stuart king) they began taking the part of the Puritan ministers against the king and bishops, and boldly informed James that "the Kings of England" have no power "either to alter religion . . . or to make any laws concerning the same," save "by consent of Parliament." They also quarreled with James about money. Partly because of rising prices and partly because James, though a Scotsman, was more extravagant than Elizabeth, he needed more money than had his predecessor. Finding Parliament stingy, James and his councilors increased the import and export duties to secure more revenue. Constitutionally, it was then part of the royal prerogative to regulate trade by levying export and import dues, but to levy these dues just for revenue was a questionable use of this power, although the courts supported James. The Commons vigorously protested the increased levies in the session of 1610. When James warned them "not to dispute of the

King's power and prerogative in imposing upon merchandise exported and imported," they moved to the level of fundamental principles. They revived the Elizabethan radicals' cry of freedom of speech, declaring it "an ancient, general, and undoubted right of Parliament to debate freely all matters which do properly concern the subject and his right or state; which freedom of debate being once foreclosed, the essence of the liberty of Parliament is withal dissolved." James did not persist. The debate on impositions occurred, and some members advanced the doctrine that whenever the king needed additional money he had to come to Parliament.

As the rift between king and Commons widened, the Commons quarreled with James about other matters — foreign policy for one. James negotiated peace with Spain in 1604. When the Thirty Years' War broke out in 1618, he refused to aid the Protestants by force of arms. He thought he could help his son-in-law, Elector Palatine Frederick, through sheer diplomacy. Here again he overestimated his capacities. He had yet other goals: a social climber, he wished to marry his son Charles to the daughter of a Habsburg, Philip III of Spain, a representative of the topmost European dynasty. But here James ran afoul of the English people. To them, Spain was the national enemy. To deny aid to the Protestants on the Continent, to dance attendance on Spain, to try to give England a Catholic queen, and at home to persecute Puritans while tolerating lay Catholics — all this looked like treason. In 1621 the Commons made bold to discuss James's foreign policy, and especially Charles's projected "match with the daughter of Spain." James ordered them to be silent on this sector of his prerogative. The Commons protested against his attempt "to abridge us of the ancient liberty of Parliament for freedom of speech." This time the king did persist. He told them that their privileges were not, as the House called them an "ancient and undoubted right and inheritance," but only "derived from the grace and permission of our ancestors and us." The House could not let this challenge pass. In the celebrated Protestation of December 18, 1621, every single member concurred

That the liberties, franchises, privileges, and jurisdictions of Parliament are the ancient and undoubted birthright and inheritance of the subjects of England; and that the arduous and urgent affairs concerning the King, State, and defence of the realm, and of the Church of England, and the maintenance and making of law, and redress of mischiefs and grievances which daily happen within this realm, are proper subjects and matter of counsel and debate in Parliament; and that in the handling and proceeding of those businesses every member of the House of Parliament hath, and of right ought to have, freedom of speech to propound, treat, reason, and bring to conclusion the same.

The country gentlemen of the House of Commons were proposing to throw off all the Tudor limitations which forbade their discussion of defense, religion, and foreign policy unless invited to do so. Little wonder that James, after dissolving the House of Commons, asked for its journal and personally ripped out the offensive page on which the Protestation was written.

And so the quarrels between king and Parliament flared up, arising when the wills of the members of the House of Commons clashed with those of Elizabeth and James. In moments of high emotion the Commons and James had raised disagreements over particular issues of church organization, money, and foreign policy to the level of debate over the ultimate principles of English government — the doctrine, ritual, and organization of the state church, the relation of the king to the judges and to the law, the relation of the king to Parliament, and the nature and origins of Parliament's power and privileges. King and Parliament went on quarreling throughout the seventeenth century, involving Englishmen in events no one had intended and leading in the end to consequences no one had foreseen.

Charles I, Civil War, and the Restoration
Settlement of 1660

James, who had not done so well in lecturing Parliament, did better with his son and successor, Charles I. From childhood Charles had been indoctrinated by his father in the sanctity and responsibility of the sovereign's part. When, elegant and refined, Charles became king in 1625 at the age of twenty-four, he espoused the religion of monarchy. He believed that he held his throne of God by hereditary right, and that it was his Christian duty to exercise his absolute authority to insure equal justice, order, and peace to his good people, just as it was their Christian duty to accept his commands with unquestioning obedience. In the spirit, as he believed, of his deceased father, Charles revised the coronation oath, swearing to maintain the liberties and laws of the country only in so far as they did not clash with his prerogative. At the same time, the distrustful, aggressive mood of his first House of Commons was clearly shown in its proposing to grant him tonnage and poundage (the usual customs duties on imports) for one year only, instead of for life as was customary.

Charles continued to collect tonnage and poundage anyway. Needing additional sums, he brought pressure on his subjects to lend money to the Crown. Until they paid the forced loan, poor men were forced to serve as soldiers or to accept soldiers quartered on their land, and rich men were arrested by the Privy Council and imprisoned. When Parliament met again in 1628, Edward Coke led it to pass a Petition of Right. This petition declared that no man should be compelled to make any gift or loan, or to pay any tax without common consent by act of Parliament, that no free man should be detained in prison without cause shown, and that soldiers should not be billeted upon people without their assent. Finding its way from fact to fact, from year to year, from stubborn king to stubborn king, Parliament was coming across the basic principles of a revolution.

Charles dissolved Parliament and tried ruling without it, from 1629 to 1640. At first he was not unsuccessful. The executive power was his. Obstinate judges had been dismissed by his father and himself. For the moment there were enough statutes so that he did not need a parliament to enact new ones. His councilors were so ingenious in devising new, legal fiscal exactions that by 1635 the budget was nearly balanced. However, the exactions were of such a nature as to arouse every substantial group in the kingdom. Tonnage and poundage continued to be levied upon the merchants by royal authority alone. Anyone refusing to pay was jailed by either the Council or the Star Chamber. An old law was enforced requiring the owners of an estate worth 40 pounds a year to receive knighthood. Gentry who had neglected the obligation had to pay heavy penalties. The king's rights over land that had once been forest were revived. Peers were fined huge sums to retain land no longer forested. Consumers suffered from the sale of monopoly rights in articles of necessary use, such as soap. The most notorious device of all was ship money. For many years in time of war or threat of war, the king had asked seaport towns to provide war vessels or money to construct them. However, Charles extended the levy to inland counties and exacted it in peacetime in three successive years, 1634, 1635, 1636. Ship money was fast becoming a permanent tax. A country squire, John Hampden, refused to pay. The judges decided against him, by a vote of 7 to 5. Nevertheless, the argument of his lawyers struck home and was noticed, that if the king could "levy taxes on his subjects at will, the foundation of property itself was attacked and no man could possess anything but 'at the goodness and mercy of the King' — a proposition evidently at variance with the accepted principles and practice of English law."[3] Again the king won the skirmish and lost the country. Disaffection with Charles grew, and returns from the ship money tax came in more slowly.

There were other grievances, in fact there were nearly as many grievances as royal schemes. Charles was the first English monarch to have been reared from childhood in the Church of England. His predecessors had accepted it in maturity, as a convenience, but he believed in it. Also, he had been won over by those non-Puritan bishops who made much of an elegant ritual. In 1633 he appointed one of them, William Laud, archbishop of Canterbury. A conscientious little man, Laud went about England thoroughly insisting that clergymen wear the surplice and that the communion table be moved to the east end of the church in an altar position. These measures were hated by the Puritan

[3] *Ibid.*, p. 192.

members of the Anglican church and feared by nearly everyone as portending a return to Roman Catholicism. Charles was too thorough an Anglican to desire that, but other facts supported the same misinterpretation of his intent. He tolerated lay Catholics, had a French Catholic queen, allowed her to have around her Catholic priests and friends who pursued missionary enterprise, and all the while followed a policy of benevolent neutrality toward Catholic Spain. His foreign policy also hampered the efforts of colonial promoters among the peers, gentry, and London merchants who wished to break into the Spanish colonial monopoly.

Nevertheless, Charles might have continued to govern England without Parliament for an indefinite period had not he and Archbishop Laud decided to put their religious ideas to practice in the Scottish church. But the Scots were more Calvinist than the English. They followed a harder line of Protestanism, and they could not tolerate "popish" practices. When Laud prescribed the use of a new prayer book after the Anglican model, they rose in armed rebellion. Charles, needing tremendous sums of money to subdue them, was forced to call Parliament, twice in 1640. When the members of the House of Commons finally met, they had had twelve years of changes in religion, favor to Roman Catholics and to Spain, monopolies, ship money, fines, and subjection of the courts to the "evil counsellors" of the king. An astute parliamentarian, John Pym, used their discontent and the king's need for money to lead Parliament to strip the king of his powers, one by one. The two houses enacted — and Charles accepted — acts which insured that not more than three years should elapse without a Parliament being summoned; stipulated that this Parliament could not be dissolved without its consent; legalized the tonnage and poundage prerogative levies that had been made, but prohibited them for the future; declared ship money unlawful; restored the boundaries of royal forests and outlawed vexatious proceedings concerning knighthood; abolished the Star Chamber and other prerogative courts; and deprived the Privy Council of its power to give judgment in civil and criminal cases and subjected its commitment of accused persons to review by common law courts. In sum, Parliament had insured that the king could not legally govern unless it met on a regular basis nor obtain money without its consent, nor punish his opponents without the good will of the juries of the common law courts.

Probably at least half of the members of the House of Commons wished to stop here. They had gathered to end what they considered to be the abusive use of royal power; they had no desire to replace an authoritative monarch with an authoritative Parliament. However, Pym and his allies suspected that Charles was merely biding his time. The Irish had just rebelled against English rule. An army had to be sent against them. Who should control that army, king or Parliament? If the king, he might use it against Parliament. If Parliament, then he could never regain his powers. On this issue, neither side felt it could retreat without irretrievably compromising its position and endangering its security. In November, 1641, the Commons broadened the issue by petitioning the king to appoint only such councilors, ambassadors, and other ministers as might be approved by Parliament, thus asking that the control of the executive be transferred from the Crown to the two Houses. In 1642 the Parliament simply assumed supreme executive authority. It began to organize its own army and to issue orders to the justices of the peace. The king, challenged in the exercise of his executive power, fled to York, calling upon the gentry to follow him.

The ensuing Civil War went on and on and acquired an intricacy and an atmosphere of hourly confusion and urgency beyond the power of this brief account to represent. It began as a clearcut struggle for power, phrased in constitutional terms, between two groups: on the one hand, the king and his supporters among the Lords and gentry, on the other, the majority of the Commons and its supporters among the Lords, gentry, and merchants. At the start, then, it was a contest among members of the ruling groups, but as it continued unexpectedly for years, other men, interests, and ideas were drawn in, and each side had to improvise. With the king absent and an enemy, the Commons had to improvise an executive council, a system of taxation, and an army; administer a navy; regulate trade; conduct foreign relations; and deal with religion. It had to do what the kings had been doing, and it had to debate and govern in areas from which it perennially had been warned off by the Tudors and Stuarts. Parliament was never quite the same again for the experience. At the end of 1643, Parliament secured the Scots as allies on the condition (in effect) that the episcopacy and the Book of Common Prayer of the Anglican church be replaced by Presbyterian organization and ritual. Parliament at this stage of events became identified with Presbyterianism, and the king with episcopal Anglicanism. A year later, Parliament replaced its early raw levies with a "New Model" paid regular army, commanded by two generals of merit, Lord Fairfax and Oliver Cromwell. The intervention of the Scots, the army reorganization, and Cromwell's genius proved decisive: the king's army was defeated at the battle of Marston Moor (July 2, 1644) and destroyed at Naseby (June 14, 1645).

The three victors, Parliament, the New Model Army, and the Scots, then fell out among themselves, while their prisoner, Charles, was passed from one group to another. The New Model Army was composed of Independents, who held that each person and each congregation should be allowed to seek God independently and in freedom. They opposed a state church, whether Anglican or Presbyterian. Many of them also held democratic views about government. Cromwell shared the passion of the Independents for religious toleration, but not their democratic notions. In the three-cornered conflict, the New Model Army won out. In 1648 the army defeated the Scots and purged

Parliament of its Presbyterian members. In 1649 it had the king executed, the monarchy and House of Lords abolished, and a Commonwealth or republic declared. The army's leading general, Cromwell, became governor of the country, a military dictator with ill-defined powers. Through several written constitutions he tried to improvise a legislative assembly and legitimize his position, but not one of his experiments succeeded. After his death in 1658 the English people by almost common consent restored the hereditary monarchy and in 1660 welcomed the return to England of Charles's son Charles II.

The Restoration of 1660, as the complex events of that year came to be called, restored the ancient institutions of government (the Crown, the House of Lords, the House of Commons, the established Anglican church) and continued the judges of the common law and the justices of peace, who never had ceased to operate during the civil wars. By the Restoration arrangements the king retained considerable power. The executive power was his, and he still conducted the government. He disbursed the revenue, commanded the army, administered the navy, declared war and made peace, conducted foreign relations, negotiated treaties, and appointed and dismissed councilors, judges, and officers of the armed forces. He still could veto bills passed by the Lords and Commons. Under certain conditions he still could suspend the operation of the laws and dispense people from their penalties.

At the same time, Charles II, Parliament, and the common law judges accepted as valid the legislation enacted by Parliament (King, Lords, and Commons) until the outbreak of the Civil War in 1642. This acceptance signified the curtailment of the king's power, the enhancement of the position of the common law judges and of Parliament, and the settlement of many issues that had agitated the English ruling groups since the accession of Elizabeth a century before in 1559. No longer could the king exercise the royal judicial power and attempt to secure the execution of policy through the prerogative courts. These courts remained abolished, as did the power of the Privy Council to decide civil and criminal cases. The courts of the common law and of Chancery now found themselves in possession of long-disputed jurisdiction, while the Court of King's Bench decided jurisdictional disputes among the remaining courts. "English constitutional law was [now] bound . . . to assume a bias, appropriate to the Common Law tradition, in favor of individual rights and property, and on the whole adverse to the claims of the State to a freedom of action determined by considerations of public policy."[4] Also, no longer could the king attempt to raise money by his

_____

[4] David Keir, *The Constitutional History of Modern Britain since 1485*, (seventh edition), pp. 233-34. The bias was strengthened by the Habeas Corpus Act (1679), which required judges to order jailers to produce a prisoner within three days of imprisonment and show cause of dentention; the judges then either released the prisoner or set an early date for trial.

own devices, such as forced loans, tonnage and poundage, and ship money. When he needed funds, beyond the diminished revenue from his property, it seemed that he had to turn to Parliament. Nor could the king attempt exceptional legislation through his Privy Council in proclamation and ordinance. Legislation was henceforth to be grounded upon clear majorities in legally elected Parliaments. Parliament's consent was now necessary to both taxation and legislation. Parliament could now freely discuss any issue involving the welfare of the kingdom.

Parliament's power over legislation was nowhere more clearly demonstrated than in church affairs. The Elizabethan church settlement, though made law by Parliament, had been mainly the work of the Queen and her chief councilor, William Cecil. The church settlement of the Restoration was the work of Parliament, over the objections of Charles II and his chief minister, the Earl of Clarendon. Charles himself wanted to tolerate all Christians save a few radical Protestant sects. Clarendon advocated that the doctrine, ritual, and government of the Anglican church be so broadly defined as to comprehend the Presbyterians. Parliament followed neither policy. It re-established the Anglican church as the state church and retained the episcopal organization and the doctrine and ritual of the Prayer Book of the Elizabethan settlement, thus excluding Presbyterians and all other sects. Taught by the events of the Civil War to identify Puritan non-conformity with rebellion, Parliament then introduced persecution. It required all municipal officers to take the sacraments according to the rites of the Church of England, ejected two thousand pastors who refused to conform to the Anglican liturgy, forbade them to come within five miles of any city, borough, or corporate town, and imposed penalties upon all present at a non-Anglican religious meeting. The outcome was the division of the English people into Anglicans, who conformed at least outwardly to the rites of the established church, and Protestant Dissenters, who were outside the pale of official approval. There were also a few persecuted Roman Catholics.

We must be sure not to miss one feature of the Restoration. Although Charles II's acceptance of the statutes enacted prior to the outbreak of the Civil War in 1642 established limits on the king's power, the ultimate result of the resistance of his father Charles I and his supporters had been to prevent the parliamentary majority from triumphing on those very issues — namely, the control of the army and the appointment of the king's councilors — that had precipitated the war. Out of the clash of wills — Parliament vs. king — had arisen the compromise arrangements of 1660 which no one had willed. The arrangements left unanswered — and open — many questions about the relations of Parliament to royal executive action.

The Stuarts' Second Chance

Charles II was pleasure-loving, affable, and shrewd. Born in 1630, he had spent most of his early years in exile, and after 1660 he was resolved not "to go on his travels again." Though more tactful than his father and grandfather, he too believed that he held his throne of God by hereditary right and was tenacious in his pursuit of influence and power. He was much more aware than his predecessors of the tricky dangers of the whole situation. He must have felt something like a snake charmer, entering a cage, handling a bundle of snakes (Parliament) that had already proved their venom. He no longer considered himself immune, and he maneuvered carefully. Accepting for a time the frequent meeting of Parliament as one of the facts of life, he tried to coax and gradually lead away some of its members. Pensions and offices for them or their relatives were the bait he used most often.

At first he was not always successful in winning influence. Twice, in 1662 and 1672, Charles tried to carry out his policy of religious toleration by issuing a declaration of indulgence which suspended the penal laws against Dissenters and Roman Catholics. In each case the Commons protested, giving him to know that there would be no money if the declaration remained in effect. Indeed, in 1673 Parliament forced Charles to accept the Test Act, which imposed on all holders of office under the Crown the obligation of receiving communion according to the usages of the Church of England. Throughout his reign Charles attempted to use his royal power over the conduct of foreign relations to direct English foreign policy, only to encounter parliamentary objections. At that time, Louis XIV was seeking to extend the frontiers of France northward and eastward. He warred with Spain (1667-1668) to enforce his claim to the Spanish Netherlands, and was checked in full career of conquest by the Triple Alliance of Holland, England, and Sweden. Turning his fury on the Dutch, Louis persuaded Charles to join him in an attack on Holland in 1672. Though the Dutch were the traditional enemies and trade rivals of England, Parliament was strongly anti-Catholic, did not care to have England allied with a great Catholic power against a Protestant state, and compelled Charles to withdraw from the war.

From 1681 until he died in 1685, however, Charles stopped making concessions to Parliament and successfully defended the royal prerogative. In 1679-1681, controversy developed in the royal court and in Parliament over whether Charles's brother and heir, James, a known Roman Catholic, should be excluded from the throne by an act of Parliament. The exclusionists, who wanted parliamentary limitations on the Crown and toleration for Protestants only, were labeled "Whigs" and were led by the Earl of Shaftesbury. The "Tory" label was applied to those who were supporters of hereditary succession and the prerogative. The two groups represented tendencies rather than parties; the groups themselves were composed of factions and individuals; each leading individual had his nuance of support and opposition to the Crown: and the individuals, factions, and groups disagreed not only about principles but competed for office and power, so that the nuance of principle was always being affected by the pressures of personal and factional ambition. Nevertheless, at this time it seems possible to speak of a Whig tendency toward emphasis on Parliament in governmental relations and of a Tory tendency toward emphasis on the power and activity of the Crown. By 1680, the Whig lords, squires, and merchants were sufficiently influential to pass an Exclusion Bill in the Commons, though it was defeated in the Lords.

With the Commons against him at home, Charles turned to France. In 1681, he arranged with Louis for a subsidy of £400,000 in the next three years, in return for English neutrality in foreign affairs. He dissolved Parliament and did not call another. He imprisoned the Whig leader Shaftesbury in the Tower, though a London grand jury later freed him. There followed a series of more or less repressive measures. Charles enforced the Test Act, which required civil and military officeholders to take the sacrament of the Lord's Supper according to the Anglican rite. While a number of Roman Catholics were released from jail, the local justices of the peace rounded up dissenting ministers and teachers. Judges who were inclined to side against the king in cases involving the royal prerogative were dismissed and replaced by more dependable magistrates. Legal grounds were discovered for proceeding against the Whig strongholds of London and other municipalities and permitted them to affirm their local influence as justices of the peace and lords lieutenants in the countries. In turn, they approved of employment of the royal prerogative against their enemies: the Shaftesbury Whigs, the Presbyterians, and the more rabid Republicans. Charles also moved in accord with a large body of political theory of the time: that good government meant strong government, that strong government meant an effective monarchy, that a monarchy to be effective had to be hereditary, and that obedience to a hereditary king was a moral obligation.

Charles's successor, his brother James II, inherited from him in 1685 a monarchical authority that seemed firmly reestablished. Yet in only three years James II undid Charles's work, so much did the strength of the monarchy still depend on the character of the monarch. Like a good Stuart, James was firmly convinced of the right, and of the duty, of a king to exercise wide powers of government. However, James was also a convert to Roman Catholicism and a religious zealot. He confided to one counselor, the Earl of Sunderland, that his ultimate aim was the re-establishment of the Catholic church and the reconciliation of England with the Holy See. When another advisor protested that this policy might mean trouble, James replied that in that case he looked forward to having his red-letter day on the calendar as a Roman Catholic martyr. During the early autumn he dispensed a few Roman Catholics from the operation of the Test Act and appointed them army officers. James's first Parliament in May, 1685, had been friendly, but in November it was cool and even hostile. Louis XIV's Revocation of the Edict of Nantes was only a few weeks old, and the use the French army was being put to, to harry the Huguenots into compliance with Catholicism, was well known. When James asked Parliament to approve his appointment of Catholic officers and to repeal the Test Act, it refused. The act safeguarded the maintenance of Protestant government in England and besides gave the Anglicans a monopoly of government positions. James dissolved Parliament. He secured an opinion of the judges that he might indeed dispense with the Test Act in the appointment of individual candidates to office. Seeking to assure the election of a friendly House of Commons, he dismissed the Tory Anglicans from their posts of lord lieutenant and justice of peace in the counties and replaced them with Roman Catholics and sometimes Dissenters. He thus struck at the local influence of the Tory Anglicans, the basis of their power. He dismissed from the Privy Council Anglicans who refused to convert and substituted Roman Catholics. He appointed Catholics even to benefices in the Anglican church. To be ready in case of trouble, he strengthened the small standing army Charles II had maintained, encamped it just outside London, and continued to staff it with Roman Catholic officers. He followed these actions with a Declaration of Indulgence (April, 1687), which suspended all penal laws against Dissenters and Roman Catholics alike, and allowed to both freedom of public worship. He calculated that Dissenters would be so overjoyed with their freedom that they would overlook the toleration accorded Catholics.

However, James failed to appreciate the shrill fear of popery that existed among English townsmen, Anglicans and Dissenters alike. Nor did he realize that by now his measures had alienated nearly every element in the kingdom. Many peers and country gentlemen were sincerely loyal to the national Anglican church. Those of a whiggish tendency found outrageous James's extensive use of royal prerogative. On principle the Tory Anglicans could not object to an active employment of the royal authority, but they opposed James's proposal to repeal the Test Act, which safeguarded Protestant government and their own positions, and they resented his use of his prerogative to dismiss them from office. Individual Tory peers were angry at being outpaced by political rivals who "converted" to Roman Catholicism. Several Dissenters, such as William Penn, accepted as sincere James's offer of toleration, but most Dissenters were taught by their fear of popery and by Tory and Whig propaganda to view the offer as a popish trick in the game of winning England for Catholicism. The same propaganda led them to expect from a freely elected Parliament the toleration they desired. From 1686 a succession of leading Englishmen visited William of Orange, the Protestant stadtholder of five of the seven Dutch provinces and captain-general of the Dutch army. Would he come over, make a show of force, and compel James to behave — to abandon his Catholic course, to withdraw the Declaration of Indulgence, to summon a freely elected Parliament, to dismiss his Roman Catholic officials, and to appoint Anglicans? The English leaders apparently had no thought of dethroning James and making William king.

William finally consented, but for his own purposes. He was the son, born in 1650, of the sister of Charles II and James II, and as such the nearest Protestant male heir to the English throne and the third in line after James's two daughters, the Protestants Mary and Anne. William was a frail, diminutive figure, afflicted with chronic asthma, but his appearance was deceptive. He probably dreamed very early of some day becoming king of England by succession. In 1677, he married his cousin Mary, partly to prevent her marrying someone who might prove a enemy and partly to strengthen his own chance of being king. In 1686-1687, he kept himself informed of the daily changes in the English situation. England seemed once again to be drifting toward anarchy, civil war, and a republic. The throne to which his wife and he had claims would be then non-existent. Also, as captain-general of the Dutch forces, he was responsible for. the defense of Holland against the attacks of Louis XIV. As leader and architect of a growing European coalition against aggressive France, he needed to be able to call upon the resources of England. In April, 1688, he told the latest English emissary, Edward Russell, that he had decided to intervene in English affairs with armed force if he received a formal invitation from English men of quality. On June 20, a son and heir was born to James. It was obvious that the Catholic tendencies of this reign would be continued into the next. On June 30, seven Tory and Whig peers invited William to make an armed intervention to protect the English people until they could protect themselves. As in any enterprise of great moment, there were operating in the English leaders many motives, mingled differently in different individuals and in the same individual at different times. Desire for office, concern for English laws and liberties, hatred of political rivals, devotion to the national church, fear of popery — all no doubt played their role. At bottom, though, the English leaders intended to *use* William — to compel James to dismiss the Roman Catholic officials, call a freely elected Parliament, and appoint Anglicans to office. William, however, had privately decided to use them and the occasion to place himself on the English throne to assure the application of England's resources against France.

The English leaders wished William to arrive with a large fleet and a small army. Once on land, he would then be dependent on them, and they would be able to exploit any initial successes he achieved. However, to be ready for any eventuality and to render himself independent of any English faction,

William prepared a powerful expedition of 16,000 experienced soldiers, 60 ships-of-line, 200 transport vessels, and adequate carts and horses for land travel. He landed on November 5, 1688, in southwest England. He marched toward London, and, when James fled to France, entered the city and installed himself in one of the royal palances. At the suggestion of English leaders, he summoned a convention which was a freely elected parliament in all respects except that the summons lacked the signature and seal of the king. When the leading Tory and Whig peers in the convention were discussing the next step — whether Mary should be queen and William her powerless consort or whether William should serve for a time as regent — William let it be known that he had not come over to be gentleman usher for his wife; he had come over to be king and if they did not like it, he would take his army home and they could hang on the gallows for their treasonable intrigues against James. So the convention was forced to accept William as king of England and joint ruler with Mary as queen, an outcome the English leaders had not intended.

To justify what was occurring, the convention passed a whiggish resolution declaring that "King James II, having endeavored to subvert the constitution of the kingdom by breaking the original contract between the king and people, and having by the advice of Jesuits and other wicked people violated the fundamental laws and withdrawn himself out of the kingdom, the throne is hereby vacant." The convention then offered the crown to William and Mary as joint sovereigns, the administration of the government to be in the hands of William. The offer was conditional on their acceptance of a Declaration of Rights that listed English liberties they as sovereigns promised to respect. The Declaration was subsequently enacted by a regular Parliament as a Bill of Rights (1689). When William objected to the Declaration as a curb on his royal prerogative, he was assured that it only defined existing law. This was easy enough to say to a foreigner who was not well-versed in the whole story — part fact, part interpretation, and part jungle — of English law. However easy to say, it was scarcely accurate. To be sure, the Bill of Rights did reaffirm certain elements of the Restoration Settlement of 1660, such as freedom of speech in Parliament, the levy of money only with Parliament's consent, and the right to jury trial. It went on, however, to outlaw royal suspension of laws, royal dispensation of individuals from the operation of laws, and royal maintenance of a peacetime standing army without Parliament's consent — all royal powers that James II had enjoyed and abused.

In the same year Parliament also enacted an Act of Toleration which retained (by implication) an exclusive Anglican church and the Test Act requiring membership in it of all officeholders, while extending toleration to all other Christians, except Catholics and Unitarians. However, after 1689 even Unitarians and Catholics were not interfered with much as long as they were loyal to the government. By the Act of Settlement of 1701, usually associated by historians with the events of 1688-1689, Parliament stipulated that the throne should pass only to a Protestant. The act also provided that the king could not dismiss judges; while he still appointed them, they were to hold office during good behavior and could be removed only after conviction in the courts of law or in response to addresses from both houses of Parliament. The act went a long way toward making the judiciary independent in its action of the other branches of government and tended to decide the legal issue in favor of an independent judiciary applying a law that safeguarded the individual and limited the king. Judicial freedom flowed into a broader stream, merging with the liberty of the individual. As the decisions embodied in the Bill of Rights, Toleration Act, and Act of Settlement endured for over a century, the Revolution of 1688 can be said to have settled the religious and legal issues of the sixteenth and seventeenth centuries and to have further curtailed the powers of the king.

The Revolution of 1688 still left unsettled many aspects of the relations between king and Parliament, which in part were worked out during the reigns of William (1689-1702) and Anne (1702-1714). As William intended, he enlisted England in a war against France. The war, in two stages, continued on a world-wide scale for nearly a quarter of a century (War of the League of Augsburg, 1689-1697, and War of the Spanish Succession, 1701-1714). Since only the king and his ministers could direct military operations and conduct diplomatic negotiations, the war greatly increased the activity and importance of the royal executive. But it also enhanced the importance of Parliament. Because the war was on a new scale involving tremendous expenses, William and then Anne had to summon Parliament each year to vote taxes and loans, until the annual meeting of Parliament became customary. Since the sums were huge, Parliament began to appropriate them for specific purposes and to audit the accounts of the treasury officials. It began, in other words, to encroach on the royal power to disburse revenue. Since government borrowings were large and could not be paid during a single reign, Parliament began underwriting them and establishing them as a lien on the credit of the nation rather than on the credit of the king. It also founded the Bank of England to make it easier to float government loans. The king still appointed ministers to govern the country and he was still the center of the government, but he now had to appoint ministers who possessed the abilities both to administer the government and to secure parliamentary approval of appropriations and policies. For Parliament now gave the money, and Parliament now debated policy, and debating and money-giving were one complex process. So Parliament was powerful in a way, and largely as a result of the war its regular meeting became an accepted part of government procedure.

Just as important as what happened in the Revolution of 1688 was what people thought happened. The phrases that James had violated "original contract" and the "fundamental laws" and the wording of the Declaration of Rights to imply that the acceptance of William and Mary as sovereigns was contingent upon their promise to respect the ancient rights and liberties of Englishmen — all this helped to start an influential and enduring legend. A myth grew up and spread throughout the Western world. It was this: in 1688 a great people, outraged by the oppressive acts of a tyrannical king, overthrew him, replaced him with another monarch who agreed to respect their liberties, and thus accomplished a successful revolution for freedom. This story of a Glorious Revolution was helped along by the ignorance of most people of the complicated intrigues and motives of William and the Tory and Whig leaders. It was reinforced by the publication in 1689 of a *Second Treatise on Government* by a noted philosopher, John Locke. In 1680-1681, the Whig leader Shaftesbury was preparing an armed uprising against Charles II and had his friend Locke compose a treatise in defense of armed rebellion against an arbitrary king. Shaftesbury's uprising never came off, and Locke laid aside his manuscript. In 1689, still a friend of the Whig leaders, he retrieved the manuscript, touched it up, added a foreword suggesting that King William's title lay "in the consent of the people," and issued the book to justify the actions of his Whig friends and their associates in rebelling against James II.

In the work, Locke argued that originally in a state of nature individual men or families lived apart. Each individual had natural liberty — that is, perfect freedom to do what he wished with his person and possessions within the bounds of reason, even to the extent of judging and punishing any individual who attacked him; and natural equality — that is, men were equal with respect to the jurisdiction of one over another. But this state of nature had certain inconveniences. Owing to the presence of ill-intentioned men, individual life, liberty, and possessions often were insecure. Consequently, individual men by unanimous agreement entered into a contract with each other to form a society. Then, by majority vote they entered into a second contract with a government, which agreed to protect their individual rights to life, liberty, and property. It followed that when the government ceased to protect those rights, it might be legitimately altered or overthrown by the majority of the people. Locke thus defended the right of revolution under certain circumstances and generalized the significance of the legendary English example for all peoples.

Concluding Remarks

As Great Britain entered the second and third decades of the eighteenth century the judicial, executive, and legislative branches of the British government were separated and yet inter-connected. The judicial power was entrusted to a relatively independent judiciary, but the king appointed the judges, Parliament might dismiss them, and the House of Lords still served as a high court of appeal. Local justices of the peace still performed both judicial and administrative functions. The king conducted the government. The executive power was his, but he exercised it in accord with the common law of the judges and the statute law of Parliament. He also exercised it through ministers who sat in Parliament and who had to persuade both houses to support their executive policies. Parliament was the supreme legislative authority. The royal power to veto bills was no longer exercised after 1708, and the practice of making law by royal proclamation was narrowly restricted. However, through the distribution of pensions and offices to members of Parliament and their relatives and friends, the king could often secure from Parliament the legislation he and his ministers desired. Moreover, large sectors of the law were embedded in common law precedents and had never been enacted by Parliament into statute law, while even statute law was interpreted by the judges.

Such complicated arrangements had arisen from the clash of wills in the sixteenth and seventeenth centuries, and depended for successful operation in the eighteenth century on the essential harmony of wills with respect to the basic principles of government. It is a temptation to portray the eighteenth-century constitution as the result of the triumph of idealistic common law judges and champions of Parliament over selfish, villainous Tory defenders of the king and the royal prerogative. Actually, there was idealism and self-interest, heroism and cowardice on both sides, and usually in the same persons. The continuing strength of the king into the eighteenth century owed much to a long line of Tory partisans. The balance of judiciary, Parliament, and Crown in the eighteenth century was the consequence, unintended and unforeseen, of the competition of volitions, not of the triumph of any one of them.

In any case, by the eighteenth century the government of Great Britain was different from the governments in continental Europe. The first great difference was the existence of civil liberties. Some of these were embedded in common law procedures and helped to protect the individual from arbitrary arrest, imprisonment, and trial. They included such devices as a search warrant, writ of habeas corpus, indictment by a rand jury, access of the accused to legal counsel, public trial by petty jury, and equality of the law and its penalties for everyone, noble and commoner. Other civil liberties were expressed in statute law or in its omissions. These liberties included freedom of the press from prior censorship (secured in 1694), legal religious toleration of all Christians save Catholics and Unitarians, and practical toleration for Christians who kept the peace. The second great difference which set English government apart was the existence of a central legislative assembly that met regularly, possessed the powers of taxation and legislation, and influenced executive policy. The third great difference was that in the crucible of internal conflict a sense of national identity had become fused with the values of freedom. The inhabitants of England were now proud not simply of being Englishmen but also of being *free-born* Englishmen. If France became the prototype, as we shall see, for the administrative monarchies in continental Europe and for her colonies, Great Britain became the prototype for her own colonies and for changes in France and other administrative monarchies.

An Invitation to Further Inquiry and Reflection

The history of England, especially the history of England during the seventeenth century, often seems inexplicable, mysterious, and baffling. Usually, in the history of Franc, or Prussia, or Austria, or Russia, we can find a reason why events took a given course; English history, on the other hand, at times seems to go haywire, and one is reduced to telling a story.

Still, we continue to inquire. Why, for example, did English institutions increasingly diverge from those of the continental monarchies? England, we say, was the great exception. Why did it become so? By now we should know how to handle a question of this type. This is a comparison, and we need to discover both resemblances and differences. What, for example, were the resemblances between French and English institutions in the seventeenth century. The resemblances may tell us something of the characteristics of European civilization as a whole, especially if they exist in Prussia, Austria, and Russia as well. The resemblances may help us also to define the differences. So, what were the divergencies between seventeenth-century French and English institutions? When did each divergence first appear? In each instance, why? The question may lead us to relations hitherto unnoticed.

Or again, why did the Civil War break out in England in 1642? The first answer of course is that the two sides confronted each other over an issue, the control of the army, on which neither could retreat without jeopardizing its security. But we press the question further back and deeper. How far back? To the installation of a foreign king, James I? Was that the reason for the Civil war? And deeper. What were the two sides? And why had they emerged? Was it simply because certain men in the Commons were devoted to the rule of law and possessed by buring religious conviction? Really, did men become heated about independence of the judiciary, survival of representative instiutions, freedom from arbitrary arrest, defense against arbitrary fiscal exactions by the state, and preservation of the Anglican church from Popish practices? Or were these issues merely the expression of social discontent, of the resentment of rising men who knew they were good and hated their exclusion from a position of importance? In other words, we seem to know the political, constitutional, and religious story; we are coming to know the social and economic story; were the two stories connected, and what do we need to know to *demonstrate* that they were?

For Further Reading

(For general reading)

Maurice Ashley, *Oliver Cromwell and the Puritan Revolution*

————, *The Glorious Revolution* (1967)

Stephen Baxter, *William III and the Defense of European Liberty, 1650-1702* (1966)

B. W. Beckingsale, *Burghley: Tudor statesman, 1520-1598* (1967)

Catherine D. Bowen, *The Lion and the Throne: The Life and Times of Sir Edward Coke (1552-1634)* (1957)

Carl Bridenbaugh, *Vexed and Troubled Englishmen, 1590-1642* (1968)

Andrew Browning, *Thomas Osborne, Earl of Danby and Duke of Leeds 1632-1712*. 2 volumes (1944)

Arthur Bryant, *Samuel Pepys: the Man in the Making* (1934)

————, *Samuel Pepys: The Years of Peril* (1935)

————, *Samuel Pepys: The Savior of the Navy* (1939)

John Buchan, *Oliver Cromwell* (1934)

Maurice Cranston, *John Locke: A Biography* (1957)

H. C. Foxcroft, *A Character of the Trimmer, Being A Short Life of the First Marquis of Halifax* (1946)

J. P. Kenyon, *Robert Spencer, Earl of Sunderland 1641-1702* (1958)

G. Mattingly, *The Defeat of the Armada* (1959)

John Neale, *Elizabeth I and Her Parliament, 1559-1581* (1953)

————, *Elizabeth I and Her Parliament, 1584-1601* (1957)

————, *Queen Elizabeth* (1934)

David B. Quinn, *Raleigh and the British Empire* (1947)

Conyers Read, *Lord Burghley and Queen Elizabeth* (1960)

————, *The Tudors: Personalities and Practical Politics in Sixteenth Century England* (1936)

Alfred L. Rowse, *The England of Elizabeth: the Structure of Society* (1951)

————, *The Expansion of Elizabethan England* (1955)

————, *The Elizabethan Renaissance: The Cultural Achievement* (1972)

George H. Sabine, *A History of Political Theory* (3rd ed., 1963)

J. J. Scarisbrick, *Henry VIII* (1968)

Giles Lytton Strachey, *Elizabeth and Essex, A Tragic History* (1930)

Cicely Wedgwood, *The King's Peace* (1957)

————, *The King's War* (1959)

J. R. Western, *Monarchy and Revolution: The English State in the 1680's* (1972)

James A. Williamson, *The Age of Drake* (2nd ed., 1946) (4th ed., 1960)

David H. Willson, *King James VI and I* (1956)

(For advanced study)

L. A. Clarkson, *The Pre-Industrial Economy of England, 1500-1750* (1972)

Charles Wilson, *England's Apprenticeship, 1603-1763* (1965)

Kenneth Pickthorn, *Early Tudor Government: Henry VIII* (1934)

G. R. Elton, *The Tudor Revolution in Government* (1953)

———, *England under the Tudors* (1955)

———, *Policy and Police: The Enforcement of the Reformation in the Age of Thomas Cromwell* (1972)

Lacey Baldwin Smith, *Henry VIII: The Mask of Royalty* (1971)

J. R. Tanner, *English Constitutional Conflicts of the Seventeenth Century, 1603-1689* (1928-1948)

David Keir, *The Constitutional History of Modern Britain since 1485* (1960)

Lawrence Stone, *Crisis of the Aristocracy 1558-1641* (1965)

R. C. Richardson, *Puritanism in North-west England: A Regional Study at the Diocese of Chester to 1642* (1972)

P. A. M. Taylor (ed.), *The Origins of the English Civil War: Conspiracy, Crusade, or Class Conflict?* (1960)

Leo F. Solt, *Saints in Arms* (1959)

Articles on origins and denouement of the 17th-century English revolution by Christopher Hill and J. H. Hexter in *The European Past*, I, 293-323.

Henry Williams and G. L. Harriss, "A Revolution in Tudor History," *Past and Present*, No. 25 (July, 1963), 3-58.

Richard H. Tawney, "The Rise of the Gentry, 1558-1640," *Economic History Review*, XI (1941), 1-38.

Lawrence Stone, "The Anatomy of the Elizabethan Aristocracy," *Economic History Review*, XXIII (1948), 1-52.

Hugh Trevor-Roper, *The Gentry*, 1540-1640 (1953)

Perez Zagorin, "The English Revolution," *Journal of World History*, II (1955), 668-81, 895-914.

Cicely Wedgwood, "The Causes of the English Civil War," *History Today*, V (October, 1955), 670-76.

Lawrence Stone, "The Inflation of Honours 1558-1641," *Past and Present*, No. 14 (November, 1958), 45-70.

Jack H. Hexter, "Storm over the Gentry," *Encounter*, X (May, 1958), 22-34.

H. R. Trevor-Roper, "The General Crisis of the 17th Century," *Past and Present*, No. 16 (November, 1959), 31-64.

Perez Zagorin, "The Social Interpretation of the English Revolution," *Journal of Economic History*, XIX (Sept., 1959), 376-401.

Willson H. Coates, "An Analysis of Major Conflicts in Seventeenth-Century England," in *Conflict in Stuart England* (1960) edited by William Appleton Aiken and Basil Duke Henning, pp. 15-60.

Christopher Hill, "Recent Interpretation of the Civil War," in *Puritanism and Revolution* (1958)

Perez Zagorin, "English History, 1558-1640: A Bibliographical Survey," *American Historical Review*, 68 (1962-1963), 364-384.

Lawrence Stone, "The Educational Revolution in England, 1560-1640," *Past and Present*, No. 28 (July, 1964), 41-80.

W. T. MacCaffrey, "England: "England: The Crown and the New Aristocracy, 1540-1600," *Past and Present*, No. 30 (April, 1965), 52-65.

G. E. Aylmer, "Review Article: The Crisis of the Aristocracy 1558-1641," *Past and Present*, No. 32 (December, 1965), 113-125.

Lawrence Stone, "Social Mobility in England, 1500-1700," *Past and Present*, No. 33 (April, 1966), 16-55.

Paul Hardacre, "Writings on Oliver Cromwell since 1929," *Journal of Modern History*, XXXIII (March, 1961), 1-14.

Robert Walcott, "The Later Stuarts (1660-1714): Significant Work of the Last Twenty Years (1939-1959)," *American Historical Review*, 67 (January, 1962), 352-370.

Maurice Ashley, "Is there a case for James II?", *History Today* (May, 1963), 347-52.

G. M. Strake (ed.), *The Revolution of 1688: Whig Triumph or Palace Revolution?* (1963)

Lucile Pinkham, *William III and the Respectable Revolution: The Part Played by William of Orange in the Revolution of 1688* (1954)

CHAPTER X
FRENCH AND ENGLISH COLONIAL EMPIRES COMPARED
AND CONTRASTED

We have seen how the Portuguese and Spaniards traveled overseas to America and around Africa to Asia. They carried with them some of the ideas and some of the ways of doing things which were characteristic of theeir countries at the time they left. We have noticed how they changed these ideas and practices to meet the vicissitudes, the problem-saturated conditions of new places. In new places, they developed the commercial and settlement types of empire. Toward the close of the sixteenth century, Dutch, English, and French intruders, each with their own brand of European life, entered the Spanish-American preserve. The power game in Europe began to help decide which brand of European civilization would last overseas and in what areas. By 1689 it was more or less settled that Spain woul; hold on to California, Mexico, Central America, a few islands of the West Indies, non-Brazilian South America, and the Philippines; Portugual would keep Brazil, posts along the coast of Africa and India, and Macao and Timor; and Holland would have a few Caribbean islands and a part of Guiana, part of Ceylon, and dominance of the East Indies. The prime contest overseas, after 1689, was to be between England and France. Having looked at developments in France and England during the sixteenth and seventeenth centuries, we are prepared to compare the colonies of the two countries in the seventeenth century with respect to, first, their location; second, the ideas, practices, and customs that were carried by Frenchmen and Englishmen to North American settlements and there modified; and third, the imperial economic policy followed by the two governments in regard to their colonies.

Location

England and France, entering the colonial field rather late, in the seventeenth century, developed their settlements side by side, in India, the West Indies, and North America. In India, the English went slightly ahead of the French. An English East India Company was formed in 1600; shortly thereafter, the fleets of this company ousted the Portuguese from several key towns on the west coast between Goa and Diu and seized strategic ports, such as Madras, on the east coast. The French East India Company was formed in 1604, but the first French trading post (at Pondichéry near Madras) was not established until 1668, and the French did not seriously compete with the English and Dutch in India until the end of the seventeenth century. In the West Indies, both countries acquired a number of islands and developed them as sugar plantations. British emigrants settled the Bermudas in 1612, half of St. Kitts and the Barbados in 1625, Nevis in 1628, Antigua in 1632, Jamaica and the Bahamas later. At the same time, the French occupied the other half of St. Kitts, Martinique, Guadeloupd, and the western portion of San Domingo.

In North America, the first successful English settlement was made at Jamestown, Virginia, in 1607. Somehow the English took root in this country, and the land began to hold them. They kept settling along a strip of the Atlantic seaboard from what is now Maine southward to South Carolina. Then there were English fur-trading posts in the Hudson Bay region. The French maintained a few precarious villages along the Atlantic seaboard in Acadia (Nova Scotia) and Newfoundland, but their main effort was farther inland. There explorers, soldiers, Catholic (and particularly Jesuit) missionaries, and fur traders entered the bottleneck of the St. Lawrence River, founded Quebeck in 1608 and Montreal in 1642, and fanned out over the rivers and lakes of the North American continent. They learned the Indian lore of wilderness travel and forest warfare. As the fur-bearing animals were killed off near Quebec and Montreal, the fur traders had to go farther and farther west. New France was drawn into expansion, almost in spite of itself. The fur traders fraternized with the Indians, often taking native wives. The royal government entered into treaty alliances with Indian tribes and by the close of the seventeenth century was constructing a series of fortified posts from Quebec along the Great Lakes and down the Illinois, Ohio, and Mississippi river valleys to New Orleans.

French and English Settlements in North America

The settlement of Canada, as distinquished from its exploration, was the work of the French royal government, and especially of Louis XIV and Colbert. They took a paternal interest in the colony. In keeping with their policy of mercantilism they wished it to become self-supporting financially and a source of raw materials and a market for France. They were fashioning the emerging administrative monarchy of France and were trying to direct everything from Paris. They naturally sought to help and guide from Paris the development of Canada in every way.

Their penetrating attention to the minutiae of frontier life was illustrated by their efforts to increase the Canadian population and to develop its agriculture. When Louis XIV began ruling in 1661, the entire French population in Canada — priests, nuns, traders, soldiers, and settlers — numbered no more than 2,500 people. Louis and Colbert took measures to collect in France and to send to Canada at least three hundred men a year, each merchant ship being required to carry some. But these were mostly single men who needed wives. So Louis and Colbert recruited women in France, exercising care that they were of good character and that besides being strong and healthy they were "free from any natural blemish or anything personally repulsive." An annual consignment of young French women was shipped over. The French administrators made sure that the emigrants, male and female, were of Catholic persuasion, for no Huguenot was allowed in the colony. At the same time that emigration was encouraged, measures were employed to stimulate a natural increase of population in Canada. Early marriage was rewarded. A youth who married at or before the age of twenty was entitled to a gift of 20 livres, called "the king's gift." Fathers who had not married their sons at twenty and their daughters at sixteen were penalized. Bounties were given to parents who had as many as ten living children. Bachelors were given fifteen days after the arrival of a shipload of girls to find a wife – if they had no luck, they were fined 300 livres. These measures and other factors were not without effect. The French population of Canada increased to about 15,000 by 1700, and to some 65,000 by 1760, mostly by reason of a high birth rate.

After a couple were married, the king (through his Canadian agents) tried to arrange that they receive a grant of land upon conditions of tenure already familiar in France. Louis and Colbert naturally started with what they knew, the French feudal-manorial regime, and used certain features and modifications of it to promote in Canada the distribution and development of agricultural land. The king granted to civil officials, retired army officers, and the church large segments of forested land, about four miles by six, along both sides of St. Lawrence River on condition that they swear fealty and homage to him, clear and cultivate the land, and not sell it save as a totality. The individual seigneur, as the grantee was called, would erect a manor house and a flour mill and keep part of his estate for his own cultivation.

The term "seigneur" conjures up feudalism. An this echo does not lead us too far astray. Since the seigneur could not personally cultivate all his estate, or sell parcels of it on the market, he was led to sub-grant sections of it to young married couples, provided they work their land and render him certain manorial dues and obligations. In the beginning these people were not paying rent to a landlord, so much as services and dues to a lord.

Louis and Colbert had expected the young families would follow the French custom and cluster in villages – not only expected but hoped, since villages would be easy to control from a center of authority, and easy to defend. A royal intendant even laid out in Canada three villages showing the colonists how settlement should be organized. But it was wishful thinking. There were no roads to and from the villages, and each couple wished to live on the colony's only highway, the St. Lawrence River. The seigneurs were forced to divide their estates into long, narrow strips that would border the St. Lawrence River for about a thousand feet and extend inland for a mile to three miles. Also, to keep settlers from taking to the woods as trappers, the seigneur lightened the burden of manorial obligations and the tithe. For the right to cultivate such a strip a couple would pay a seigneur an annual money due of a few pence; give him annually perhaps a half-dozen chickens or a bushel of grain for every 60 acres; grind their grain at his mill, and leave the fourteenth part in payment; work on his land one day each in the seasons of plowing, seedtime, and harvest; surrender about 5 per cent of the sale price if the land were sold; and submit to his rough-and-ready justice in lesser cases, with the right of appeal to the local royal courts. As each seigniory became a parish and received a parish priest, the married couples would build a chapel and give a tithe (one twenty-sixth, in this case) of their grain to the priest. The church also collected dues and labor from married couples on its own seigniories. In Canada, as in France, the church was the largest single landholder: it had received one-fourth of the granted land.

The manorial regime was thus transferred to Canada and modified in the meeting of practical problems. To secure the development of agricultural land, Louis had added to the usual condition of fealty and homage the provision that the grant be cleared and cultivated and not sold save as a totality. To meet the settler's need of transportation, the seigneur had sub-divided the grant into long, narrow strips that fronted the St. Lawrence. To keep the settler working the land, the seigneur had reduced the burden of manorial obligations and the tithe, while the royal government refrained from exacting a direct tax. So modified, the manorial regime seemed to work. A traveler who descended the St. Lawrence from Montreal past Quebec in 1760 sailed between two rows of neat, whitewashed farmhouses, back of which stretched on either hand waving fields of grain as far as the eye could see.

Louis also transferred to Canada, with modifications, the government of a French frontier province. He appointed a bishop for the Canadian church, a governor as military commander, and an intendant for the administration of justice, police, finance, agriculture, commerce, industry, and in general anything that concerned the welfare of the colony. Bishop, governor, intendant, and a few local notables appointed by the king formed a Superior Council. This appointive council laid down the rules for daily public relationships, binding the loose-knit frontier life together. It issued decrees for the civil, commercial, and financial government of the colony. The council also served as a court, giving judgment in civil and criminal cases according to royal ordinances and the Custom of Paris. The intendant likewise issued regulations with the force of law. These "were usually read to the people at the doors of churches after mass, or sometimes by the priest from his pulpit."

They dealt with the whole unexplored horizon of the intendant's responsibility in a frontier region — the "regulation of inns and markets, poaching, preservation of game, sale of brandy, rent of pews, stray hogs, mad dogs, tithes, matrimonial quarrels, fast driving, wards and guardians, weights and measures, nuisances, value of coinage, trespass on lands, building churches, observance of Sunday, preservation of timber, seignior and vassal, settlement of boundaries, and many others."[1] As in France, a church could not be repaired not a road mended without the consent of the intendant. Public meetings were discouraged. A harmless, semi-annual meeting of the inhabitants of Quebec to discuss the supply of firewood, the quality of bread, and similar matters was discontinued. An assembly of the parishioners held under the eye of the priest to estimate the cost of a new church required a special license from the intendant. The king would grant his colonists every stimulus except a voice in their own government.

Nevertheless, there gradually developed in the central St. Lawrence valley under royal supervision a fresh and exploratory way of life, having echoes of both France and the wilderness, accommodating the work rythms of Norman farms to St. Lawrence grainfields: a self-perpetuating, homespun community of French blood, language, and law, of Catholic religion, with a substantial agricultrue operating under a modified manorial regime, an industry that supplied local needs of clothing and tools, an active fur trade, two important towns (Quebec and Montreal), and a centralized administration that took its direction largely from Parris.

English settlers on the Atlantic seaboard, like the first-generation French Canadians, were bearers of a European, Christian culture. Also, the process of adaptation by which the two settlements developed was essentially the same. Like the French, the English came over bearing a heavy load of ideas, moods, ideals, patterns of behavior, institutions, and ambitions characteristic of their former homes. In coping with the wilderness, they changed their lives, they changed their ideas, and they changed the institutions of their common heritage. They developed a new civilization which came to differ from that of their mother country.

Yet the contrasts between the English and French colonies were probably more striking than the resemblances. Though the essential process of adaptation was the same, its content was different. the settlement of Canada was the work of a cental will, which we can locate in a particular place in Europe — Paris — a will already institutionalized in the administrative monarchy of France. But the English colonies were the product of many primarily private initiatives. English individuals and companies, for their own specific purposes, either settled or sent settlers overseas. They often incorporated themselves and asked the government's sanction for their

[1] Francis Parkman, *The Old Regime in Canada*, p. 340.

activity, but English kings and ministers, unlike Louis XIV and Colbert, rarely took the lead. Certainly they never had a deliberate overall plan of overseas colonization. In the seventeenth century, English colonial activity largely went of itself. Also, whereas the French government carefully screened the settlers for Canada (barring Huguenots, for instance), England did not hinder the migration overseas of any religious or political dissenter. Puritans, Catholics, Jews, Quakers, Anabaptists as well as members of the Church of England, supporters of Cromwell as well as supporters of the kind, all could find asylum in North America. Irish, Germans, and French Huguenots were accepted too. Furthermore, whereas the 65,000 (1760) French settlers formed around Quebec and Montreal a compact, homogeneous society in a unitary environment, the 1,200,000 (1754) inhabitants of the thirteen English colonies were scattered from Maine to Georgia in a wide variety of geographic and climatic conditions. Adaptation of the settlers to varying local conditions resulted in colonial economies and societies that differed both from those of England and from each other. In New England agriculture consisted of small, subsistence farms, and cash income came from furs, fishing, lumber, shipbuilding, and commerce, but the medium-sized farms in the middle colonies produced a surplus of wheat, pork, beef, and flour for export through thriving commercial ports, and the plantations of the southern colonies yielded tobacco, rice, and indigo for sale in Europe.

However, not everything was diversity along the seaboard. Most of the settlers there were English and shared many customs in common. They naturally brought with them many of the attitudes, ideas, and practices that prevailed in seventeenth-century England at the time of their departure. They left behind them the titled nobility, Parliament (for it was impossible to transplant King, Lords, and Commons), and bishops. But they brought along the English language; the King James version of the Bible, once characterized as the one great book of the plain people of English speech on both sides of the Atlantic; Protestantism, often of the dissenting kind; a hierarchic but fluid society; the common law, with its safeguards to individual liberty; and the habit of working with or through an assembly, sometimes a representative assembly. In all these traits, except for the hierarchic society, English colonial civilization differed from the French.

As the English settlers responded day by day to the problems of the wilderness and often to their own dreams of creating a new and better world, these inherited traits were modified in the direction of mildness and greater liberty. In religion, the founders of Virginia and Massachusetts followed prevailing English practice in starting out on the principle of the union of church and state. In each colony the inhabitants, whether church members or not, were taxed to support the established church and required to attend its services. Nonconformists were at first persecuted. When the state church was the Anglican, as in Virginia and South Carolina, the unit of church government was the parish, usually a subdivision of the county. The parish's governing body was the vestry, a group of twelve persons elected by parishioners and charged with levying assessments for the support of the local church. When the state church was not Anglican but Puritan, as in Massachusetts, the unit of government was the congregation. Each local church was independent and self-governing, with power to admit members, make choice of a pastor, and exact obedience to a puritanical code of conduct from its members.

For various reasons, actual toleration began to prevail in most of the colonies by the eighteenth century. Roger Williams and William Penn, two implacable believers in religious freedom, established liberty of conscience, respectively, in Rhode Island and Pennsylvania. George Calvert, a convert to Roman Catholicism, insisted on religious toleration in his colony of Maryland, to protect his fellow Catholics from persecution. The weakening of the intensity of religious feeling in Puritan New England promoted the growth of toleration of Anglicans and Quakers in that area. The passage of the Toleration Act of 1689 in England led to a similar one in Virginia by 1699. Anglicans in the South found it worthwhile to tolerate dissenters whose settlements guarded their Indian frontiers. By 1750, actual persecution for religious opinion had almost disappeared.

The English settlers brought with them the notion that a proper society should be organized hierarchically, like a sturdy ladder, a stairway, broad below and narrow above, with fewer people toward the top. However, another notion went with this one: namely that no unsurmountable legal barrier should be built into the ladder to keep competent white people from climbing up. The first shock of the wilderness, the experience of a single winter, for example, often knocked over the ladder and reduced the early settlers to a rough economic equality. But the notion and pattern persisted. After this early stage, classes developed, usually on the basis of differentials in wealth and income. In the Southern colonies and parts of New York the large landholders formed the most eminent group; after them came the small farmers and (in the South) the Negro slaves. In the middle and northern colonies, the merchants were apt to be the leaders, joined in New England by the ministers; after them came the small farmers and the artisans. Legislation affirmed differences based on wealth. Sumptuary laws forbade the lower classes to wear such fineries as lace, embroidery, and ruffs. People sat in church according to rank. College students at Harvard and Yale were listed not alphabetically but by the social standing of their families. Nevertheless, class differences among white colonists were not as sharply drawn as among the inhabitants of England. The extreme edges of English society — titled nobility and peasantry — did not exist. People treated each other with a greater mutual tolerance than in Europe. Since it was easier for a man to acquire property (given the abundance of land and the expanding economy), people could pass more easily up the ladder into higher social classes.

The charter of the Virginia Company, granted by James I in 1606, provided that the colonists should "have and enjoy all liberties, franchises, and immunities . . . as if they had been abiding and born within this our realm of England." The colonials used this clause and similar provisions in other charters to confirm their right to employ common-law procedures, where these seemed appropriate. As a matter of fact, in the simple colonial civilization of the early seventeenth century the English settler did not need the very complicated fabric which the common law had woven around property, and he did not at once transplant it. However, the early settler did know of indictment by grand jury and trial by petty jury, and he transplanted these. Then, as colonial civilization became more complex, other features of the common-law practice became relevant, and in the eighteenth century they too were borrowed. Features of common-law theory were also retained. Embedded in the common law was the theory that a fundamental law, interpreted by common-law judges, created and defined the powers of king and Parliament. In Great Britain the facts of constitutional development were dissolving these theories of fundamental law and judicial review. By common-law principle, legislative supremacy rested with Parliament, and statutes enacted by Parliament could alter common law. When in the eighteenth century Parliament became more important and legislated on every kind of business, there seemed to be no legal limits to what it might do in a legislative way. During the same period, the facts of colonial constitutional development were reinforcing in the colonies the concept of fundamental law and the practice of judicial review. Nea.ly every colonial charter provided that the laws passed by the colonial assembly must be consonant with the laws of England and, of course, with the articles of the charter. In a sense, the charter and English law formed the fundamental law of each colony. Laws enacted by colonial assemblies were reviewed by the Privy Council and were sometimes judicially disallowed as contrary to the laws of England. In this instance, English and colonial civilizations were diverging as they moved from common assumptions in different directions.

English settlers had long since formed the habit of working through an assembly. It was part of the culture they had brought with them. We saw this in their church government, in the meetings of the vestries of the Anglican church and of the self-governing congregations of the dissenting sects. We can also see it in their administration of justice. Here the basic unit was the county. Throughout the seaboard colonies, the justices of peace met as a county court to try small cases, such as drunkenness and stealing, and to settle civil disputes. And besides the county court, what was the jury if not an assembly? The habit of using an assembly was apparent, furthermore, in local government. In the South and in several sections of the middle colonies the county court performed administrative functions: assessed and collected local taxes, supervised the construction and maintenance of roads, relieved the poor, called up the militia, and supervised elections of delegates to colonial assemblies. In New England and sections of New York and Pennsylvania the town meeting of the township performed these duties. Every town dweller might attend the town meeting and could speak his mind, though only property owners could vote and elect local "selectmen" to execute the meeting's decisions.

The Englishman's habit of using assemblies appeared finally in the structure of the government of each colony. By the mid-eighteenth century, in each colony except Rhode Island and Connecticut, the chief executive was a governor appointed either by the king or the proprietor. The governor was advised by the council, whose members were appointed by the king or proprietor on the governor's recommendation. The council formed the upper house of the colonial legislature. The legislature was completed by a lower house, an assembly elected by voters who met certain property qualifications. English lawyers generally likened a colony to a municipal corporation: an inferior and subordinate body exercising self-governing powers within well-defined limits. The colonists saw themselves in a different light. The lower house of each colonial legislature came to think gloriously of itself as a miniature House of Commons and to copy its forms and to claim its privileges. Each colonial assembly had a speaker with a mace and gown, a sergeant-at-arms with his staff, a chaplain, a clerk, and a doorkeeper. The assemblies demanded and exercised full control over their own members, in matters of admissions, qualifications, and expulsion. They insisted that colonial taxes could be levied only with their consent and spent only upon their specific appropriation. As in England they entered pitched battle with the executive power. They argued through the decades with generations of governors. They argued about whether representative government in the colonies derived more from a mere act of grace on the part of the king or was the expression of an inherent right that colonists might claim as Englishmen; whether the assembly should meet regularly, and if so, whether it should meet once a year or once every three years; what a governor should be paid; and whether the governor could dismiss judges or whether they could hold office during good behavior. So in every phase of life, the English colonists turned to assemblies to get things done. Embedded in this habit of turning to an assembly, under the layer of what was visible, were the values of a civilization — motives, beliefs, ideas, resilient and enduring institutions, a whole complex of human relationships, which survived the sea voyages and the changing time. And this complex was considerably different from that which, a few hundred miles to the north, underlay and held together the lives of French settlers.

Imperial Economic Policy

Different though the institutions of the French and English colonies might be, the imperial economic policies of the French and English governments were similar. By the 1660's they were both trying through mercantilistic regulations to organize the colonies and the mother countrry into an exclusive, self-sufficient (raw material-manufacturing-trade-labor) economy which would operate so as to enrich the home country. Their policy was the culmination of a long development of regulations stretching back into the medieval past. In the twelfth century an economic unit was the town and the surrounding rural population. The master craftsmen of each trade in each town, seeking security, organized themselves in guilds and made regulations giving them a monopoly of this local market. The town councils, consisting of merchants and craftsmen, enforced the craft regulations and added some of their own to protect the townspeople as a unit. As exchange became interregional and the area of the market enlarged, the town councils of Venice and Genoa applied regulatory and protectionist policies to the Levantine trade and tried to make of it a Venetian, or Genoese, monopoly. Kings, such as Louis XI of France and Henry VII of England, issued economic regulations for their entire kingdoms. As the kingdoms of Portugal and Spain and their area of exchange enlarged to include trading posts in Africa and the Far East and colonies in America, the Portuguese and Spanish governments attempted to apply the policy of monopoly and exclusion to their new possessions.

The Dutch introduced a new aggressive element. The Hollanders and Zeelanders long had been a seafaring people and made money from fisheries and the carrying trade. As long as they were inferior to other maritime powers and outside the walls of the Portuguese and Spanish monopolies, they preached freedom of the seas and freedom to trade anywhere. Once, though, they had breached the Portuguese monopoly in the Far East and seized the commerce of the Spice Islands, they thoroughly enforced a policy of exclusion. Remorselessly, they threw out the English traders, excluded the French, and forced both to retire to the less lucrative trade of the peninsula of India. While restricting the traders of other states, however, the Dutch merchants continued to insist on freedom to intrude on the commerce of other countries. With rather incredible energy the Dutch sea captains made themselves masters of the African slave trade, much of the commerce of the French and English colonies, and the carrying trade of Europe. During the first half of the seventeenth century, they made the Dutch Netherlands preeminent at sea, as their merchant fleets covered the water. Colbert, the French controller-general, estimated that the Dutch owned sixteen thousand of the twenty thousand vessels engaged in Europe's trade. For English and French statesmen the Dutch Netherlands was the nation to watch and to beat, both the model to emulate and the rival to withstand and surpass.

As we have seen, the groundwork of French mercantilism had been laid long before Colbert, but he did not stop with what he inherited. He was a great builder of economic and administrative policies. In order to fight the Dutch for the trade of the two Indies, he organized the French East and West India companies. He considered the East India Company of greater importance, and eventually in the eighteenth century it justified his hopes. Nearly on the basis of equality, it contested with the English East India Company trade and territorial supremacy in India. However, in the seventeenth century the French West India Company was of more immediate significance, and Colbert's measures with respect to the French West Indies throw a clearer light on his intentions and methods.

In 1663 and 1664 Colbert looked into the problems of the fourteen French West Indian islands. French planters had been raising sugar cane there for years, but the island trade was altogether in Dutch hands. Few French vessels touched at the islands, though over one hundred Dutch merchant ships passed through every year, exchanging manufactured goods for French money and raw sugar. Once safely home this sugar was refined (the Dutch Netherlands was the leading sugar refining country in Europe) and then sold to French consumers. The French island planters needed lumber for building purposes, for repairing ships, and in the form of staves, hoops, and headings for making sugar barrels. It was brought by Dutch merchants. The planters possessed about twelve thousand Negro slaves, who had been transported from Africa by the Dutch, and they needed each year two or three thousand more. These too were imported by Dutch sea captains. Each slave consumed two pounds of beef a week; the beef, as we might expect, came from Ireland in Dutch ships. The profits of the French sugar cane plantations were passing into Dutch hands.

Colbert was well aware of this profit drain. To meet the challenge he had Louis XIV decree in 1664 that no Dutch vessel was to be received at a French West Indian island. In the same year he chartered the French West India Company and gave it a monopoly of the island trade. When by 1666-1667 it was able to muster only sixty vessels to meet the needs formerly supplied by over one hundred Dutch ships, Colbert made the company admit French private traders. Then he began work on the French half of the mercantilistic equation. To encourage sugar refining in France he placed a very high import duty on foreign refined sugar, subsidized the establishement of sugar refineries in France, and lowered the export duty on the sugar they produced. To encourage French refineries to use raw sugar from the French West Indies, he imposed a heavy duty on the non-French product from Brazil and a low one on all raw sugar from the French colonies. Anxious to persuade French sugar planters to purchase their cloth, clothing, and household utensils from France, he abrogated the duties ordinarily levied on such exports to the colonies from France. He founded first one Company of the Senegal and then another to transport African Negroes to the French islands. He urged the French Canadians to produce lumber and beef for shipment in French and Canadian vessels to the West Indies.

Colbert met his different problems more or less pragmatically, one by one, to meet particular aspects of the French West India situation, but he saw no one of them separately from all the others or from their context. Each had a place in his total vision. Implicit in each particular measure was the overall aim to create a self-sufficient commercial empire of mutually complementary parts which would operate so as to increase the gold and wealth of the mother country. In this ideal empire the colonies would supply the raw materials (sugar cane and, from Canada, lumber, furs, fish, and beef); France, the manufacturing skill (to refine sugar and to manufacture cloth, clothing, and utensils); France and the colonies, the shipping; and France, the colonies, and Africa, the labor (native Frenchmen, French colonists, and Negro slaves). Ideally, the system would form a balanced whole: French Canada would produce just the amount of lumber and beef the French West Indies could consume, the French islands would grow just enough sugar cane to enable French sugar refineries to meet the needs of French and foreign consumption, and Africa would furnish the necessary number of slaves. No embarrassing surpluses would develop. Ideally, also, the system would operate so that France would export more to the colonies than she imported, and gold would flow to France. It seemed a good risk that this would happen since, as a rule, French-manufactured articles had greater value than did sugar cane. But France would profit not only over the islands; France and the islands would profit over the world, as the export of raw sugar drew gold to the system.

Many of Colbert's measures were immediately successful, but the overall ideal was never as closely approximated as he and his successors desired. Though the French West India Company soon went bankrupt, private French traders, having grasped a foothold, were able to shut out the Dutch. The number of private French merchant ships calling on the islands increased from three or four in 1662 to one hundred and thirty-one in 1674 and to two hundred and five in 1683. French merchants built a lucrative trade transporting French-manufactured articles to the islands and returning with raw sugar. By 1683 there were in France twenty-nine sugar refineries, processing annually 17,700,000 pounds of raw sugar. France now exported, rather than imported, raw sugar and in the eighteenth century became the leading sugar refining country in Europe. However, French Canada never produced enough lumber nor enough beef to meet the needs of the French islands. Beef was still brought from Ireland. The second Senegal company imported over a thousand slaves a year, but never the three thousand which the islands needed. And there were other unexpected problems. The island sugar cane industry yielded valuable by-products, molasses and rum, which could not be marketed in France. The typical Frenchman, it seems, had no taste for molasses, while the government kept out the rum for fear he might like it too much and stop buying French brandy. When French island settlers petitioned in 1680 for permission to trade molasses and rum to New England merchants for salt, meat, lumber, and livestock, Colbert, following the mercantilistic principle of a closed economic system, said no. The decision retarded the colony's economic growth. Only in the eighteenth century, when this exchange was tolerated, did the French sugar islands flourish.

The experience of English administrators was similar to that of the French. English kings had long put some restrictions on trade, but to meet specific needs, not to carry out an economic theory. Henry VII, for example, restricted the import of French wine to English vessels. Elizabeth chartered companies for trade in the Baltic, in Spain, in Venice, in Turkey, on the African coast, and in the East Indies. To stop the drain of money paid for Spanish tobacco, the councilors of James I and Charles I encouraged the growth of the "weed" in Virginia and other colonies. They allowed no tobacco planting in England and no tobacco imports from foreign countries. In return for this monopoly market, colonial planters were required to send all their crop to England even if it were to be re-exported elsewhere.

In the 1650's and 1660's English statesmen and theorists, provoked in part by Dutch success, began to consider English commercial and colonial policy in terms of achieving a self-sufficient empire by the broader use of mercantilistic measures. During the anarchy of the English civil wars in the 1640's the Dutch traders had taken over much of English trade with her own colonies and with Europe. In 1650 Parliament appointed a commission to study the state of the nation's trade and the affairs of the colonies, to see "how they may be best managed and made useful for the Commonwealth; how the commodities thereof may be so multiplied and improved with what it necessarily wants." The next year Parliament passed a comprehensive Navigation Act, designed to exclude Dutch merchants from the trade of carrying the products of Asia, Africa, America, and Europe to England and to reserve it, as far as possible, for English merchants. This policy worked its way into the English mind on a theoretical level. During the Restoration, thinkers like Thomas Mun, Josiah Child, and John Cary began to speak of England and her colonies as forming "one great body" or economic unit.

For more than a century after 1651 Parliament enacted numerous economic regulations, each one usually designed to meet the needs and demands of some special interest group of English merchants and manufacturers. Hovering behind the short-range goal of each bill, however, was the long-range ideal: to mold the empire into a self-sufficient economic unit operating to England's

benefit. To encourage the colonies to produce raw materials and semi-manu-
factured goods needed in England, import duties on English colonial ginger,
indigo, cotton, sugar, and tobacco were made much lower than on the foreign
competing products (tariff of 1660); bounties were paid on naval stores of
pitch, resin, turpentine, hemp, and masts (act of 1705); and some goods such
as pig and bar iron were freed from import dues (Iron Act of 1750). To
maintain the supremacy of English manufacturers, Parliament prohibited the
export from England of raw wool, prescribed standards of quality for woolen
cloth, forbade the import of silks and calicoes from India, and placed an
embargo on the emigration of skilled workmen and the export of special tools
and secret processes. Parliament also placed restrictions on rival colonial
manufactures: the Woolens Act of 1699 interdicted the export of wool and
woolens from the colonies to the British Isles, to foreign countries, and from
one colony to another; the Hat Act of 1732 forbade the exportation of
American-made hats from the colony in which they were produced and
limited each hatmaker to two apprentices; the celebrated Iron Act of 1750
allowed the colonists to manufacture iron but forbade them to work it up
into finished products.

To assure the English plantation colonies an adequate supply of slaves and
to free them from dependence on Dutch slave traders, the government of
Charles II chartered in 1672 the successful Royal African Company to establish forts and trading stations in West Africa and to barter English products
for Negroes. Finally, the navigation acts of 1660, 1663, 1673, and 1696
sought to control the flow of trade within the system. Foreigners and foreign
ships were barred from the colonial trade. No goods might be shipped to or
from the colonies except in English or colonial ships. Certain enumerated
colonial raw materials needed by England, including sugar, molasses, tobacco,
cotton, wool, indigo, dyewoods, and naval stores, had to be exported first to
England even if proceeding later to other European countries. European
manufactured goods headed for the colonies also had to touch base in
England. This last provision, if enforced, would prevent the colonies from
developing a direct import trade of their own and tend to compel them to
buy English-manufactured articles. By the Molasses Act of 1733, high import
duties were placed upon sugar, molasses, and rum imported into the British
colonies from foreign plantations. This act was designed to compel New
England merchants to trade within the system and to purchase their rum and
molasses from the British, instead of the French, West Indies.

Since these regulations were laxly enforced until 1764, it is difficult to
estimate their effect upon the imperial economy. For whatever reason —
mercantilistic laws or colonial dependence on English manufacturers — the
system did drain gold from the colonies to England. In 1700 the colonial
balance of payments owing England amounted to about £50,000, and in 1760

to about £2,000,000. On the other hand, since the different regions within the empire did not always develop at the same rate, they did not always balance each other. By the eighteenth century, for example, New England was producing more lumber and catching more fish than the sugar islands of the British West Indies could take and was consuming more rum and molasses than the British islands could supply.

Whether the French and English acts of trade were effective and prudent was perhaps of less importance than that statesmen believed they were. Contemporary statesmen believed that a colonial empire, regulated and administered in this fashion, was a decisive asset in the continuing rivalry among the powers. A self-sufficient empire, they thought, would mean wealth, so necessary in the struggle for power. An empire would free the state from dependency on rivals for raw materials, giving it greater freedom of action in choosing its allies and enemies. If England could obtain masts from New England, for instance, it would not have to curry the favor of Sweden, another source of timber. Because colonies were desirable, a state would do well to acquire as many as possible, including those of its rivals. The colonies of a rival, furthermore, offered a vulnerable spot through which it might be attacked. As objects of desire and targets for attack, colonial empires continued to be involved in European events of diplomacy and war. Another dimension was added to the tangle of Machiavellian calculations: the dimension of far-flung, problematic, and unprecedented situations overseas, distant from the center of authority. It became more difficult to define what was a European event: European events were happening everywhere.

An Invitation to Further Inquiry and Reflection

Several decades ago Professor Herbert Bolton of the University of California advanced the thesis that in addition to having histories of the United States, histories of Canada, histories of Mexico, histories of Argentina, and so on, country by country, we should have an overall history of America. That history, he argued, has unity of time, unity of place, and unity of process. When the histories of the several colonial undertakings and later of the several countries are viewed in this perspective and compared with each other, new historical relationships will be perceived. There are really two Americas, one critic observed, Latin America and Anglo-America; the difference between their histories is so great they cannot be subsumed under a single rubric, and comparison is valueless, except to reveal divergence. Still Bolton's concept has its champions, notably Silvio Zavala, and we might test it against what we know of the history of the Spanish, Portuguese, French, and English colonies in America.

In starting our probe, we might ask, what criteria should such a concept meet if we are to accept it? Might one criterion be, its correspondence to historical reality? In the history of these four colonial enterprises are there cultural similarities deriving from a common European origin? If so, what are they? In the transplantation of European institutions to a new environment, are there similarities of process? of problems and opportunities in the new environment? of results? Might a second criterion be, does the concept set up useful and stimulating comparisons, so that the phenomena clarify each other and perhaps demonstrate the existence of historical relationships hitherto ignored or only surmised? For example, might not a comparison of Negro slave plantations in the Caribbean area under Spanish, French, English, Dutch, and Portuguese flags help us isolate what characteristics of plantation society were due to Europeans in general, to Africans in general, to the problems and opportunities of the tropical environment, to the operation of the processes of institutional transplantation and development, and to the peculiar contribution of the Spanish, French, English, Dutch, or Portuguese settlers, and, perhaps, of different African tribes? Can we think of any other comparisons of compound phenomena that might be set up and analyzed, to discover the structure, processes, and relations involved? Then, might a third criterion be, that the concept is good provided it does not lead us to perceive non-existent similarities, to blur the distinctive features and individuality of each colonial enterprise, and to forget that the explanation of what occurs is frequently to be found in a *detailed* narration of particular, unique circumstances?

In the light of these criteria, should we accept Bolton's concept?

For Further Reading

(For general reading)

Morris Bishop, *Champlain: The Life of Fortitude* (1948)
Daniel J. Boorstin, *The Americans: The Colonial Experience* (1958)
W. J. Eccles, *Canada under Louis XIV, 1663-1701* (1964)
————, *The Canadian Frontier, 1534-1760* (1969)
————, *Frontenac: The Courtier Governor* (1959) (1965)
Gerald S. Graham, *Canada* (1950)
W. M. Munro, *The Seigneurs of Old Canada* (1935)
Francis Parkman, *Count Frontenac and New France under Louis XIV* (1897)
————, *The Old Régime in Canada* (1893) (1921)
J. H. Parry, *Trade and Dominion: The European Overseas Empires in the Eighteenth Century* (1971)
Max Savelle, *Seeds of History* (1948)
Charles S. Sydnor, *Gentlemen Freeholders: Political Practices in Washington's Virginia* (1952)
Louis B. Wright, *The Atlantic Frontier: Colonial American Civilization 1607-1763* (1947)

(For advanced study)

Charles M. Andrews, *The Colonial Period of American History* (4 vols.; 1934, 1938)
George Louis Beer, *The Origins of the British Colonial System 1578-1660* (1908)
————, *The Old Colonial System 1660-1688* (2 vols.; 1912)
Thomas C. Cochran, *Business in American Life: A History* (1972)
Rhys Isaac, "Order and Growth, Authority and Meaning in Colonial New England," *American Historical Review*, 76 (1971), 728-737.
Philip A. Means, *The Spanish Main: Focus of Envy, 1492-1700* (1935)
Stewart L. Mims, *Colbert's West Indian Policy* (1912)

CHAPTER XI

THE EMERGING ADMINISTRATIVE MONARCHY: CENTRAL
EUROPE – AUSTRIA AND PRUSSIA

Western Europe had expanded not only overseas to the Americas and India
but also overland to the east in Germany into the territory of the Slavs. At
the beginning of the ninth century, the Slavic tribes, here and there loosely
confederated into kingdoms, had occupied an enormous area extending from
the mouth of the Elbe River in the northwest to the Peloponnesus in the
southwest and from the Saale River in the west to the Volga in the east. In
the ninth century this more-or-less uniform Slavic world was disrupted by the
invasion of a Mongolian-blooded people, the Asiatic Magyars, who settled on
the Hungarian plain and were converted to Roman Catholicism. Thereafter, it
is possible to speak of southern, eastern, and western Slavs. Most southern
Slavs – Romanians, the bulk of the Serbs, Montenegrins, Bulgarians, and the
now largely Slavic inhabitants of Greece – received their alphabet and the
Greek orthodox form of Christianity from Constantinople. They warred
against the Byzantine Empire and among themselves until in the fifteenth
century they passed, along with the Byzantine Empire, under the rule of the
Ottoman Turks, and withdrew from Western eyes, behind the Mohammedan
veil, for four hundred years. Of the southern Slavs, only the northwestern
Serbs, known as Croats, fell under the sway of the Magyars and adopted the
customs and Roman Catholic religion of the west. The eastern Slavs founded
states at Kiev, and later at Moscow, and adopted both the alphabet and the
Orthodox religion of Byzantium before bowing to Mongolian domination in
the thirteenth century. Two centuries later the leaders at Moscow shook off
the Mongol yoke, and laid the foundation of the later Russian Empire. The
western Slavs – Bohemians (Czechs), Slovaks, and Poles – accepted Roman
Catholicism and the civilization of western Europe, while engaging in intermittent struggles with each other and with Germans, Magyars, and Turks.

German eastward attack and (often peaceable) colonization, split by the
Bohemian mountain ranges, pointed in two directions: to the southeast down
the Danube through eastern Bavaria and Austria; to the northeast along the
shores of the Baltic through Brandenburg, Prussia, modern Lithuania, Latvia,
and Estonia. By the latter part of the seventeenth century, a great power had
begun to rise for each prong – in the southeast, the conglomerate Habsburg
monarchy of Austria; in the northeast, the military state of Brandenburg-Prussia. At the same time, the great Slavic state of Russia was emerging. These

three states, Austria, Prussia, and Russia, were arising along an inland frontier, on the Great Lowland and Danubian plains, which were as inscrutable and elemental as the oceans which had baffled the Portuguese. The three states were arising in "colonial" Europe east of the Elbe and Saale rivers. There distances were longer, interregional trade was slighter, towns were fewer, landed estates were larger and more sprawling, and intellectual activity was less intense than in western Europe, and the only important classes were the leading noble families and country gentry who owned the land and the peasant serfs who worked it. Nevertheless, the history of each of these states resembled in many respects the history of France, and by the eighteenth century they were all tending toward the establishment of administrative monarchies. The Hohenzollerns of Prussia and the Romanovs of Russia were also helping to form in their respective countries traditions fateful for the history of Europe and the world.

A Glance at the Holy Roman Empire in Early Modern Times and at the Habsburg Monarchy to 1740

By the late Middle Ages the Germans had failed to achieve an effective government or national unity. During the fifteenth century the power of their central government, the Holy Roman Empire, instead of rising to greater authority as in England and France, had declined. The independence of the territorial princes, instead of being curbed, had increased. The pulse of German national sentiment in individuals beat feebly or irregularly or not at all. Large portions of the borderlands were drifting away from the empire.

The Reformation and the religious wars during the sixteenth and seventeenth centuries sharpened the tendencies toward division. The religious issue introduced cleavages between Catholic south and Protestant north, and later between Lutherans and Calvinists, that set Germans to fighting each other. The authority each Protestant and Catholic prince acquired over the administration of his territorial church and the freedom he exercised in forming alliances and conducting military campaigns during the religious wars greatly extended his power. France and Sweden utilized Germany's troubles to fight their wars on German land and to keep more than a little of it for themselves. The authority of the Catholic emperors was debased by successive defeats, while the prosperity of the townsmen was ruined by the devastation of the Thirty Years' War.

The Treaty of Westphalia, which concluded the war in 1648, registered the triumph of the princes and the virtual dissolution of the Holy Roman Empire. France was allowed to take Alsace, and Sweden to have western Pomerania and the bishoprics of Bremen and Verden, which placed her across the mouths of the Oder, Elbe, and Weser rivers. The highland Swiss cantons at the

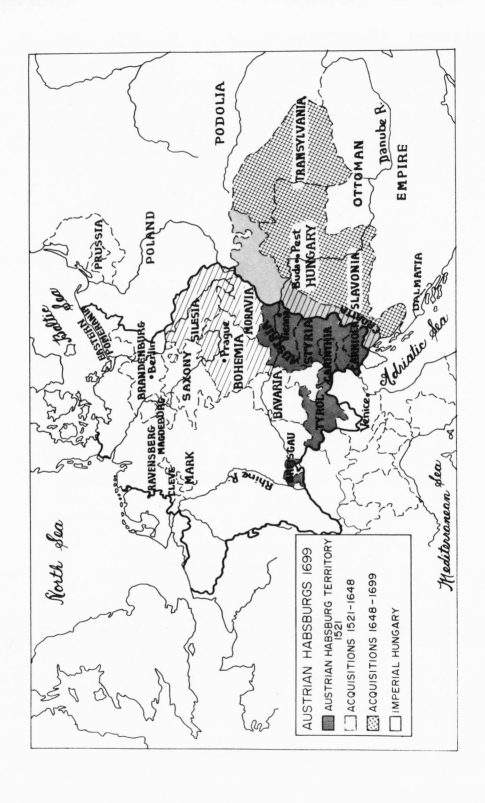

PODOLIA

TRANSYLVANIA

Danube R.

OTTOMAN

EMPIRE

PRUSSIA

POLAND

Buda·Pest HUNGARY

SLAVONIA

DALMATIA

Baltic Sea

EASTERN POMERANIA

BRANDENBURG

·Berlin

SAXONY

SILESIA

MORAVIA

·Prague

BOHEMIA

VIENNA

Vienna

STYRIA

CARINTHIA

CARNIOLA

Adriatic Sea

RAVENSBERG

MAGDEBURG

·CLEVE

MARK

BAVARIA

TYROL

Venice

FRIBURG

Rhine R.

North Sea

Mediterranean Sea

AUSTRIAN HABSBURGS 1699

AUSTRIAN HABSBURG TERRITORY 1521

ACQUISITIONS 1521-1648

ACQUISITIONS 1648-1699

IMPERIAL HUNGARY

headwaters of the Rhine and the Dutch Netherlands at its mouth obtained their independence. Since Turkey held the outlet of the Danube, the mouths of all the great rivers flowing through Germany were imprisoned in the hands of foreigners. The treaty confirmed the division of Germany into a complicated patchwork of some three hundred states. These varied in size from the free imperial cities like Hamburg and the Lilliputian knighthoods of Thuringia through states of medium extent, such as Bavaria, Saxony, Hanover, and Brandenburg, to the sizable Habsburg lands of Austria and Bohemia. Each separate German state, the treaty declared, was sovereign within its own domain. Each German ruler might choose whether he and his subjects be Lutheran, Calvinist, or Catholic, might form alliances and declare war against anyone except the emperor and the empire, and might establish his own army, coinage, laws, weights and measures, tolls and customs houses. True, an outline of a central organization still survived — a Holy Roman Emperor who was elected by the eight leading princes, an imperial Diet or legislature, and an imperial tribunal. But the emperor, without an army or administration, enjoyed an official annual revenue of only 8,000 talers — the price of a good farm. The delegates of the over 300 states who formed the imperial Diet disagreed on nearly everything except their opposition to the emperor. The imperial tribunal was so inadequately staffed as to fall decades behind in the decision of cases. The Diet ordered a commission to assemble in November, 1654, to investigate the judicial delays. Incredibly, the commission did not hold its first session until May, 1767, one hundred and thirteen years later. By then the imperial tribunal had 61,223 unsettled cases on its books, some of them one hundred and eighty years old. The Holy Roman Empire was a phantom organization which, as Voltaire observed, was neither Holy nor Roman nor an empire. After 1648, the empire, properly speaking, had no history of its own, as each ruler, mindless of the welfare of Germany, pursued his own advantage.

For centuries, one of the leading German families had been the Habsburg dukes of Austria. *Ostarrichi* meant "the land in the east" in old German, and we can perhaps hear in its evocative name something of the spell these white Alpine slopes, blue rivers, and green valleys cast over the eastward-moving Germans. During the tenth century and several centuries thereafter, German nobles, bishops, and abbots had settled German serfs in Austria proper around Vienna and also (side by side with Slav serfs) in the neighboring lands of Styria, Carinthia, and Carniola. In 1273 the south German Count Rudolf of Habsburg was elected Holy Roman Emperor and shortly after acquired Austria, Styria, Carinthia, and Carniola. His successors added the Tyrol in 1363. They continued intermittently to enlarge their Austrian foothold through marriage, bargaining, and war. After 1438 they were able to monopolize the title of Holy Roman Emperor. Emperor Charles V, who faced Martin Luther at Worms, granted in 1522 the administration of his Austrian lands to his brother, Ferdinand I, who was soon elected king of Bohemia and king of Hungary. The Bohemian complex then included the predominantly Slavic lands of Bohemia, Moravia, and Silesia; Hungary comprised only a western strip that had been left free by the Turks. Though the Reformation weakened the authority of the Austrian Habsburgs as emperors, the Counter-Reformation and the Thirty Years' War enabled them to re-impose Roman Catholic uniformity in their own dominions. Leopold I (1658-1705) and Charles VI (1711-1740) recovered from Turkey all of Hungary, the province of Transylvania, and part of Croatia, thus giving the Austrian Habsburgs a massive block of territory in the middle Danube. Charles VI acquired through the War of the Spanish Succession and later treaties of exchange the Spanish Netherlands (Belgium) and the Italian territories of Milan, Tuscany, Parma, and Piacenza. The Austrian House of Habsburg, by virtue of its vast, multilingual possessions, was by the early eighteenth century stronger than any other German princely family. By 1700 there had been ten straight generations of Habsburg emperors. No other German family had broken their streak; no other family seemed in competition with them.

Nevertheless, the authority of the Habsburgs in their own possessions was by no means absolute. As they had acquired separate territories in the middle Danube, they also acquired in each territory leading families of nobles who exacted dues and labor from peasant serfs, acted as local police officers and justices, enjoyed immunity from the direct land tax, and sat with representatives of the clergy and towns in local territorial assemblies known as diets. Austria itself was not one land but three (Upper, Lower, and Inner), each with its own diet. Diets also existed in Styria, Carinthia, Carniola, Bohemia, Moravia, and Hungary, making nine in all.[a] The consent of each diet, that is, in effect, of the leading noble families, had to be obtained before the land tax could be levied in its territory. Each diet, in fact, assessed and collected the land tax through its own administrative officer. It also arranged for the recruiting, provisioning, and quartering of troops and supervised the administration of police and justice by the local nobility.

The Habsburgs, especially Ferdinand I in the sixteenth century and Leopold I in the seventeenth, developed at Vienna a few central institutions, largely to co-ordinate their relations with the various diets. These institutions included a Privy Council of a few intimates with whom the emperor took counsel; five chancelleries in Vienna which corresponded with foreign powers and with the diets and officials in Austria proper, the Bohemian complex,

---

[a]The Assembly in Hungary, which was always more independent of the Habsburgs than the other provinces, was composed not of three houses (clergy, nobles, and townsmen) but of two — a House of Magnates, in which the great nobles and bishops sat, and the Table of Estates, for representatives of the country gentry and the towns.

Hungary, the Netherlands, and the Italian possessions; a Finance Council to receive and expend revenue from the royal domain, excise taxes on wine and beer, and the direct land tax; a War Council to organize the imperial army; and a Commerce Council to develop ports, overseas trading companies, and silk manufactories and to diminish provincial tariffs. By 1740 the Habsburg monarchy was a vast, multilingual, loosely-organized, rather easygoing complex of territories whose central administration negotiated largely with the leading noble families and rarely touched the inarticulate, illiterate peasant masses below. The Habsburgs were building, mostly from immediate need, institutions and usages that were making for unity: a few central administrative boards in Vienna; a dominant Roman Catholic church; a cosmpolitan imperial army with its own *esprit de corps* and loyalty to the dynasty; and an economic totality, as exchange within the Habsburg possessions increased. But the loose-jointed monarchy was still so laxly and superficially put together than it could not effectively organize the considerable resources it did possess.

Brandenburg-Prussia until 1786

The fate of Germany, as it turned out, lay not with Habsburg Austria but with the military, Protestant, northern German state of Brandenburg-Prussia. Nature did not make Brandenburg-Prussia great. The German knights and peasants who settled it found sandy soil, cold, white skies, and scraggy forests. Nature appeared to condemn them to poverty and powerlessness. But as they fought nature and other enemies, they came to have three leaders who made a difference – the Great Elector, Frederick William (1640-1688), King Frederick William I (1713-1740), and Frederick II, the Great (1740-1786). Of these the most significant, perhaps, was the Great Elector, for he launched those solutions of the continuing problems of his dynasty which his successors needed only to develop.

The problems were the outgrowth of centuries of history. For three centuries, the twelfth, thirteenth, and fourteenth, German migrants had crossed the Elbe, Oder, and Vistula rivers in search of land and easier tenures. They either settled among or exterminated the Slavs. Each German peasant householder was granted a village plot. If it was not always the best plot, he could leave when he chose, and he could not be removed without his consent. Each peasant family need pay only a few annual dues, usually in kind, to the local German knight and work a few days annually on his estate, which lay close to the village. Peasants and knights alike owed allegiance to an overlord. Between the Elbe and Oder rivers it was the margrave (later elector) of Brandenburg. At the mouth of the Oder it was the duke of Pomerania. Beyond the Vistula, it was the leader of the Teutonic Knights (after 1525 the duke of Prussia). In 1417 the electorate of Brandenburg was conferred on a rather obscure south German family, the Hohenzollern. The Hohenzollern elector acquired in 1614 through marriage and inheritance the duchy of Cleves and the counties of Mark and Ravensberg near the border of Holland and added in 1618 (also by inheritance) the duchy of (East) Prussia. The Great Elector thus had in his hands, on his accession in 1640, three rather small, rather bleak fragments of northern Europe, dispersed across the north German plain.

Each fragment of his inheritance had its own coinage, weights and measures, army, law, administration, and diet. In each diet the leading noble families gave tongue to their recalcitrance and to their selfish, local interests. The landlord families of Brandenburg and of Prussia had become especially formidable. As the new money economy had reached them in the late fourteenth century, the German knights east of the Elbe were tempted to raise grain in large quantities for export and sale. They brought into cultivation waste lands. When these were not enough, they incorporated peasant holdings, even whole villages, into their own estates, often on the scantiest pretexts. They slowly tightened their grip on the peasantry under their influence, replacing, piece by piece, the relatively loose fabric of manorial obligations with manacles. They gradually increased the labor traditionally owed the lord from several days each year to three or four days each week. They reduced the peasants from relatively free men who could move away to serfs irrevocably bound to the soil. Meanwhile, the knights continued to exercise the right to administer justice, to exercise police power, to appoint village magistrates, and to serve as local tax collectors. They gradually changed their title from *Ritter*, that is, knight, to *Junker*, that is, young gentleman or nobleman.

The money economy did not always produce these effects. It could work the other way. West of the Elbe it often did, where in a wholly different social and economic context onetime serfs, having a little currency, became renters, their obligations became money payments, and their lords, landlords who lived off their rent. In these cases the money in circulation loosened up their lives. But east of the Elbe it was a different story. There the money economy transformed the relatively free peasants into serfs supporting a cruel burden of obligatory services, and it elevated the knight into a Junker who administered the capitalistic exploitation by service labor of several thousand acres of land. In their managerial occupation the Junkers gained a pride in family, a comfortable habit of command, and a sense of solid assurance even in the presence of dukes and electors. The Junkers sat with the town representatives in the diets of Brandenburg and of Prussia and took advantage of the fiscal needs of the electors and of the dukes to exact the right of increased participation in the government. By 1640, the diets of Prussia, of Brandenburg, and of Cleves claimed extraordinary privileges. Taxes could not

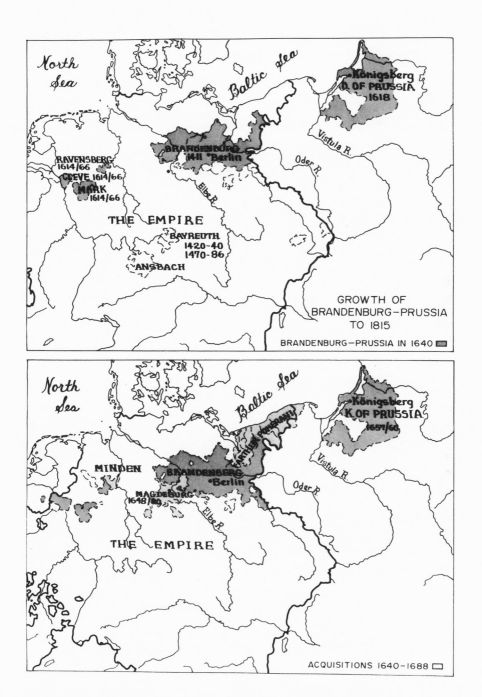

North Sea

Baltic Sea

Königsberg
D. OF PRUSSIA
1618

Vistula R.

BRANDENBURG
1411 Berlin

Oder R.

RAVENSBERG
1614/66
CLEVE 1614/66
MARK
1614/66

Elbe R.

THE EMPIRE

BAYREUTH
1420-40
1470-86

ANSBACH

GROWTH OF
BRANDENBURG-PRUSSIA
TO 1815

BRANDENBURG-PRUSSIA IN 1640 ▨

North Sea

Baltic Sea

Königsberg
K. OF PRUSSIA
1657/60

Vistula R.

FARTHER POMERANIA

MINDEN

BRANDENBURG
Berlin

Oder R.

MAGDEBURG
1648/80

Elbe R.

THE EMPIRE

ACQUISITIONS 1640-1688 ▢

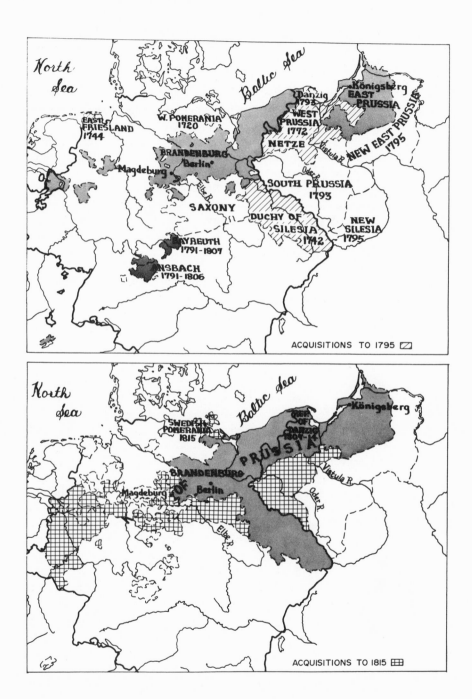

North Sea

Baltic Sea

Königsberg
EAST PRUSSIA

Danzig 1793
WEST PRUSSIA 1772

EAST FRIESLAND 1744

W. POMERANIA 1720

NETZE

NEW EAST PRUSSIA 1795

Vistula R.

BRANDENBURG 'Berlin'

Magdeburg

Oder R.

SOUTH PRUSSIA 1793

SAXONY

DUCHY OF SILESIA 1742

NEW SILESIA 1795

BAYREUTH 1791-1807

ANSBACH 1791-1806

ACQUISITIONS TO 1795 ▨

North Sea

Baltic Sea

Königsberg

SWEDISH POMERANIA 1815

Q'DOM OF DANZIG 1807-14

P R U S S I A

BRANDENBURG

Magdeburg

OF

Berlin

Vistula R.

Oder R.

Elbe R.

ACQUISITIONS TO 1815 ⊞

be levied nor troops maintained nor foreign alliances negotiated without their consent, while only the native-born (of Prussia, Brandenburg, or Cleves) were eligible for administrative office.

Each fragment of the Great Elector's heritage was also exposed to attack and harassment during the Thirty Years' War. The Great Elector's father, George William (1620-1640), was a well-meaning, not unintelligent man, but too vacillating and soft to defend the neutrality of his land against the marauding armies of both sides which crossed and re-crossed and ravaged it. The story is told that George William was once reduced to wandering with his councilors in the woods muttering, *"Que faire! Ils ont des canons"* ("What to do? They have cannon!"). By 1640 the Rhenish possession of Cleves-Mark, ringed by Dutch, Imperial, and Spanish armies, and invaded by each in turn, was completely out of control; Brandenburg, plundered and almost desolate, was occupied by the Swedes except for a few fortresses and its capital, Berlin; Prussia, free of foreign troops, was yet caught up in the complexities of Polish-Swedish enmity.

The Great Elector was in 1640 a sober, practical, intelligent young man of twenty years of age. The defense and extension of three feeble, disconnected possessions, he realized, required an army. "Alliances," he later observed, "are good; but a force of one's own, on which one can rely, is better." On his accession, he disbanded the mercenary force which had gotten out of hand and refounded a new army of 4,000 in 1641, increased it to 8,000 by 1655, then to a wartime force of 27,000 by 1660, and to a permanent peacetime army of 30,000 by 1688. At first the troops of the Elector's various lands were organized under separate commands, but after 1655 they were placed under the command of a single general. There was thus one general before there was one state. The soldiers recruited in Cleves might now serve in East Prussia, and all soldiers knew no authority save the Elector's. Well equipped and disciplined, the army won its reputation when at the battle of Fehrbellin in 1675 it defeated the Swedish infantry, then considered after the French the best in Europe.

An army led to taxes, and these in turn to the manipulation in each diet of the leading noble families who often refused to vote revenue grants. The Great Elector reached a virtual compromise with the Junkers of Brandenburg and of Prussia. He agreed that the Junkers were not simple knights but were nobles, that their lands were exempt from taxation, and that noble land could be transferred by testament or sale only to nobles. He confirmed their right to hold the peasants in serfdom and to exercise local police jurisdiction over peasant villages. The Elector also accepted Junkers as officers in the army and administration, thus inaugurating a working alliance between nobles and ruler that was to be one of the continuing characteristics of the Prussian state. Since the Junkers lived in a backward country of poor soil, they were not rich and they came to welcome the opportunity of finding a career or supplementing their income through royal employment. At the same time, the Elector insisted on obedience and gradually deprived the diets of Brandenburg, of Prussia, and of Cleves-Mark of the power to hobble his activity. When they granted money for a period of years, he continued to collect it beyond the stipulated period. When they refused money, he collected it anyway. Eventually, the Elector and his successors were sufficiently strong to bypass the diets almost entirely.

An army led to taxes, to a compromise with the Junkers, to a disabling of the diets — and also to a central administration. A united army under a single command by 1668 led to the formation of a group of officers into a general staff at Berlin which considered questions of strategy and leadership in the field. A united army led to the establishment at Berlin of a central administrative board, the General Commissariat, which saw to the recruiting, provisioning, and quartering of troops in all the Elector's land. It also appointed subordinate local officials who collected the excise tax on beer, wine, and other articles in the towns, and the direct land tax from the peasants. The Elector (and his successor) also set up a central board at Berlin to administer the royal domains in all his territories.

An army led to attempts to increase the yield of taxes by promoting the prosperity of a poor country through government supervision, regulation, and aid. The Great Elector encouraged immigration. He settled seventy Frisian families, acquainted with better agricultural methods, in Brandenburg; then a few Swiss; then he attracted 20,000 refugee French Huguenots by giving them land, building materials, and exemption from taxation for six years. He established a postal system, ran a botanical garden in front of the Berlin palace to try out foreign trees and plants for suitability in his sandy soil, organized a model farm, stipulated that no bridegroom might marry until he had planted at least six new fruit-trees, all the while vigorously regulating the quality of the product of established industries and encouraging by subsidies and tariffs the development of new ones. He also constructed a canal which joined the Oder River with the Spree, thus opening an uninterrupted waterway from the Oder, down the Spree, the Havel, and the Elbe, to the North Sea.

He ruled always with the army at his back, and on the frontiers. He used the army and a shrewd diplomacy to cut down the distances between his three disconnected territories. By the Peace of Westphalia (1648), which concluded the Thirty Years' War, the Great Elector secured eastern Pomerania, a finger of land stretching from Brandenburg along the Baltic seacoast toward East Prussia, and the bishoprics of Halberstadt, Cammin, Minden, and Magdeburg, which extended from Brandenburg toward the Rhineland. By the settlement of 1648 the head of the house of Hohenzollern controlled a larger area of territory than any other German prince except the head of the house of Habsburg.

The Great Elector's son, Frederick I (1688-1713), was a misshapen, unmilitary spendthrift who yet wangled the permission of the Holy Roman Emperor (a Habsburg) to assume the title of King in Prussia. The work of the Great Elector was resumed by his grandson, Frederick William I (1713-1740). Faced by the same problem as the Great Elector — to defend and extend scattered possessions of low productivity — Frederick William continued the same policies and solutions, with even greater stress on the army. A harsh, literal-minded man whom Carlyle tagged the Royal Drill Sergeant of Prussia, Frederick William was engrossed in military affairs. "If one wishes to decide anything in the world," he remarked, "it cannot be done with the pen if it is not supported by the power of the sword." He wore the army uniform throughout his life, and when at his deathbed they were chanting, "Naked I came into the world, and naked I shall leave it," he broke in seriously, "That is not so; I shall be buried in my uniform."

An army in a poor land, he realized, required thrift, the development of the land's resources, and a diligent civil administration. His spendthrift father had not been dead for half an hour when Frederick William called for the royal household accounts and dismissed two-thirds of the court officials, lackeys, and pages. When his father had journeyed to Königsberg for his coronation in 1701, he traveled for fourteen days with a train of 2,000 horses and spent 5,000,000 talers. Frederick William went there for the same purpose in four days with 50 horses and spent 2,547 talers. Like the Great Elector, he steadily attempted to promote the material prosperity of his possessions through government direction and aid. He settled waste places with thrifty colonists, increased the tariff on woolens and grain, and encouraged by subsidies new industries. Building on the foundations laid by the Great Elector, he re-organized the administration. He brought the separate administrations of War, Finance, and Domain into the hands of a single administrative board, the General Directory, with which he worked. Whereas the Great Elector had usually been forced to promise that officials be used only in their native province, Frederick William insisted that they be transferred out of their own provinces into others, thus cutting them loose from local connections and local sentiments and persuading them to devote themselves to the service of the king in all his separate lands. He attracted into the administration members of both the middle class and the Junkers, thus absorbing "into the service of the monarchy the most industrious and intelligent section of the population, and binding their interests closly to those of the state."[1] He

---

[1] Walter L. Dorn, "The Prussian Bureaucracy in the Eighteenth Century," *Political Science Quarterly*, XLVI (1931), 407-408.

exacted from his officials punctuality and diligence. He himself was up at five o'clock every morning, busy reading reports. Accounts, under him, were carefully audited, and corruption extirpated. He set a tradition which for two hundred years made the Prussian civil service one of the best in the world, noted for service, honesty, and devotion to duty. Partly as a result of his measures, the material product of the Prussian economy tripled during his reign, while the royal revenue increased from 3,655,000 to nearly 7,000,000 talers.

Nearly all of this money was spent by him on the military forces. Of the annual revenue of seven million talers, one million was spent on education, civil service, and the court, one million was saved, and five million was expended on the army. Frederick William increased the size of the army from 38,000 in 1713 to 83,000 in 1740 and shaped it by stern discipline and incessant drill into the most precise military machine in Europe. Prussia with 2.2 million people ranked twelfth in population among the European states but placed fourth (just after Russia, France, and Austria) in the size of its army. The House of Austria, with its enormous territories and nearly ten times as many subjects as the king of Prussia, had an army of only 100,000 men. Industry, commerce, agriculture, taxation, administration, and the organization of society were all geared in Prussia to the creation of a fine army. The privates were increasingly drawn from the native peasantry, who were declared to be universally liable to military service. The officers were more and more frequently Junkers, who became devoted to the Hohenzollern dynasty which they had once defied. Accustomed to command peasants at home, they easily learned to command them in the field, and they became pillars of the Prussian monarchy. The revenue for military purposes was increasingly derived from the townsmen, who were usually exempt from military duty. Contemporaries were wont to repeat: "Prussia is not a state which possesses an army, but an army which possesses a state." A Frenchman visiting Berlin in 1733 wrote: "Soldiers form the majority of the inhabitants of this capital. The conversation of doctors, pastors, townsfolk, even ladies, turns on military topics, and one hears nothing but drilling and marching." So dearly did Frederick William love his "blue boys" that he dared risk his army only once in war, against Sweden. He was then able to add in 1720 the mouth of the Oder River and the good Baltic seaport of Stettin.

The basic policies which the Great Elector started and Frederick William intensified — government regulation of and aid to the economy, an efficient bureaucracy directed by the ruler, devotion of five-sevenths of the annual revenue to the army, incorporation of the Junkers into the bureaucracy and army, and acquisition of territory — were continued by Frederick the Great (1740-1786). Frederick, a gifted general, used the army his father had forged to nearly double the area of Prussia and more than double its population. He annexed without much excuse Silesia, the fairest province of the Habsburg Empress Maria Theresa, and defended his grab in the First Silesian War (1740-1742), the Second Silesian War (1744-1745), and the Seven Years' War (1756-1763). In the last war he was matched against three empires, Austria, France, and Russia, each of whose armies was greater than his and whose combined populations were far greater than that of Prussia. Frederick, aided only by English subsidies and an Anglo-Hanoverian force, "campaigned across his ravaged dominions as cunning and as desperate as a wolf at bay" and in the end kept Silesia. He participated with Austria and Russia in the First Partition of Poland in 1772 and took as his share West Prussia, which filled in the gap between Pomerania and East Prussia. By his death in 1786 the population of Prussia had risen from 2.2 to 5.7 million and the number of soldiers from 83,000 to 200,000. The Great Elector had inaugurated the solution (army, bureaucracy, incorporation of nobility, and mercantilism) to the continuing problems of the dynasty; Frederick William I had imbued the bureaucracy with a sense of duty and accentuated the concentration of will and resources on the army; Frederick the Great carried the army and Prussia to victory.

By the end of the eighteenth century the three rulers had accomplished the impossible: out of scattered units open to attack on the poor, sandy soil of the northern German plain, they had created a great power able to challenge the Austrian Habsburgs for leadership in Germany and to compete as equals with France and Russia in Europe. Thereafter, the future of Germany hung on the outcome of the rivalry between Austria and Prussia. The Prussian rulers, in the process of solving their problems and repeating the solutions, had shaped traditional policies and institutions that endured through the passage of time. Working from above more or less alone, within narrow limits, they had woven these memorable patterns surprisingly deep into the experience of the royal family and the Junkers.

The first element of this Prussian tradition, which became in time part of the German tradition, was acceptance of and belief in the value of the military and power aspects of life. "The first duty of the prince," observed Frederick the Great, "is to maintain himself and the second to improve his position." A Hohenzollern would feel disgraced if he did not leave the kingdom larger than he found it. For the execution of these duties a strong army was necessary. "Negotiations without arms," again to quote Frederick, "are music without instruments." Construction of a fine army was the first concern of the ruler; service in the army, the first and supreme duty of the subject. War and preparation for war, observed the eighteenth-century writer, Mirabeau, was "the national industry of Prussia." Belief in a strong army implied a faith in force — why shouldn't the Hohenzollerns have a faith in force; had it not always in the long run been successful?

The second element of the tradition was the heavy emphasis placed on a disciplined civil administration. In more than one way this civil service was the complement of the military service: it was carefully graded, co-ordinated and organized, and responsible to the sovereign alone; it was animated by a sense of duty and by devotion to the state. Third, the administration and all the power and treasure of the monarch were to be used to promote the material prosperity of the country through government intervention and aid. Enterprises were to be encouraged, to be subsidized, to be protected by tariffs, but they were also to be guided, to be directed, to be regulated. Fourth, the Junkers were integrated as loyal servants into the administration and army. In the France of Louis XIV something different was happening: the nobles were being uprooted from participation in military and political affairs by the encroachments of the centralized administration on the manorial regime, by their ceremonial life at Versailles, and by the preference of the monarch for bourgeois councilors. In Prussia, the Junker at home on his estate was the local police official, justice of the peace, tax collector, and recruiting officer, as well as capitalistic entrepreneur. Away from home he was the king's comrade in arms and his faithful administrator.

The fifth element in the tradition was a philosophy that stressed the state rather than the individual. From the laborious king on down, the individual must sacrifice himself in the service of the state. "I am the first servant of the State," was Frederick the Great's oft-repeated motto. When a delegation of townspeople thanked him for his generous donation of money that enabled them to rebuild their houses destroyed by fire, Frederick, "visibly moved," replied characteristically: "You have no need to thank me; it was my duty; that is what I am here for!" The service of the state was the highest form of all service. In that service, in performing his duty, the individual found his life and fulfilled it. Greatness and a sense of greatness were not to be gained by individual, personal achievement or development, but in being the obedient part of a larger whole. As the greatness of Prussia increased, so did the sense of greatness of each Prussian. Although the separate elements of this tradition were not peculiar to Prussia, their concentrated combination and sustained application were unique.

These three rulers, acting in response to their daily needs, desires, and dreams, and without being aware of the full consequences of their acts, had founded not only a state and a tradition — they were also in the way of forming, without intending it, a Prussian nation. In the late Middle Ages we noted how the activities of the central governments of England and France were bringing their respective peoples together. Here in the history of Prussia we watch by the illumination of modern documents a similar process. When the Great Elector took charge in 1640, each of his dominions, Cleves-Mark, Brandenburg, and Prussia, had a separate coinage, law, army, administration, capital, legislature, and (in a sense) a separate titular ruler — the duke of Cleves or the elector of Brandenburg or the duke of Prussia, though he was the same person. The inhabitants of the three possessions, having little in common except the German language, had a sense of separateness. If they lived in Cleves-Mark, for example, they thought of the Great Elector as a duke of Cleves, who had other dominions scattered throughout Germany which were doubtless his care but with which they had nothing to do. Brandenburg-Prussia had so little sense of nation that inhabitants of Brandenburg around Berlin looked upon the Pomeranians immediately to the north as foreigners and tried to refuse them military aid, though they were under the same ruler.

The Great Elector, on the contrary, looked upon his separate possessions as forming a single unit. He overawed the separate legislatures and formed a single army in which soldiers from Cleves-Mark, Brandenburg, and Prussia fought side by side under a single flag and a single leader for the single common purpose of strengthening the Hohenzollern dynasty. He established at Berlin central administrative councils and boards on which natives from all his possessions considered together the problems of all his dominions. With the assumption by the Great Elector's son of the title of king "in Prussia," the subjects of his separate lands now served together in the Royal Prussian Army and accepted the orders of the Royal Prussian Administration. Frederick William forwarded the process by forbidding officials to serve in the native province. He also established a common code of criminal procedure for all Prussian courts of law, and Frederick the Great issued a uniform civil procedure. The subjects of the Hohenzollern kings came to have a sense of living under the same ruler and administration and of being tried by the same procedure.

The awareness, however, came gradually and was at first only intellectual. As late as the 1750's, Frederick the Great still referred to his possessions as "mes états" (my states), instead of "my state," while a preacher in Berlin spoke from his pulpit "of all these provinces which we must regard as our fatherland." But the terrible Seven Years' War, in which Frederick the Great was matched against Russia, Austria, and France, brought the people closer to each other and to their monarch. The common experience of a great struggle, the common suffering and the common effort, aroused in the inhabitants a lively sense of cohesion, of belonging together, and they rallied around their heroic king. Frederick began to speak of the *esprit de corps et de nation* of his army officers and civil servants. The citizens of Magdeburg (just across the river from Brandenburg) collected money for the relief of the Pomeranians, now looked upon as fellow Prussians. As the war receded into the past, the feeling of belonging together cooled, but it remained latent and was to be refired and reaffirmed in the War of Liberation against Napoleon. It had taken two wars to forge the Prussian nation, just as it probably required two wars (the Hundred Years' War against France and the War against Spain) to fuse the English. Part of the Prussian tradition, in any case, was pride in being Prussian. "Prussians we are and Prussians we will remain," Otto von Bismarck wrote later with Prussia's history in mind, "and I hope to God that we will still long remain Prussians when this sheet of paper is forgotten like a withered autumn leaf."

The Habsburg Monarchy, 1740-1780

Frederick the Great's successful annexation of Silesia shocked the Austrian Habsburgs into realizing that the new and upstart Hohenzollerns, whom they had once despised, had passed them in administrative efficiency and military power. The Empress Maria Theresa (1740-1780), a warm-hearted, intelligent *Hausfrau* with a tact for circumstances, was astounded that her cumbersome administrative arrangements let her maintain only two cavalry regiments in Silesia while Frederick sustained there an army. After losing Silesia, she dreamed of getting it back. With the coming of peace in 1748 she set about to reorganize the monarchy. Her measures, like those of her Prussian rival, grew out of the need for a larger, more effective army, which in turn required a larger revenue and an efficient administrative network behind it. She allowed the diets of her Austrian-Bohemian lands to meet annually, but she deprived them of the right to consent to taxes, to administer the collection of taxes, and to supervise the recruiting, quartering, or provisioning of troops. These lands were now divided into ten districts, each one administered by an imperial official whose subordinates collected taxes and recruited soldiers. The officials reported to a unified Austrian-Bohemian Treasury at Vienna. At the capital were also a centralized war office, a foreign office, a ministry of commerce, and a high court of justice.

The bypassing of the diets and the extension of the administration from Vienna to the remotest town or village brought Maria Theresa into contact with the condition of the peasant serfs. She came to realize that the size of her revenue and the health of her monarchy depended to a considerable degree on their prosperity. Since the leading noble families of Bohemia and Austria were generally wealthier than the Prussian Junkers, they had not entered the imperial army and civil service in large numbers. There was less reason and also less likelihood for the imperial government to be considerate of their feelings. Measures were taken to tax the nobles and to set a minimum acreage for the use of each serf and a maximum of obligations for their burdens. As Maria Theresa said, "I must do justice both to the rich and the poor, I must satisfy my conscience and I won't lose my soul for the interest of some magnates and noble persons."

The Habsburg monarchy was too sprawling and multilingual and its administrative integration had started too late for it ever to become an intense national unit like Prussia. Maria Theresa was never able, for example, to apply her administrative and social reforms to Hungary, Lombardy, and Belgium, whose leading noble families remained nearly as independent as before. Nevertheless, the reforms she did achieve brought the monarchy abreast of current administrative practice, revived it as a vital going concern, and enabled it to field a far better army in the Seven Years' War than it had ten years before.

An Invitation to Further Inquiry and Reflection

In the third chapter we reflected on the rise of the national monarchy in France and England, the delayed consolidation of Spain, and the negative examples of Italy and Germany to reach a hypothesis about how nation-states were being formed at that time in Europe. The hypothesis was being held tentatively, for the examples were few and the data incomplete and scattered. Now, we have the opportunity to check the hypothesis against another positive example, the formation of the Prussian nation-state. To conduct the check as a thought-experiment, what steps must we follow? Would it not be well, as a first step, to list the propositions that the hypothesis asserts about the formation of a nation-state? Next to check each proposition against the Prussian experience? Then to note which propositions stand up, which do not, and which, perhaps, need re-phrasing in the light of the new evidence? And, at the same time, to derive from the Prussian example additional propositions that need to be checked against the earlier French, English, and Spanish instances? Having done this, are we then ready to build one model of the formation of nation-states in Western culture? What would that model be? What do we mean by "model"? Are we ready to formulate a theory about the formation of nation-states in Western culture? What do we mean by theory and when do we have one? And how does a theory differ from a hypothesis?

For Further Reading

(For general reading)

Walter H. Bruford, *Germany in the Eighteenth Century — The Social Background of the Literary Revival* (1935)

Henri De Catt, *Frederick the Great, the Memoirs of His Reader, Henri De Catt* (1930)

Walter Dorn, *Competition for Empire, 1740-1763* (1940)

Robert Ergang, *The Potsdam Führer: Frederick I, Father of Prussian Militarism* (1941)

P. Frischauer, *The Imperial Crown: The Story of the Rise and Fall of the Holy Roman and the Austrian Empires* (1939)

———, *Prince Eugene, 1663-1763: A Man and a Hundred Years of History* (1934)

Pierre Gaxotte, *Frederick the Great* (1942)

George P. Gooch, *Courts and Cabinets* (1946)

George Peabody Gooch, *Frederick the Great: The Ruler, the Writer, the Man* (1947)

Ferdinand Schevill, *The Great Elector* (1947)

(For advanced study)

Paul Bernard, *Joseph II* (1968)

John A. R. Marriott and Charles G. Robertson,   *The Evolution of Prussia* (1915)

H. Rosenberg, "The Rise of the Junkers in Brandenburg-Prussia, 1410-1653," *American Historical Review*, 49 (1943-1944), 1-22, 228-42

Chapter XII
THE RISE OF RUSSIA

Meanwhile, on the eastern fringe of Europe, still another star was arising, from the forest clearings around Moscow. At first this seems to be something we have seen before: Moscow, a clearing in the wilderness, was gradually transformed (like Paris, Vienna, and Berlin) into the center of a state. The process of development was a lingering one, spread out through many centuries and generations. As with the formation of France, Austria, and Prussia, so with Russia: a princely family started obscurely in an overgrown village; it subdued and came to terms with the leading noble families living in the forests immediately adjacent, used the resources of this inner domain to acquire other territories, gropingly devised administrative practices to secure obedience in the enlarged kingdom, and gradually became a focus of regard for a wider society.

But then in the seventeenth and eighteenth centuries the organic growth of Russian society was interrupted. The technology, economy, and military and administrative organization of Muscovy had lagged behind that of western Europe. When the Muscovite princes came face to face with the superior power of the other European states they tried to catch up. They adopted or accentuated practices that usually increased the power of their state but also widened the rift between the great mass of the peasants on the one hand and the nobles and government on the other. They thus introduced a fault (to use a geological term) in Russian society and history. The key figure in the continuation and the interruption of Russian history was Peter the Great, perhaps the most significant ruler of Russia before Lenin.

The Kievan Period (to 1132)

A salient feature of Russia is the vastness of the Russian land. The immense plain that Russia came to occupy stretches almost without a break from the Baltic Sea, East Prussia, and Poland across the Eurasian continent to the Pacific Ocean, a territory that is more than twice the size of the United States. The Ural Mountains, which technically divide Europe from Asia, are a low range of wooded highlands, rarely rising higher than forty-five hundred feet above sea level. From north to south the plain is divided geographically into four broad bands which merge the one into the next: the bleak tundra of frozen waste stretching along the shore of the Arctic Sea; the zone of deep forested wilderness which extends as far south as Kiev-Kazan and through which the rivers (to use a figure of Bernard Pares) draw lines of light; the low-rolling, arable, treeless prairie (the steppe), producing grasses that in summer grow high enough to give cover to a horse; and, as the moisture diminishes, the sun-baked semideserts and deserts of the south. From time immemorial the steppe was the invasion route of mounted Asiatic nomads, who riding like monkeys on their horses swept periodically from central Asia across southern Russia into Europe.

The original home of the Slavic tribes who came to inhabit this land had been north of the Carpathian Mountains, in the region of the Pripet river, a tributary of the Dnieper. From that center they had migrated toward the west, the south, and east in the first centuries of the Christian era. Those that had moved east into the forested wilderness and the steppes of present-day Russia had reached the Don river by the sixth century, the Volga by the eighth. They had settled mostly in and around commercial towns, such as Kiev, Novgorod, Smolensk, and Rostov. These lay along the water trade routes from the Baltic area, either down the Dnieper River to the Black Sea and thence to the Byzantine capital of Constantinople or down the Volga River to the Caspian Sea and thence to the Moslem capital of Baghdad. The Slavs participated in this trade and, like the Venetians in the Mediterranean, exchanged slaves, amber, salt, furs, honey, and wax for the fine silks and gold work of the Greek and Arabic craftsmen. The Slavs acquired from Constantinople an alphabet that resembled the Greek, a new religion (the Orthodox version of Christianity), and a style of architecture. They evolved a form of political organization by accepting the leadership of the princes of Kiev, and they gradually began to rise, like the contemporary western Europeans, from crudity toward civilization.

Their progress was retarded after 1132 for three hundred and fifty years by the renewed attacks of the Asiatic nomads, first of the Cumans and then of the Mongolian Tartars. From 1236 to 1462, for example, there were forty-eight Tartar invasions. Killing, looting, taking prisoners, and exacting tribute, the well-organized nomads severed the trade and cultural contacts of the Russians with Constantinople, scattering the Slavs around Kiev in three directions. Some Slavs retired westward to Galicia, the home of their ancestors north of the Carpathian Mountains. Others fled northward along the Dnieper to join their brethren around Smolensk and Novgorod. These two groups, around Galicia and Smolensk and Novgorod, eventually fell under the large Roman Catholic state of Lithuania-Poland. Still other Slavs stole off northeastward along the rivers into the sheltering forests at the headwaters of the Volga River. Here in the backwoods there gradually emerged around Moscow a new Great-Russian society and a Muscovite tsar.

RUSSIAN EMPIRE 1796
ALASKA
SIBERIA
RUSSIA
PRUSSIA
AUSTRIA
MONGOLIA
TURKESTAN
CHINA

Arctic Ocean

TERRITORY ACQUIRED 1462-1505

URAL MTS.
Obi
Dvina
BOUNDARY OF THE GOLDEN HORDE
UNTIL 1480

SWEDEN
FINLAND
1743
KARELIA St. Petersburg
INGRIA 1721
LIVONIA
1510
Novgorod

SIBERIA
URAL MTS.

Baltic Sea

PRUSSIA
Pripet
ACQUIRED BY PARTITION OF POLAND 1772-1795

Moscow
Smolensk
1617
MUSCOVY 1462

TERRITORY ACQUIRED 1505-1682

Ural R.

Kiev
ACQUIRED 1725-1796

Volga

Carpathian Mts.

AUSTRIAN EMPIRE
Dniester R.
Dnieper
Don
Azov
Caspian Sea
Aral Sea

OTTOMAN
1725-1796
Black Sea
Constantinople
EMPIRE
Aegean Sea

EXPANSION OF RUSSIA 1300-1796
1300-1462   1505-1682
1462-1505   1682-1725
1725-1796

The Emergence of Muscovy (1132-1682)

At the base of the Great Russian society from the twelfth century until Soviet Communism was the patriarchal peasant household, composed of father, mother, sons, daughters, grandsons, granddaughters, brothers, sisters, cousins, and in-laws, all tumbling over each other in a single cottage or several. At first, in the twelfth and thirteenth centuries and even later a single household would occupy and own a clearing in the wilderness as far as the plow and ax could reach. Gradually, three or four other households would be added to form a village. By the sixteenth century the village had usually adopted the western three-field system of cultivation where each household held several strips in each of the three fields. In Russia the village came to hold periodic meetings to decide when to plow, when to sow, and when to reap. The meetings were also beginning by the sixteenth century to apportion or reapportion land among the households. At the same time, from the twelfth century to the fifteenth most peasant households, for reasons that are obscure, ceased to be independent landowners and became renters. In return for protection and cleared land, the household paid the noble (or ecclesiastical) landlord a rent in kind or money and worked his land. The household in the sixteenth century was still in law a free tenant: it could still leave if it discharged its obligations. Nevertheless, as the noble mounted, his peasants sank under him to form a kind of pedestal. An insidious relationship set in, then, early in this story, between his social position and their social abasement.

Above the noble landlords, who were called boyars, were princes of varying degrees of property and importance. Gradually the prince of Moscow pulled ahead of the others. The first Moscow prince of importance was Prince Yuri (1304-1324) of the House of Rurik. Moscow and Yuri in 1304 corresponded to Paris and Hugh Capet in 987. (The time lag is interesting though not necessarily crucial, since both Vienna and Berlin, the Habsburgs and the Hohenzollerns, also had started late.) Yuri secured from the grand khan of the Mongolian Tartars the profitable privilege of collecting from the Russians the annual tribute for the Golden Horde and thus gained financial supervision over the rival princes. Yuri and his immediate successors struggled with the princes and with recalcitrant boyars until Vasili II (1425-1462) gained undisputed mastery of the 15,000 square miles around Moscow, just as the Capetian Louis the Fat (1108-1137) had mastered the Île-de-France. Striking out from there, using the men and other resources their base afforded them, Vasili's successors added the northern principalities of Yaroslav (1436), Rostov (1474), Tver (1485), Viatka (1489), and Novgorod (1471) to give Moscow an outlet on the Arctic Sea. They threw off the Tartar yoke in 1480, and annexed the Tartar Khanates of Kazan (1552) and Astrakhan (1556), thus acquiring the entire basin of the Volga River. By conquests from Lithuania-Poland they also pushed back the western frontier with the acquisition of Smolensk (1522) and the east bank of the Dnieper as well as the city of Kiev on the west bank (1667, 1686). Meanwhile, from the latter part of the sixteenth century, individual adventurers, trappers, traders, and peasants had passed the Urals, entered largely uninhabited Siberia, and reached the Pacific Ocean by 1600 in an eastward expansion that for the most part went of itself. Muscovy, by the mid-seventeenth century, had acquired the outlines of a world power.

The princes of Moscow, like the Capetian kings, the Habsburg emperors, and the Hohenzollern electors, gropingly devised administrative practices that would enable them to govern their enlarged domain. They owned in name far more than they controlled in fact. They faced again the winner's old problem: of spreading out their administration and sinking it down. Since Moscow was at the center of a vast wilderness where trade was relatively slight, towns few, and the middle class inconsiderable, the Moscow princes had to rely, to a greater degree even than the Habsburgs and Hohenzollerns, on the scattered, landed nobility. They came to grant land only upon condition that services be rendered. Gradually they imposed the obligation that services must be returned by all nobles who held land. Each noble was expected to lead into campaign (and each village was expected to provide) a specified number of peasant soldiers. This wartime militia proving inadequate, the Muscovite princes developed a standing army of mercenaries, often instructed in the rudiments of warfare by foreign soldiers of fortune. By 1681 the ruler of Moscow had dispersed across his territory a wartime army of 164,000, part mercenary, some of it armed with muskets, some with bows and arrows.

An army this big required considerable money. Each village and town was assigned its quota of taxes. The village meeting apportioned the taxes among the different peasant households, then gave the required sum to the landlord, who passed it on to the district tax collector, who transmitted it to the governor of the province, who sent it to Moscow. As business increased and new administrative problems arose, the Muscovite princes created new central administrative offices one by one, according to the needs and indications of the moment, until by 1650 they had nearly reached the wondrous number of fifty. There were four offices that dealt with military affairs, the Office of Infantry, the Office of Cavalry, the Office of Foreign Troops, and the Office of Apothecaries (Physicians), not to mention the Office for the Ransoming of Prisoners. Several offices shared the right to collect taxes. The effective operation of these military and financial measures required a firmly settled population in villages and towns that could be counted on to cultivate the land of the noble, supply recruits for the army, and pay taxes. Since the peasant tenants tended to flee to the steppe or the outlying wilderness to

escape the murderous extortions of landlord and state, the central government
issued during the sixteenth and seventeenth centuries a series of edicts which
at first limited and then prohibited the free movement of agricultural workers.
The great bulk of the free tenants disappeared into serfdom. All the while, the
Russian branch of the Orthodox church supported the princes of Moscow.
The metropolitan see of "All Russia" was transferred to Moscow in 1326 and
raised to the patriarchate in 1589. It continued the Byzantine tradition of
subservience of the Orthodox church to the state, going so far as to affirm
that a breach of allegiance to the ruler of Moscow was a crime against the
church.

All this spelled the prince's gain. It spelled the peasant's ruin; and, strangely, it spelled the boyar's loss. They were losing, like the peasants under them,
the right to leave the service of their own lord, the prince of Moscow, and to
accept service with another. They could no longer own hereditary estates
unencumbered by an obligation to render services to the prince. The boyar
duma, an informal council of high government officials drawn from the
boyars, was rarely called. The Muscovite princes, sustained by the church,
asserted ever more extravagant pretensions to absolute and autocratic rule,
unlimited by law. They assumed ever more extravagant titles to go with their
increasing possessions and power. Ivan III (1462-1505) married in 1472
Sophie Paleologue, a niece of the last Byzantine emperor. Adopting the
double eagle of the Byzantine Empire for his coat-of-arms, he styled himself
"by the Grace of God, Tsar (Caesar), Autocrat, Lord of All Russia, Grand
Prince of Moscow, Prince of Tver, etc." He was regarded by his people as the
chosen of God, protector of the Orthodox faith. Ivan IV (1553-1584) claimed
that his power came of God alone, and was subject to no limitations of
human origin. The early princes and tsars of Moscow had gradually acquired a
moral and even an autocratic authority which their successors, under the stress
of war with European states, could wield to initiate reform.

The Early Expansion of Russia Toward Europe and
Its Consequences (1613-1725)

The immediate predecessors of Peter the Great — Ivan III, Vasili III
(1504-1533), Ivan IV, and the rulers of the new Romanov dynasty, Michael'
(1613-1645) and Alexis (1645-1675) — had driven east against shadowy,
slippery nomadic enemies, and had found rather easy going. But when they
turned west and south, however, they faced powerful foes. Russia could make
no headway against Sweden, which then excluded her from the shore of the
Baltic Sea, nor against Turkey, which after 1475 denied her access to the
Black Sea, while she could barely defeat Poland.

The Russian army and administration had progressed during the sixteenth and seventeenth centuries, but the technological, administrative, and military organization of the other European states had also advanced, and Russia still remained behind. Muscovy in the seventeenth century was still a vast, wooded, landlocked country at the edge of European agricultural settlement, with the nomadic tribes of central Asia just beyond. As in tenth-century western Europe, there were in Muscovy few trading towns, and fewer valuable manufactures. Men were unskilled in agriculture, home industries, and trade. Craftsmen were unable to build ships, work metals, or finish cloth with western proficiency. Merchants did not know how to figure and hence were cheated while the finest scholars, it was said, did not understand fourth-grade arithmetic, let alone higher mathematics. The army was scattered and poorly equipped; the administrators, barbarous, corrupt, and inefficient. The great mass of Russians, landlords and peasants, were untidy and superstitious. The men were bearded, for they believed that man was made in the image of God with a beard, and they wore conical bonnets and the long, flowing robes of the oriental caftan that excited hilarity among the Europeans. The Russians were boundlessly ignorant and boundlessly attached to their customs and were persuaded that the "Third Rome" of Muscovite Orthodoxy stood superior and alone in a sinful and heretical world.

As often happens, it may have been a cannonball that woke up her leaders. Repeated military defeats, especially at the hands of Sweden and Turkey, forced the tsars to face the hard facts of military inferiority, to swallow their pride, and occasionally to adopt a Western practice. Foreign mercenary troops were imported. Foreign soldiers of fortune engaged to train Russian mercenaries. Muskets were purchased from Europe. In 1632 a Dutch merchant was hired to erect the Tula armament works, to which a batch of peasant-serfs was assigned. Trained craftsmen of other skills were brought in — weavers, watchmakers, masons, smelters, ironmasters, painters — and settled in the "German" quarter in Moscow. These unco-ordinated sporadic efforts brought modest results, but their effect did not end there. The German quarter served as a kind of miniature world's fair, hovering in the back streets, remote and alien, yet evocative. Together with the military defeats it brought other members of the Russian ruling group to recognize both the inferiority of Russian technology and military organization and the necessity of imitating the West.

The military problems were not the only ones, but they provided a focus for the others. And they, above all the others, spurred Peter the Great (1682-1725) to accelerate the borrowing of Western practices. Peter was one of the giants of history, both in physical stature and achievement. He was nearly seven feet tall, and he gloried in feats of physical strength. He rolled up silver plates into tubes with his hands and severed pieces of cloth with a knife when they were thrown into the air. When he came to actual rule in 1695, at the age of twenty-three, Peter had no complete or elaborate plan of reform.

His reforms came piecemeal, as necessity arose. He became a reformer, as it were, incidentally; he was drawn into the role perhaps unwillingly. War led him on and on.

He plunged into war with Turkey in 1695 to obtain the fortress of Azov and thus come closer to the Black Sea. For want of a fleet, he was catastrophically defeated. That winter he moved into the city of Voronezh and set up a vast shipbuilding enterprise. A supremely sanguine, restless, and driven giant, he worked sixteen hours a day with ax, saw, and plane, while making the Russians about him work as they never had before. Following a Dutch model, he built the first galley with his own hands. By April he had thirty war vessels and about thirteen hundred smaller craft. In the summer of 1696 Azov was taken.

To gain further victories against Turkey, Russia needed a sea-going fleet. Russia had never been a naval power. Her people were accustomed to navigate rivers, but not the sea. They were incompetent in constructing naval vessels of any size. Peter was a direct thinker. In his youth, he had associated with several members of the "German" quarter in Moscow and had become aware of the superior technological world to the west. Once faced with the problem of construction of a sea-going fleet, he dispatched fifty young noblemen to the maritime countries of western Europe to study the science of navigation. He himself followed and traveled for eighteen months (1697-1698) through Prussia, Holland, and England to acquire a knowledge of naval affairs. He worked as a simple carpenter in a private shipyard in Holland. He visited factories, workshops, hospitals, educational institutions, and military and industrial establishments, entertained and called upon foreigners, and recruited over 750 experts for service in Russia.

On the way home he passed through Poland. This country, which had been a great Slav power in early modern times and had extended from the Baltic to the Black Sea, was now reversing the process of state-formation. The power of the center — the elective king — was dissolving, that of the nobles was increasing, and the result was anarchy. The current ruler, Augustus II of Saxony, however, was unscrupulous and strong, and he conspired with Peter to partition Sweden. Under Gustavus Adolphus and his successors, Sweden had acquired a Baltic empire, which her neighbors coveted. Hanover wanted the bishoprics of Verden and Bremen, which dominated the mouths of the Elbe and Weser; Brandenburg-Prussia desired Western Pomerania; Denmark, Holstein-Gottorp, whose duke led the Swedish armies; Poland, Livonia; and Peter, Ingria and Karelia, which would open Russia to the Baltic. So Denmark, Poland, and Russia plotted Sweden's humiliation.

Peter, after gaining Azov, dropped the conflict against Turkey and in 1700 plunged into war against Sweden. The war lasted twenty-one years. The allies had reckoned without the young King Charles XII (1697-1718) of Sweden, a brilliant soldier who put Denmark out of the war before Russia entered, routed 40,000 Russians with 8.000 Swedes at the battle of Narva (1700), and went on to ravage Poland. For Peter defeats were always lessons, preludes to later triumphs. Abolishing the old-time militia, he organized and recruited a new army, brigaded and equipped after the Western fashion. A specified number of peasant and town households, usually twenty, were required to supply one recruit to serve for twenty-five years. If he died or deserted, the same households were compelled to replace him. This system of conscription lasted until 1874. The nobility were called upon to give unlimited military service and usually served as privates in the two crack Guards regiments before receiving their epaulets as officers. After taking Estonia, Ingria, and Livonia with the renewed army in 1701-1704 and establishing a new capital, St. Petersburg, on the Gulf of Finland, Peter started the construction of a Baltic fleet. At his death, Russia had one of the largest armies in Europe, 200,000 regulars and 100,000 Cossack and Tartar irregulars, and a Baltic navy of 48 large warships, 787 smaller ones, and 28,000 sailors.

Peter's war against Sweden also required a vigorous policy of industrialization. His trip to western Europe had left him with an ineffaceable impression of Western wealth, trade, manufactures, and knowledge and what it all meant to a country in terms of power. He became acquainted with current mercantile theory that a country should produce nearly all it consumed, that exports should exceed imports, and that the state might well take action to promote that favorable balance. He dreamed of a Russia that would be independent of industrial imports. But it was war necessities, not general concepts, that jolted him into action. He needed guns, ships, canvas for sails, and woolen cloth for uniforms. He granted manufacturers subsidies, exemptions from taxation, high tariff protection, and serfs. He built iron mills, munition plants, leather, cloth, and cordage manufactories, and turned them over to private individuals. Of all Peter's enterprises, the iron foundries of the Urals were most productive. To them he forcibly assigned 25,000 serfs. In 1718, at these and similar works in Russia, 104,464 tons of iron were smelted when only 17,000 tons were produced in all England. The iron from the mountain foundries was sent to the arsenals, and in 1725 the artillery stood at 16,000 guns, not counting those of the fleet.

There was still another level of solutions, supporting the weight of the others. Russia needed a specialized, highly trained staff for the army, navy, bureaucracy, and industry. This implied the introduction of education, schools, and books. Peter was chiefly concerned with the training of young nobles, from whom he drew most of his army and navy officers and his civil servants. Until adequate instruction was available, he dispatched them to European cities. Upon their return they had to pass examinations at which Peter himself might be present. Eventually, Peter built state technical schools, a Russian naval academy, a school of army engineers, and an artillery school, in which such subjects as mathematics, navigation, and engineering were studied by young nobles. Peter also sent Russian artisans and merchants abroad to "pick the brains of the Westerners," imported foreign technicians, and opened various trade schools in conjunction with some of the more important industrial enterprises.

Army, navy, industry, and schools needed to be interwoven into a network which would not only control them separately but bind them together in a single enterprise, to benefit the state. This was the task of the government. Partly to meet the new demands Peter gradually formed a governmental structure which in its essentials remained intact up to the Revolution of 1905. Segments of it continued in existence until the Bolshevik Revolution of 1917, and some of its traditions are still in operation today. The center of the structure was the autocratic tsar, who now assumed the European title of "Emperor" and was the source of all legislative, executive, judicial, military, and religious authority. The fifty-odd administrative offices were consolidated into approximately nine departments: army, navy, foreign affairs, commerce, state revenue, state expenditure, justice, industry, and mining. Over each department was a board consisting of a president and ten others who acted by a majority vote, after the administrative procedure of contemporary Sweden and Prussia. An administrative board (the Synod), appointed by the emperor, replaced the patriarch as the governing body of the Orthodox church in Russia, and the church became in effect a department of the government. The country, for local administration, was divided into provinces, with a governor over each, and the provinces into districts. At the lowest level, the local landlord came to serve as tax collector, conscription sergeant, policeman, and judge over the serf village. A governing Senate of nine personages appointed by the tsar was instructed to supervise and co-ordinate the administration. When the Senate proved inefficient and corrupt, a procurator-general was appointed to watch and to preside over the Senate. When the procurator-general and his assistants proved dishonest, Peter elaborated the organization of the security police to keep an eye on the administration, the Senate, and the procurator-general. Spies, informers, and accusers became the order of the day and a Russian tradition. The more rational administrative organization plus heavier taxes enabled the government to increase its revenue from 1.4 million rubles in 1680 to 8.5 million in 1724. Of the last figure, military expenditures took three-fourths.

Peter struggled to keep his bureaucracy honest, but in vain. Thievery was rife; embezzlement and fraud were almost universal. Peter's failure to establish an efficient, honest administration is to be attributed not so much to his own shortcomings as to the material which Russia provided. Other monarchs of his period had inherited better-established executive and judicial institutions, while the French kings found in the middle class useful public servants for their administration. Peter found none of these things. He worked with what he had — indolent, sly, landowning nobles and hostile peasants — and imposed on all of them the obligation to perform state service. He drove the nobles to school and to serve as officers in the army, the navy, and the administration. He extended the net of serfdom to catch laborers who had remained free and tightened its bonds by providing that a serf might not even travel from his village without the written permission of his lord. He did not stop there, either. He drafted peasants into the army and navy, forced them to work in factories and mines, and compelled them to pay taxes to the treasury. When the burdens became unbearable and peasant revolts broke out, Peter was merciless with the rebels and wreaked fearful vengeance.

So working at many levels, Peter came back at Charles XII, and beat him at the battle of Poltava, in 1709. He then shared in the partition of the Swedish Empire that was arranged by the treaties of Stockholm, Frederiksborg, and Nystad in 1719, 1720, and 1721. By the treaties Hanover received Bremen and Verden; Prussia, Stettin and part of Pomerania; Denmark, the Gottrop portion of Schleswig; Augustus II, recognition of his right to sit on the Polish throne; and Russia, Livonia, Estonia, Ingria, Karelia, and the fortress of Viborg. Sweden retained Finland, but the great Swedish empire was destroyed.

It would be idle to pretend that Peter the Great had transformed Russia. The bulk of the Russians were peasant serfs, and the round of life in the Orthodox serf villages went on much as before. Nevertheless, his efforts had results both immediate and long-range, both surface and profound, both intended and unforeseen. He defeated Sweden and gained an outlet to the Baltic Sea. Using the personal autocratic authority inherited from his predecessors, he made of Russia a great military power, able to participate in the coalitions of European diplomacy and war as equal to any other country. In the same movement of forced growth, he had both accelerated the Westernization of the government and the landowning nobles and aggravated the lot of the peasant serf, thus widening the rift between the ruling class (nobles) and the ruled (peasants). The community which had emerged in the forests around Moscow had been, down to the beginning of the seventeenth century, morally and spiritually homogeneous, despite the social cleavage. The basic plan of the palace of the tsar and the mansions of the nobles was the same as that of the peasant's hut, the nobles and peasants learned the same catechism, and society still formed a moral whole. During the seventeenth century a few nobles adopted Western furniture, while Peter insisted that his courtiers and nobles use razors and shave their beards, abandon the long flowing robes of the oriental caftan for European knee breeches, and bring their wives out of oriental seclusion into the light and gaiety of mixed social assemblies. Because of his efforts and of increasing contacts with Europe, after his reign there came to be two Russias, different in speech, dress, manners, and outlook: the peasant smock culture of the illiterate, Orthodox village; the smart Europeanized (we can later say the Frenchified) civilization of the landowning nobles.

Peter had no coherent plan of reform, though toward the end he attempted to arrange his changes in a more orderly way. He took on problems as they came to him at different levels, tried this and that method or device, ordered and counter-ordered. But "he goes farthest who knows not where he goes." That was true of Peter. On the other hand, some rulers "walk after current affairs and allow life itself to tie the knots with which later generations do not know what to do." That also, to a degree, was true of Peter. As it turned out, he continued and accentuated the autocratic authority of the tsar and the social division that he had inherited from ancient Muscovy, and he borrowed from the West those military, economic, and administrative techniques that would enable Russia to resist the West. His emphasis on compulsion and the Westernization of the landowning nobles unintentionally hastened a process in Russian life which was splitting the ruling class from the ruled and was creating a state "not organically one with its people and a people not organically one with" each other. [1]

Each of these central and eastern European countries had a source of strain which, responded to in a certain way, warped its history. The multilingual composition of the Habsburg Empire, when handled autocratically and insensitively, would bring the empire's dissolution. The poverty and defenselessness of the scattered units of Brandenburg-Prussia, when combined with Hohenzollern ambition and drive, produced a tradition of disciplined militarism. The backwardness and inferiority of Russia, when united with the international ambition of its princes and the impetuosity of a Peter, yielded serfdom, the Westernization of the landowning nobility, a more pronounced cleavage between the classes, and an interruption of the organic growth of Russian institutions and society.

The Eighteenth Century (1725-1801)

Although the theory of autocracy had been expressed by earlier tsars, Peter was the first to give it legislative recognition. The army regulations of 1716 proclaimed that "His Majesty is an absolute monarch who is not responsible to anyone in the world for his deeds; but he has the right and power to govern his realm and his lands, as a Christian sovereign according to his will and wisdom." The church statute used a formula that was retained until

[1] John Maynard, *Russia in Flux*, p. 7.

1917: "The power of the monarchs is autocratic, and to obey it conscientiously is ordained by God himself." Even the most absolute monarchs of
Western Europe were limited by law. The French kings, for example, were
governed by the Salic Law of succession, that the French throne passed in the
male line of inheritance. Prussians prided themselves that theirs was a *Recht-
staat*: the Prussian king made the law, but he governed according to the law
he had made. The tsars were controlled by no constitutional or legal limitations. Old Muscovy lacked even a law of succession, although in fact the
throne usually passed to the eldest son. However, in line with autocratic
theory, Peter decreed in 1722 that the tsar might choose his successor. He
himself did not get to exercise his choice. Dramatically, just as he was saying,
"Give all to —," he died.

With no law of regular succession, there ensued a period of palace revolutions, from 1725 to 1801. A few favorites, officials, and noble members of
the Guard regiments engaged in perennial intrigues to make and depose tsars.
From 1725 to 1762 the throne passed from Peter to his second wife, to his
grandson, to his step-niece, to his half-brother's great grandson, to his daughter, to another grandson, and then to that grandson's wife. In 1797, Paul I
(1797-1801) finally promulgated a law that made the throne hereditary in the
house of Romanov and defined the order of succession.

In the period 1725 to 1801 there were two able rulers, both of them
women: Elizabeth (1741-1762) and Catherine II (1762-1796). Throughout the
period, the tendencies of Russian life which Peter had affirmed, initiated, or
fought continued. The personal autocracy, ruling largely through fear, continued. Though the nobility was entrenched as a class, individual nobles as well
as individual peasants were subject to the whims and vagaries of the tsar and
secret police. The major organs of the central administration – Senate,
procurator-general, the ministerial departments of the army, navy, and foreign
affairs, the Holy Synod, and the secret police – survived. In the interests of
securing execution of the tsar's will in the localities, Catherine refined the
system of local government that Peter had started. The number of provinces
was increased from eight to fifty. The provincial governor appointed by the
tsar was accountable to the Senate; provincial boards for finance, police, and
social welfare as well as provincial civil and criminal courts reported to the
procurator-general. However, despite reforms, the administration remained
slovenly, corrupt, inadequately staffed, and myopic, unable to comprehend
the vast country below them or the horizons (incredibly distant) of their
responsibility. It is indicative that during Elizabeth's reign only one-third of
the taxes ever reached the central treasury.

After Peter's death, the nobility gained in privileges and importance
throughout the rest of the eighteenth century. Noble members of the Guard
regiments made and unmade tsars. Nobles held key positions in the central

and provincial administration, while in the villages the country gentry served as local policemen, magistrates, and tax collectors. In 1762 Peter II released them from *obligatory* service to the state. Catherine II's Charter of the Nobility in 1785 freed them from corporal punishment, exempted them from direct taxes, and permitted them to meet together in provincial assemblies. The lot of the serfs, meanwhile, deteriorated further. The nobles gained the unrestricted right to sell their serfs with or without land, singly or in families. The cultural cleavage between the landowners and the serfs was accentuated, as the French language, fashions, and manners gained a distinct ascendancy among the noble landowning class. It has been observed that Peter had started building at the top, and built down. After him, the nobility kept rising legally and culturally, the peasants kept sinking, and the gap widened between the upper and lower stories. Very few messages passed either way. The state could not afford a communicating stairway, for the state depended on the gap; the power of the high, the impotence of the low. Its foundations rested precisely in the riddled community. Perhaps, then, the downfall was implicated in the building, and it was made to be undermined.

Russia, after Peter, also continued its territorial expansion. Catherine II, through two wars with Turkey, acquired the northern shore of the Black Sea and, through sharing with Austria and Prussia in the three partitions of Poland (1771, 1793, 1795), advanced the western frontier of Russia to a line running from the mouth of the Niemen River on the north to that of the Dniester on the south. The three partitions of Poland brought Russia face to face with Prussia and Austria, while the great victories over the Turks opened trade with the Black Sea region and brought Russia within sight of Constantinople, a second outlet to the West. Vast Russia was more than ever an important factor in European affairs.

An Invitation to Further Inquiry and Reflection

Decisive years in Russian history were the years of the Tartar invasions, and to a degree the history of Russia is the history of things left out. Until 1132 the Slav society around Kiev was evolving at approximately the same rate as the societies of Western Europe, and conceivably its contacts with Mediterranean culture might have accelerated that evolution as similar contacts accelerated the evolution of the Western societies. But the Tartars, from 1132 to 1462, isolated Russia from contact with a superior culture. The isolation of landlocked Muscovy then continued for nearly two hundred additional years. Meanwhile, what was happening in Western Europe from 1132 to, let us say, 1632? What many things were being added to Western culture during those five centuries, by borrowing and by native innovation?

Then, once Muscovy recovered its contact with the West and discovered its inferiority in the power aspects of life, Peter inaugurated the practice of forced input of Western tools, institutions, and ideas. He was the first of a series of Russian rulers, and, later, intellectuals who borrow from the West, Lenin and the Marxists being among the latest. But in the West these tools, institutions, and ideas arose, so to speak, in a native development. In Muscovy they intrude upon another native development out of sequence. Marxian socialism, for example, was the outgrowth of the early Industrial Revolution and was intended to be the next step in that revolution. It was designed for a heavily industrialized state with a large industrial plant and a numerous industrial proletariat. In Russia it was applied out of sequence to a vast peasant country. If only for that reason the consequences were different from what was anticipated. No wonder Russian intellectuals since the 1830's have reflected, as we might reflect, on the nature of Russian culture, of European civilization, and of the historical and optimum relationship between the two.

For Further Reading

(For general reading)

Russia to 1796

S. T. Aksakov, *A Russian Gentleman* (1923, 1943)
G. P. Gooch, *Catherine the Great and Other Studies* (1954)
Stephen Graham, *Ivan the Terrible: Life of Ivan IV of Russia* (1933)
V. Klyuchevsky, *Peter the Great* (1958)
B. H. Sumner, *Peter the Great and the Emergence of Russia* (Teach Yourself History Library, 1951)

Gladys Thomson, *Catherine the Great and the Expansion of Russia* (Teach Yourself History Library, 1947)

Voltaire, *History of Charles XII* (1731)

(For advanced study):

Michael Florinsky, *Russia: A History and an Interpretation* (1953)

M. Raeff, *Peter the Great: Reformer or Revolutionary?* (1964)

Reinhard Wittram, *Peter I, Czar and Kaiser: Zur Geschichte Peters des Grossen in Seiner Zeit* (1964)

Jerome Blum, *Lord and Peasant in Russia from the Ninth to the Nineteenth Century* (1961)

CHAPTER XIII

FEUDING AND FIGHTING, 1689-1763

From 1494 until 1659, the central rivalry in European diplomacy and war was between France and the Habsburg power of Spain and Austria, a contest that France won. For over a hundred years, until about 1635, Spain had threatened to dominate Europe, but she could not last. Her own weaknesses and a coalition of powers brought her down. The central rivalry from 1689 to 1815 was between France and Great Britain, a conflict in which Great Britain triumphed. Twice, under Louis XIV (1661-1715) and under Napoleon (1799-1815), France was the single strongest military power and, like Spain before her, threatened to dominate Europe, until a coalition of countries brought *her* down. The period 1689 to 1815 saw three eras of great wars: the first era at the close of Louis XIV's reign, the War of the League of Augsburg (1689-1697) and the War of the Spanish Succession (1702-1713); the second era in mid-eighteenth century, the War of the Austrian Succession (1740-1748) and the Seven Years' War (1756-1763); and the third era, the wars of the French Revolution and Napoleon (1792-1815). This chapter deals with the wars of the first two eras. These great wars (to 1763), which were maintained on a scale never before seen in the Western world, accelerated the extension of the administration of the modern state, quickened the development of industry, commerce, and finance to sustain the military and naval forces, and evoked the emergence in diplomacy of balance-of-power considerations on a continental scale. By 1763 Great Britain had emerged as the commercial, colonial, and naval leader of the West.

The wars of the first era originated in the ambitions of Louis XIV, whose personal rule of France began in 1661. Louis sought glory in diplomacy, war, and the acquisition of territory. He was encouraged in his dreams of conquest by the strength of France and the divisions among his potential enemies. France then formed a compact territory, possessed internal lines of communications, and had in her sixteen to twenty million people a population larger than that of any European country and twice that of its immediate rival, Spain. France was thriving. Her commerce was expanding, her treasury was sound, and her young king had at his disposal an array of leaders (Colbert as controller-general, Louvois as minister of war, and Lionne in diplomacy, the generals Condé, Turenne, and Vauban) who were among the most forceful and competent in Europe. After some time, the Habsburgs were divided into two

branches, the Spanish and the Austrian, not always in agreement; Italy and
Germany were still partitioned among lesser princes who could be bribed or
intimidated; and the two maritime powers, Holland and England, still vied
with each other for commercial supremacy.

Louis XIV was the son of one Spanish Habsburg princess, Anne, and the
husband of another, Maria Theresa, the daughter of Philip IV of Spain. When
Louis married the Spanish Infanta, he renounced all claims to her Spanish
heritage on condition that her dowry of 500,000 gold crowns be promptly
paid. When Spain failed to pay the dowry, Louis XIV maintained that his
renunciation was without force. When Philip IV died in 1665, he left the
Spanish throne and empire to his son, Charles II, a man so sickly it was clear
that he would have no children and that his death, when it came, would
precipitate a scramble for the Spanish inheritance. Louis XIV, however, did
not wait for Charles to die; he set his lawyers to work, to justify his wife's
claim to the Spanish Netherlands (later Belgium). The lawyers discovered that
in certain provinces of the Netherlands the local custom provided that on the
death of a parent all children shared the inheritance. The French queen thus
seemed to have a legal claim to portions of the provinces, a claim the French
experts enlarged to include all the Spanish Netherlands. In support of her
claim, Louis XIV mobilized a careful diplomacy: he married a French princess to the King of Portugal and subsidized the latter in his war with Spain;
he negotiated alliances with the duke of Neuburg, the bishop of Münster, and
the electors of Cologne and Mainz, Rhineland princes who could block the
movement of Austrian Habsburg troops to the Spanish Netherlands; he be-
mused the Austrian Habsburg emperor with plans to divide the Spanish
Empire between them; he persuaded Charles II of England to promise not to
enter into an agreement against France for a year and he maintained alliances
with Sweden and Brandenburg. When all was ready, Louis XIV entered the
Spanish Netherlands in May, 1667, at the head of a powerful French army
captained by Turenne. Easily the French forces captured a string of border
fortresses, and militarily the Spanish Netherlands lay open to their advance.
However, the revelation of overwhelming French power alarmed the other
European governments. The Dutch, who desired the French as friends but not
as neighbors, mediated peace between Portugal and Spain and organized a
triple alliance of England, Holland, and Sweden to impose restraint on Louis
XIV. In the ensuing peace treaty of Aix-la-Chapelle, May 2, 1668, France
acquired in the Spanish Netherlands twelve border towns, including Armen-
tières, Lille, Douai, and Tournai, and their dependencies. Strategically, the
acquisition was important in pushing the northwestern French frontier farther
from Paris, but in effect Louis XIV had been stopped.

Louis did not take throttling very well, especially at the hands of a few
Calvinist merchants. He correctly blamed the Dutch for his check, and decided

to crush them. Again, he made careful diplomatic preparation. The emperor, concerned for his eastern frontier with Turkey, was persuaded to disinterest himself with respect to the Dutch, provided the war did not involve the Holy Roman Empire. Sweden was induced to keep troops in Pomerania to distract the elector of Brandenburg, who was inclined to befriend Holland. Charles II of England, needing money in his quarrels with Parliament, accepted Louis XIV's subsidies and agreed to go to war against Holland. The German Rhineland princes, in return for French money, granted to the French army unopposed passage through their states on its way to Holland. Again, the French won spectacular early success. In May, 1672, the French forces of more than 160,000 men bypassed the Spanish Netherlands, promenaded down the Meuse River valley, and, virtually unchallenged, crossed the relatively unfortified eastern frontier of Holland. Amsterdam and the other major Dutch cities apparently lay at French mercy. However, Louis XIV, instead of striking directly for Amsterdam as his general Condé advised, settled down to besiege the minor Dutch fortresses, one by one. The Dutch cut their dikes, the captain-general of their troops, William of Orange, maintained the contest, and the other European governments, again shocked by the spectacular revelation of French power, rallied to the aid of Holland. The emperor, the king of Spain, the king of Denmark, the duke of Lorraine, the elector of Brandenburg, the archbishops of Mainz and Trier, and other German princes joined Holland in a grand coalition against Louis. Parliament and public opinion forced Charles II to withdraw England from the war and then to make peace with the Dutch in 1674. Louis XIV, however, continued to pay Charles II subsidies to keep England from joining Holland. France, with only a single ally, Sweden, was now fighting a defensive war against most of Europe. The course of the war, which lasted from 1672 to 1678, and the concluding peace of Nimwegen, by which Spain ceded Franche Comté and a number of towns in the Spanish Netherlands to France, indicated that France alone was still more powerful than any coalition of states that did not include England. The maintenance of a balance of power in Europe between France and an opposing coalition depended on whether England joined the coalition. And her decision, in turn, depended on the internal balance of power between Parliament and the Stuart kings. No wonder Louis XIV paid subsidies to Charles II, to render him independent of Parliament and to enable him to keep England from joining France's enemies.

From 1678 to 1689 Louis XIV continued his aggressions and depredations in time of peace. He declared that all territories that had ever been dependencies of lands assigned to France by treaty during the preceding half-century belonged to the French crown. On his instructions French "Chambers of Reunion" adjudged to France piece after piece of land in Alsace, including the city of Strasburg itself. There seemed no way to check this policy of blatant annexation. Louis XIV's aspiration to have himself or his son elected Holy Roman Emperor and his standing claim to the Spanish heritage, whenever Charles II of Spain should die, rendered him the natural enemy of Emperor Leopold I, an Austrian Habsburg who had rival claims in both Germany and Spain. In 1682 Louis XIV, His Most Christian Majesty, assured the government of the Ottoman Empire that he would not support Leopold should the Moslem Turks invade Austria. Relying on this assurance, the Turkish army entered Austria, besieged Vienna in 1683, and initiated a war on Austria's eastern frontier that raged for years. Louis XIV, meanwhile, pursued his haughty course. His persecution of French Huguenots and the revocation of the Edict of Nantes embittered Protestants throughout Europe. The Dutch, especially, were antagonized when Louis persecuted Dutch merchants who had settled in France and had become naturalized French citizens on the understanding that they would not be molested because of their religion. Meanwhile Genoa was bombarded by the French for refusing to surrender a portion of its fleet to France, and its doge had personally to apologize to Louis XIV at Versailles. The duke of Savoy, despite his protests, was forced to accept a French army sent to extirpate the Savoyard Protestants. The pope himself was bullied, as the French ambassador in Rome claimed diplomatic immunity not simply for the ambassadorial palace but also for the whole quarter in which it lay. By 1688 Louis XIV was feared and hated throughout Europe. Among the European governments there was a growing realization that only force would check his insolence.

William of Orange, stadholder of the Dutch provinces as well as captain-general of their forces, undertook to bring together the European states in a grand coalition against the great aggressor. To be successful a coalition had to include Austria and England. But Austria was distracted by the war against the Turks, while England's king, James II, a Stuart and a Catholic, was accessible to French influence. However, by the close of 1688, victorious Austrian armies had occupied Hungary, invaded Transylvania, and taken Belgrade and could now stand on the defensive in the east, while William of Orange had seized the English throne, with the deliberate intent of involving England in a war against France. In 1689, a Grand Alliance of the United Netherlands, England, Austria, Spain, Sweden, Savoy, and a number of German princes was formed to bring Louis to order.

The ensuing War of the League of Augsburg (1689-1697) was long and hard. It was fought not only in Europe but also in North America and India and on the high seas. In a sense, the effort of every member of the coalition was needed to bring down France. In the end, the subsidies, armies, fleets, and diplomacy of the two maritime states, England and Holland, as perseveringly managed by William of Orange, proved decisive. The main French battle fleet was beaten at the battle of La Hogue (1692) and bottled up; the French armies were contained, and French resources were exhausted. A tell-tale symptom: Louis XIV was so short of funds that he suspended work on the palace of Versailles. By the Treaty of Ryswick (1697) Louis recognized William III as king of England, allowed the Dutch to garrison a line of fortresses in the Spanish Netherlands, and, while keeping Alsace, restored the overwhelming majority of his "reunions" in the Spanish Netherlands and the German empire. Later, by the Treaty of Carlowitz (1699) with Turkey, victorious Austria acquired Hungary, Transylvania, and the Siebenbürgen, except the Banat of Temesvar. The two treaties registered a check to Louis XIV's expansionist dreams, the tipping of the balance of power against France, and the emergence of England and Austria as more powerful factors in European diplomacy.

The fourth war of Louis XIV was over the Spanish succession. On November 1, 1700, Charles II of Spain finally died and willed the entire Spanish Empire to Philip of Anjou, grandson of Louis XIV. If Philip declined the throne, it was to go to the Habsburg Archduke Charles, second son of Emperor Leopold I. The Spanish heritage was still huge. It included Spain; the lands of the Spanish Netherlands; Milan, Naples, Sicily, and Sardinia; the colonial possessions in America from Mexico to Patagonia; and the Philippine Islands. Louis XIV, by now, was weary of war. The War of the League of Augsburg had been a terrible ordeal, which he did not wish to experience again. Yet, he faced a dilemma. If he accepted the Spanish throne for his grandson, he would acquire a dominating position in the Western world, but he would probably have to fight to defend it. If he did not accept, the Spanish heritage would pass to his enemy, the Austrian Habsburgs, and he would still have to fight to overthrow them. He accepted the heritage for Philip of Anjou and refused to permit Philip to renounce his claim to the throne of France.

Strangely, the Dutch and English, themselves weary of conflict, would probably have accepted the accomplished union of the French and Spanish empires if Louis XIV had granted a few conciliating commercial concessions. But Louis XIV, incorrigibly arrogant and obtuse, was provocative. He replaced the Dutch garrisons in the barrier fortresses of the Spanish Netherlands with French troops, thus placing in French hands fortresses and ports from which the United Netherlands and England could be attacked. He had published administrative regulations giving French merchants special privileges in the Spanish wool, hardware, and leather trade, in which English and Dutch merchants had been engaged. He arranged an alliance between Spain, France, and Portugal; by this diplomatic stroke he deprived the maritime powers of a naval base, Lisbon, from which they had been able to control the Straits of Gibraltar and the western Mediterranean. Acts such as these drove the European states once again to form a Grand Alliance against Louis XIV. The alliance included England, the United Netherlands, Austria, and most of the lesser German states. Louis XIV had on his side the elector of Bavaria, who aspired to be Holy Roman Emperor, the duke of Savoy, the king of Portugal, and, of course, Spain.

Defensively, his position seemed very strong, with the approaches to France now guarded by the Spanish Netherlands, Alsace, Savoy, and Spain. However, the brilliantly aggressive strategy and tactics of two coalition commanders, the duke of Marlborough of the Anglo-Dutch forces and Prince Eugene of the imperial-Austrian, and increasing English sea power brought France once again to its knees. By the battle of Blenheim (1704), Eugene and Marlborough denied southern Germany to a French advance. By the battle of Ramillies (1706), Marlborough expelled them from the Spanish Netherlands, while in the same year Eugene by the successful siege of Turin was driving them from Savoy. By the battle of Oudenarde and the capture of Lille, both in 1708, Marlborough invaded France itself. The last battle of Malpaquet (1709) and a crop failure in the same year brought France close to ruin. Meanwhile, at sea England obtained naval supremacy in the North Sea, the English Channel, and the western Mediterranean. She used her naval superiority to blockade France, to ravage French commerce, to intercept the Spanish treasure fleets, to capture the islands of Gibraltar and Minorca, and to send a few men-of-war and marines to help the northern Anglo-American colonies conquer Nova Scotia and Newfoundland.

By 1711, France, ruined, was ready for peace. So were Great Britain and the United Netherlands. France was obviously so exhausted as to be no longer a threat to the maritime states or to the European balance of power. Archduke Charles, the Austrian claimant to the Spanish heritage, had succeeded his brother as emperor and wished to continue the struggle. However, the British and Dutch were not inclined to continue a war merely to replace a Franco-Spanish combine with an Austro-Spanish one. Great Britain initiated negotiations that eventuated in the peace treaties of Utrecht (1713) and Rastatt (1714). The treaties registered and tried to guarantee the realities established in war: a European balance of power and British maritime supremacy. The Spanish heritage was partitioned. Philip of Anjou as Philip V retained Spain and its overseas empire but renounced his claim to the French throne; the specter of a great Franco-Spanish combination was thus exorcised. The Spanish Netherlands, Milan, Sardinia, and Naples were allotted to the Austrian Habsburgs. The Dutch re-acquired the right to garrison fortresses in the "Austrian" Netherlands. Austria and the United Netherlands were thus placed as sentinels to check French northward expansion. Yet the presence of Austria, an inland power, on the coast of the North Sea did not threaten Great Britain. Sicily was given to the duke of Savoy. England received Gibraltar and Minorca, islands that strengthened her naval control of the western Mediterranean. France ceded her Nova Scotia, Newfoundland, the island of St. Kitts, and the right to develop the Hudson Bay region. An earlier commercial treaty with Portugal and a new one with Spain opened to British merchants the vista of invading the commercial empires of these two states.

Measured by the intentions of its negotiators — to mirror and to establish a European equilibrium — the peace of Utrecht was successful: from 1713 to 1792 the great states *in* Europe, Great Britain, France, Spain, Austria, and Russia, *were* evenly balanced in power. To be sure, during the century shifts in power and in power relations occurred. Prussia, under Frederick the Great, took its place as a great power. Great Britain enlarged its maritime supremacy. Russia intruded as a military factor in the power combinations of central and western Europe. Indeed, the balance-of-power situation seemed to facilitate these shifts. In an age when the great states had grown small, a small state, Prussia, might grow great. Great Britain, also, might maneuver balance-of-power politics to divert her chief rival, France, from concentration on naval and colonial enterprise and so assure her own triumph overseas. Similarly, Russia, another flanking power, could intrigue to its own advantage in European diplomacy. However, even with these shifts in power relations, no country during these years menaced the security of all the others by its overwhelming preponderance.

The maritime supremacy of Great Britain and the great-power status of Prussia were affirmed in the two central wars of the eighteenth century, the War of the Austrian Succession and the Seven Years' War. The first began inconspicuously in the maritime field. British merchants had been smuggling goods into the Spanish Empire for years. By the 1730's they were becoming infuriated with the actions of the Spanish coast guard when it searched British vessels on the high seas. By 1739 they had communicated their fury to other elements of the British population and were carrying a reluctant British government into conflict against Spain. In anticipation of war the French government, hoping to be able for the first time to concentrate its resources on the naval, colonial, and commercial struggle, readied two fleets to attack British possessions in the Caribbean. As they were setting out on their mission, war coincidentally flared on the European continent.

It began in Central Europe, with a new king and a new archduchess. In May, 1740, Frederick, a young man of twenty-eight years, came to the throne of Prussia. On October 6, Emperor Charles VI of Austria died, and the Austrian inheritance passed to a young woman, Maria Theresa. On December 16, the Prussian army invaded Silesia, the fairest province of Maria Theresa's heritage, thus violating the solemn treaty promise of Frederick's father that Prussia would respect the integrity of Austria. In justification of the invasion, Frederick explained to the Silesians that he was guided by his concern for their liberties, which Austria was not powerful enough to protect; to the world he declared that Prussia had a good legal claim to Silesia; to himself Frederick merely said, if not on this occasion — then later "I take what I want; there will always be plenty of professors to justify what I do."

The two wars — the one maritime, the other land — merged. In the war on Austria, Frederick was soon joined by France, Spain, Saxony, Bavaria, each seeking a portion of Maria Theresa's inheritance. The situation seemed very dark for her. However, by her charm she rallied the Hungarian nobility to her aid. The British government, believing the dismemberment of Austria would jeopardize British security, gave her money subsidies and supported an Anglo-German-Dutch army in the defense of the Austrian Netherlands. Cabinet ministers and members of Parliament in Great Britain who favored the course of intervention on the European continent argued: the only state that threatened Great Britain was France, and it was impossible to create any confederacy against France without a strong Austria; if France should once acquire an established superiority in Europe, she would have the power to close the ports of Portugal, Italy, and the Baltic to British commerce, to crush Holland, and to outbuild Britain at sea; as soon as this happened, it would be Britain's turn to be conquered. For the sea was England's gate, and superior sea-power was the key. Once Britain lost this key to France, she would be open to invasion, and everything would be lost.

The ensuing war was fought for eight years all over the world. Overseas the British and the French were in conflict in three general combat zones: North America, the Caribbean, and India. In North America, the prize was the French-held area drained by the St. Lawrence, the Great Lakes, and the Mississippi, which France wished to retain and England, eventually, to acquire. In the West Indies the two countries were fighting over the immensely wealthy sugar islands, such as French-held Guadeloupe and Martinique and British Jamaica. (As late as 1740, the trade of the British sugar islands was still more valuable to Great Britain than the trade of all the thirteen mainland colonies.) In India the long-standing French and English commercial rivalry had been channeled through chartered trading companies: the British East India Company and the French East India Company. At first, the two European companies came merely as traders; the only establishments they attempted were warehouses, and they competed only for trade. But owing to the unsettled state of the country, they had begun to fortify and arm their settlements. By 1740, the British company had strong posts at Bombay and Calcutta and badly defended ones at Madras and Cuddalose, while the French company held Pondichéry and lesser settlements at Karikal, Mahé, and Chandernagor.

Early in the war the British obtained over-all naval superiority. This was important. Despite French privateering, British commerce could actually increase during the war. British imports went from 7½ million pounds to 11½

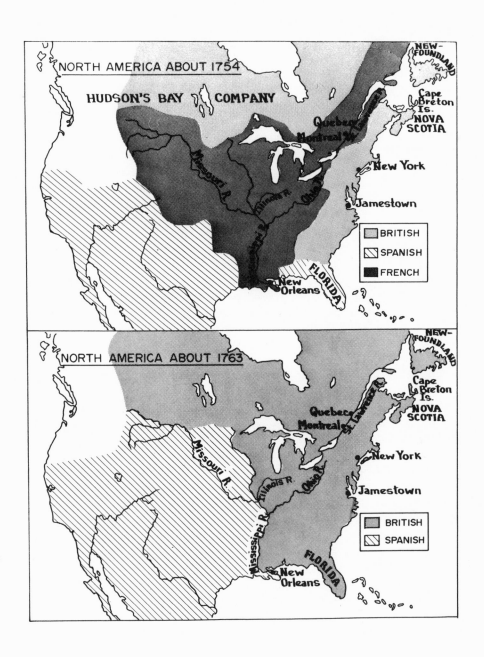

NORTH AMERICA ABOUT 1754

HUDSON'S BAY COMPANY

NEW-FOUNDLAND

Cape Breton Is.

NOVA SCOTIA

Quebec
Montreal

New York

Jamestown

Missouri R.

Illinois R.

Ohio R.

Mississippi R.

New Orleans

FLORIDA

BRITISH
SPANISH
FRENCH

NORTH AMERICA ABOUT 1763

NEW-FOUNDLAND

Cape Breton Is.

NOVA SCOTIA

Quebec
Montreal

St. Lawrence R.

New York

Jamestown

Missouri R.

Illinois R.

Ohio R.

Mississippi R.

New Orleans

FLORIDA

BRITISH
SPANISH

million a year before the war's end. Increased trade and government revenue enabled the British to sustain its own war effort and to pay money subsidies to its Continental allies. Also, by 1747 the British had imposed an effective blockade of the French coast and of the French West Indies. By 1748 the French sugar islands, short of food, faced starvation. French industry and commerce, cut off from their overseas markets and sources of raw materials, languished. The French treasury, receiving decreasing revenue, was nearing bankruptcy. A British naval squadron aided the New England colonists to capture the French fortress of Louisburg on Cape Breton Island, an armed sentinel that guarded the entrance to the St. Lawrence River. Temporary and local French naval superiority in Indian waters enabled the French commander Joseph Dupleix to take Madras, but the restoration of British naval control prevented him from receiving supplies and from making anything of his victory. Overseas the balance of success was definitely tipped toward the British. But on the European continent it was a different story. There the balance tipped toward France and her ally, Prussia. Although Maria Theresa maintained intact the core of her dominions, she could not recover Silesia from Frederick, whose brilliant generalship now won him the sobriquet of "the Great," nor could she defend the Austrian Netherlands against a conquering French army under an able soldier of fortune, Marshal de Saxe. Between Britain and France there was a strategic stalemate. Again, the concluding peace treaty, Aix-la-Chapelle (1748), reflected the realities of the military situation. By its provisions Britain and France returned their conquests, France relinquishing Madras and in effect restoring the Austrian Netherlands to recover Louisburg. Prussia retained Silesia.

The peace proved but an armed truce, as statesman at home and colonial administrators abroad prepared for the next encounter. In India Dupleix schemed to extend French commerce. He placed French officers and soldiers at the disposal of friendly native princes, who accepted French advisers and military aid and in return granted Frenchmen special trade privileges and a fixed portion of the state revenue. The British leader, Robert Clive, not to be outdone, likewise loaned to native princes British troops and demanded similar trade and taxation privileges. The British and French East India companies, competing for influence and trade, began to fight each other through their native allies. In North America, the French constructed a line of forts from Fort Presentation on the St. Lawrence to Crevecoeur in the Illinois country. The last fort in the chain, Fort Duquesne, at the junction of the Alleghany and Monongahela rivers, was finished in 1754. In 1755, before war had been declared, Great Britain dispatched four expeditions to seize four French forts, Beausejour (on the Nova Scotian frontier), Crown Point, Niagara, and Duquesne. Only the first expedition was successful; the others were turned back by the French defenders. Meanwhile, in Europe the Austrian Chancellor

Kaunitz perserveringly conspired to form a league of Austria, Russia, and France against Prussia to recover Silesia. He found a willing listener in Tsaritsa Elizabeth, who detested Frederick the Great and was not averse to acquiring East Prussia. France, Prussia's ally, was at first cool to Kaunitz' approaches. But in 1756, in an intricate series of diplomatic maneuvers in which the diplomats themselves did not always know what was happening, England and France switched partners. England became the ally of Prussia, and France of Austria and Russia. Meanwhile, Frederick had been building his army and accumulating a war treasure. Hearing something of the conspiracies of Austria and Russia against him and suspecting more, he decided to forestall the allied attack. Believing Saxons to be involved in the anti-Prussian intrigue, he invaded Saxony on August 29, 1756, and the war was on.

Frederick's situation was desperate from the start. Prussia's population of four million was one-third that of Austria and one-fifth that of France. Austria, Russia, and France could each bring to bear an army equal in size to that of Frederick the Great. He no sooner fought one invading army than he had to turn and fight a second, then turn and fight a third, and then re-turn and re-fight the second or first, and so on. He was saved by his military genius and heroic tenacity and by something totally out of his control, the good fortune that Great Britain had from 1757 to 1761 a great war minister, William Pitt. An arrogant genius ("I know I can save England, and I know no one else can"), Pitt mobilized the disparate elements of British policy into a glorious, co-ordinated effort to win the war. He paid Frederick large money subsidies to keep him fighting and to divert France's resources from the construction of a large fleet. He supported a sizable Anglo-German army in northwest Germany, to defend Hanover (the king of England was then elector of Hanover) and to keep the French army off Frederick's back. Frederick then had to deal with the armies of only Austria and Russia. At the same time, Pitt launched amphibious assaults on French coastal fortresses (Rochefort, St. Malo, Cherbourg, and Belleisle) to immobilize several French contingents and to weaken their effort against Hanover and Prussia. Meanwhile, the British fleet again won naval superiority and set up a blockade of the French coast that protected British commerce, ruined French trade and the industries dependent on it, and prevented the French from sending supplies and reinforcements to their beleaguered garrisons overseas. Pitt then dispatched expeditions to pick up the French colonies, as withered fruit from a severed vine. The expeditions were commanded by young men whom Pitt had inspired with his own patriotic ardor and stringency. They swept the French out of the North American continent, the West Indies, and India, capturing such celebrated strongholds as Louisburg, Fort Duquesne, Quebec, Montreal, Guadeloupe, Martinique, and Pondichery. When in 1761 Spain entered the war as an ally of France, Pitt's lieutenants added Havana and Manila to their trophies. These

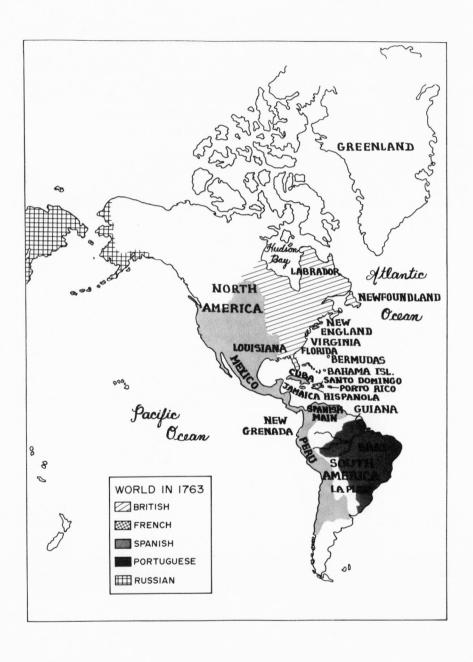

GREENLAND

Hudson Bay

LABRADOR

NORTH AMERICA

Atlantic

NEWFOUNDLAND

Ocean

NEW ENGLAND

VIRGINIA

LOUISIANA

FLORIDA

BERMUDAS

MEXICO

CUBA

BAHAMA ISL.

SANTO DOMINGO

PORTO RICO

JAMAICA HISPANOLA

SPANISH MAIN

GUIANA

Pacific

Ocean

NEW GRENADA

PERU

BRAZIL

SOUTH AMERICA

LA PLATA

WORLD IN 1763

BRITISH

FRENCH

SPANISH

PORTUGUESE

RUSSIAN

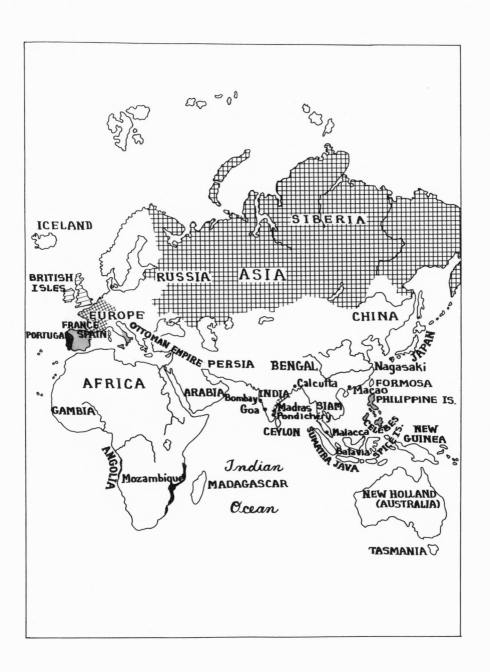

ICELAND

BRITISH
ISLES

EUROPE
FRANCE
PORTUGAL SPAIN

RUSSIA   ASIA   SIBERIA

CHINA

JAPAN

OTTOMAN EMPIRE   PERSIA   BENGAL   Nagasaki

AFRICA   ARABIA   INDIA   Calcutta   Macao   FORMOSA
                        Bombay   PHILIPPINE IS.
GAMBIA   Goa   Madras SIAM
                              Pondichery

                        CEYLON   Malacca   NEW
                                                GUINEA
ANGOLA   SUMATRA   Batavia SPICE IS.
        Mozambique   Indian   JAVA
                        MADAGASCAR

                        Ocean   NEW HOLLAND
                                       (AUSTRALIA)

                                       TASMANIA

multiple policies were effective. In 1761, Frederick was still fighting and with the Anglo-German army was still diverting French energies from the maritime struggle. France had not conquered Hanover and had nothing significant to trade to recover the lost colonies. The blockade had weakened her economy and hence her ability to wage war. Meanwhile, Great Britain had conquered an empire overseas.

The peace treaties reflected these circumstances. By the Treaty of Hubertusburg (1763) between Prussia, Austria, and Saxony (Russia had already withdrawn from the war), Prussia retained Silesia. By the Treaty of Paris (1763) between France and Great Britain, France ceded Canada and the trans-Appalachian region to the Mississippi River. In India the French were permitted to return to their posts but only as traders: their stations were neither to lodge troops nor to be fortified. To recover Cuba, Spain ceded Florida to Great Britain. To recompense Spain for her sacrifice, France gave her the Louisiana territory west of the Mississippi.

The Treaty of Paris had world historical importance. It assured that the North American continent and the sub-continent of India would be subject to Anglo-Saxon rather than to French influence. Not for the first time and certainly not for the last time had deeds of arms been decisive in setting cultural boundaries.

An Invitation to Further Inquiry and Reflection

The Italian system of states of the fifteenth century became in the next
four centuries a European system, and now in the twentieth century it is a
world system of interacting states in which the United States is inextricably
entangled. The area and the number of states involved have thus greatly
expanded, but the central features of the interaction of the states have been
continuing. We might reflect on what some of these continuing aspects were
and are. One aspect we have already considered in the chapter on the
Reformation and shall consider again in later periods of ideological disturb-
ance — the intertwining of ideological and power considerations in international politics and the consequences of the fusion on people and events. Now, in a
period of international politics, 1667-1763, when ideology was rarely a significant factor, what do we see?

We see a growing disposition of contemporary statesmen to analyse international situations in terms of balance of power and to act, on occasion,
according to balance of power calculations. The balance of power concept was
becoming a way of thinking about international relations. The concept is also
useful to us as historians and as citizens, to analyze both historical and
contemporary situations. A power situation in Europe can be represented by a
see-saw, which is even when two competing states or two opposing camps are
equal in power and which is tipped one way or the other when one state or
one camp is stronger. Thus at the opening of the War of Devolution in 1667,
France and its associates were clearly dominant.

But by 1668, Holland by mediating peace between Portugal and Spain and
negotiating the Triple Alliance of Holland, England, and Sweden, had to a
degree redressed the balance.

1668

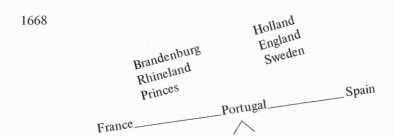

A similar analysis can be usefully performed for 1672, 1674, 1678, 1689, 1697, 1702, 1713-1714, and for other key dates in the shifting constellations of European diplomacy. What is the balance of power situation in Europe today? What is it in the world?

We can see also an emerging pattern of coalition war against a country which is considered to be a great aggressor. The pattern was foreshadowed in the coalitions against a previous aspirant to European supremacy, Emperor Charles V; it was futher developed in the wars against Louis XIV, reaching completion in the last one, the War of the Spanish Succession; and it will re-emerge in the last coalition against Napoleon, 1812-1814, and in the two coalition wars of the twentieth century against Germany, World War I and World War II. In the study of history, we are always having ideas, having new perceptions and discovering new relations. From the single example of the War of the Spanish Succession (its origin, its course, and its conclusion) can we discern this pattern of behavior that we term coalition war against a great aggressor? Then, responding to the question why, can we discover the under-lying relations which explain this pattern?

We see in addition a single country, England, gradually evolving through four wars a complicated military and foreign policy that self-consciously utilized its resources in a sophisticated way for victory. It was not a foregone conclusion that England would win over France in a contest for overseas empire. France's population was more than three times that of England, her army was seven times as large, her navy was powerful, and her economy was well-balanced. Basically, France was the strongest country on the European continent, and no mean adversary. Yet England won. Why? Accidents of leadership? William III and Marlborough vs. Louis XIV? William Pitt vs. Louis XV? Perhaps. Differences in economy, society, government, and geographic position? Maybe. What were those differences, and how did they affect English and French strength in a contest of overseas dominion? The evolution by the British, through debate in Parliament and through learning from mistakes and blunders, of a sophisticated policy which utilized the advantages of her position, wealth, and navy for overseas conflict? What was that policy, as applied to perfection by William Pitt in the Seven Years' War? Can we note the steps in its evolution in four successive wars? Is the United States evolving a similar policy with respect to Russia and China? If so, what is it? And what should it be?

For Further Reading

(For general reading)

Stephen Baxter, *William III and the Defense of European Liberty (1650-1702)* (1966)
A. Mervyn Davies, *Clive of Plassey* (1939)
Ludwig, Dehio, *The Precarious Balance* (1962)
W. L. Dorn, *Competition for Empire, 1740-1763* (1940)
Leslie Gardiner, *The British Admiralty* (1968)
P. Moon, *Warren Hastings and British India* (Teach Yourself History Library, 1947)
Francis Parkman, *Montcalm and Wolfe* (1884)
J. H. Parry, *Trade and Dominion: The European Overseas Empire in the Eighteenth Century* (1971)
C. H. Phillips, *India* (1949)
Admiral Sir Herbert Richmond, *The Navy as an Instrument of Policy, 1558-1727* (1953)
————, *British Strategy, Military and Economic: A Historical Review and its Contemporary Lessons* (1941)
————, *Statesman and Sea Power* (1946)
C. G. Robertson, *Chatham and the British Empire* (Teach Yourself History Library, 1948)
Theodore Ropp, *War in the Modern World* (1959)
John W. Stoye, *The Siege of Vienna* (1964)
John B. Wolf, *The Emergence of the Great Powers, 1685-1715* (1951)

(For advanced study)

Thomas M. Parker, *Double Eagle and Crescent: Vienna's Second Turkish Siege and its Historical Setting* (1967)
Roderic H. Davison, *Turkey* (1968)

286

288

Coen, John, 91, 154
Coeur, Jacques, 35
Coinage, see money
Coke, Sir Edward, 195, 198
Colbert, Jean-Baptiste, 269; as controller-general of France, 171-175; and Canada, 218-222; 226
Colet, John, 125
Cologne, 22; allied with France, 270
Colonial empire, 82-86; Portuguese in Far East, 86-93; Portuguese and Spanish in Americas, 93-111; English and French compared, 217-231; English, 217, 218, 221-225, 229-231; French, 217, 218-221, 226-229
Columbus, Bartholomew, 97
Columbus, Christopher, 2; early life, 93; discovers America, 94
Commerce, 1; map of medieval, 21; and crusades, 24; Mediterranean, 24; "factory", 25; technology in early, 33-34; development of early, 23-36; capitalism, 29-36; in Egypt and Syria, 86-87; caravans, 23, 25, 26, 87, 88; Venetian monopoly, 91; House of Trade, 104, 106; trading empire, 82-86, 109; joint-stock companies, 110; influence of Counter-Reformation, Calvinism, and East India Companies on, 145, 153, 154; beginnings of mercantilism, 153-155; spice trade, 25, 86, 88, 153, 154, 166; technology in 15th century French, 166; and Colbert in France, 171, 172, 174, 175; English in 17th century, 191-192; French mercantilism, 165-166, 218, 226-229; English mercantilism, 226, 229-231; in New World, 93-111, 226-231; early Russian, 254; English during War of Austrian Succession, 276
Common law, development, 50, 53, 56, 187; in New World, 224
Common Pleas court, 55, 187, 195
Commons, House of, see Parliament
Company of the Senegal, 228
Concordat of Bologna, 126
Condé, General, 269, 271
Constantinople, 11, 23, 25, 234, 254
Copernicus, 72
Cordoba, Gonsalvo, 120
Cordova, 23
Corregidor, 59
Corsica, 5, 23, 24

Cortes, 58
Cortez, Hernando, 97, 100, 155
Council of the Indies, 104
Council of Trent, 142
Counter-Reformation, 142-153, 238; and Roman Catholic Church, 141-153; in the Netherlands, 143-147; in France, 150, 151-152; Treaty of Westphalia, 152; summary, 155
Court, ducal, 10; of Admiralty, 187; of Requests, 187; of Exchequer, 50, 55, 187; Common Pleas, 55, 187, 195; Star Chamber, 187, 199, 200; King's Bench, 55, 187, 202; of Chancery, 187, 202
Craftsmen, see artisans
Cradle of civilization, 23
Cranmer, Archbishop of Canterbury, 132, 134, 135
Creole, 103, 105
Croatia, 238
Cromwell, Oliver, 201; and Commonwealth of England, 202
Crops, see agriculture
Crusades, commercial, 24; First, 24; to Egypt, 45
Cuba, 95, 101
Cuddalose, 276
Currency, see money

D

Damascus, 23
Danegeld, 48
Danube river, 237
Dauphiny, 161, 167
Debt peonage, 101
Deferents, 71
Demarcation Line, 95
Denmark, 3, 5, manorial system in 9; 22; opposed to Habsburgs, 150; and Partition of Sweden, 260, 263
Demesne, lords', 8, 28
Desima, island of, 154
De Tromp, Admiral, 152
Devolution, War of, 176
Diaz, Bartholomew, 89
Diemen, Anthony van, 154
Diet, assembly in Germany, 237
Diet of Worms, 128
Dijon, 27
Diniz, king of Portugal, 88

296

298